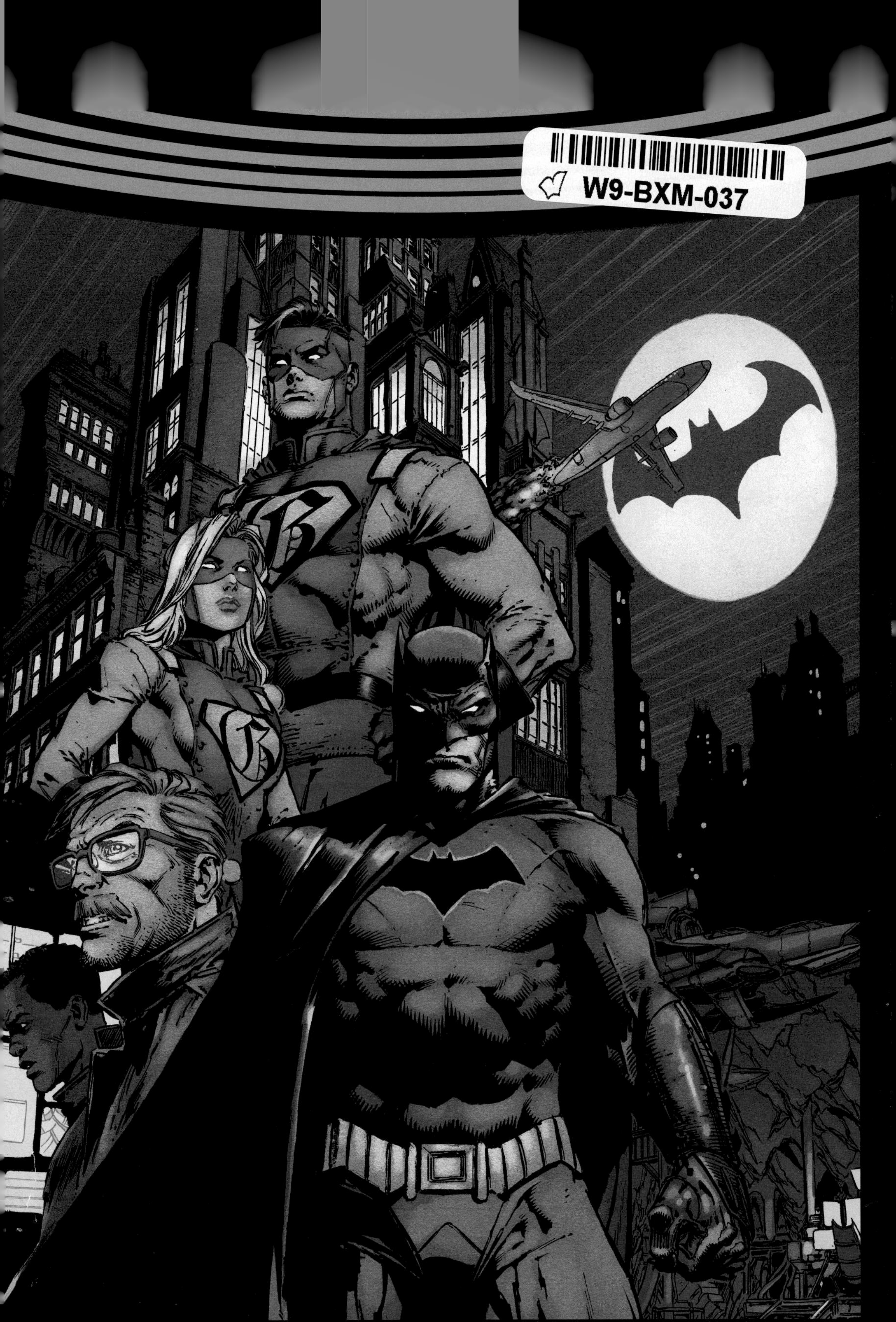

BATMAN

VOL.1 I AM GOTHAM

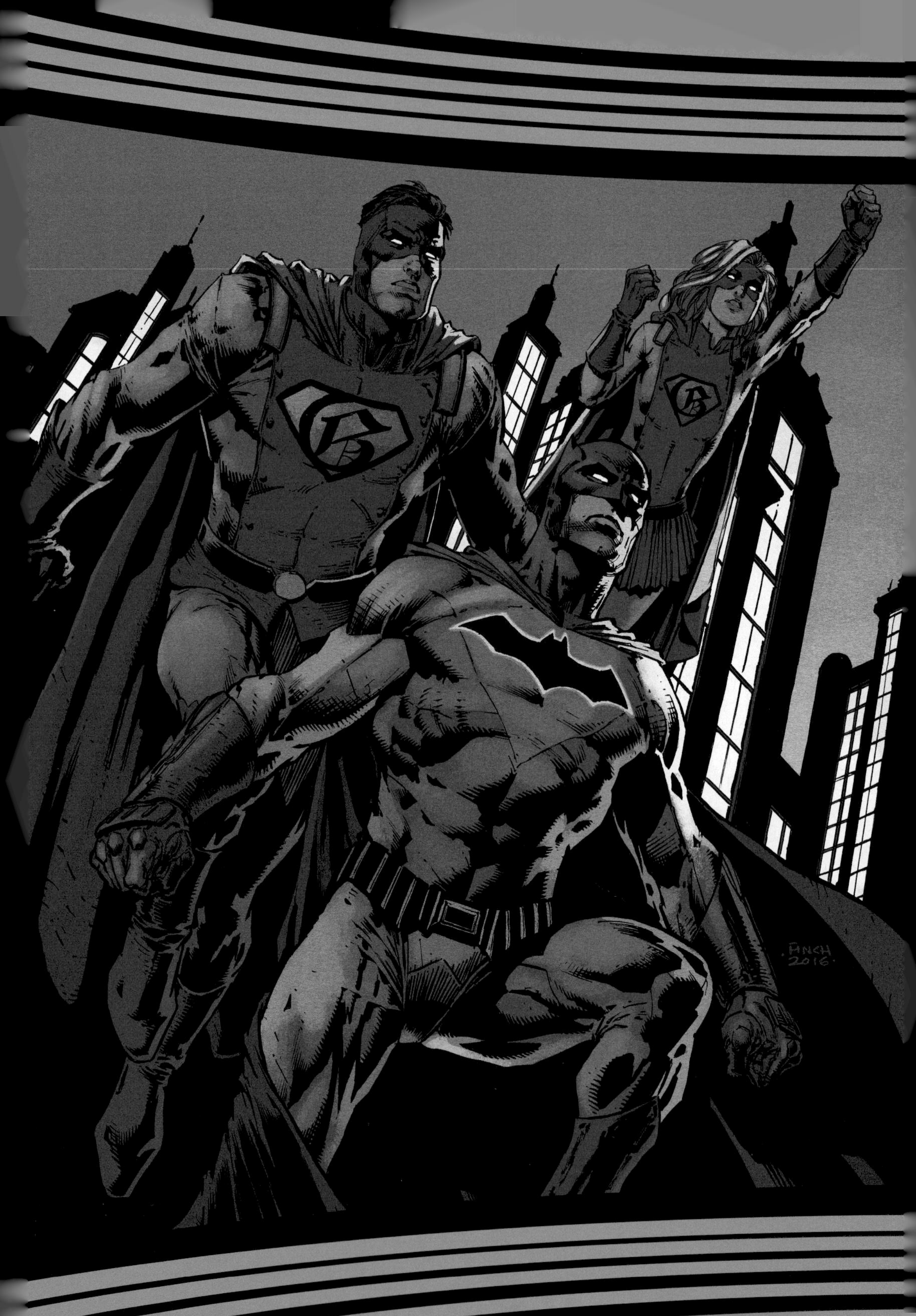
FINCH
2016

BATMAN

VOL.1 I AM GOTHAM

TOM KING
SCOTT SNYDER
writers

DAVID FINCH
MIKEL JANÍN * **IVAN REIS** * **MATT BANNING** * **DANNY MIKI** * **SANDRA HOPE**
SCOTT HANNA * **JOE PRADO** * **OCLAIR ALBERT**
artists

JORDIE BELLAIRE
JUNE CHUNG * **MARCELO MAIOLO**
colorists

JOHN WORKMAN * **DERON BENNETT**
letterers

DAVID FINCH with JORDIE BELLAIRE
collection cover artists

BATMAN created by BOB KANE with BILL FINGER
SUPERMAN created by JERRY SIEGEL and JOE SHUSTER
By special arrangement with the Jerry Siegel family

MARK DOYLE Editor - Original Series * **REBECCA TAYLOR** Associate Editor - Original Series * **JEB WOODARD** Group Editor - Collected Editions
ROBIN WILDMAN Editor - Collected Edition * **STEVE COOK** Design Director - Books * **DAMIAN RYLAND** Publication Design

BOB HARRAS Senior VP - Editor-in-Chief, DC Comics

DIANE NELSON President * **DAN DiDIO** Publisher * **JIM LEE** Publisher * **GEOFF JOHNS** President & Chief Creative Officer
AMIT DESAI Executive VP - Business & Marketing Strategy, Direct to Consumer & Global Franchise Management * **SAM ADES** Senior VP - Direct to Consumer
BOBBIE CHASE VP - Talent Development * **MARK CHIARELLO** Senior VP - Art, Design & Collected Editions
JOHN CUNNINGHAM Senior VP - Sales & Trade Marketing * **ANNE DePIES** Senior VP - Business Strategy, Finance & Administration
DON FALLETTI VP - Manufacturing Operations * **LAWRENCE GANEM** VP - Editorial Administration & Talent Relations
ALISON GILL Senior VP - Manufacturing & Operations * **HANK KANALZ** Senior VP - Editorial Strategy & Administration
JAY KOGAN VP - Legal Affairs * **THOMAS LOFTUS** VP - Business Affairs
JACK MAHAN VP - Business Affairs * **NICK J. NAPOLITANO** VP - Manufacturing Administration
EDDIE SCANNELL VP - Consumer Marketing * **COURTNEY SIMMONS** Senior VP - Publicity & Communications
JIM (SKI) SOKOLOWSKI VP - Comic Book Specialty Sales & Trade Marketing * **NANCY SPEARS** VP - Mass, Book, Digital Sales & Trade Marketing

BATMAN VOLUME 1: I AM GOTHAM

DC Comics, 2900 West Alameda Ave., Burbank, CA 91505. Printed by LSC Communications, Salem, VA, USA. 12/9/16.
First Printing. ISBN: 978-1-4012-6777-3

Library of Congress Cataloging-in-Publication Data is available.

PEFC Certified
Printed on paper from sustainably managed forests, controlled sources
www.pefc.org
PEFC
PEFC/29-31-337

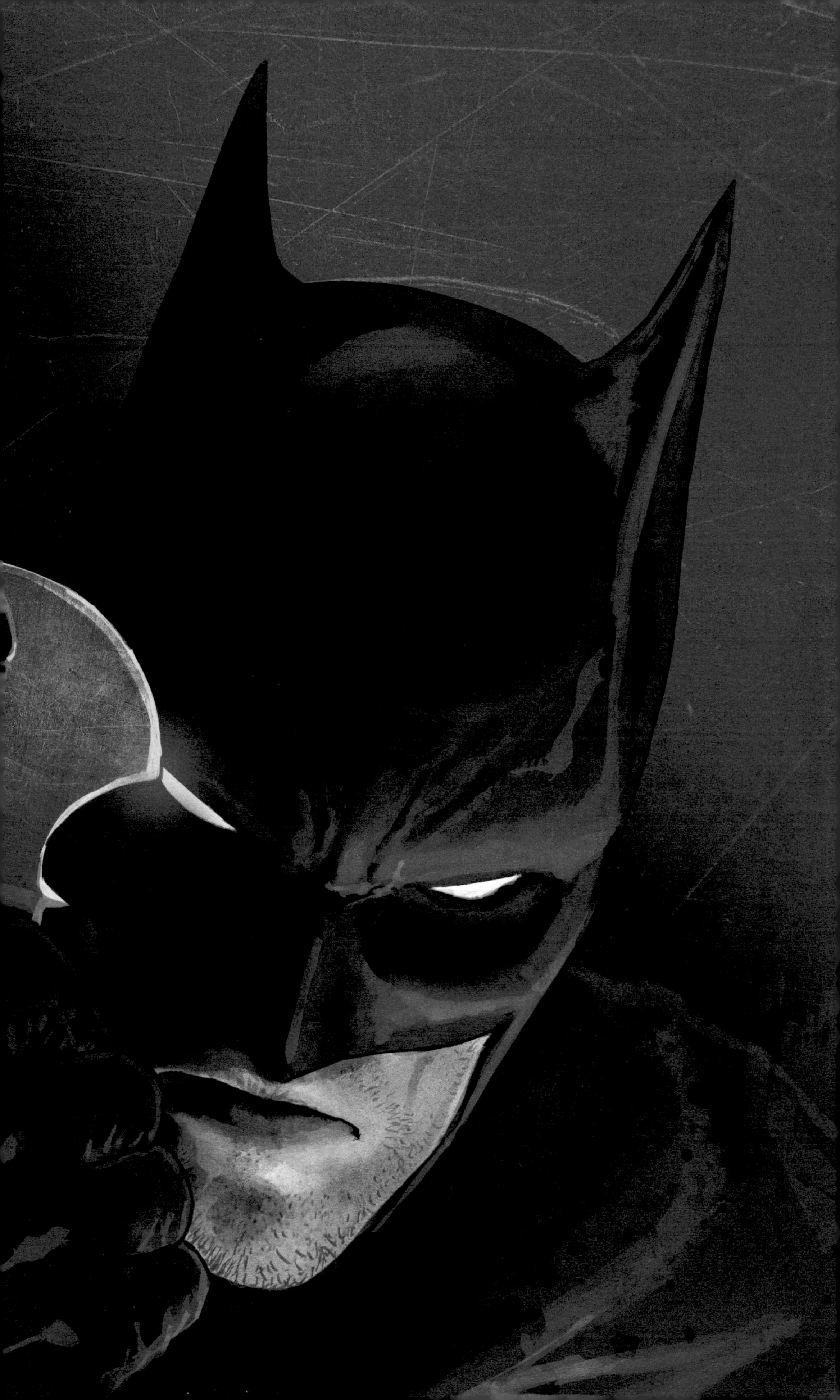

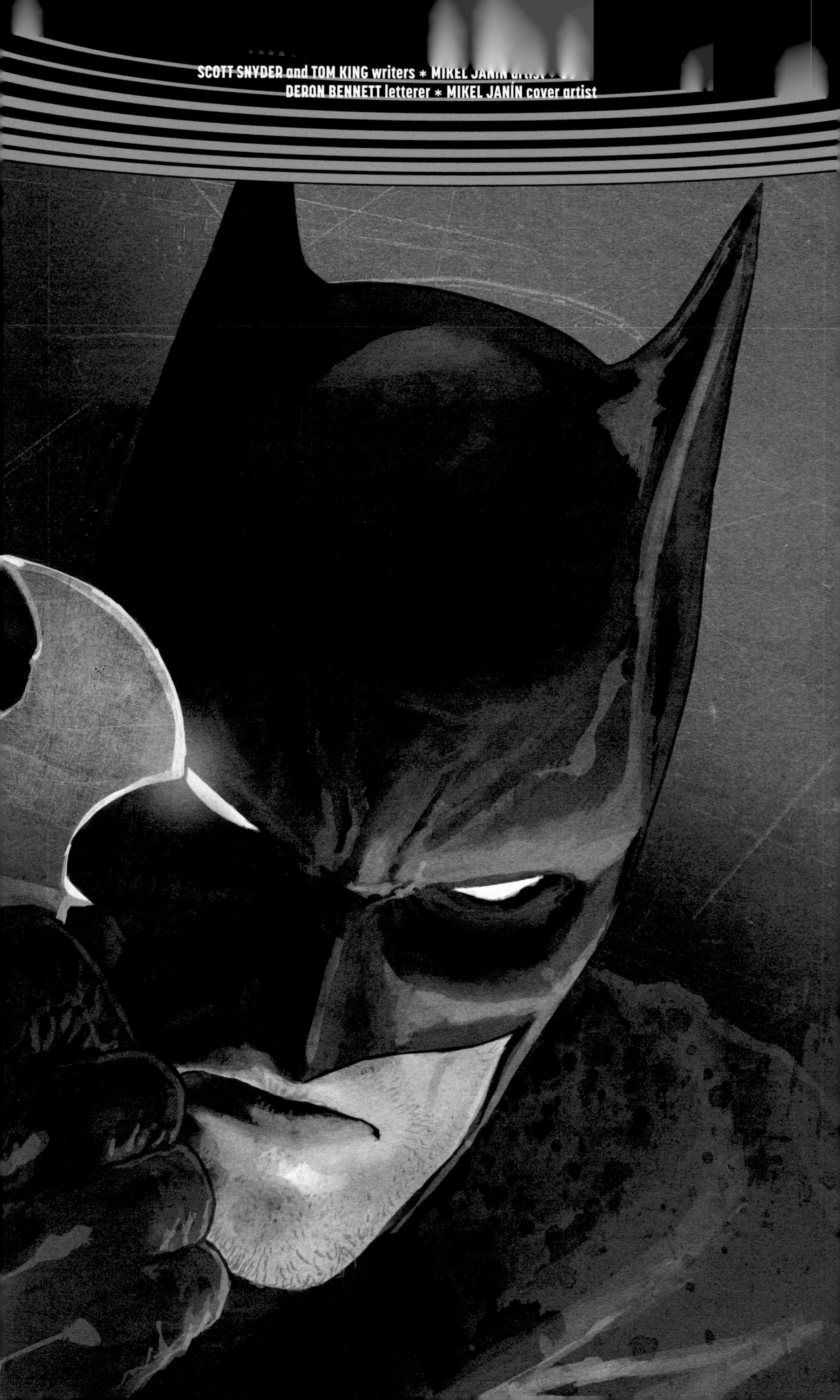
SCOTT SNYDER and TOM KING writers ∗ MIKEL JANÍN artist
DERON BENNETT letterer ∗ MIKEL JANÍN cover artist

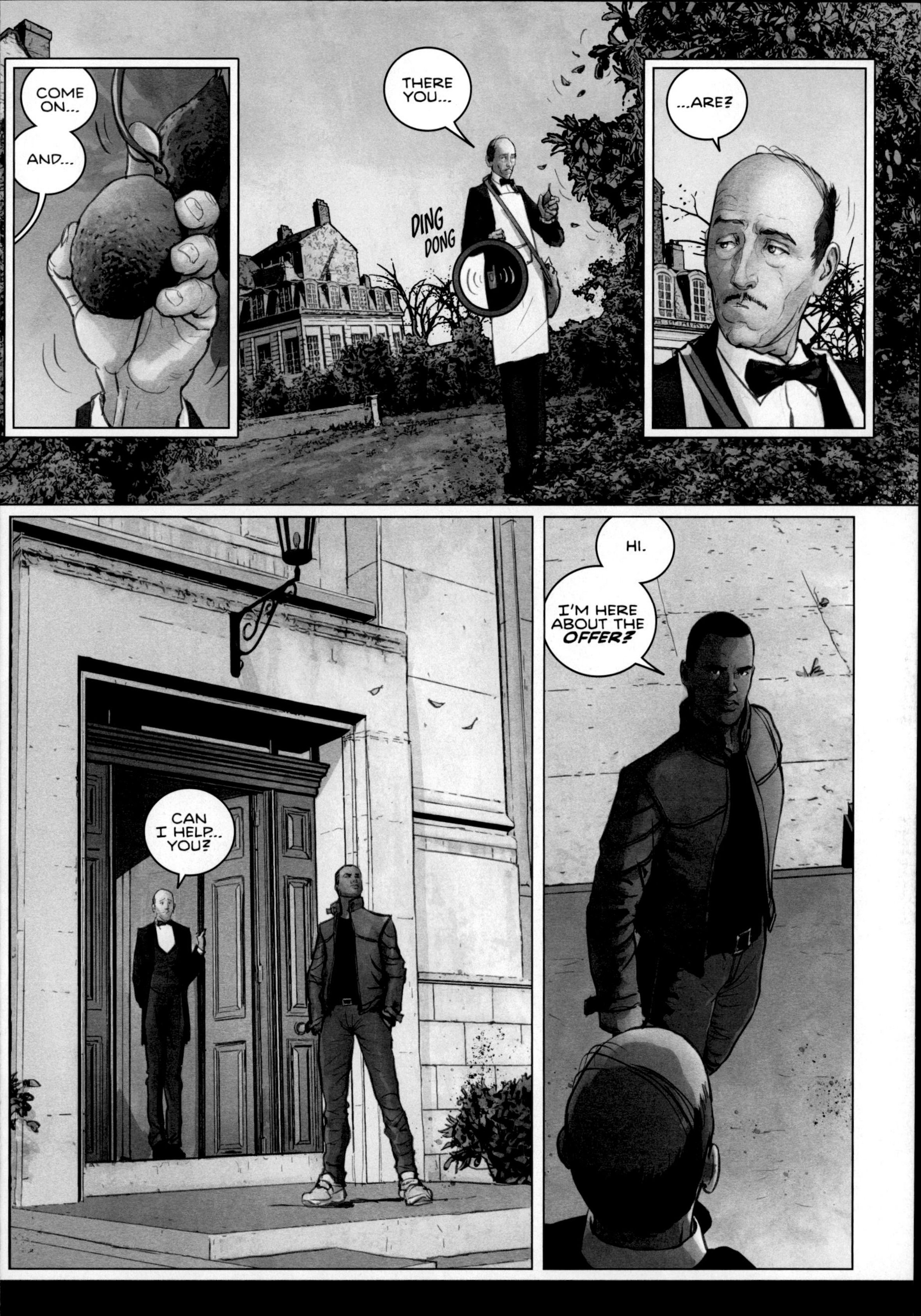
COME ON...
AND...
THERE YOU...
DING DONG
...ARE?
CAN I HELP... YOU?
HI.
I'M HERE ABOUT THE *OFFER?*

MONDAY: SPRING.

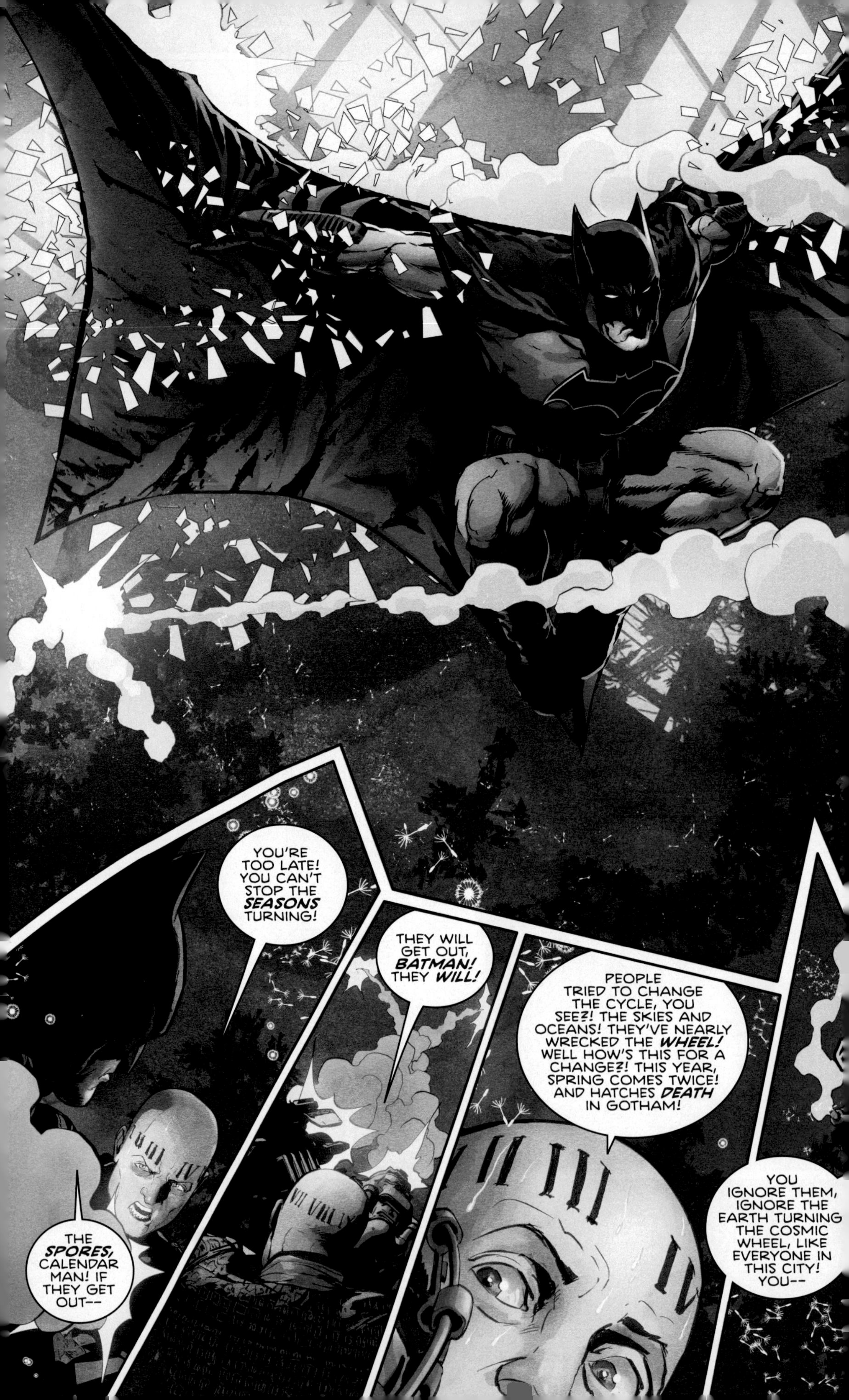
YOU'RE TOO LATE! YOU CAN'T STOP THE SEASONS TURNING!
THE SPORES, CALENDAR MAN! IF THEY GET OUT--
THEY WILL GET OUT, BATMAN! THEY WILL!
PEOPLE TRIED TO CHANGE THE CYCLE, YOU SEE?! THE SKIES AND OCEANS! THEY'VE NEARLY WRECKED THE WHEEL! WELL HOW'S THIS FOR A CHANGE?! THIS YEAR, SPRING COMES TWICE! AND HATCHES DEATH IN GOTHAM!
YOU IGNORE THEM, IGNORE THE EARTH TURNING THE COSMIC WHEEL, LIKE EVERYONE IN THIS CITY! YOU--

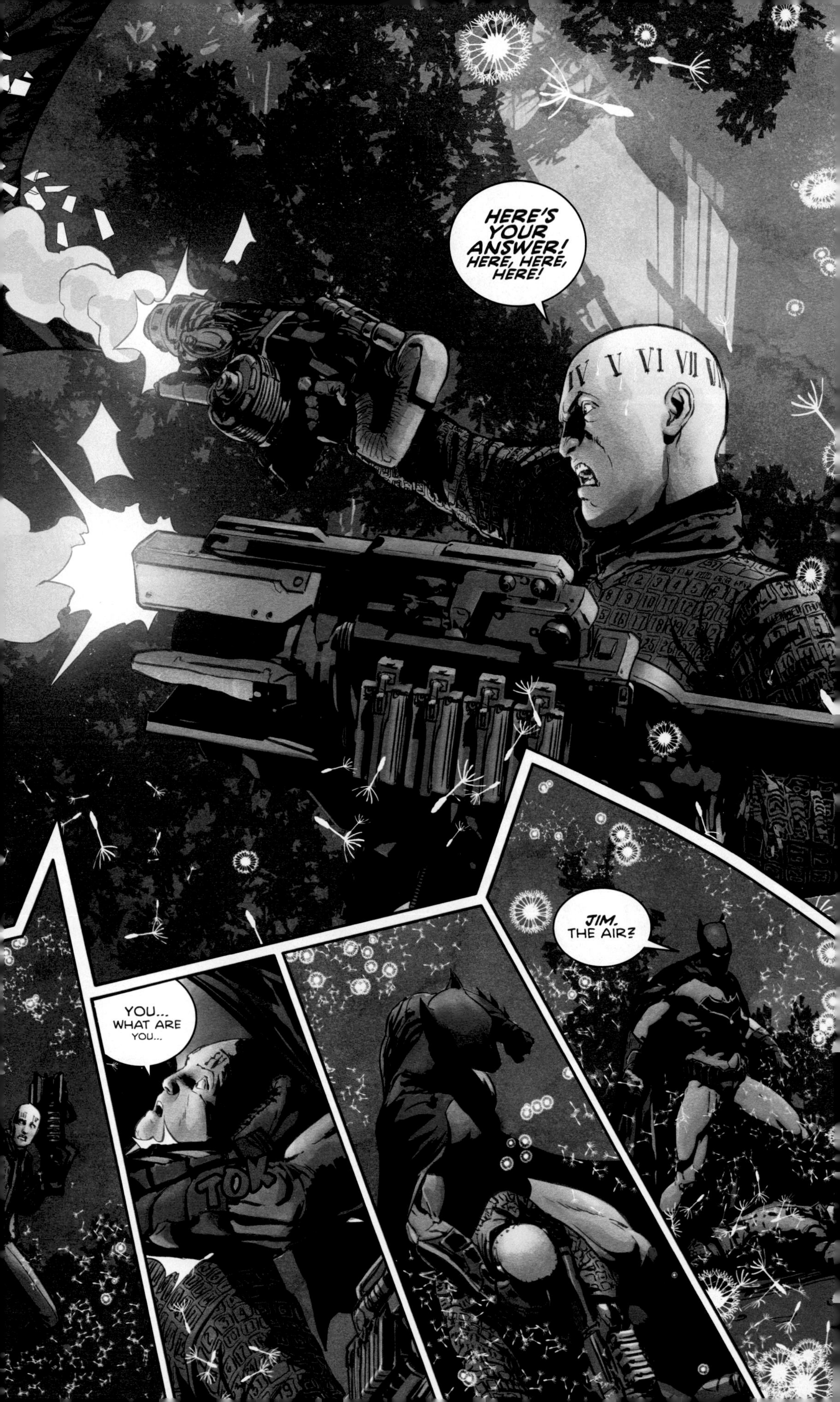
HERE'S YOUR ANSWER! HERE, HERE, HERE!
YOU... WHAT ARE YOU...
TOK
JIM. THE AIR?

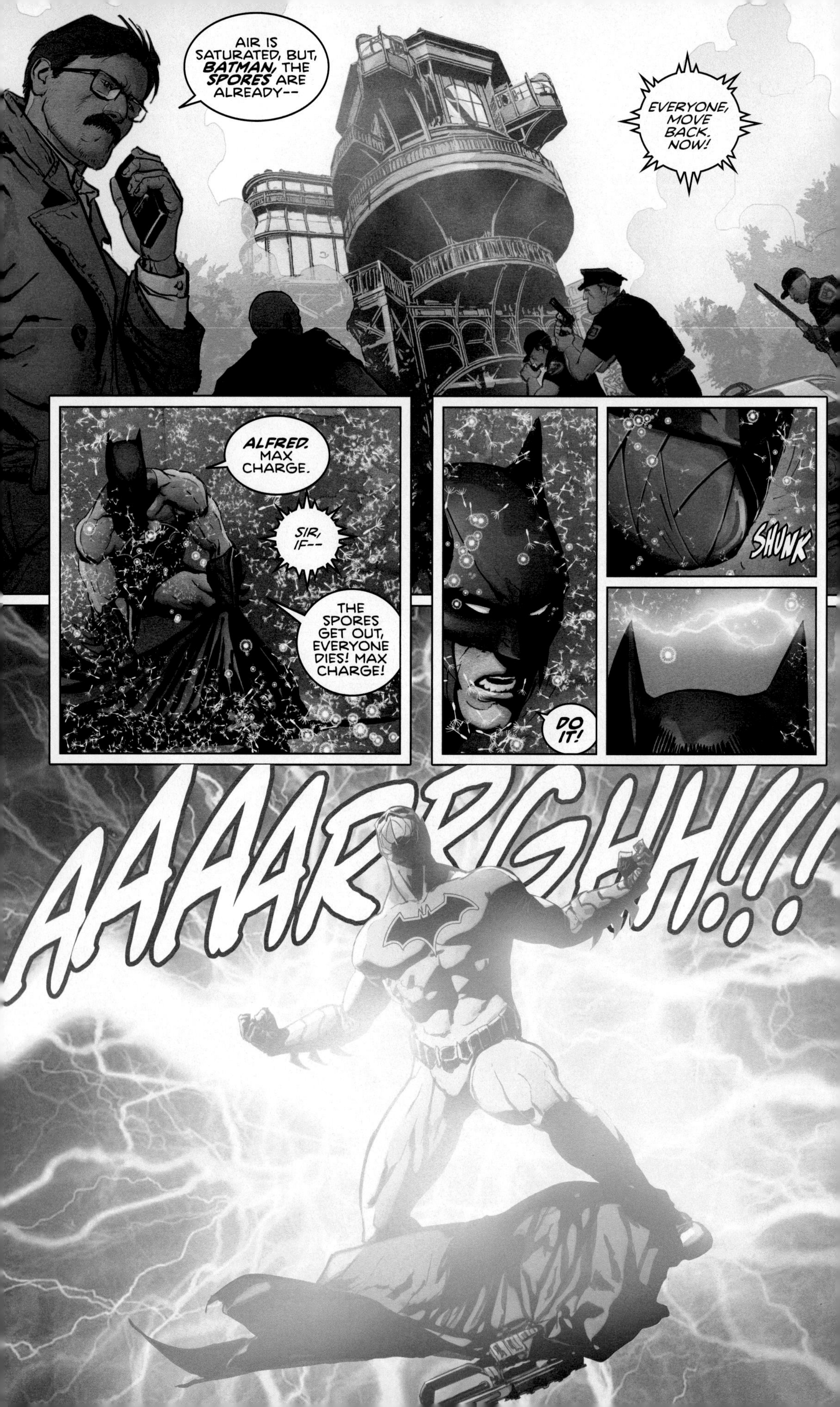
AIR IS SATURATED, BUT, BATMAN, THE SPORES ARE ALREADY--
EVERYONE, MOVE BACK. NOW!
ALFRED. MAX CHARGE.
SIR, IF--
THE SPORES GET OUT, EVERYONE DIES! MAX CHARGE!
DO IT!
SHUNK
AAAARRGHH!!!

TUESDAY. SUMMER.

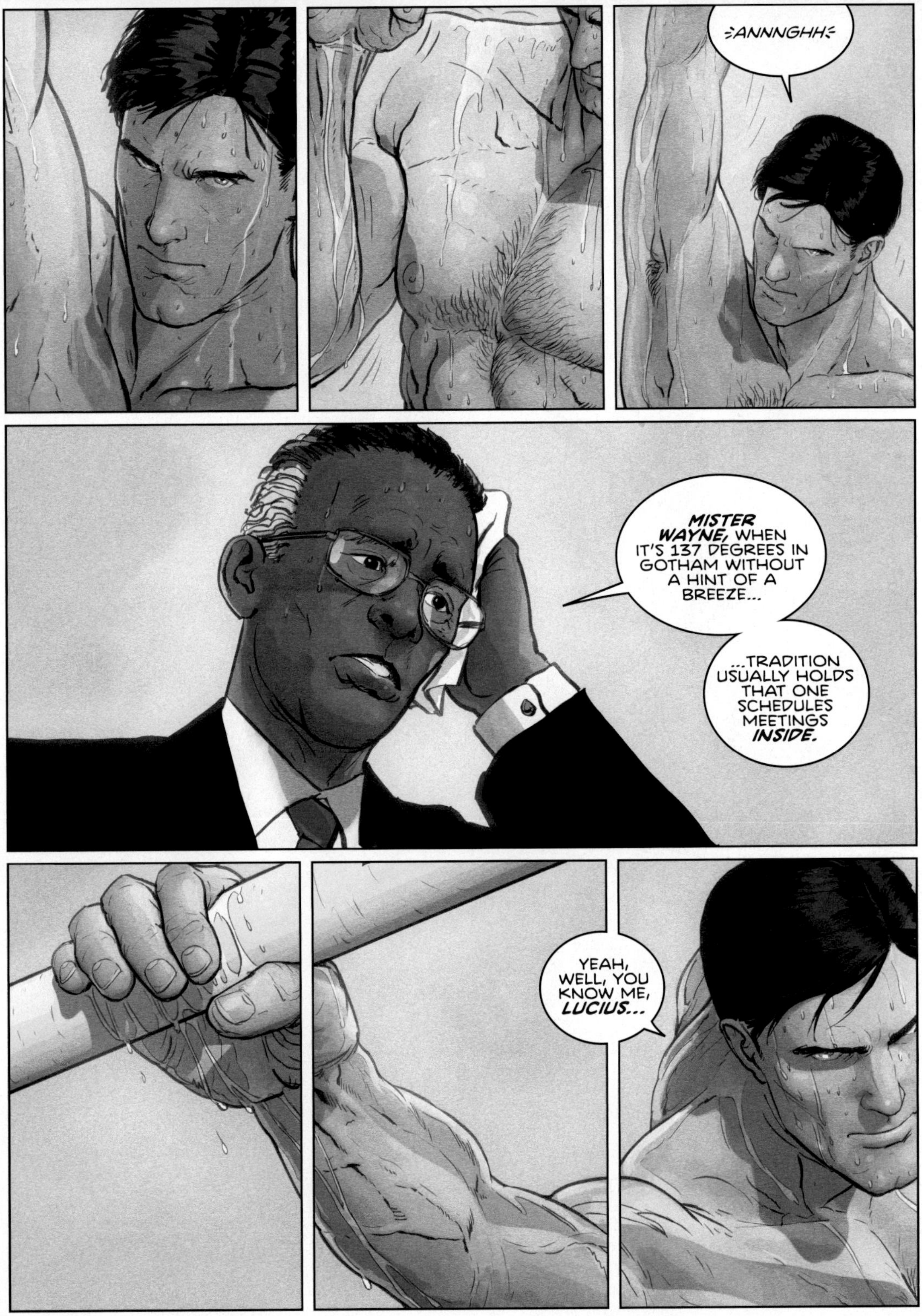
ANNNGHH
MISTER WAYNE, WHEN IT'S 137 DEGREES IN GOTHAM WITHOUT A HINT OF A BREEZE...
...TRADITION USUALLY HOLDS THAT ONE SCHEDULES MEETINGS INSIDE.
YEAH, WELL, YOU KNOW ME, LUCIUS...

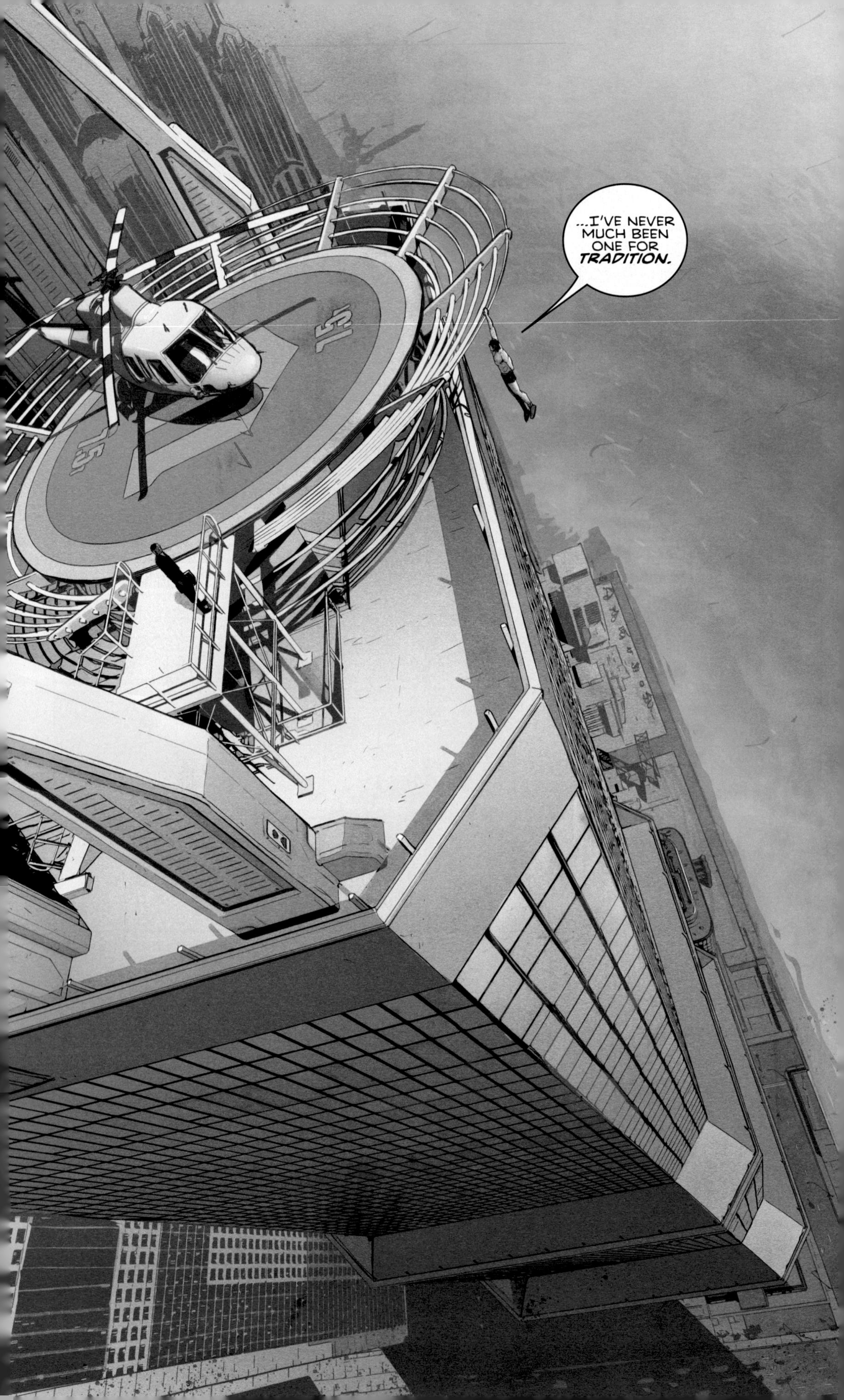
...I'VE NEVER MUCH BEEN ONE FOR TRADITION.

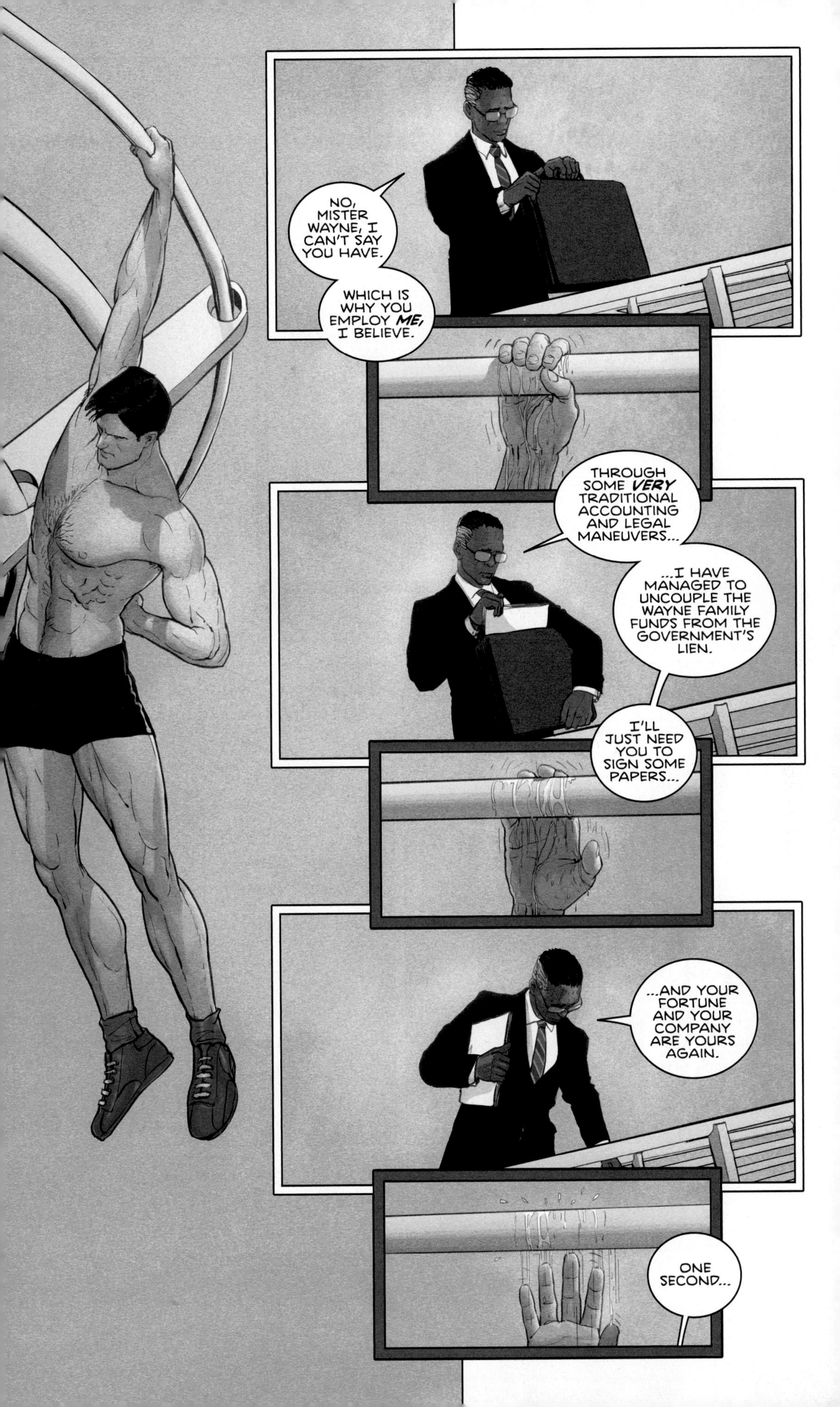
NO, MISTER WAYNE, I CAN'T SAY YOU HAVE.
WHICH IS WHY YOU EMPLOY *ME*, I BELIEVE.
THROUGH SOME *VERY* TRADITIONAL ACCOUNTING AND LEGAL MANEUVERS...
...I HAVE MANAGED TO UNCOUPLE THE WAYNE FAMILY FUNDS FROM THE GOVERNMENT'S LIEN.
I'LL JUST NEED YOU TO SIGN SOME PAPERS...
...AND YOUR FORTUNE AND YOUR COMPANY ARE YOURS AGAIN.
ONE SECOND...

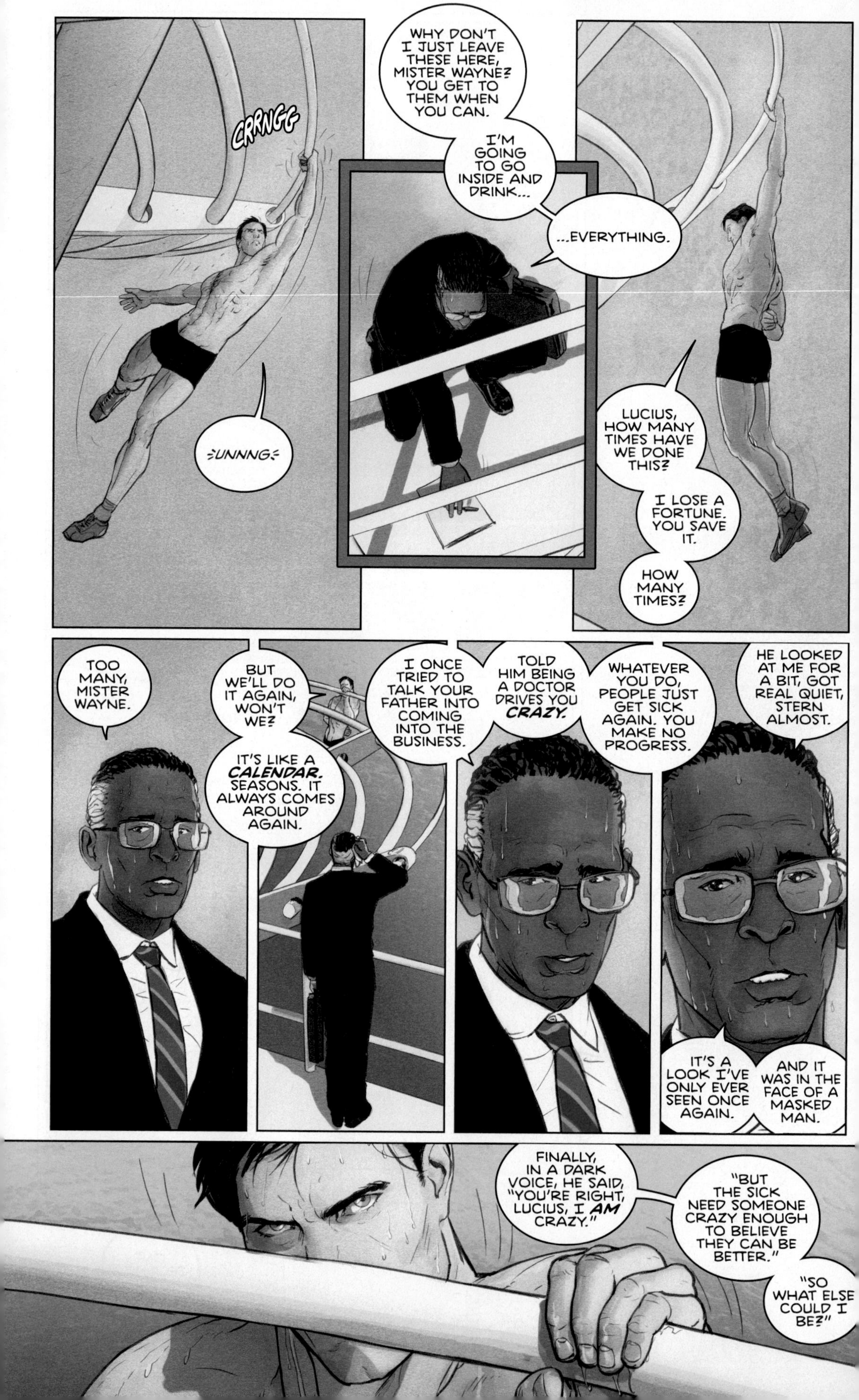
CRRNGG
≈UNNNG≈
WHY DON'T I JUST LEAVE THESE HERE, MISTER WAYNE? YOU GET TO THEM WHEN YOU CAN.
I'M GOING TO GO INSIDE AND DRINK...
...EVERYTHING.
LUCIUS, HOW MANY TIMES HAVE WE DONE THIS?
I LOSE A FORTUNE. YOU SAVE IT.
HOW MANY TIMES?
TOO MANY, MISTER WAYNE.
BUT WE'LL DO IT AGAIN, WON'T WE?
IT'S LIKE A CALENDAR. SEASONS. IT ALWAYS COMES AROUND AGAIN.
I ONCE TRIED TO TALK YOUR FATHER INTO COMING INTO THE BUSINESS.
TOLD HIM BEING A DOCTOR DRIVES YOU CRAZY.
WHATEVER YOU DO, PEOPLE JUST GET SICK AGAIN. YOU MAKE NO PROGRESS.
HE LOOKED AT ME FOR A BIT, GOT REAL QUIET, STERN ALMOST.
IT'S A LOOK I'VE ONLY EVER SEEN ONCE AGAIN.
AND IT WAS IN THE FACE OF A MASKED MAN.
FINALLY, IN A DARK VOICE, HE SAID, "YOU'RE RIGHT, LUCIUS, I AM CRAZY."
"BUT THE SICK NEED SOMEONE CRAZY ENOUGH TO BELIEVE THEY CAN BE BETTER."
"SO WHAT ELSE COULD I BE?"

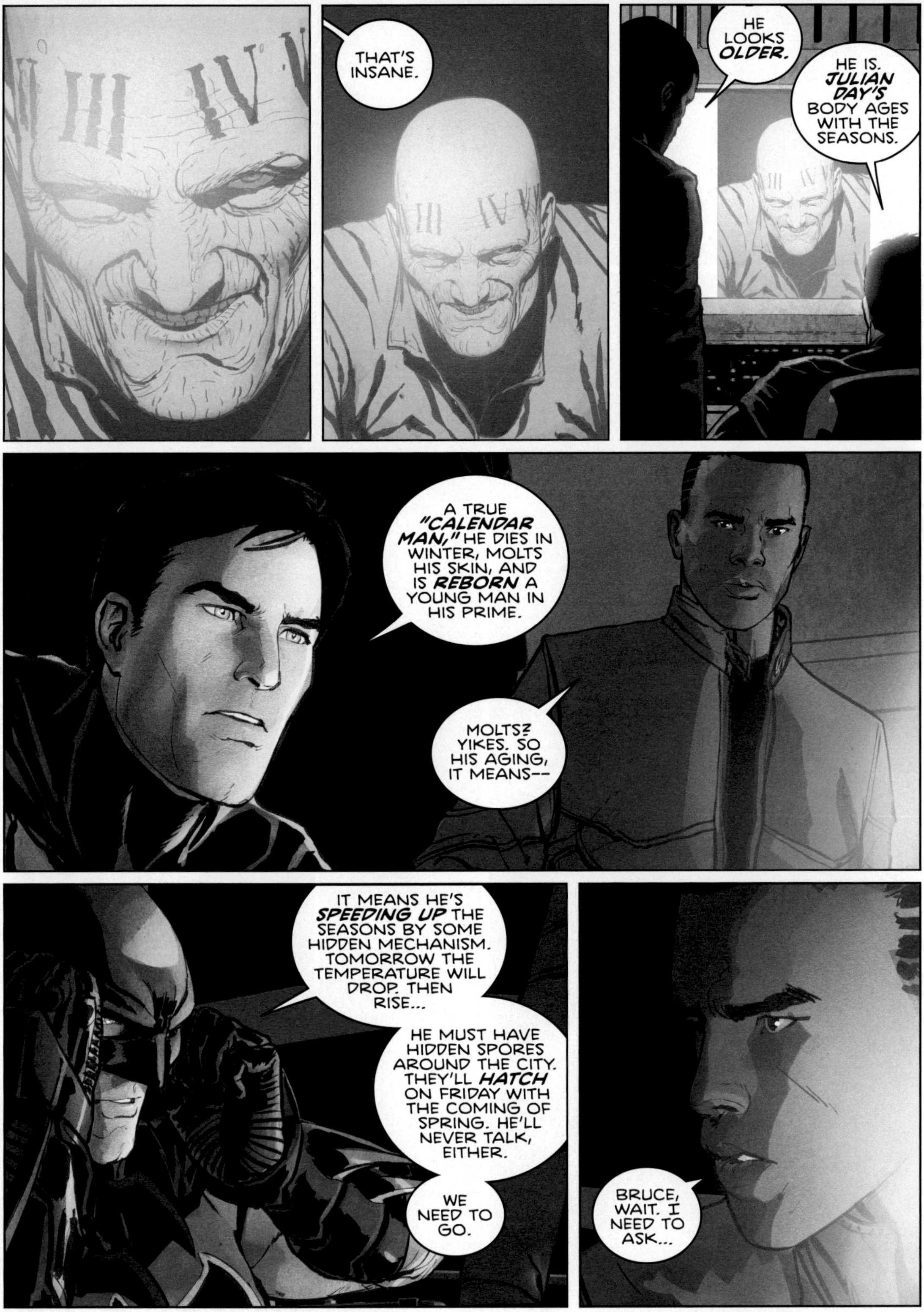
THAT'S INSANE.
HE LOOKS OLDER.
HE IS. JULIAN DAY'S BODY AGES WITH THE SEASONS.
A TRUE "CALENDAR MAN," HE DIES IN WINTER, MOLTS HIS SKIN, AND IS REBORN A YOUNG MAN IN HIS PRIME.
MOLTS? YIKES. SO HIS AGING, IT MEANS--
IT MEANS HE'S SPEEDING UP THE SEASONS BY SOME HIDDEN MECHANISM. TOMORROW THE TEMPERATURE WILL DROP. THEN RISE...
HE MUST HAVE HIDDEN SPORES AROUND THE CITY. THEY'LL HATCH ON FRIDAY WITH THE COMING OF SPRING. HE'LL NEVER TALK, EITHER.
WE NEED TO GO.
BRUCE, WAIT. I NEED TO ASK...

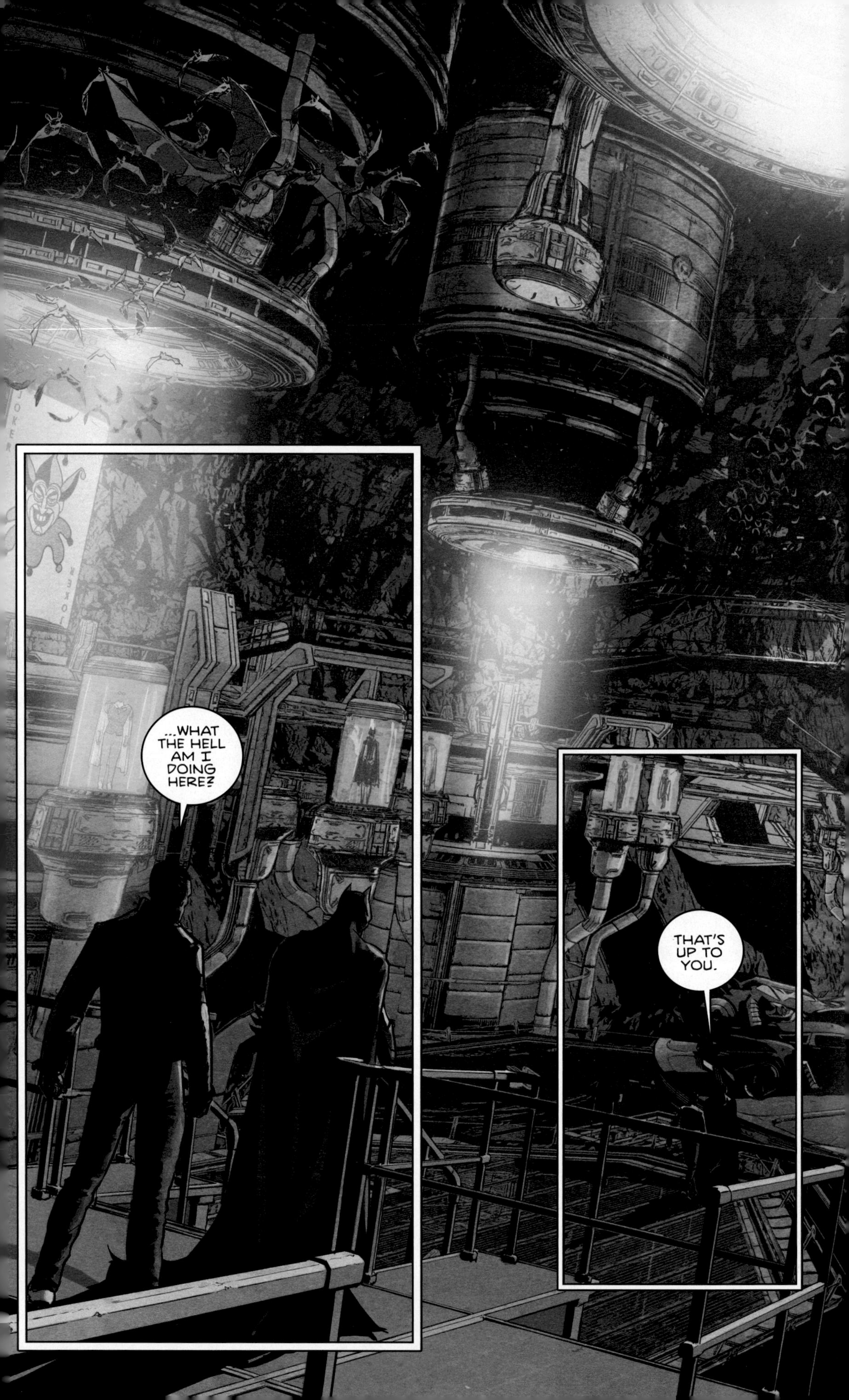
...WHAT THE HELL AM I DOING HERE?
THAT'S UP TO YOU.
JOKER

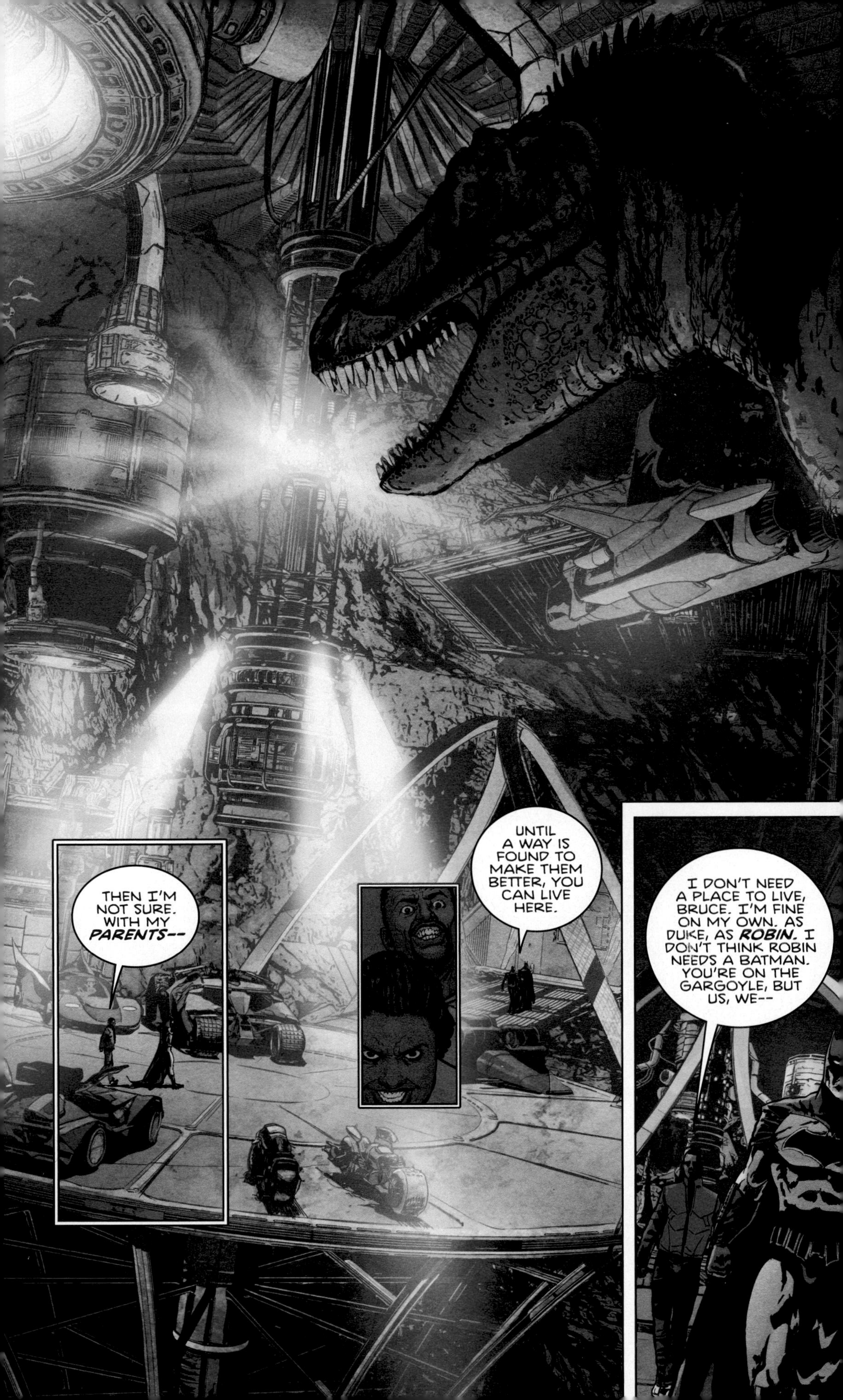
THEN I'M NOT SURE. WITH MY *PARENTS--*
UNTIL A WAY IS FOUND TO MAKE THEM BETTER, YOU CAN LIVE HERE.
I DON'T NEED A PLACE TO LIVE, BRUCE. I'M FINE ON MY OWN. AS DUKE, AS *ROBIN*. I DON'T THINK ROBIN NEEDS A BATMAN. YOU'RE ON THE GARGOYLE, BUT US, WE--

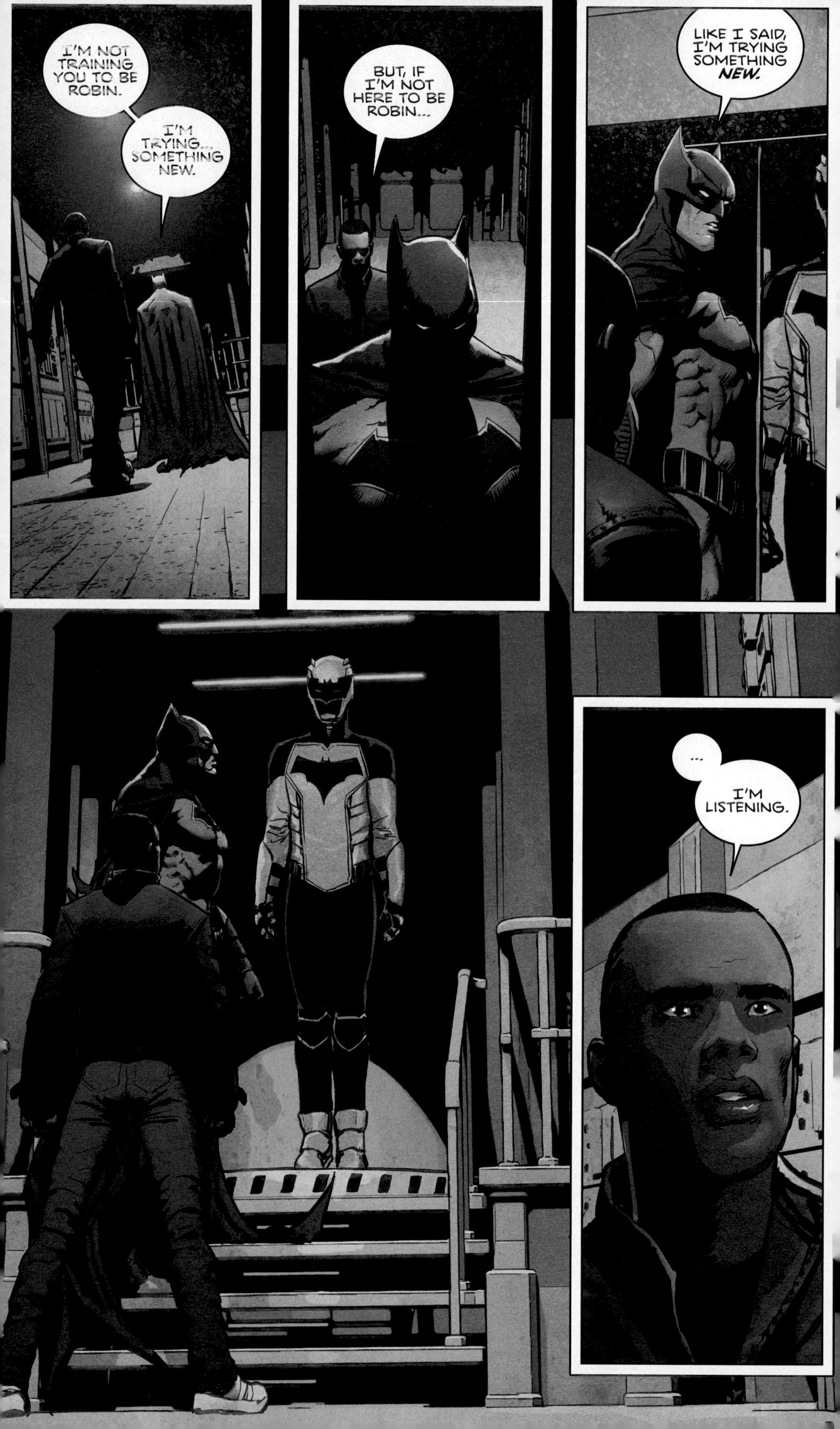
I'M NOT TRAINING YOU TO BE ROBIN.
I'M TRYING... SOMETHING NEW.
BUT, IF I'M NOT HERE TO BE ROBIN...
LIKE I SAID, I'M TRYING SOMETHING *NEW.*
...
I'M LISTENING.

THURSDAY. WINTER.

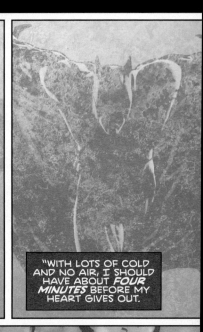

"GOOD, MISTER THOMAS.

"THEN I NEED YOU TO *COUNT.*

"OXYGEN TANK'S USELESS IN WATER THIS TEMPERATURE. FREEZES THE MAIN VALVE.

"WITH LOTS OF COLD AND NO AIR, I SHOULD HAVE ABOUT *FOUR MINUTES* BEFORE MY HEART GIVES OUT.

"IF I CAN'T FIND AND DISABLE CALENDAR'S MACHINE IN THOSE FOUR MINUTES, THE MACHINE'LL TURN THE CITY TO SPRING AGAIN.

"ALL THOSE *SPORES* WILL ACTIVATE. AND *GOTHAM* DIES.

"SO I NEED YOU TO *COUNT.*"

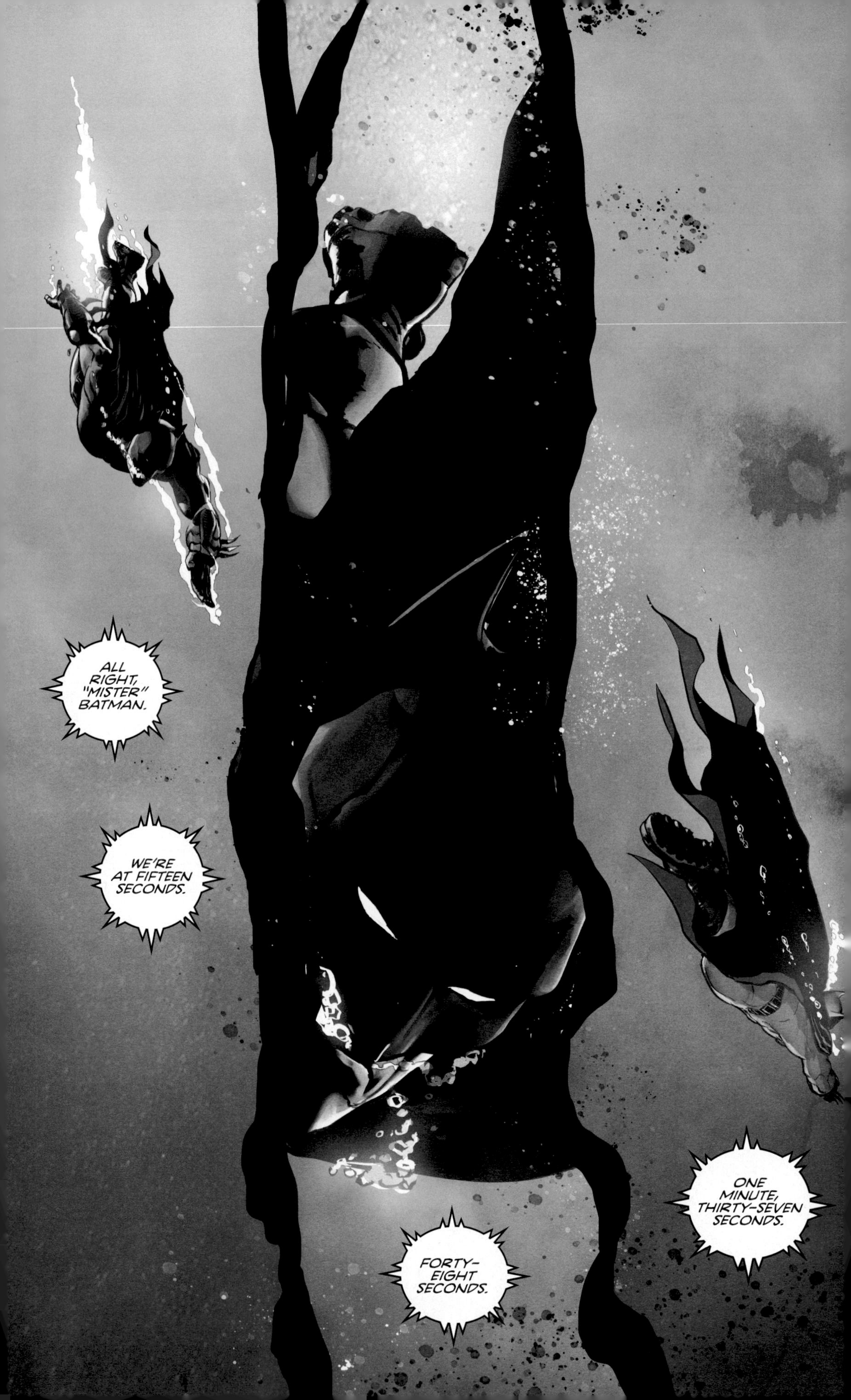
ALL RIGHT, "MISTER" BATMAN.
WE'RE AT FIFTEEN SECONDS.
FORTY-EIGHT SECONDS.
ONE MINUTE, THIRTY-SEVEN SECONDS.

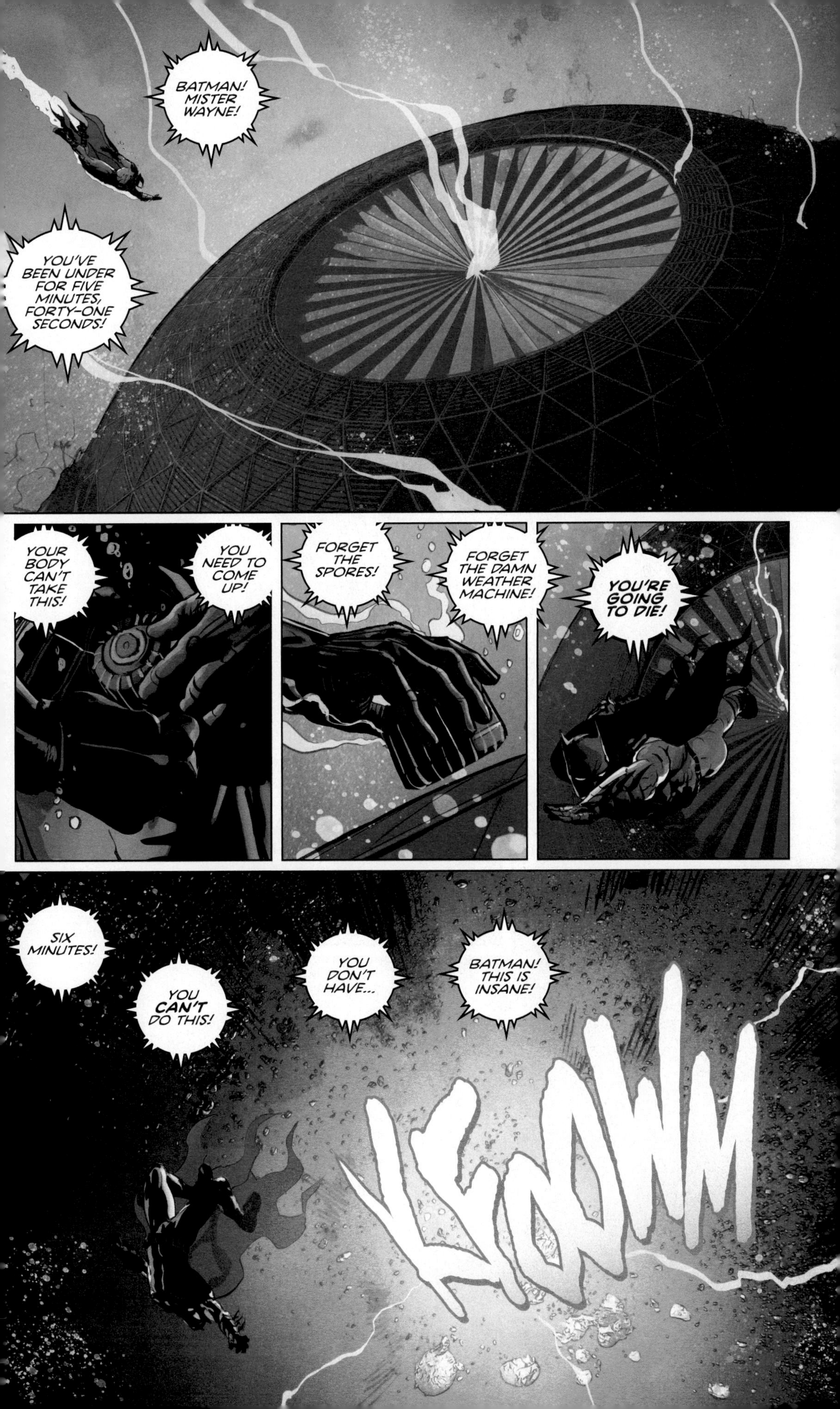
BATMAN! MISTER WAYNE!
YOU'VE BEEN UNDER FOR FIVE MINUTES, FORTY-ONE SECONDS!
YOUR BODY CAN'T TAKE THIS!
YOU NEED TO COME UP!
FORGET THE SPORES!
FORGET THE DAMN WEATHER MACHINE!
YOU'RE GOING TO DIE!
SIX MINUTES!
YOU CAN'T DO THIS!
YOU DON'T HAVE...
BATMAN! THIS IS INSANE!
KROWM

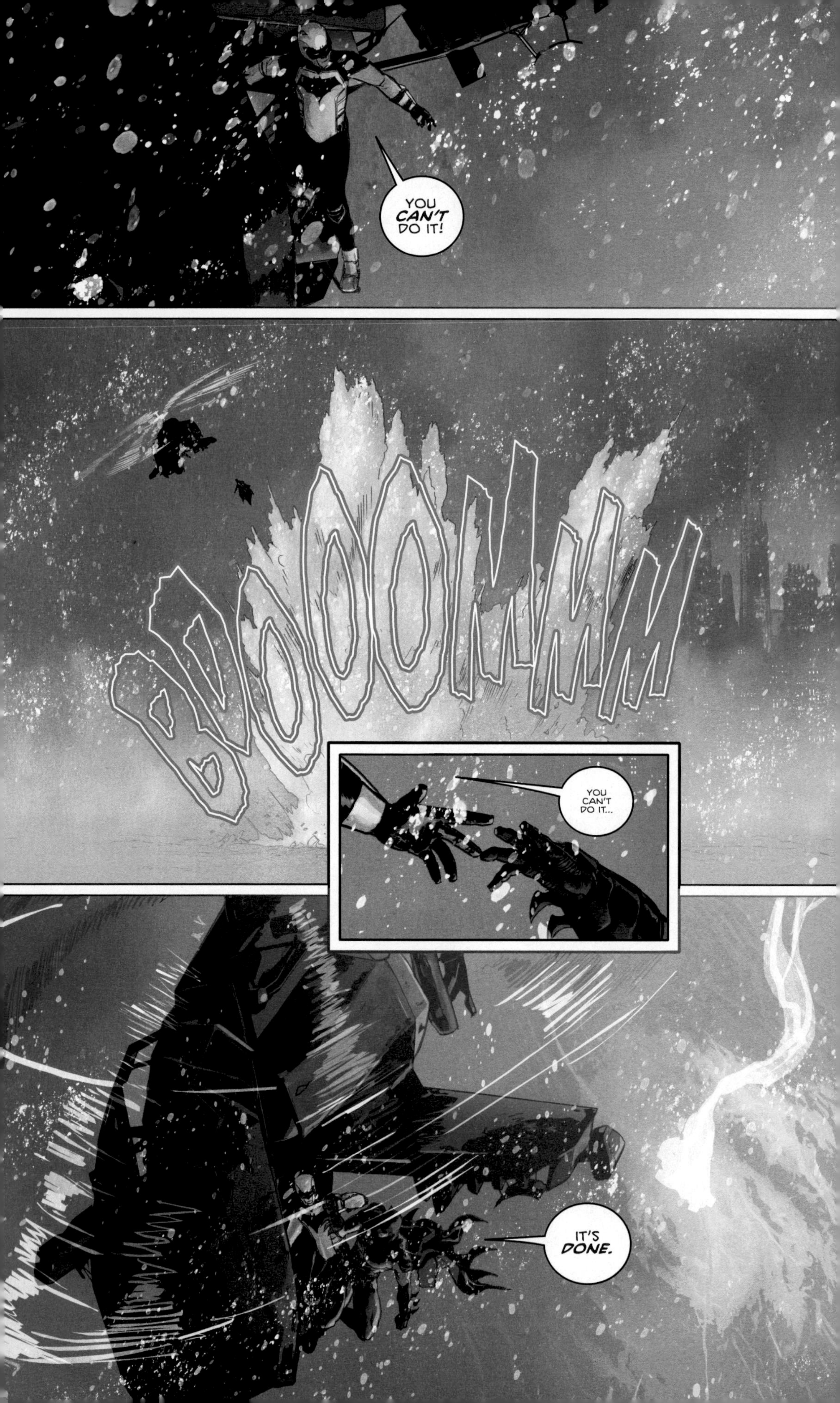
YOU CAN'T DO IT!
BOOOOMMM
YOU CAN'T DO IT...
IT'S DONE.

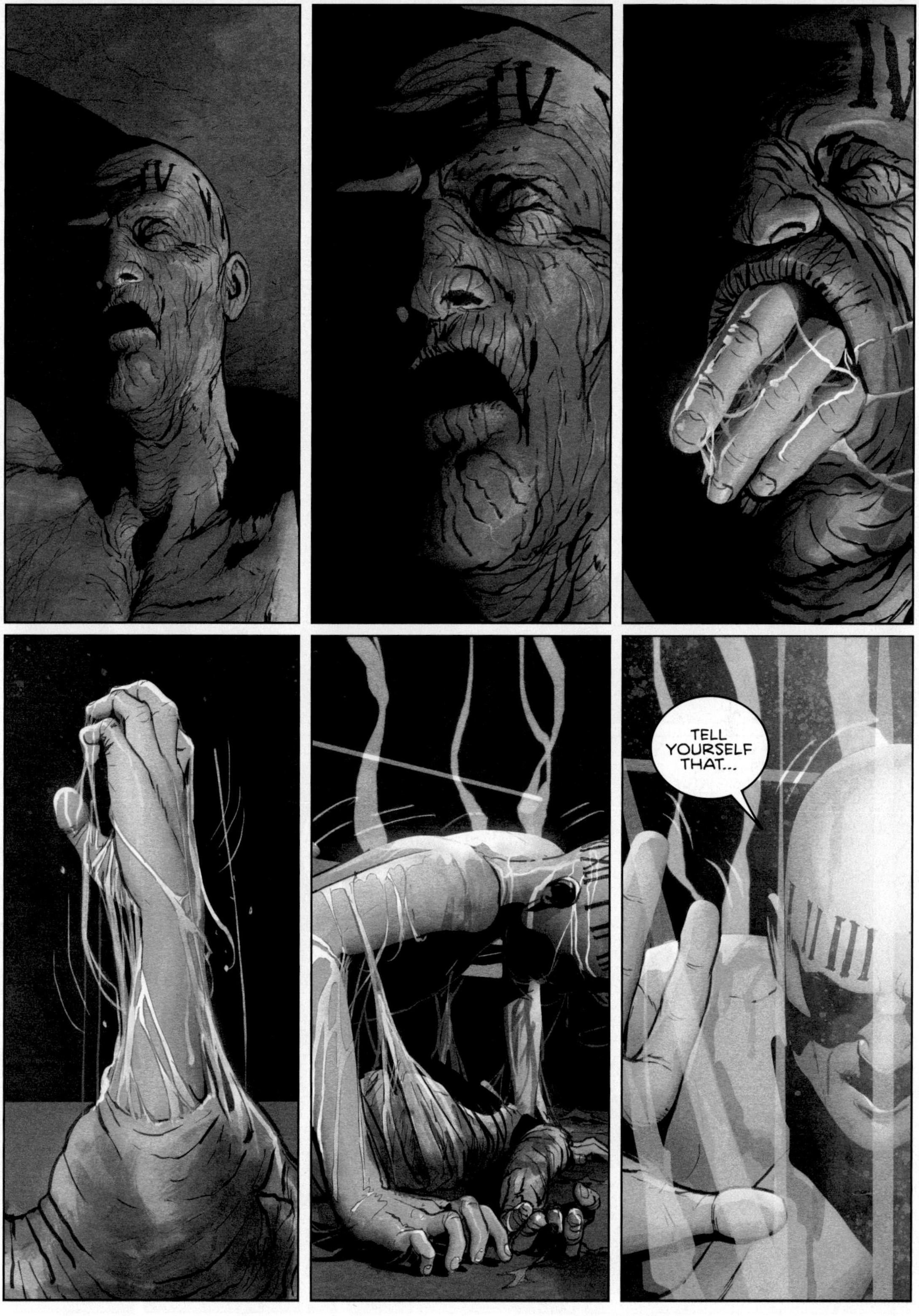
TELL YOURSELF THAT...

"...TELL YOURSELF IT'S DONE.

"BUT IT'S NEVER *DONE*."

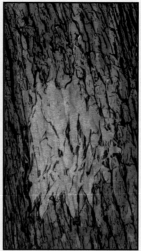

AGAIN.

HE'S BACK. RIGHT ABOUT NOW, HE'S... *HATCHING*. I WAS LOOKING AT THE FILE ON HIM.

IT SAYS THAT EVERY TIME HE COMES BACK, HE COMES BACK SLIGHTLY DIFFERENT, HIS DNA ALTERED. HE'S A DIFFERENT PERSON, BUT HE RETAINS ALL THE MEMORIES HE HAD LAST TIME.

HE'LL COME UP WITH NEW IDEAS.

THE TREE IS WINNING. YOUR POINT?

JUST THAT, HE COMES BACK *BETTER* EVERY TIME. HOW ARE WE SUPPOSED TO COMBAT THAT?

EASY. *WE* COME BACK BETTER EACH TIME, TOO.

...

YOU'RE CRAZY, YOU KNOW THAT, RIGHT?

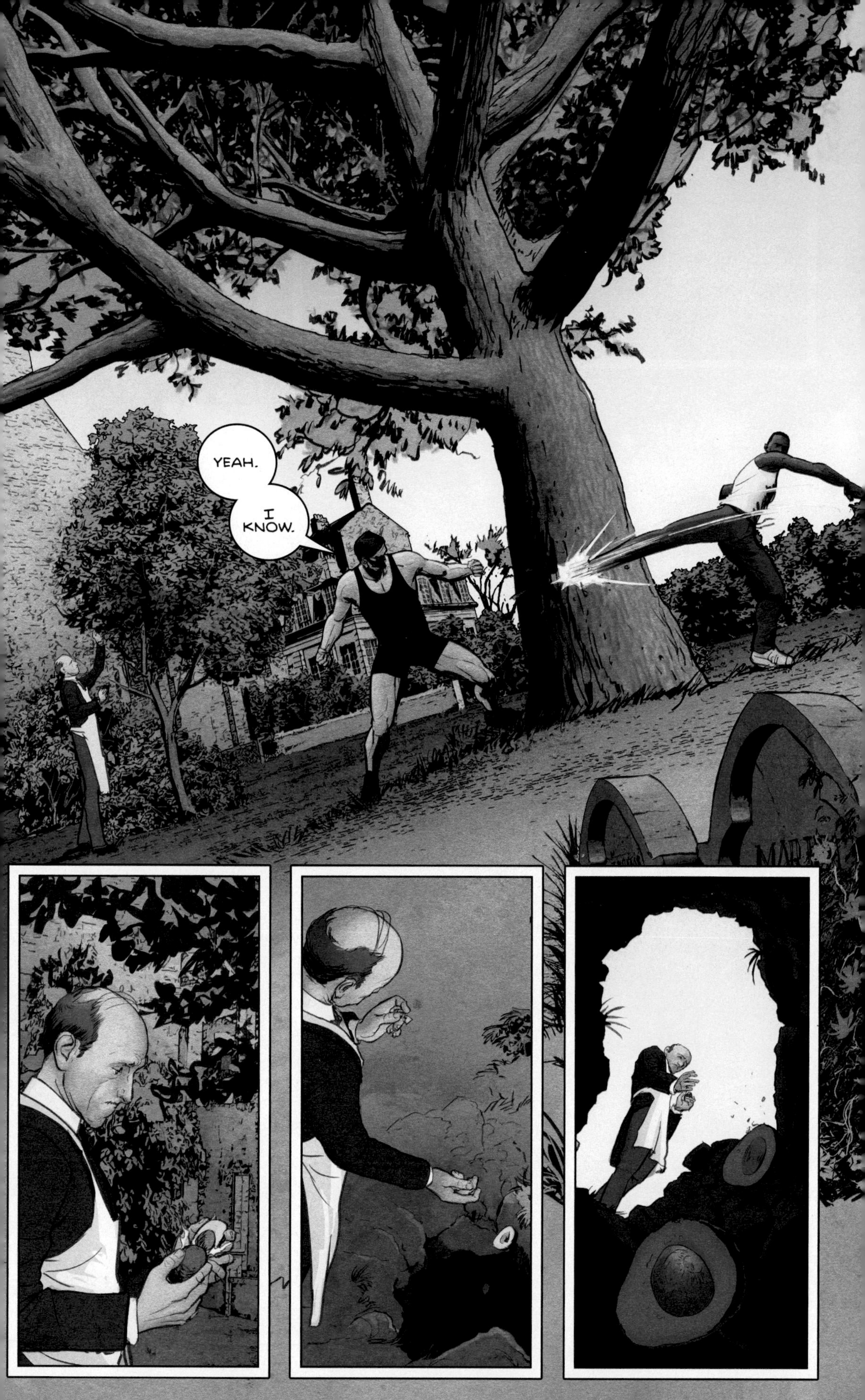
YEAH.
I KNOW.

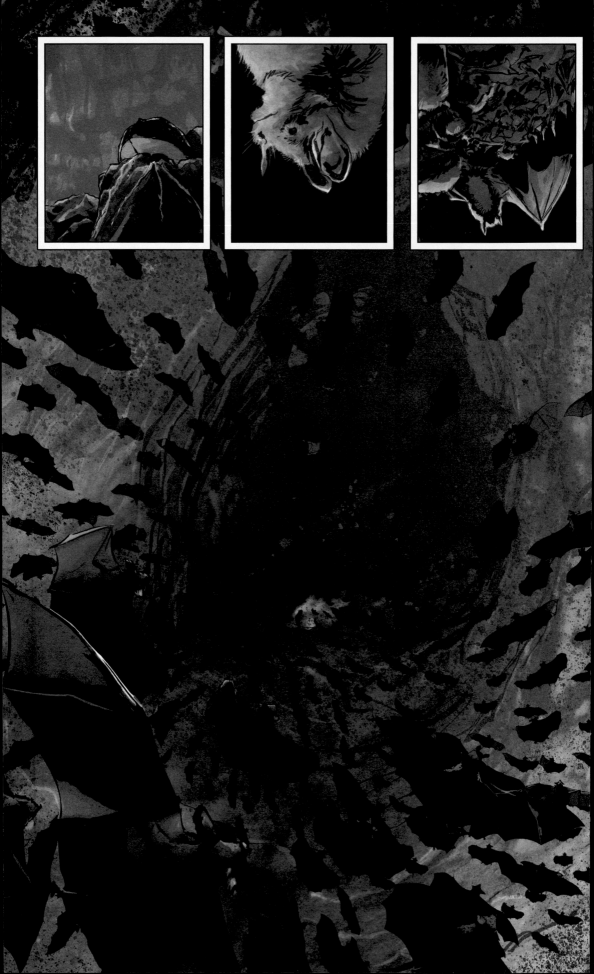

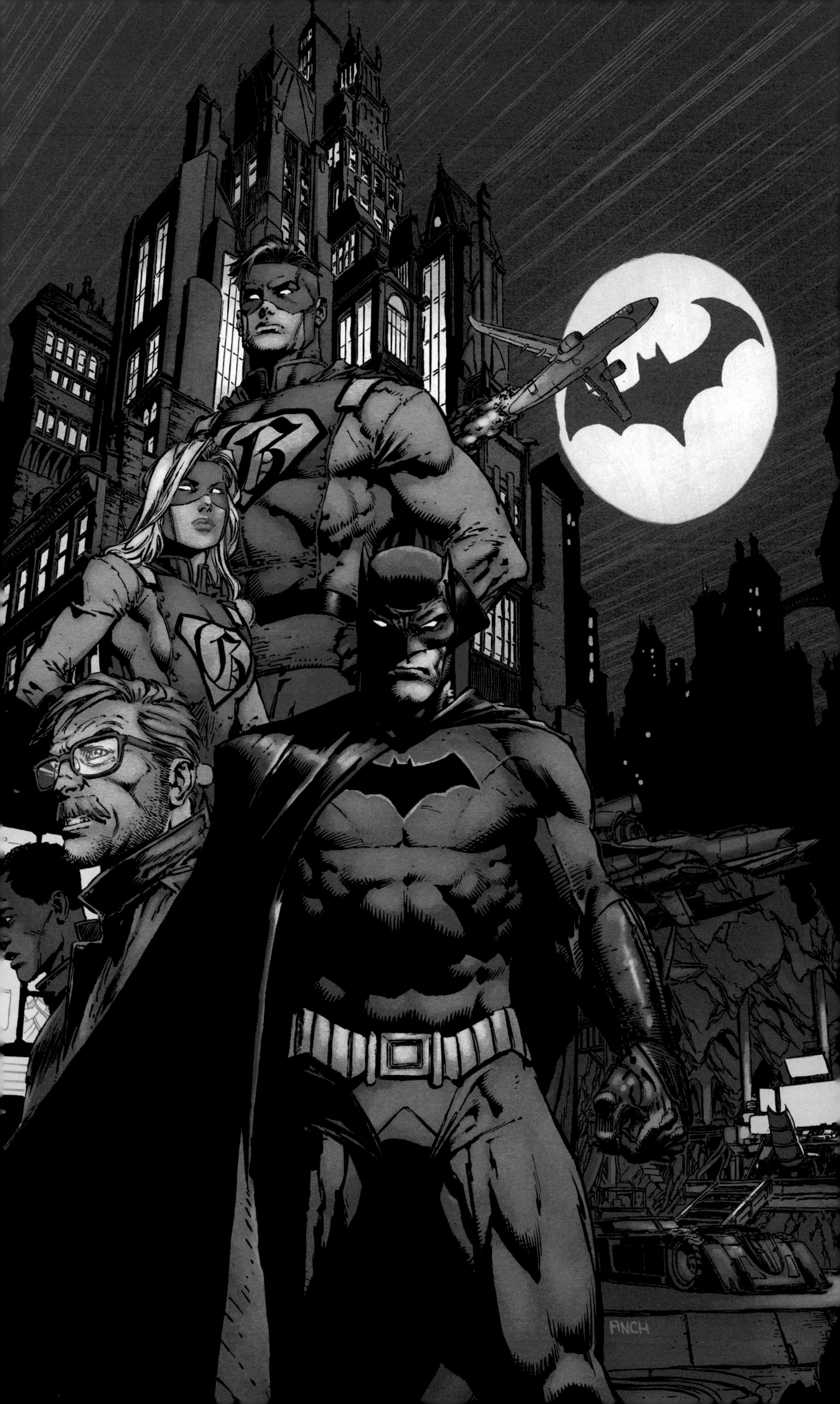
FINCH

I AM GOTHAM part one

TOM KING writer * DAVID FINCH penciller * MATT BANNING inker
JORDIE BELLAIRE colorist * JOHN WORKMAN letterer * DAVID FINCH and JORDIE BELLAIRE cover artists

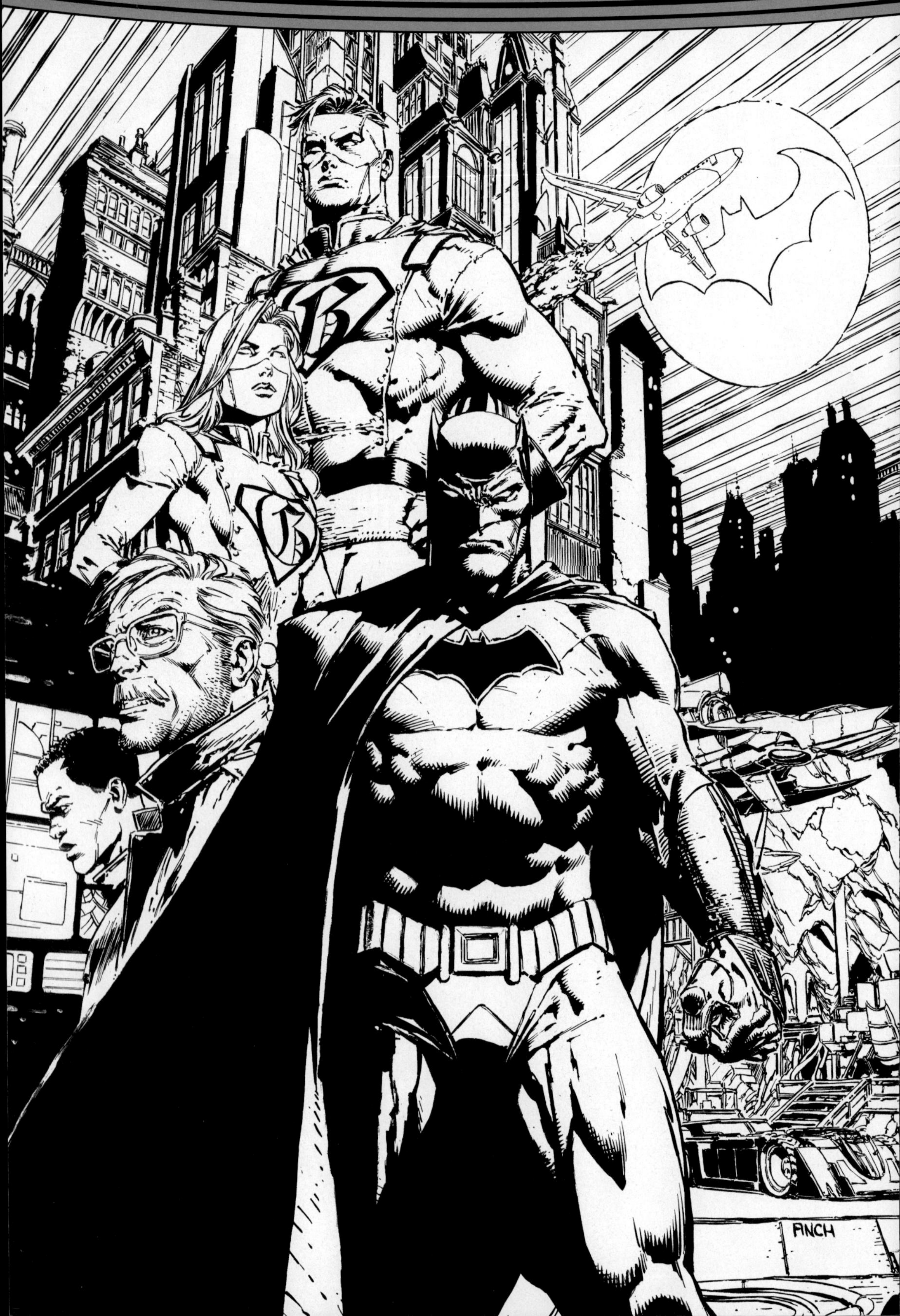
FINCH

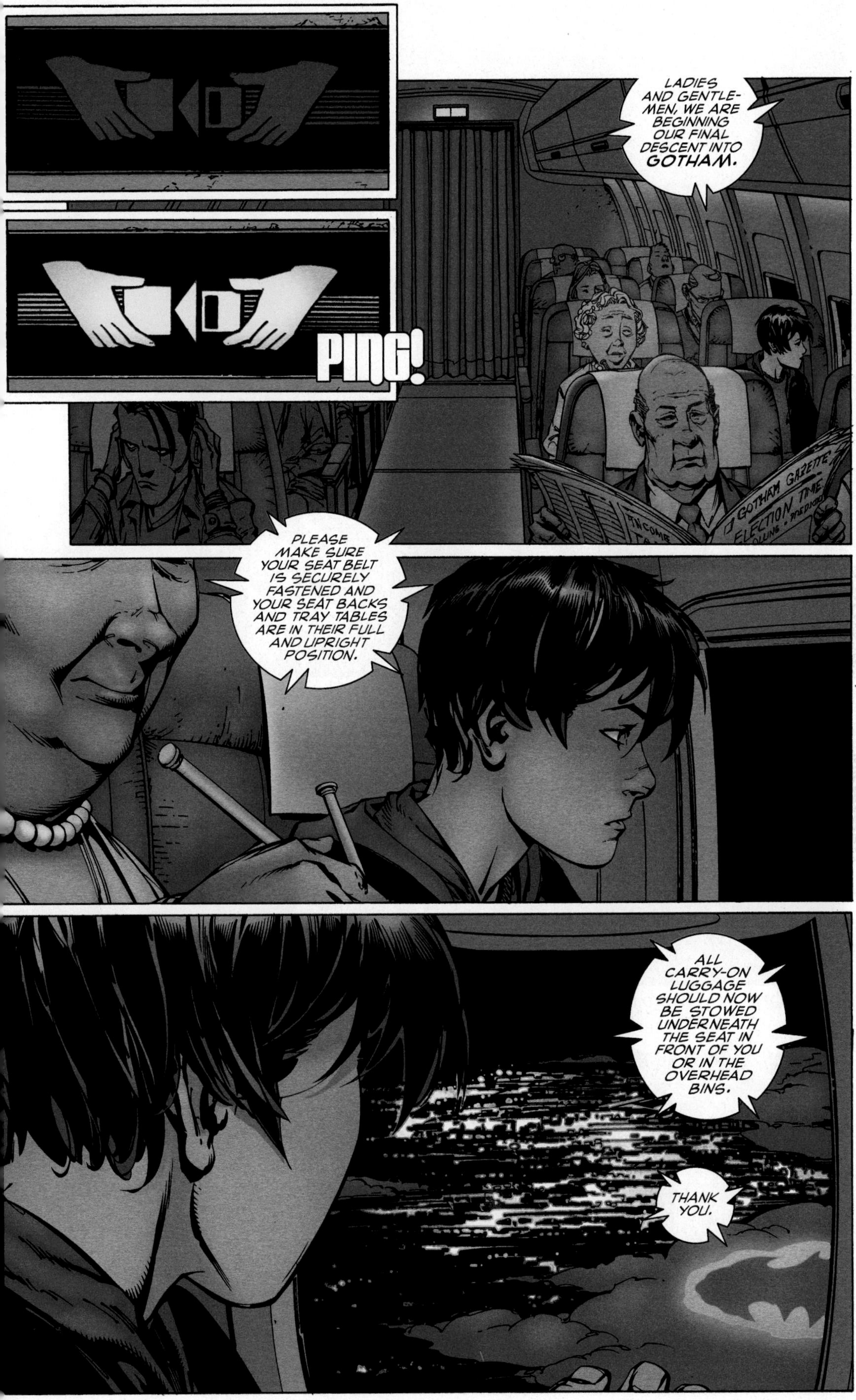
PING!
LADIES AND GENTLEMEN, WE ARE BEGINNING OUR FINAL DESCENT INTO GOTHAM.
GOTHAM GAZETTE
ELECTION TIME
PLEASE MAKE SURE YOUR SEAT BELT IS SECURELY FASTENED AND YOUR SEAT BACKS AND TRAY TABLES ARE IN THEIR FULL AND UPRIGHT POSITION.
ALL CARRY-ON LUGGAGE SHOULD NOW BE STOWED UNDERNEATH THE SEAT IN FRONT OF YOU OR IN THE OVERHEAD BINS.
THANK YOU.

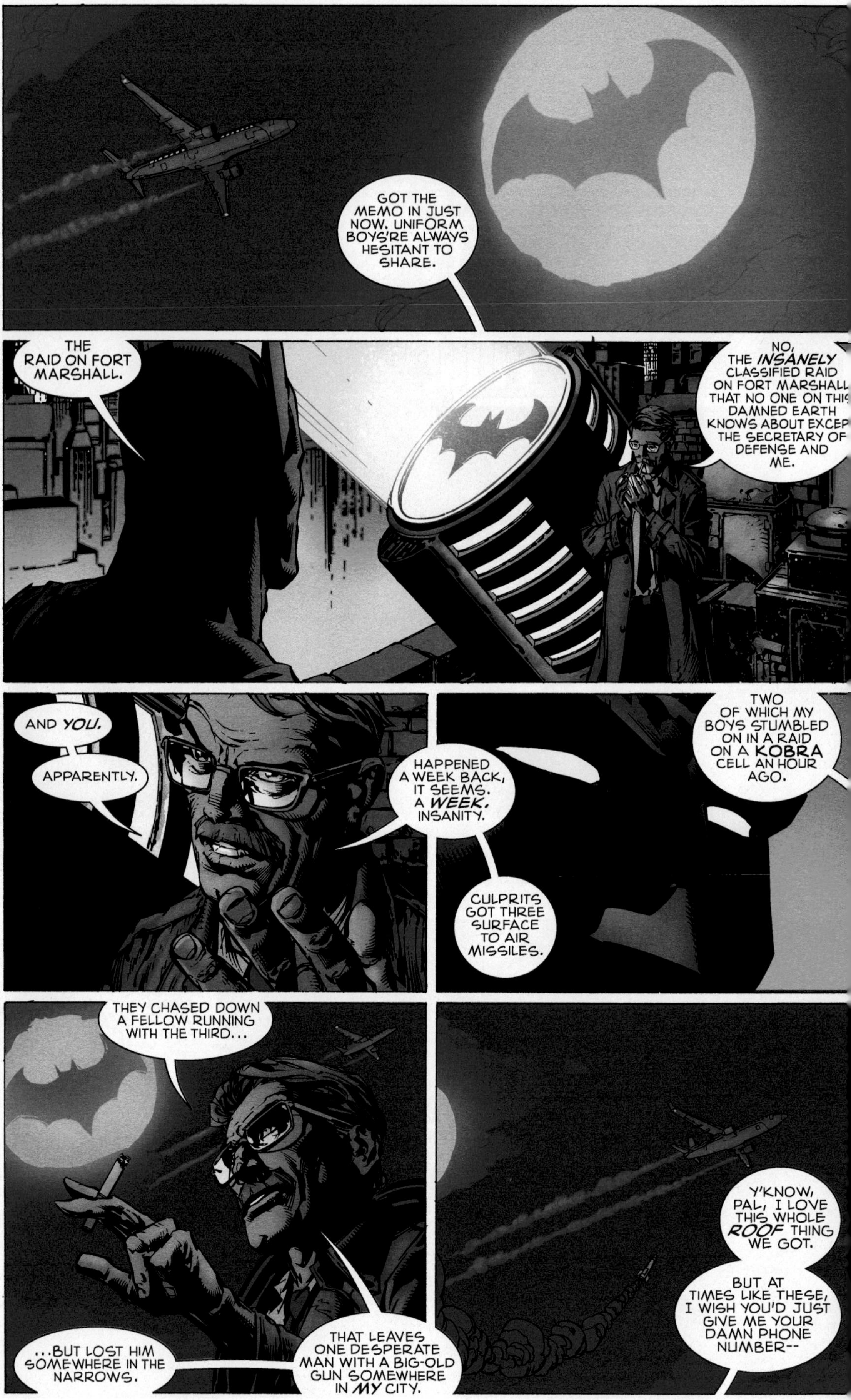
GOT THE MEMO IN JUST NOW. UNIFORM BOYS'RE ALWAYS HESITANT TO SHARE.
THE RAID ON FORT MARSHALL.
NO, THE INSANELY CLASSIFIED RAID ON FORT MARSHALL THAT NO ONE ON THIS DAMNED EARTH KNOWS ABOUT EXCEPT THE SECRETARY OF DEFENSE AND ME.
AND YOU.
APPARENTLY.
HAPPENED A WEEK BACK, IT SEEMS. A WEEK. INSANITY.
CULPRITS GOT THREE SURFACE TO AIR MISSILES.
TWO OF WHICH MY BOYS STUMBLED ON IN A RAID ON A KOBRA CELL AN HOUR AGO.
THEY CHASED DOWN A FELLOW RUNNING WITH THE THIRD...
...BUT LOST HIM SOMEWHERE IN THE NARROWS.
THAT LEAVES ONE DESPERATE MAN WITH A BIG-OLD GUN SOMEWHERE IN MY CITY.
Y'KNOW, PAL, I LOVE THIS WHOLE ROOF THING WE GOT.
BUT AT TIMES LIKE THESE, I WISH YOU'D JUST GIVE ME YOUR DAMN PHONE NUMBER--

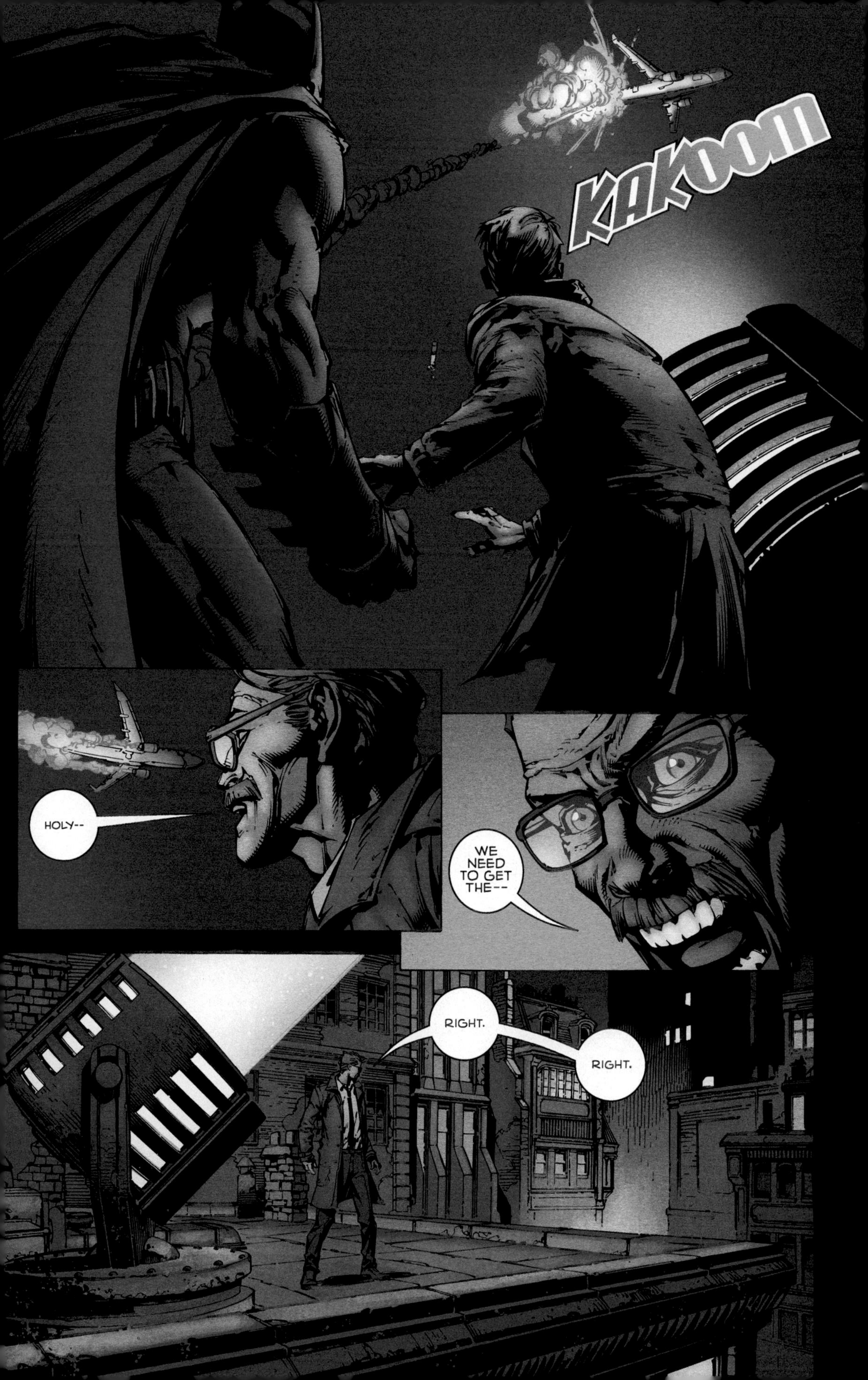
KAKOOM
HOLY--
WE NEED TO GET THE--
RIGHT.
RIGHT.

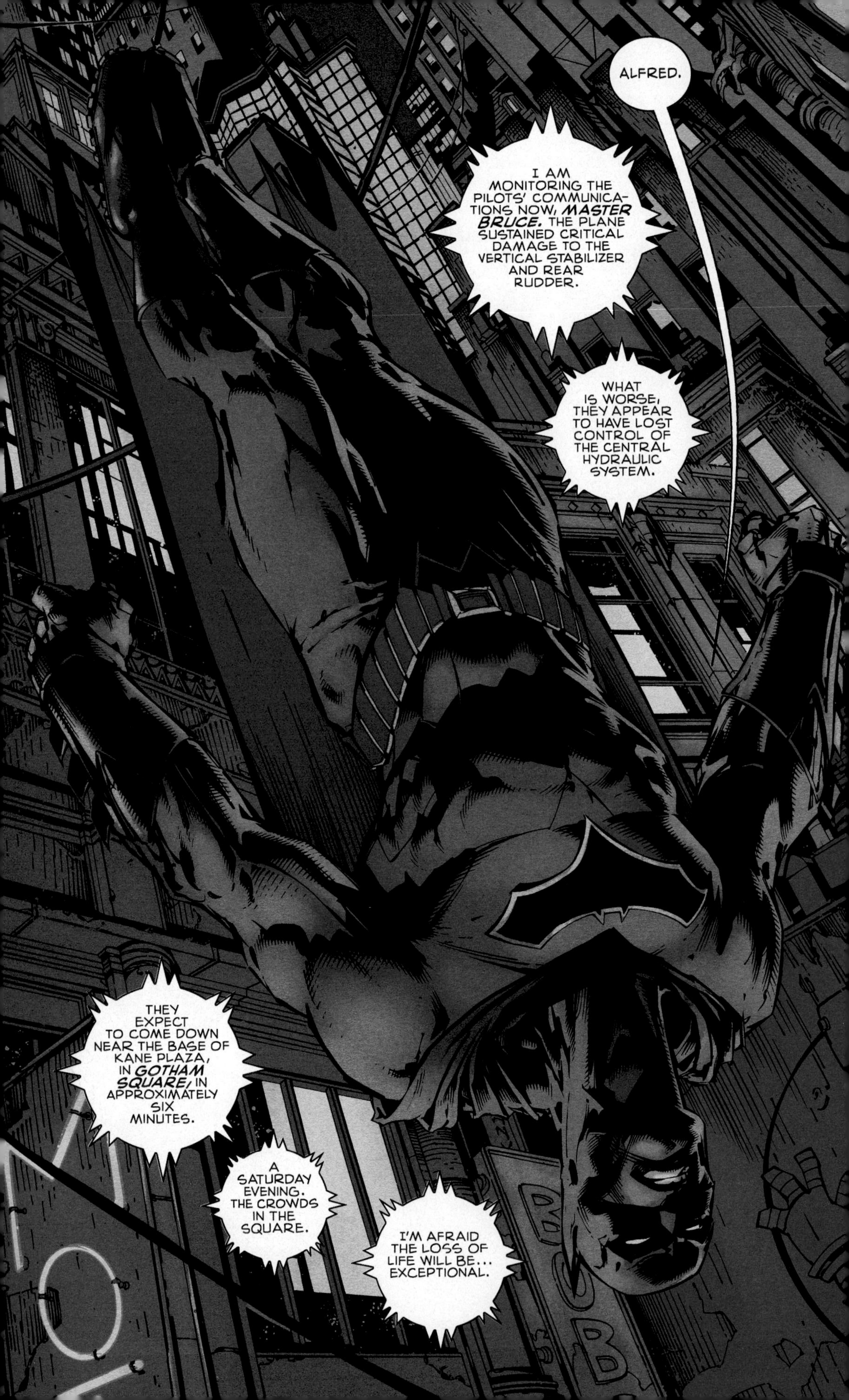

ALFRED.
I AM MONITORING THE PILOTS' COMMUNICATIONS NOW, *MASTER BRUCE.* THE PLANE SUSTAINED CRITICAL DAMAGE TO THE VERTICAL STABILIZER AND REAR RUDDER.
WHAT IS WORSE, THEY APPEAR TO HAVE LOST CONTROL OF THE CENTRAL HYDRAULIC SYSTEM.
THEY EXPECT TO COME DOWN NEAR THE BASE OF KANE PLAZA, IN *GOTHAM SQUARE,* IN APPROXIMATELY SIX MINUTES.
A SATURDAY EVENING. THE CROWDS IN THE SQUARE.
I'M AFRAID THE LOSS OF LIFE WILL BE... EXCEPTIONAL.

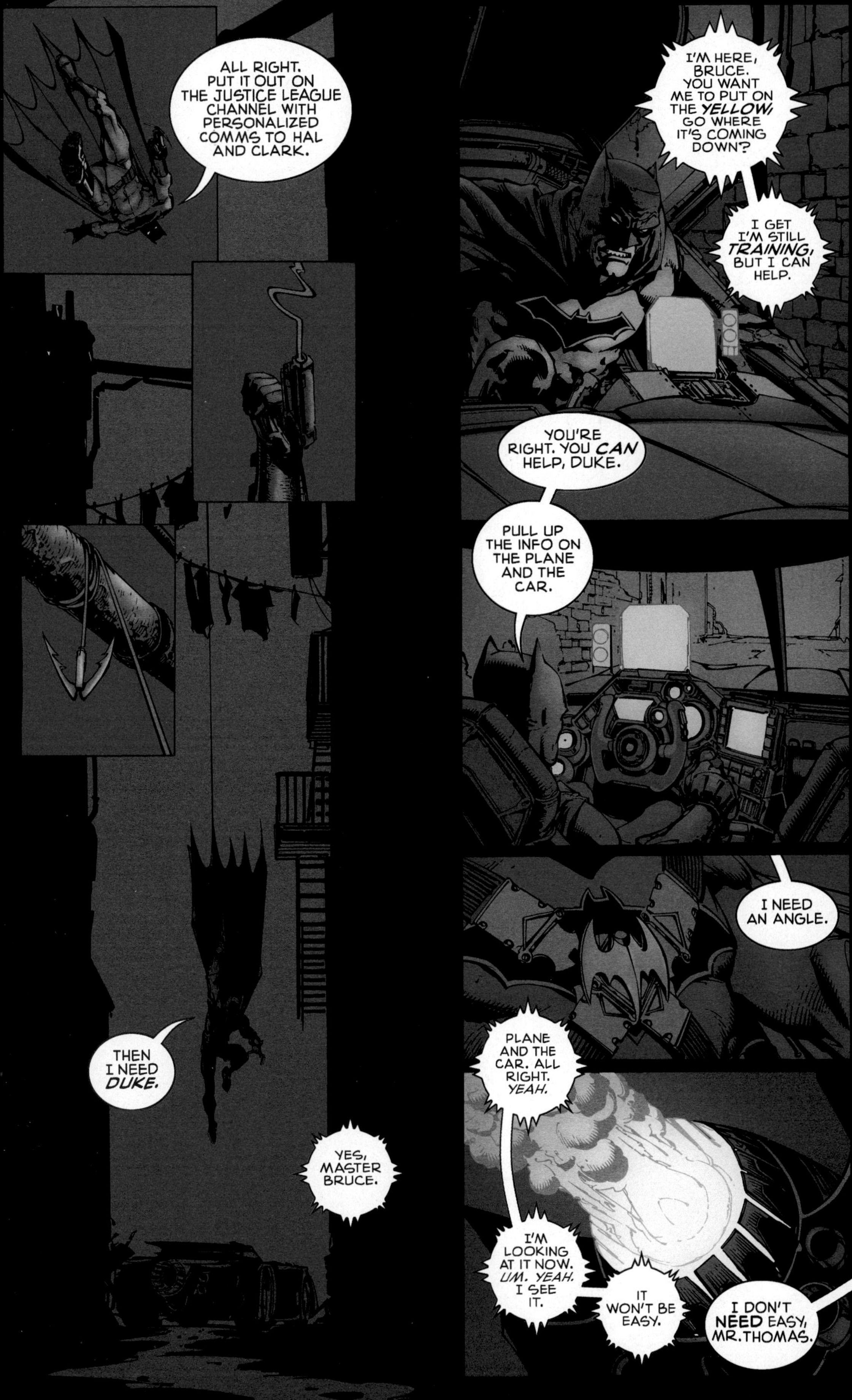
ALL RIGHT. PUT IT OUT ON THE JUSTICE LEAGUE CHANNEL WITH PERSONALIZED COMMS TO HAL AND CLARK.
THEN I NEED *DUKE.*
YES, MASTER BRUCE.
I'M HERE, BRUCE. YOU WANT ME TO PUT ON THE *YELLOW,* GO WHERE IT'S COMING DOWN?
I GET I'M STILL *TRAINING,* BUT I CAN HELP.
YOU'RE RIGHT. YOU *CAN* HELP, DUKE.
PULL UP THE INFO ON THE PLANE AND THE CAR.
I NEED AN ANGLE.
PLANE AND THE CAR. ALL RIGHT. *YEAH.*
I'M LOOKING AT IT NOW. *UM. YEAH.* I SEE IT.
IT WON'T BE EASY.
I DON'T **NEED** EASY, MR.THOMAS.

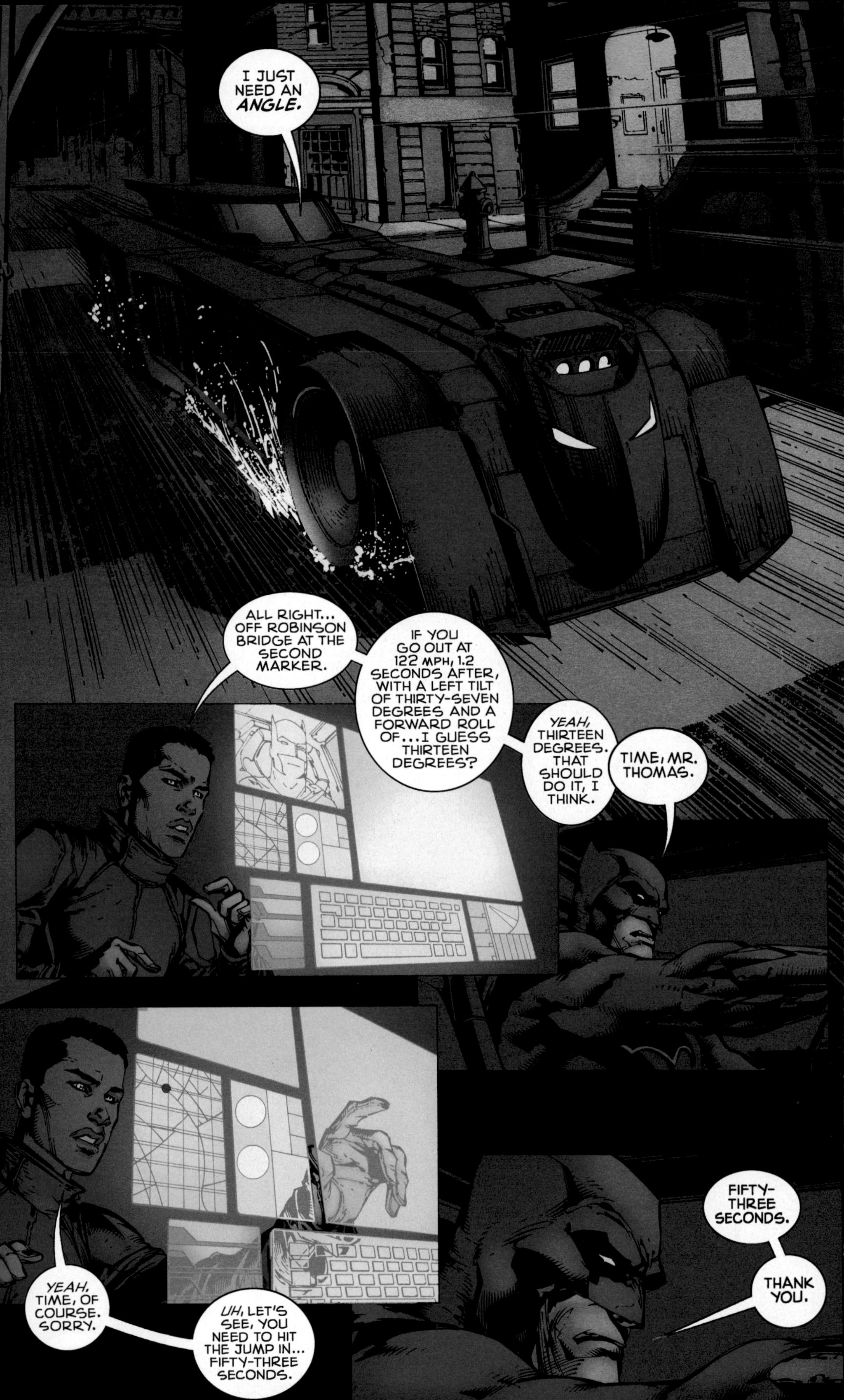
I JUST NEED AN *ANGLE.*
ALL RIGHT... OFF ROBINSON BRIDGE AT THE SECOND MARKER.
IF YOU GO OUT AT 122 MPH, 1.2 SECONDS AFTER, WITH A LEFT TILT OF THIRTY-SEVEN DEGREES AND A FORWARD ROLL OF...I GUESS THIRTEEN DEGREES?
YEAH, THIRTEEN DEGREES. THAT SHOULD DO IT, I THINK.
TIME, MR. THOMAS.
YEAH, TIME, OF COURSE. SORRY.
UH, LET'S SEE, YOU NEED TO HIT THE JUMP IN... FIFTY-THREE SECONDS.
FIFTY-THREE SECONDS.
THANK YOU.

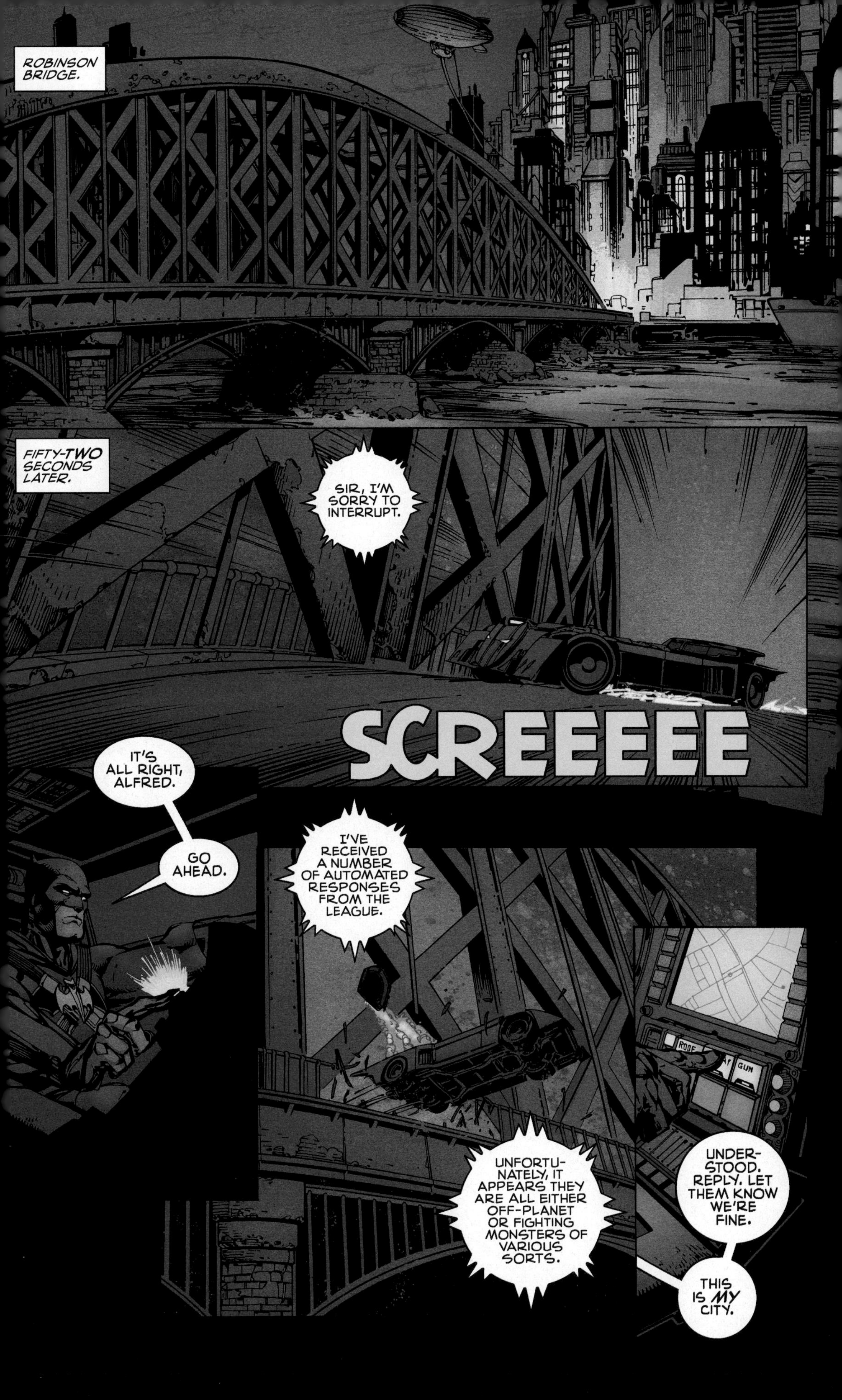

ROBINSON BRIDGE.
FIFTY-TWO SECONDS LATER.
SIR, I'M SORRY TO INTERRUPT.
SCREEEEE
IT'S ALL RIGHT, ALFRED.
GO AHEAD.
I'VE RECEIVED A NUMBER OF AUTOMATED RESPONSES FROM THE LEAGUE.
ROOF
GUN
UNFORTU-NATELY, IT APPEARS THEY ARE ALL EITHER OFF-PLANET OR FIGHTING MONSTERS OF VARIOUS SORTS.
UNDER-STOOD. REPLY. LET THEM KNOW WE'RE FINE.
THIS IS MY CITY.

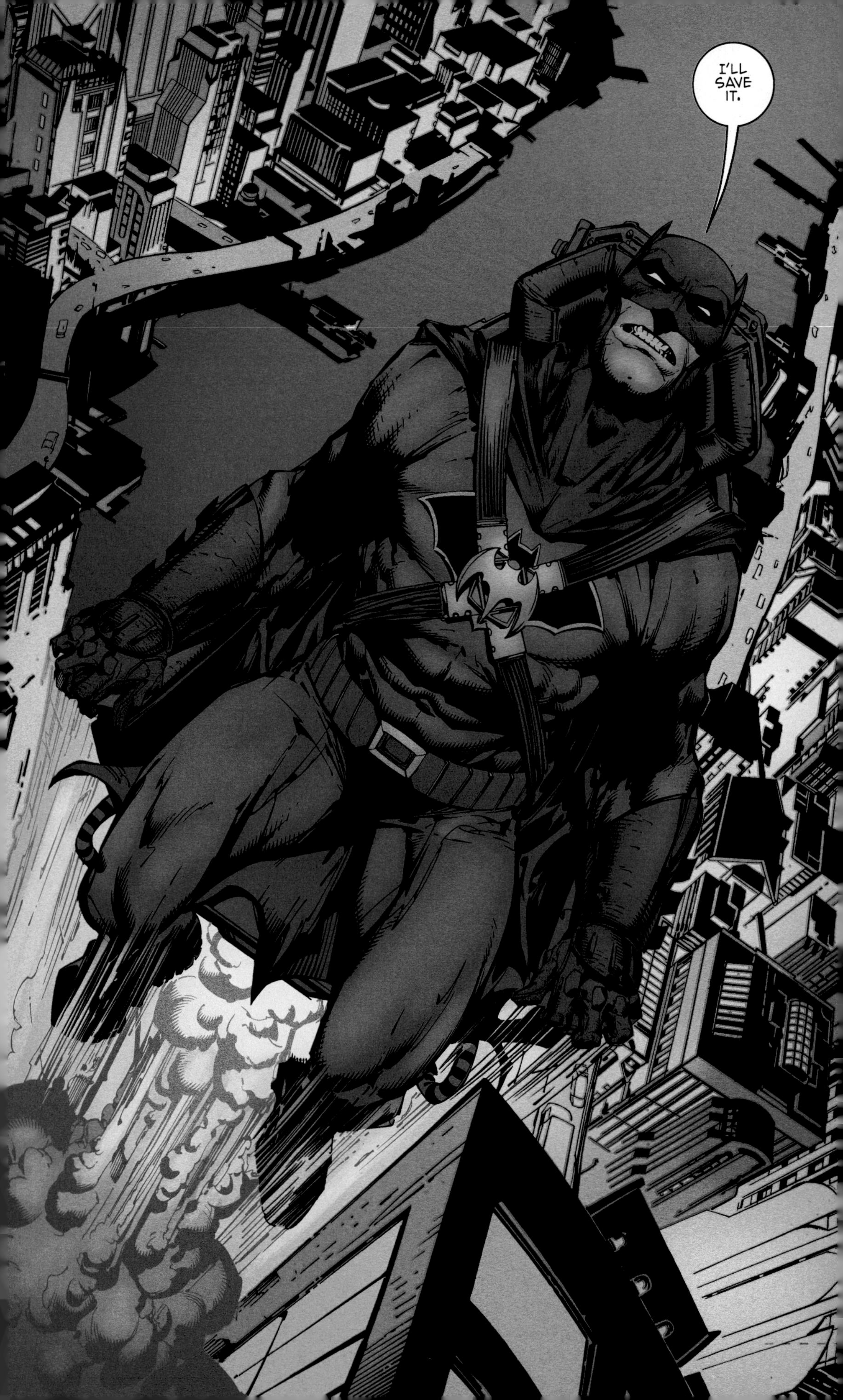
I'LL SAVE IT.

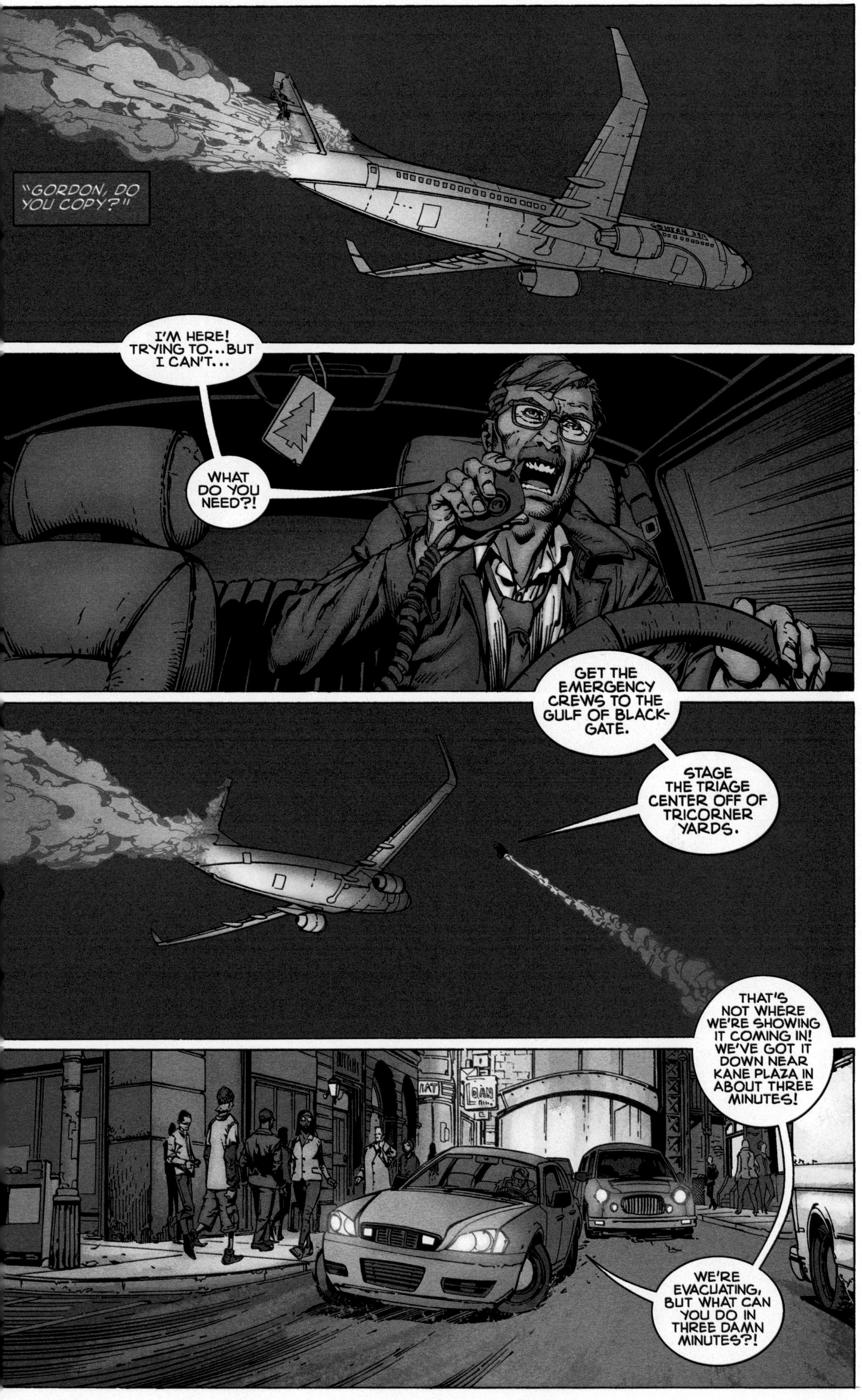
"GORDON, DO YOU COPY?"
I'M HERE! TRYING TO...BUT I CAN'T...
WHAT DO YOU NEED?!
GET THE EMERGENCY CREWS TO THE GULF OF BLACK-GATE.
STAGE THE TRIAGE CENTER OFF OF TRICORNER YARDS.
THAT'S NOT WHERE WE'RE SHOWING IT COMING IN! WE'VE GOT IT DOWN NEAR KANE PLAZA IN ABOUT THREE MINUTES!
WE'RE EVACUATING, BUT WHAT CAN YOU DO IN THREE DAMN MINUTES?!

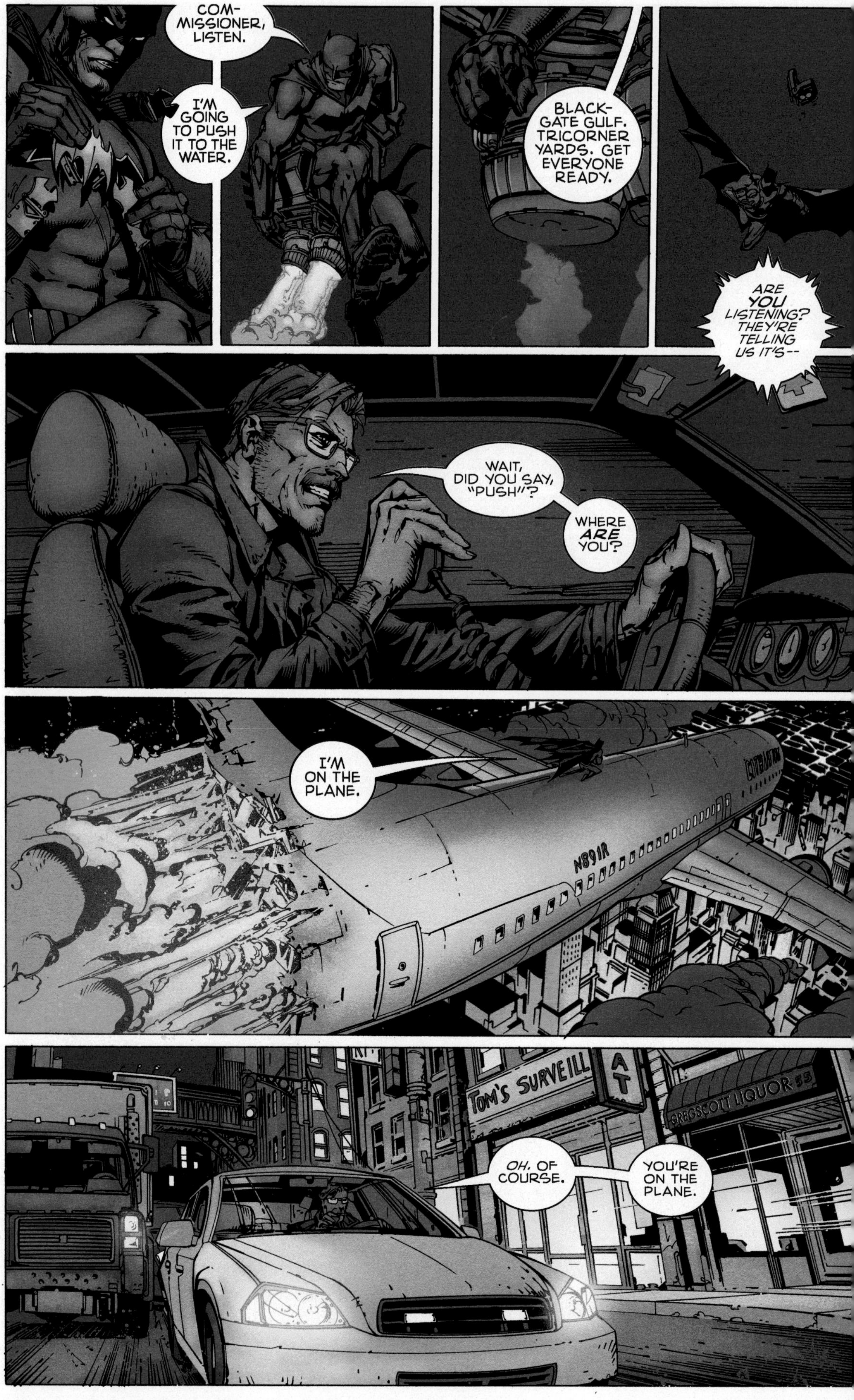
COM-MISSIONER, LISTEN.
I'M GOING TO PUSH IT TO THE WATER.
BLACK-GATE GULF. TRICORNER YARDS. GET EVERYONE READY.
ARE YOU LISTENING? THEY'RE TELLING US IT'S--
WAIT, DID YOU SAY, "PUSH"?
WHERE ARE YOU?
I'M ON THE PLANE.
N891R
TOM'S SURVEILL
GREGSCOTT LIQUOR
OH. OF COURSE.
YOU'RE ON THE PLANE.

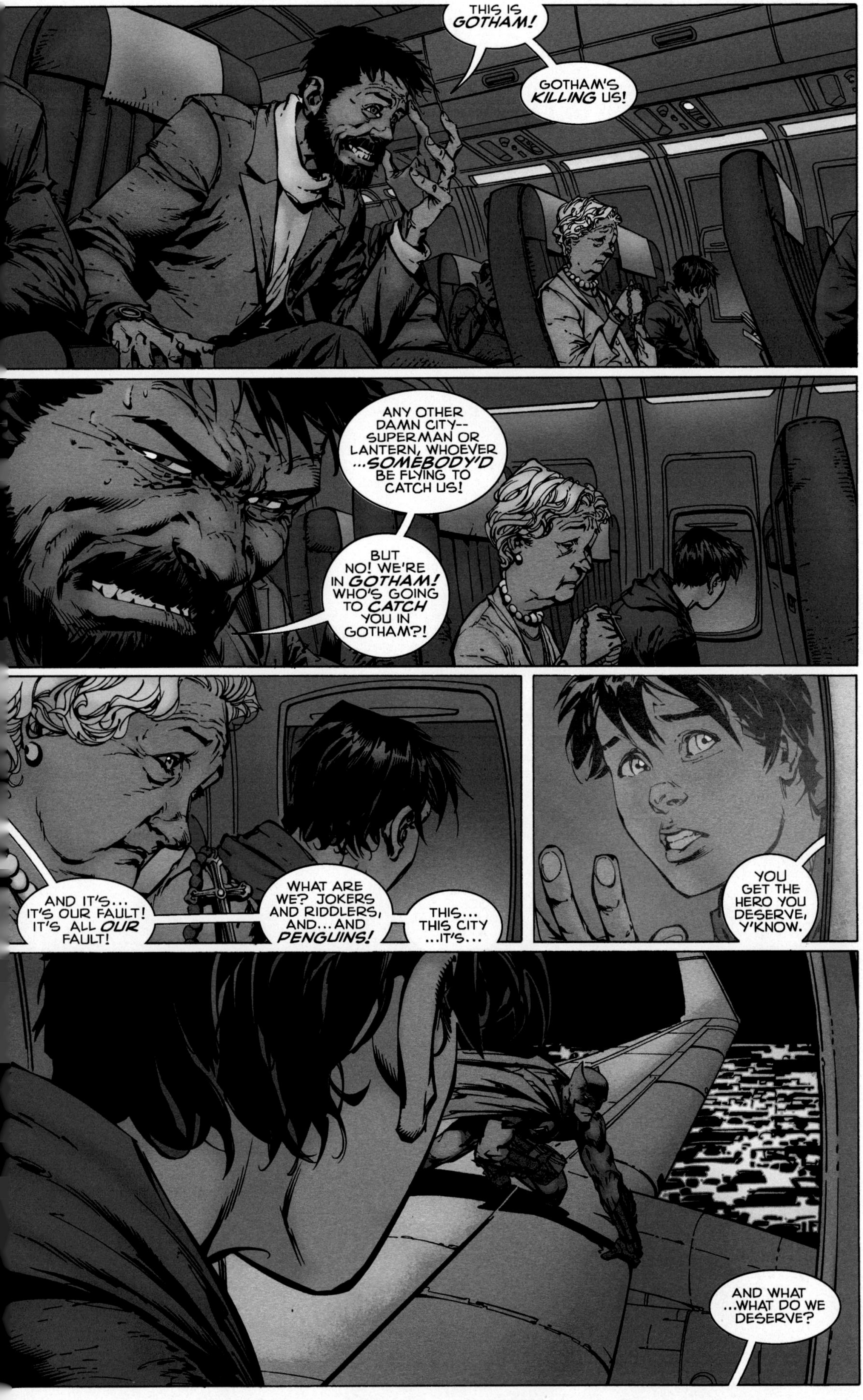
THIS IS *GOTHAM!*
GOTHAM'S *KILLING* US!
ANY OTHER DAMN CITY-- SUPERMAN OR LANTERN, WHOEVER ...*SOMEBODY'D* BE FLYING TO CATCH US!
BUT NO! WE'RE IN *GOTHAM!* WHO'S GOING TO *CATCH* YOU IN GOTHAM?!
AND IT'S... IT'S OUR FAULT! IT'S ALL *OUR* FAULT!
WHAT ARE WE? JOKERS AND RIDDLERS, AND...AND *PENGUINS!*
THIS... THIS CITY ...IT'S...
YOU GET THE HERO YOU DESERVE, Y'KNOW.
AND WHAT ...WHAT DO WE DESERVE?

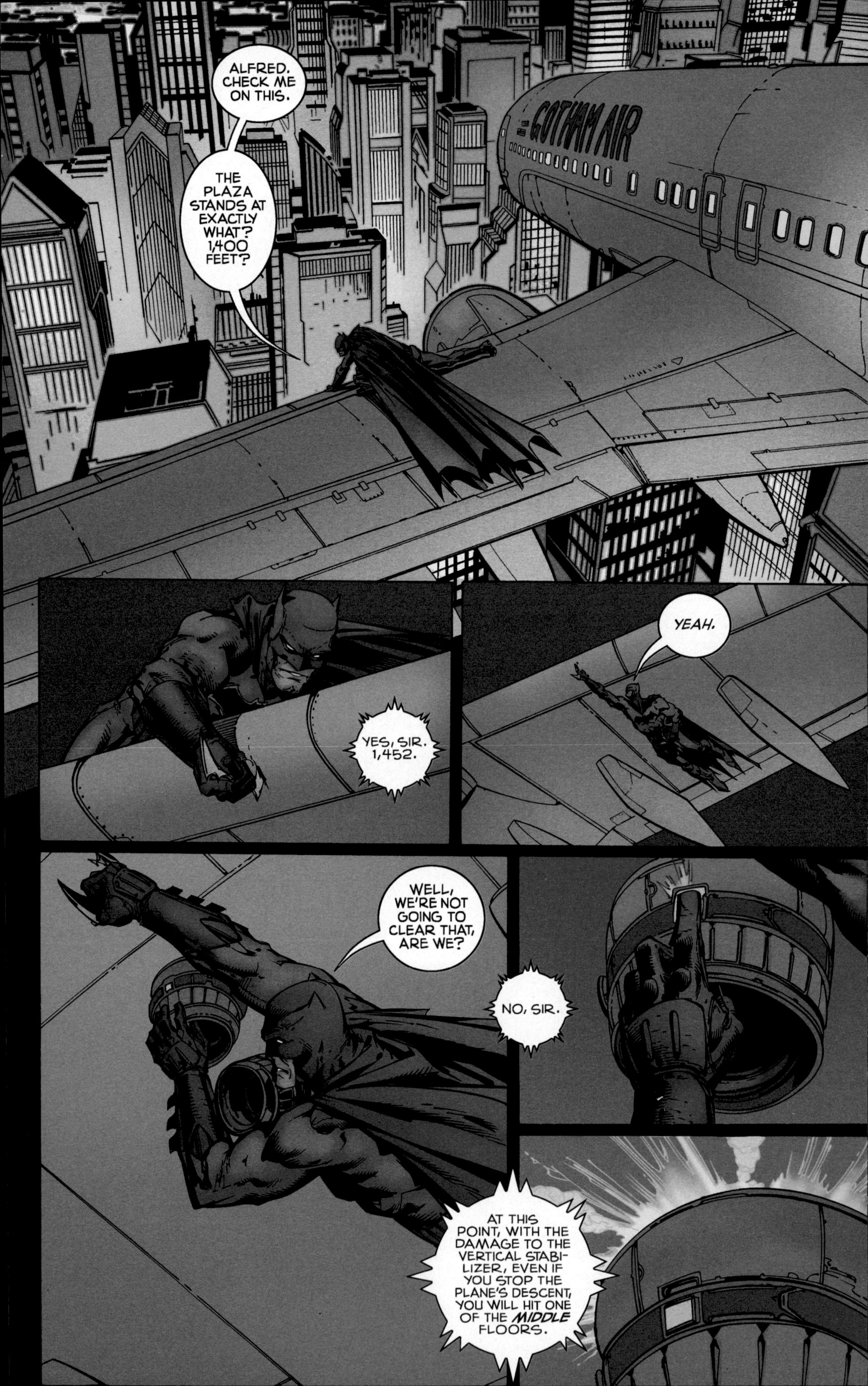

ALFRED. CHECK ME ON THIS.
THE PLAZA STANDS AT EXACTLY WHAT? 1,400 FEET?
GOTHAM AIR
YES, SIR. 1,452.
YEAH.
WELL, WE'RE NOT GOING TO CLEAR THAT, ARE WE?
NO, SIR.
AT THIS POINT, WITH THE DAMAGE TO THE VERTICAL STABILIZER, EVEN IF YOU STOP THE PLANE'S DESCENT, YOU WILL HIT ONE OF THE *MIDDLE* FLOORS.

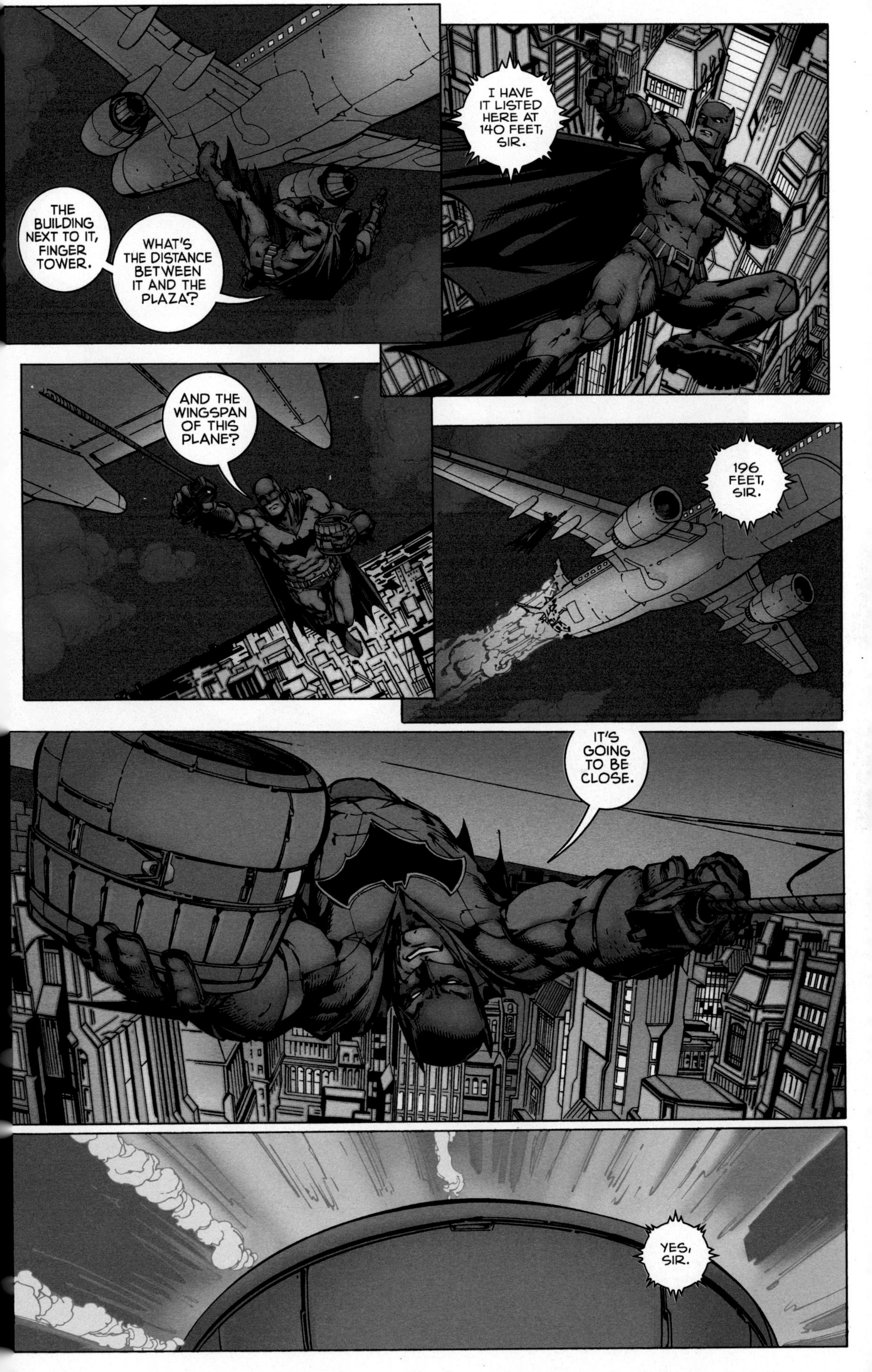
THE BUILDING NEXT TO IT, FINGER TOWER.
WHAT'S THE DISTANCE BETWEEN IT AND THE PLAZA?
I HAVE IT LISTED HERE AT 140 FEET, SIR.
AND THE WINGSPAN OF THIS PLANE?
196 FEET, SIR.
IT'S GOING TO BE CLOSE.
YES, SIR.

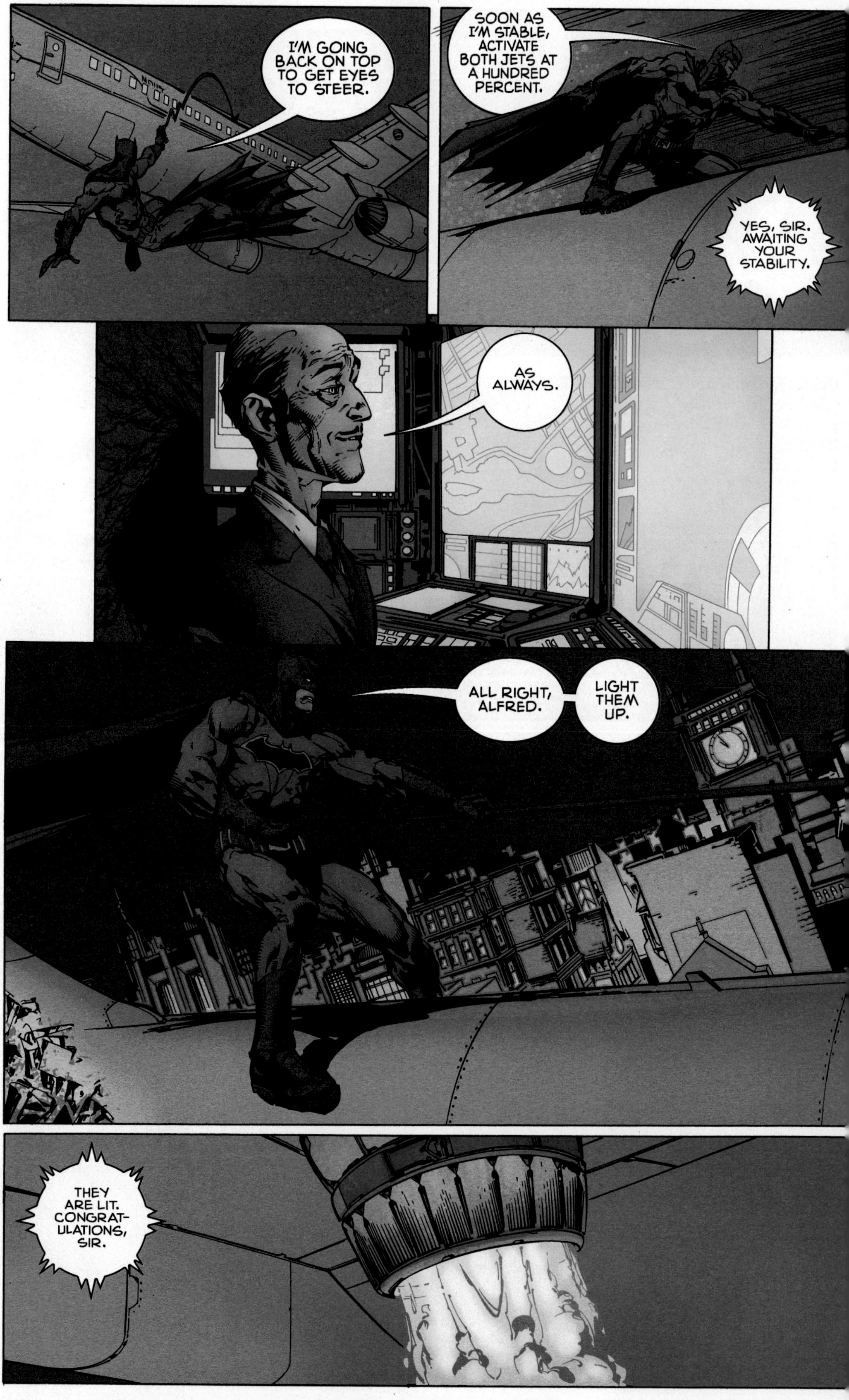
I'M GOING BACK ON TOP TO GET EYES TO STEER.
SOON AS I'M STABLE, ACTIVATE BOTH JETS AT A HUNDRED PERCENT.
YES, SIR. AWAITING YOUR STABILITY.
AS ALWAYS.
ALL RIGHT, ALFRED.
LIGHT THEM UP.
THEY ARE LIT. CONGRAT-ULATIONS, SIR.

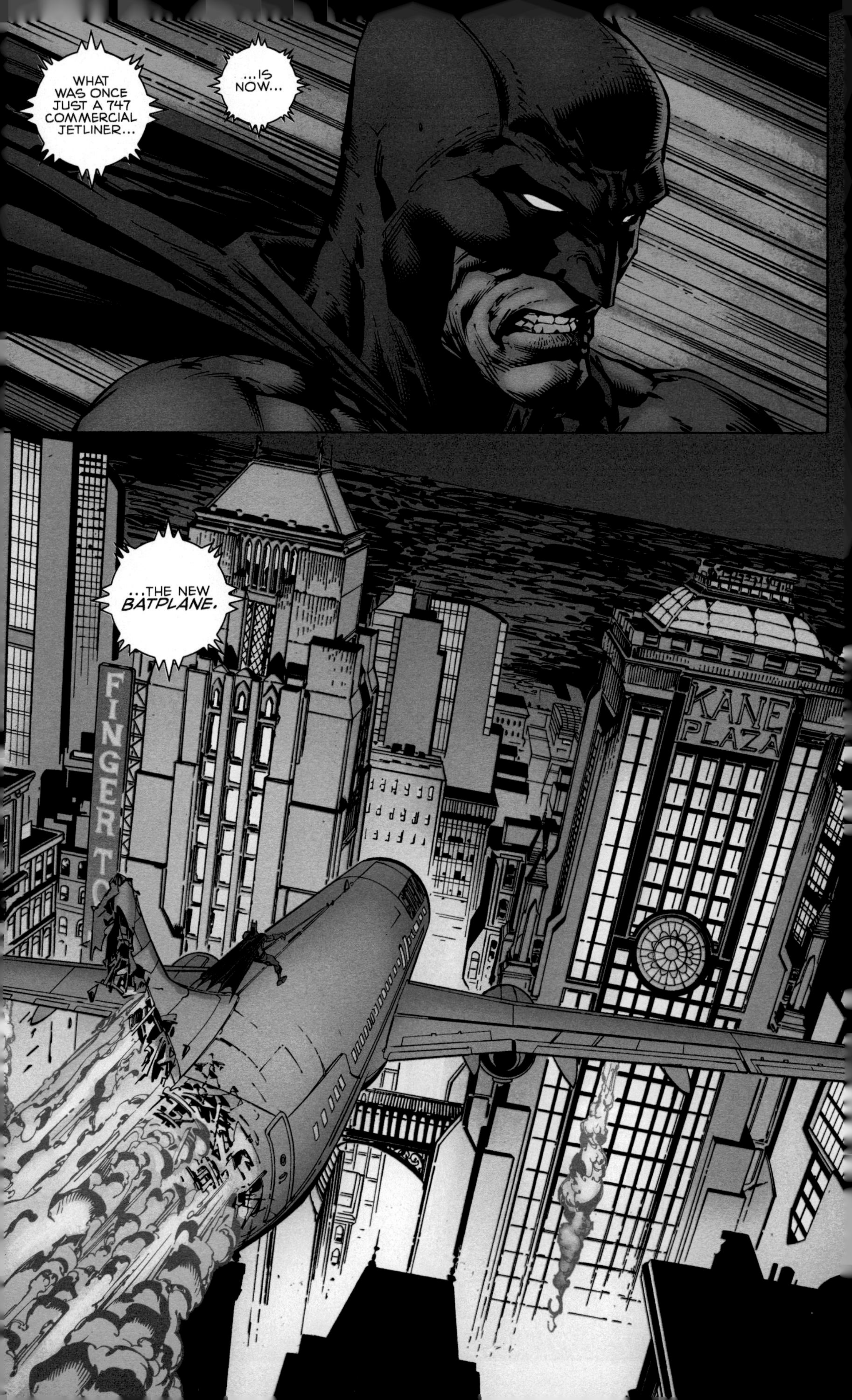

WHAT WAS ONCE JUST A 747 COMMERCIAL JETLINER...
...IS NOW...
...THE NEW BATPLANE.
FINGER TO
KANE PLAZA

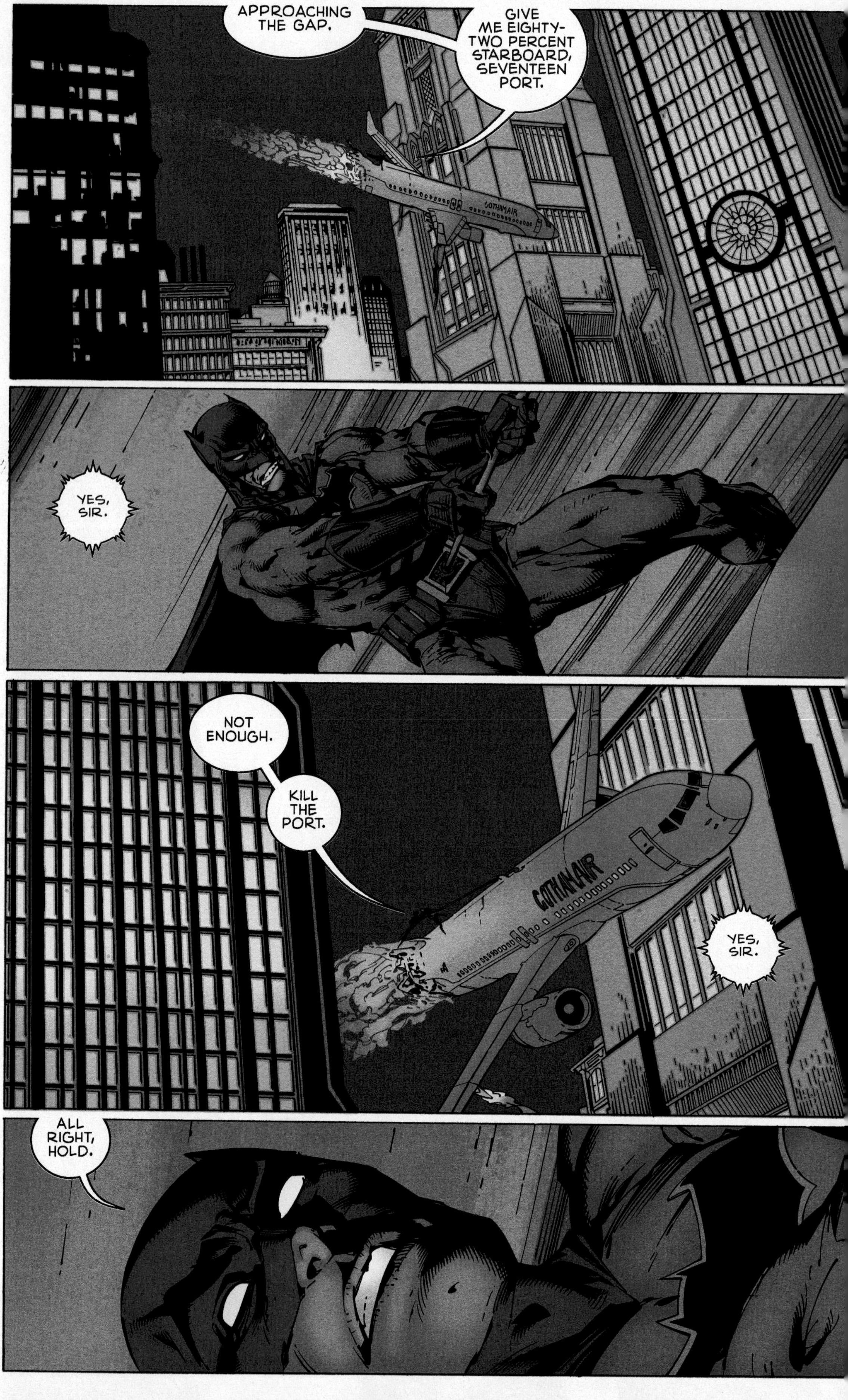
APPROACHING THE GAP.
GIVE ME EIGHTY-TWO PERCENT STARBOARD, SEVENTEEN PORT.
YES, SIR.
NOT ENOUGH.
KILL THE PORT.
YES, SIR.
ALL RIGHT, HOLD.

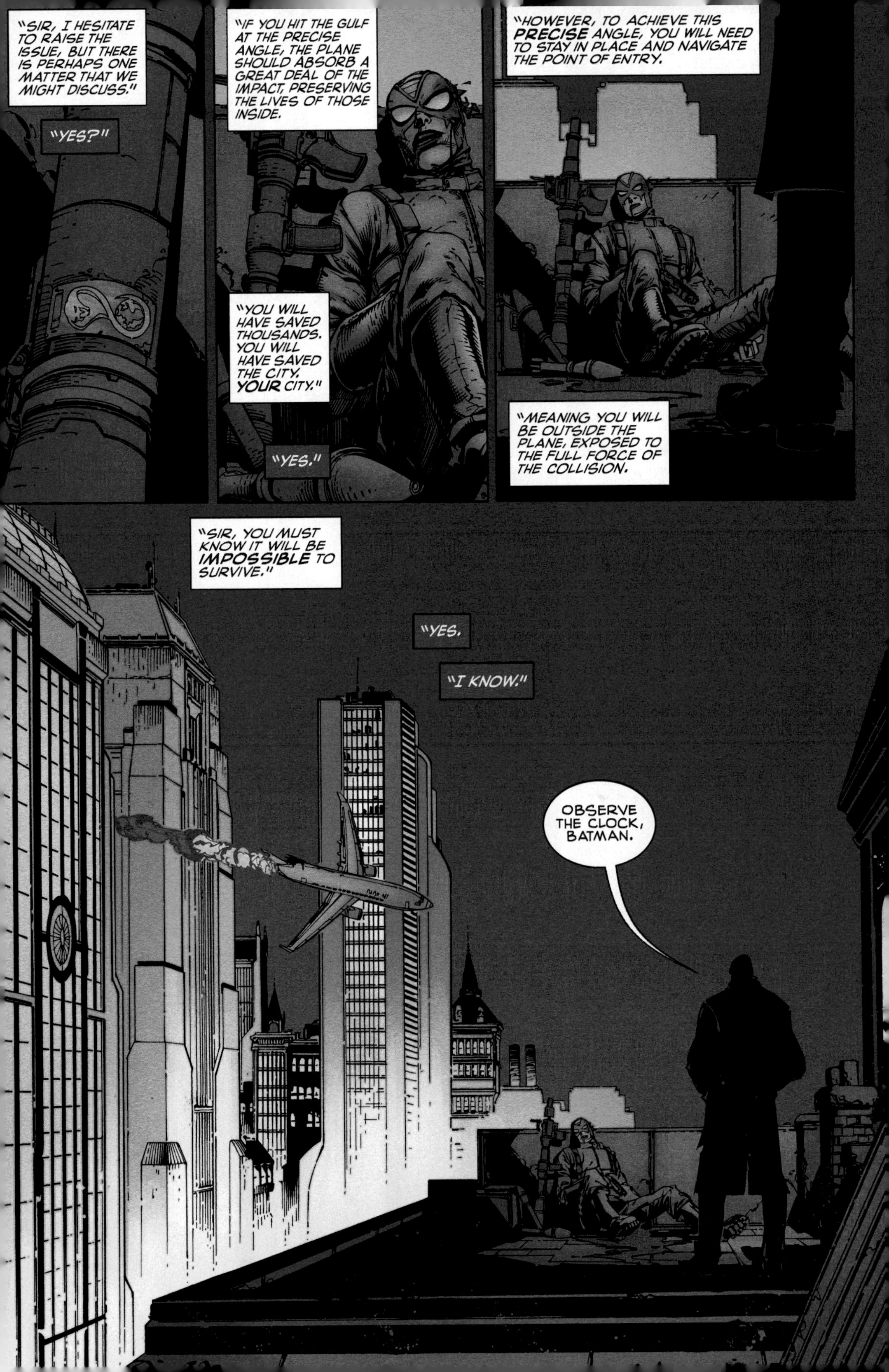
"SIR, I HESITATE TO RAISE THE ISSUE, BUT THERE IS PERHAPS ONE MATTER THAT WE MIGHT DISCUSS."
"YES?"
"IF YOU HIT THE GULF AT THE PRECISE ANGLE, THE PLANE SHOULD ABSORB A GREAT DEAL OF THE IMPACT, PRESERVING THE LIVES OF THOSE INSIDE.
"YOU WILL HAVE SAVED THOUSANDS. YOU WILL HAVE SAVED THE CITY. YOUR CITY."
"YES."
"HOWEVER, TO ACHIEVE THIS PRECISE ANGLE, YOU WILL NEED TO STAY IN PLACE AND NAVIGATE THE POINT OF ENTRY.
"MEANING YOU WILL BE OUTSIDE THE PLANE, EXPOSED TO THE FULL FORCE OF THE COLLISION.
"SIR, YOU MUST KNOW IT WILL BE IMPOSSIBLE TO SURVIVE."
"YES.
"I KNOW."
OBSERVE THE CLOCK, BATMAN.

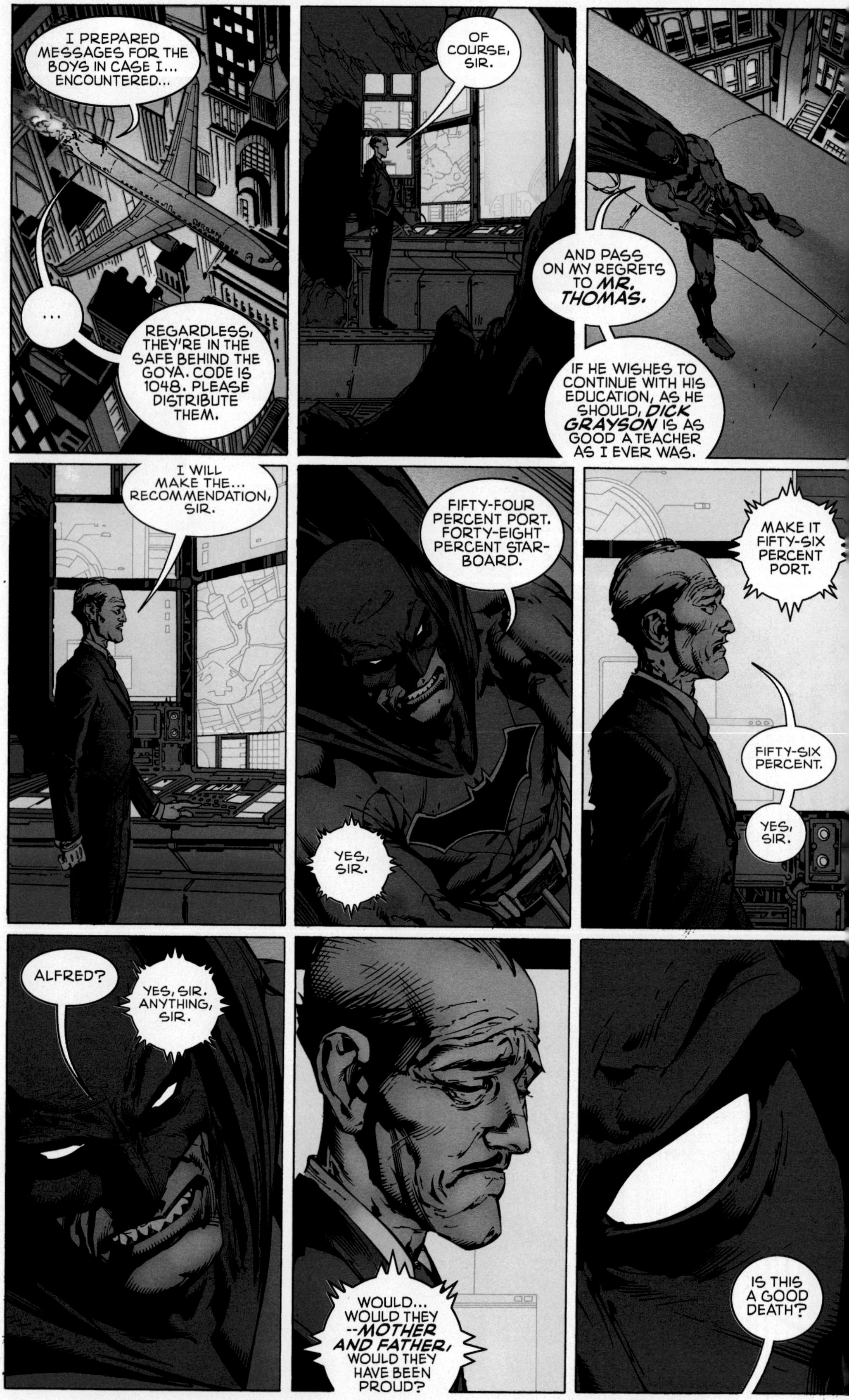
I PREPARED MESSAGES FOR THE BOYS IN CASE I... ENCOUNTERED...
...
REGARDLESS, THEY'RE IN THE SAFE BEHIND THE GOYA. CODE IS 1048. PLEASE DISTRIBUTE THEM.
OF COURSE, SIR.
AND PASS ON MY REGRETS TO MR. THOMAS.
IF HE WISHES TO CONTINUE WITH HIS EDUCATION, AS HE SHOULD, DICK GRAYSON IS AS GOOD A TEACHER AS I EVER WAS.
I WILL MAKE THE... RECOMMENDATION, SIR.
FIFTY-FOUR PERCENT PORT. FORTY-EIGHT PERCENT STAR-BOARD.
YES, SIR.
MAKE IT FIFTY-SIX PERCENT PORT.
FIFTY-SIX PERCENT.
YES, SIR.
ALFRED?
YES, SIR. ANYTHING, SIR.
WOULD... WOULD THEY --MOTHER AND FATHER, WOULD THEY HAVE BEEN PROUD?
IS THIS A GOOD DEATH?

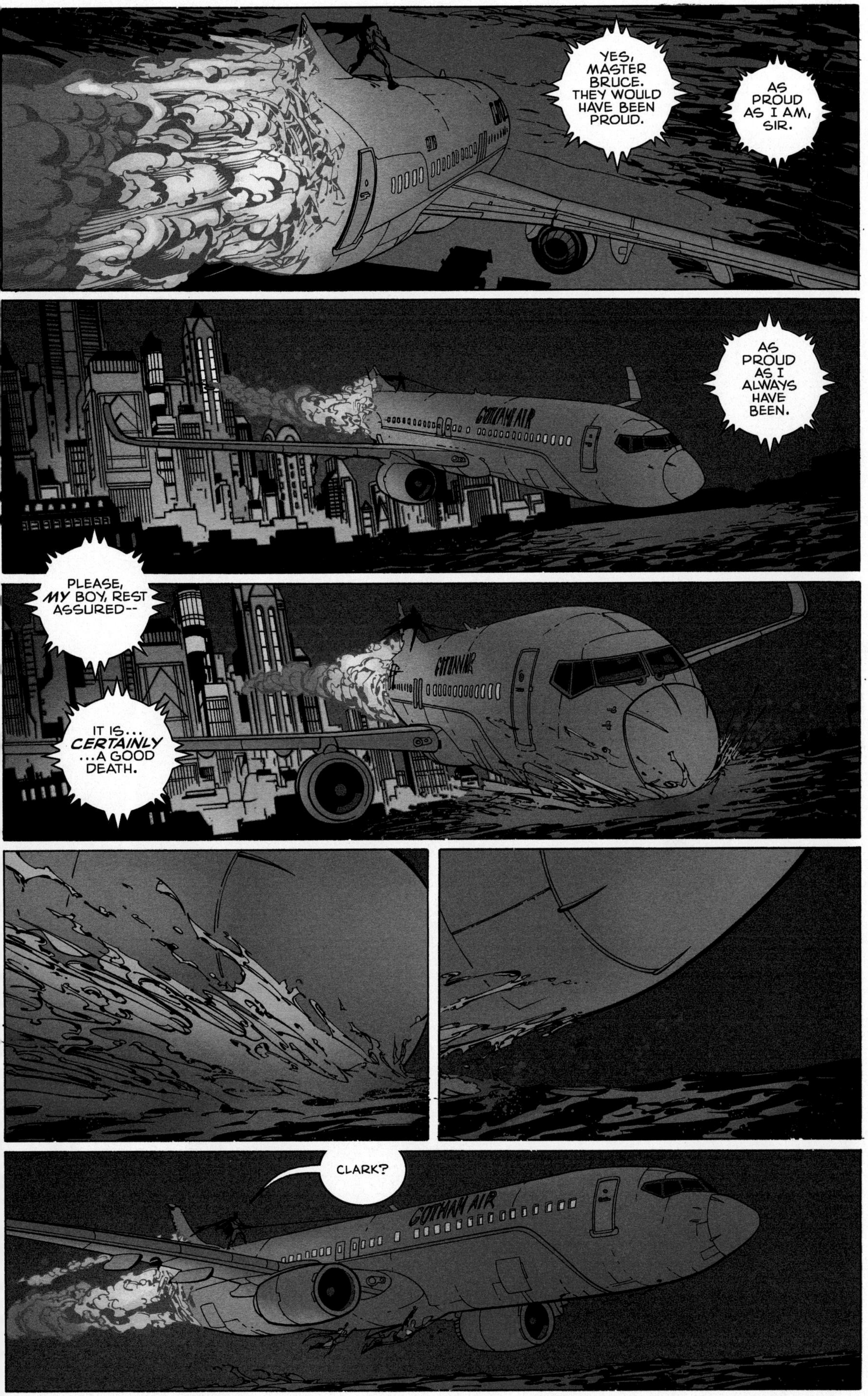
YES, MASTER BRUCE. THEY WOULD HAVE BEEN PROUD.
AS PROUD AS I AM, SIR.
AS PROUD AS I ALWAYS HAVE BEEN.
PLEASE, *MY* BOY, REST ASSURED--
IT IS... *CERTAINLY* ...A GOOD DEATH.
CLARK?
GOTHAM AIR

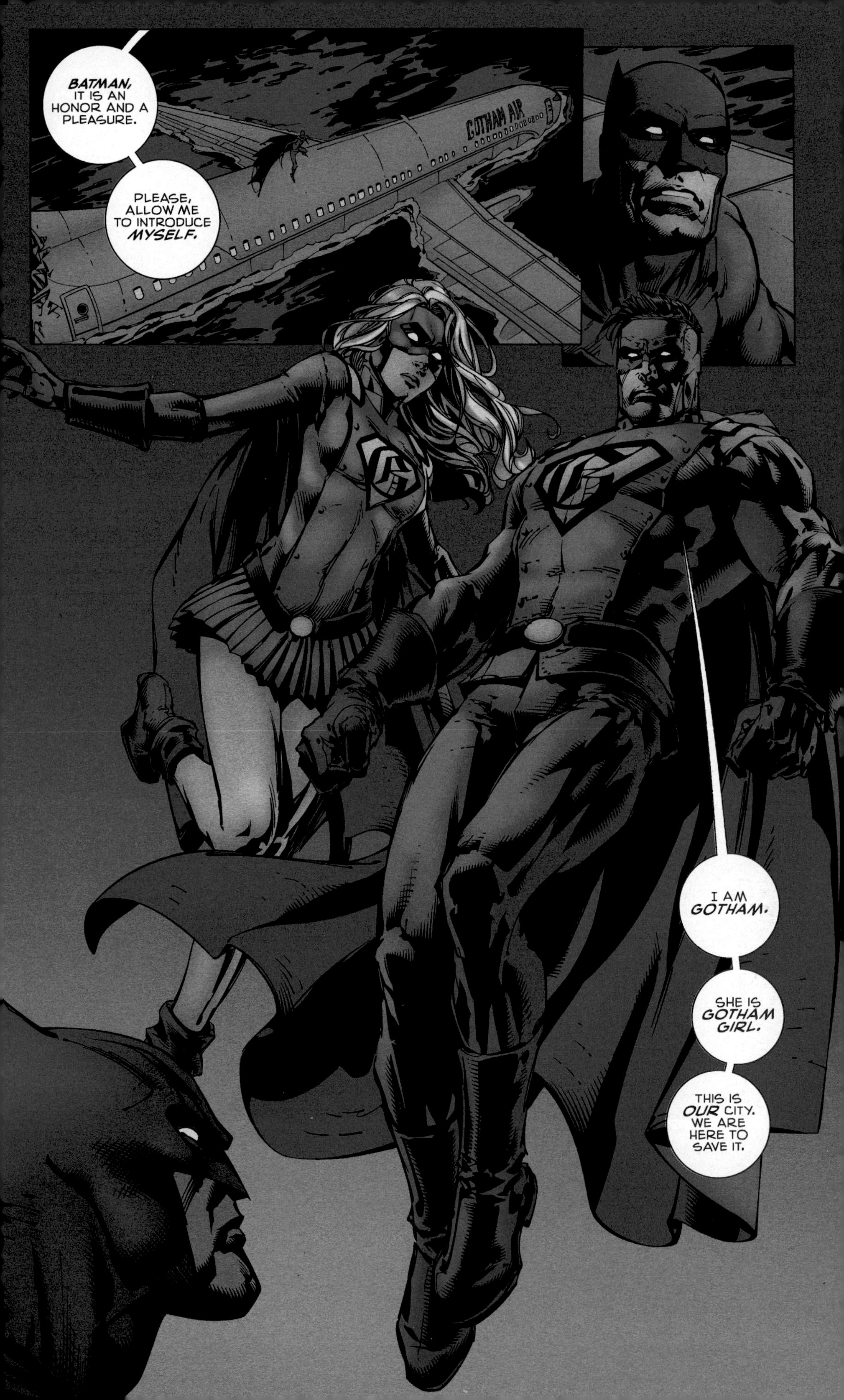

BATMAN, IT IS AN HONOR AND A PLEASURE.
PLEASE, ALLOW ME TO INTRODUCE MYSELF.
GOTHAM AIR
I AM GOTHAM.
SHE IS GOTHAM GIRL.
THIS IS OUR CITY. WE ARE HERE TO SAVE IT.

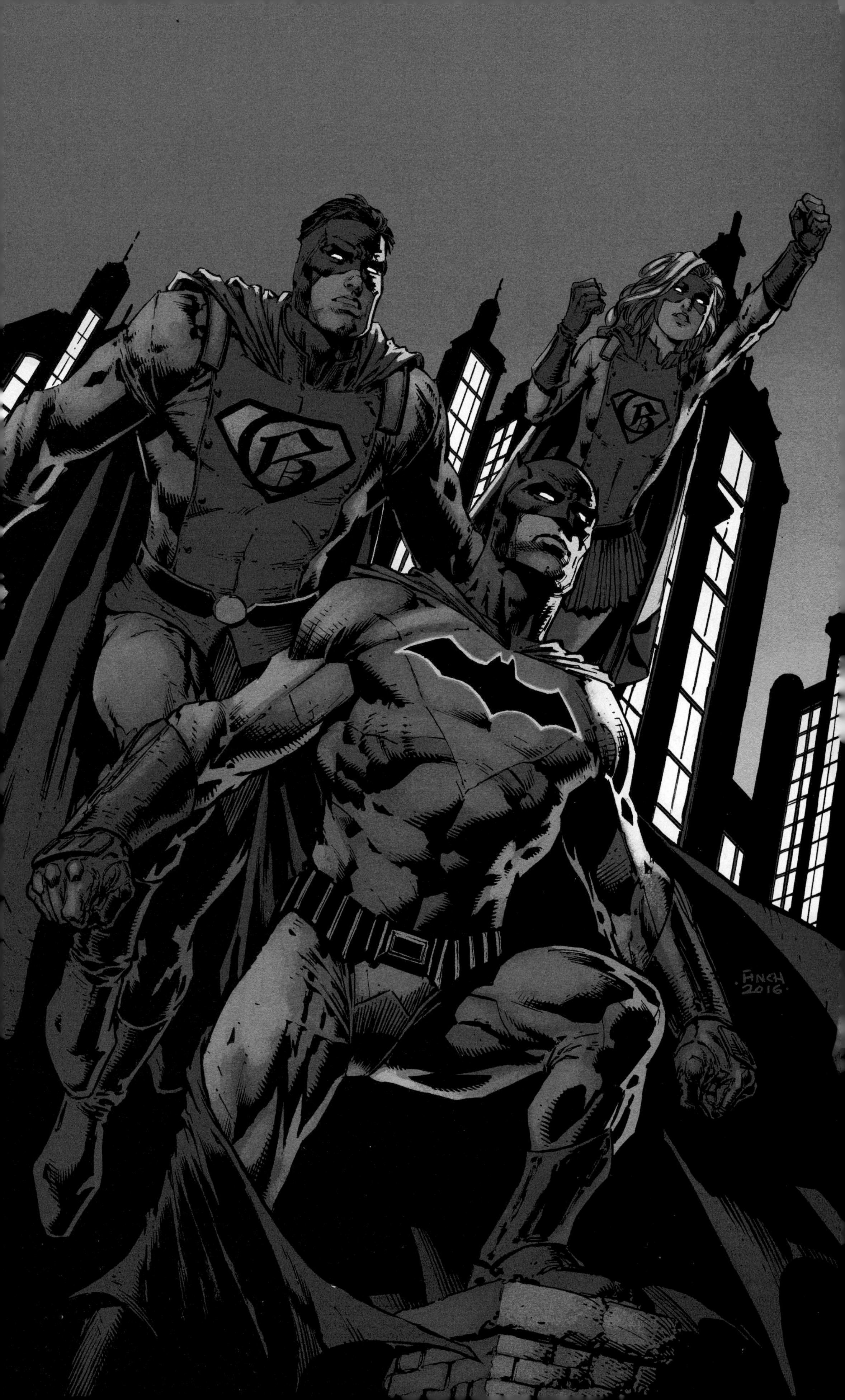
FINCH
2016

TOM KING writer * DAVID FINCH penciller * MATT BANNING and

JORDIE BELLAIRE colorist * JOHN WORKMAN letterer * DAVID FINCH and JORDIE BELLAIRE cover artists

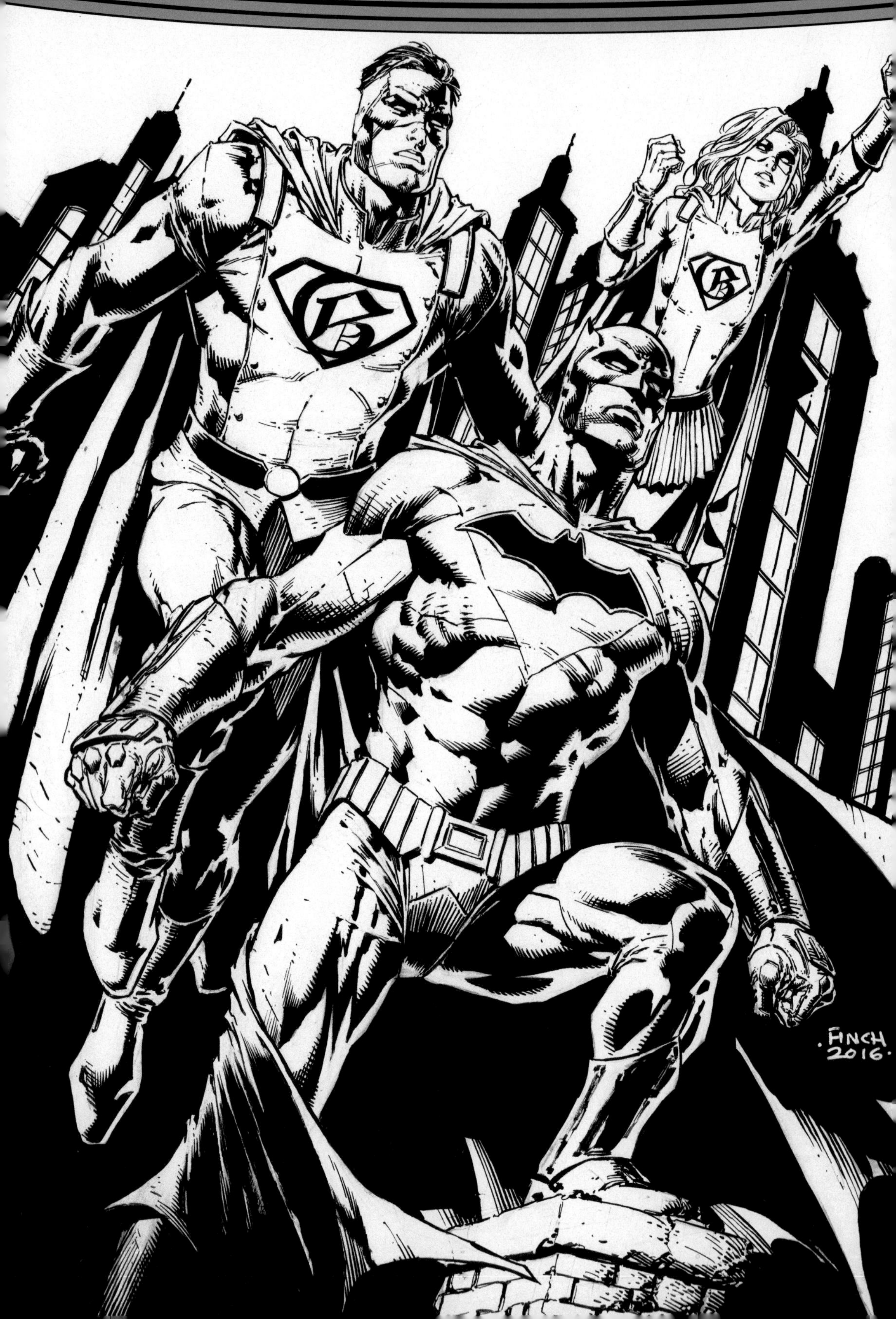
FINCH
2016

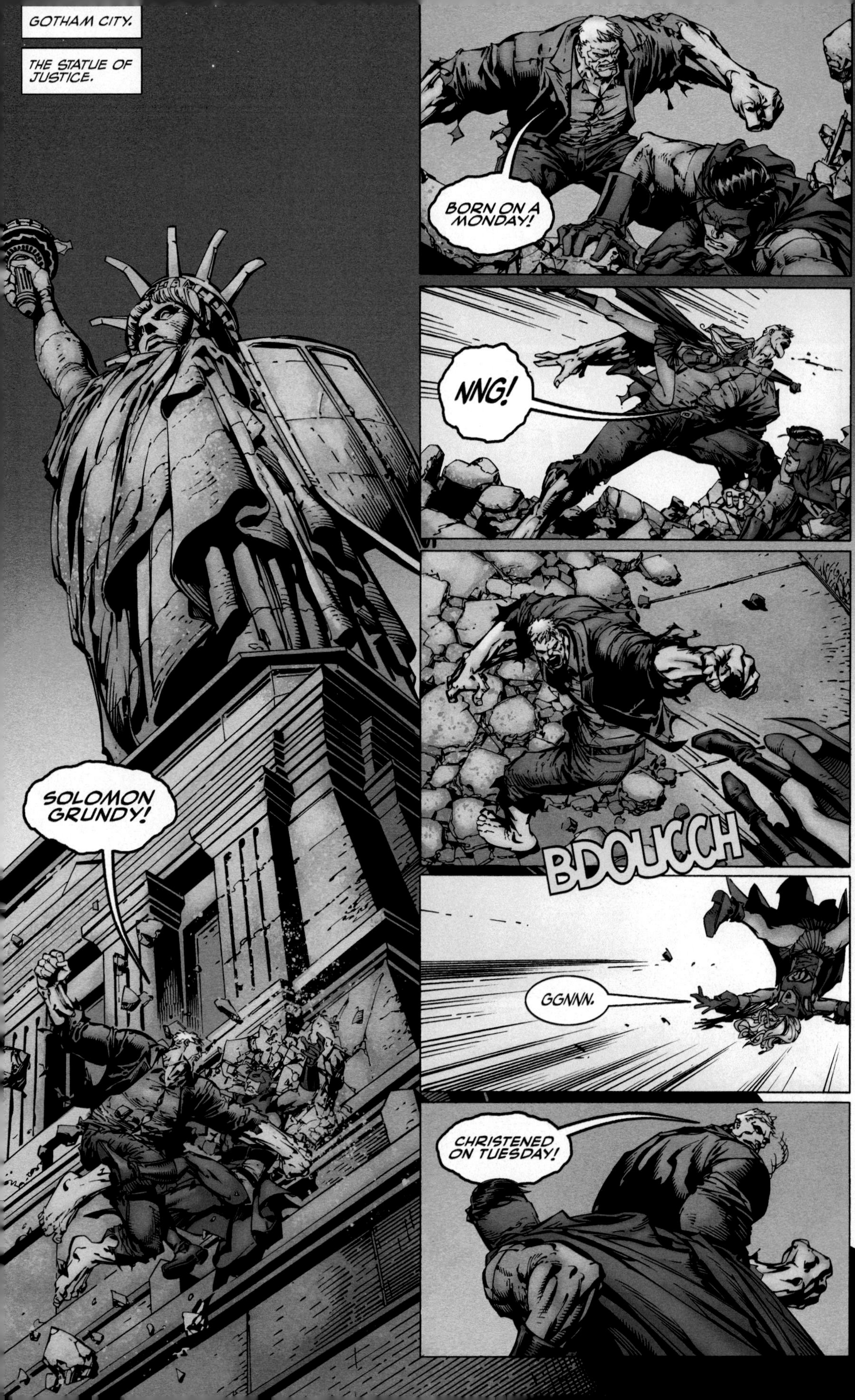
GOTHAM CITY.
THE STATUE OF JUSTICE.
SOLOMON GRUNDY!
BORN ON A MONDAY!
NNG!
BDOUCCH
GGNNN.
CHRISTENED ON TUESDAY!

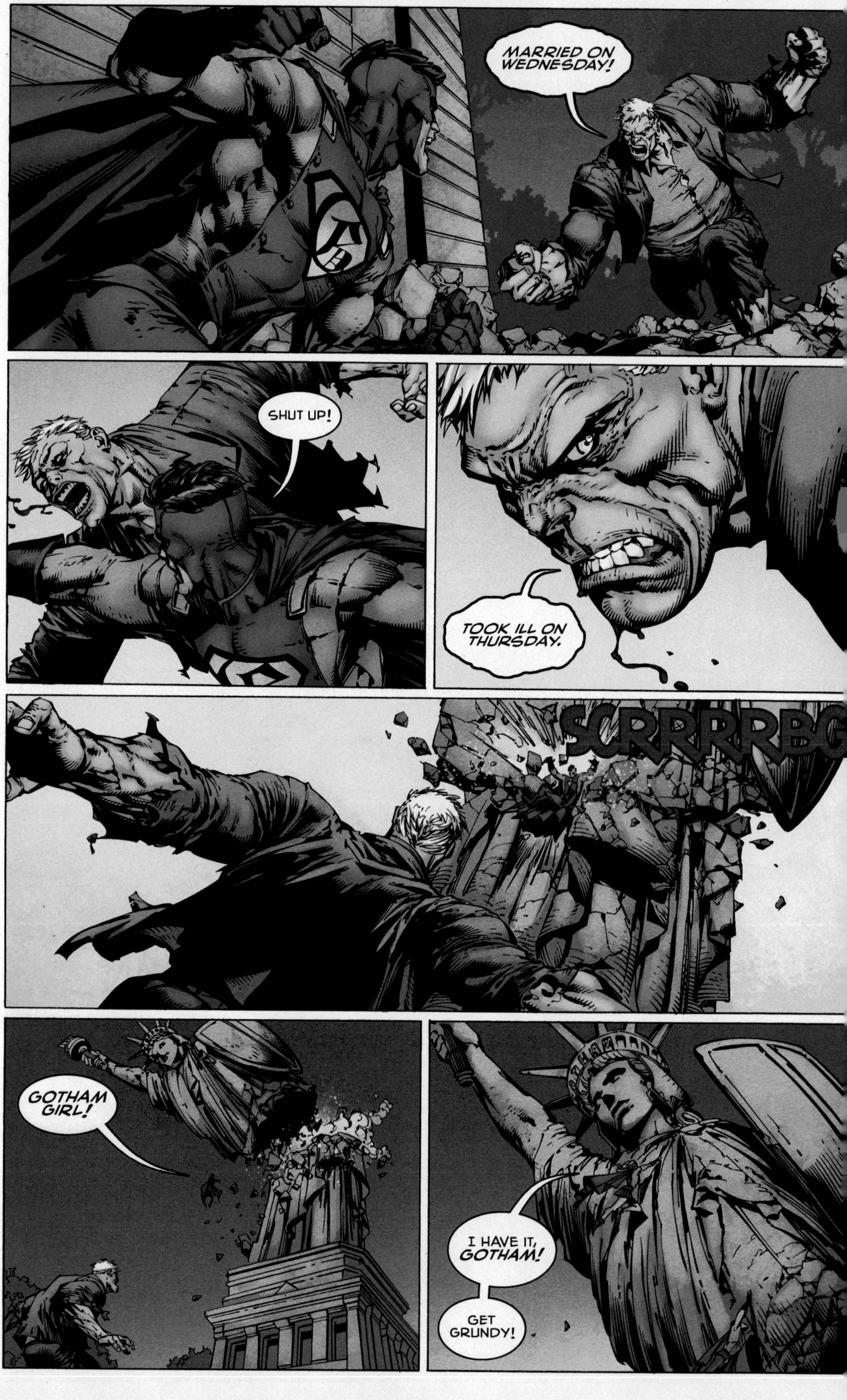
MARRIED ON WEDNESDAY!
SHUT UP!
TOOK ILL ON THURSDAY.
SCRRRRBG
GOTHAM GIRL!
I HAVE IT, GOTHAM!
GET GRUNDY!

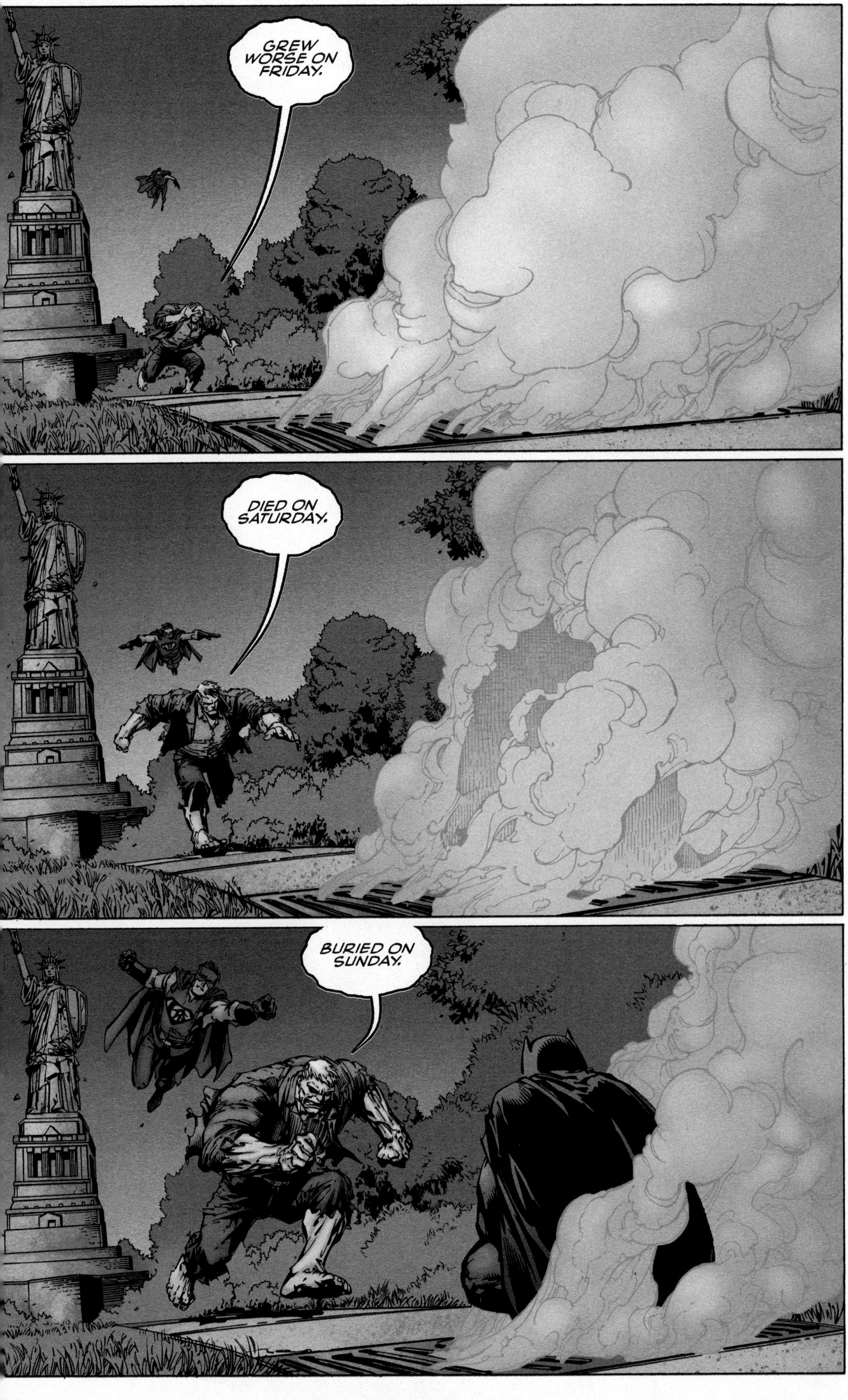
GREW WORSE ON FRIDAY.
DIED ON SATURDAY.
BURIED ON SUNDAY.

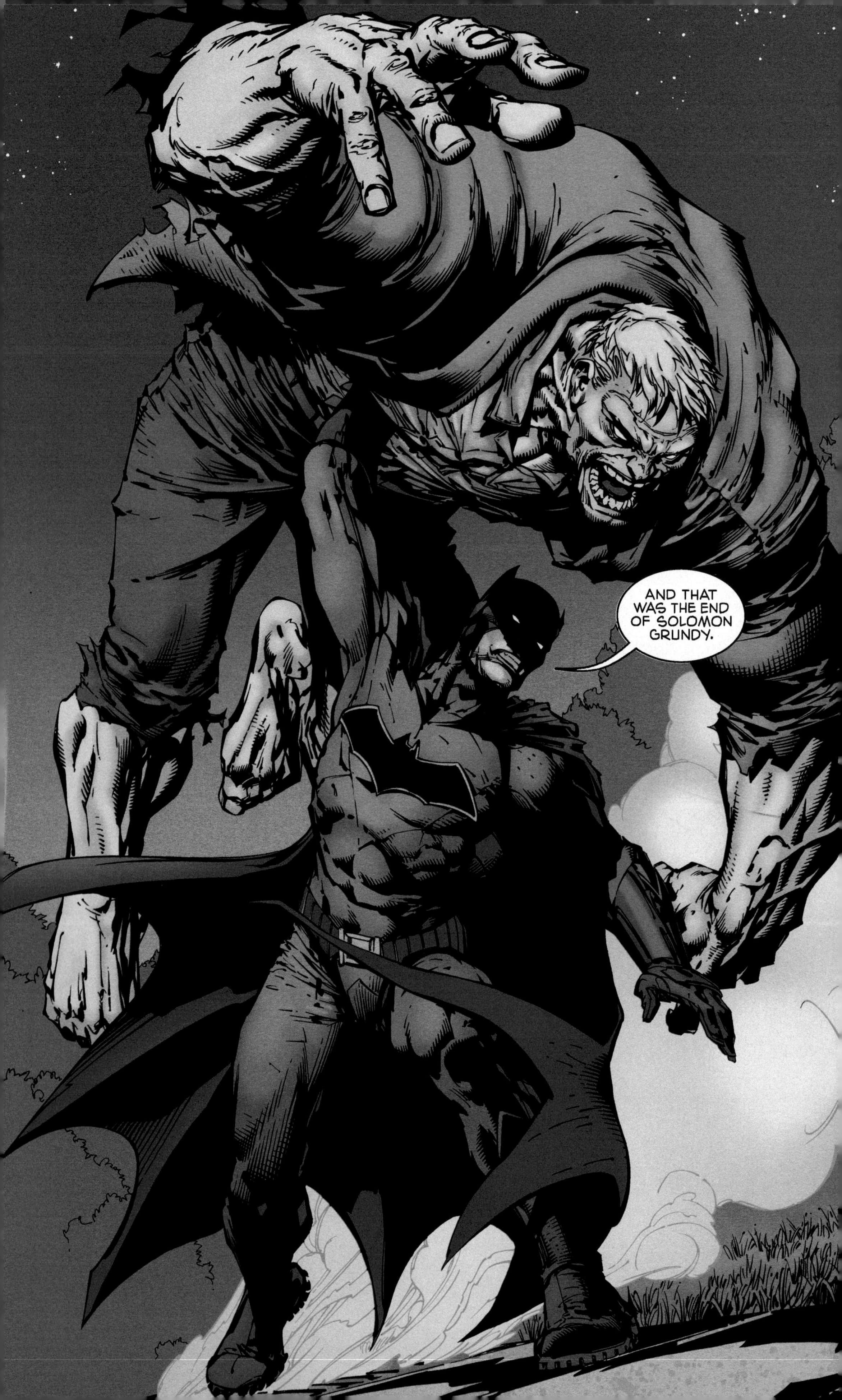
AND THAT WAS THE END OF SOLOMON GRUNDY.

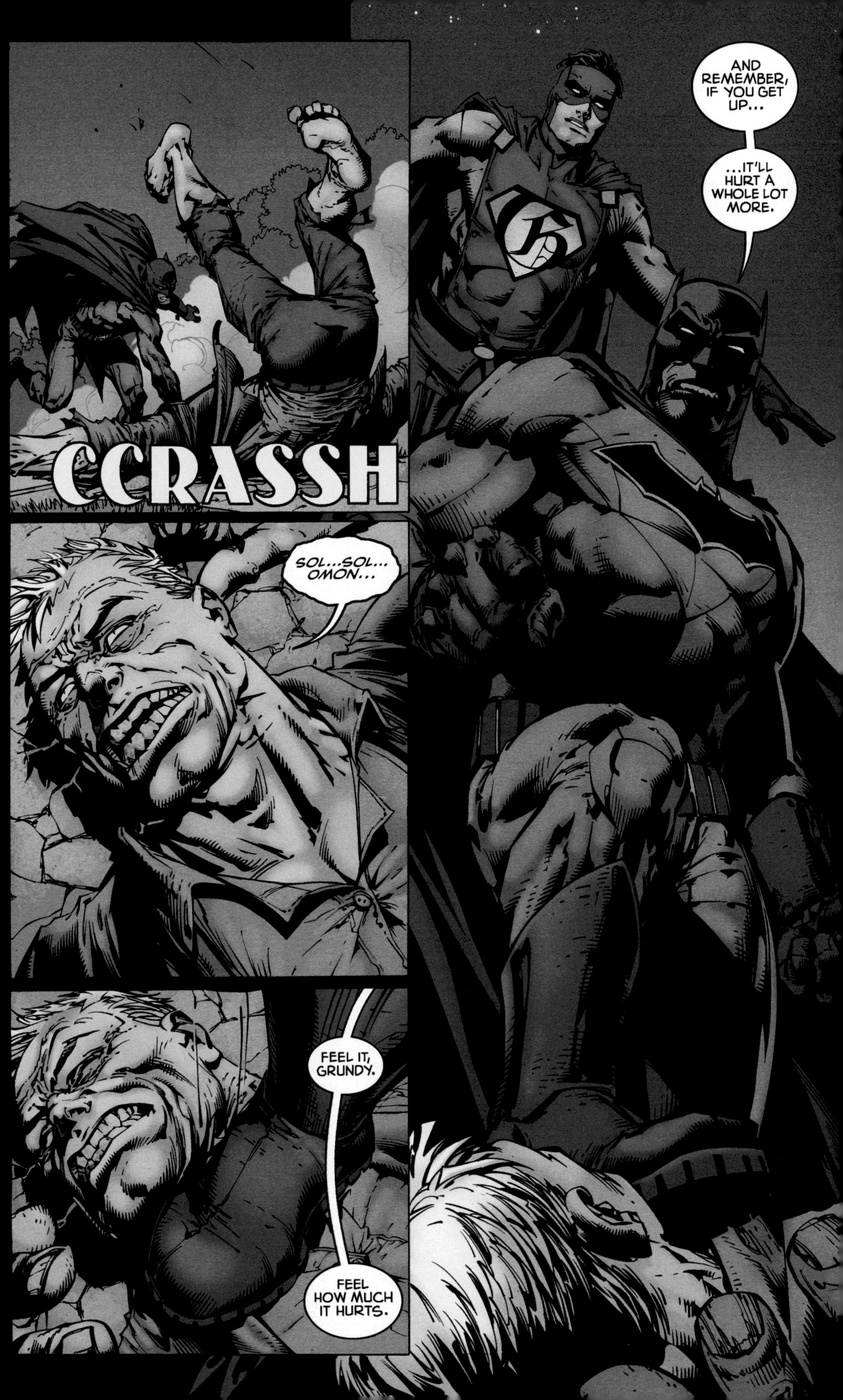
CCRASSH
AND REMEMBER, IF YOU GET UP...
...IT'LL HURT A WHOLE LOT MORE.
SOL...SOL... OMON...
FEEL IT, GRUNDY.
FEEL HOW MUCH IT HURTS.

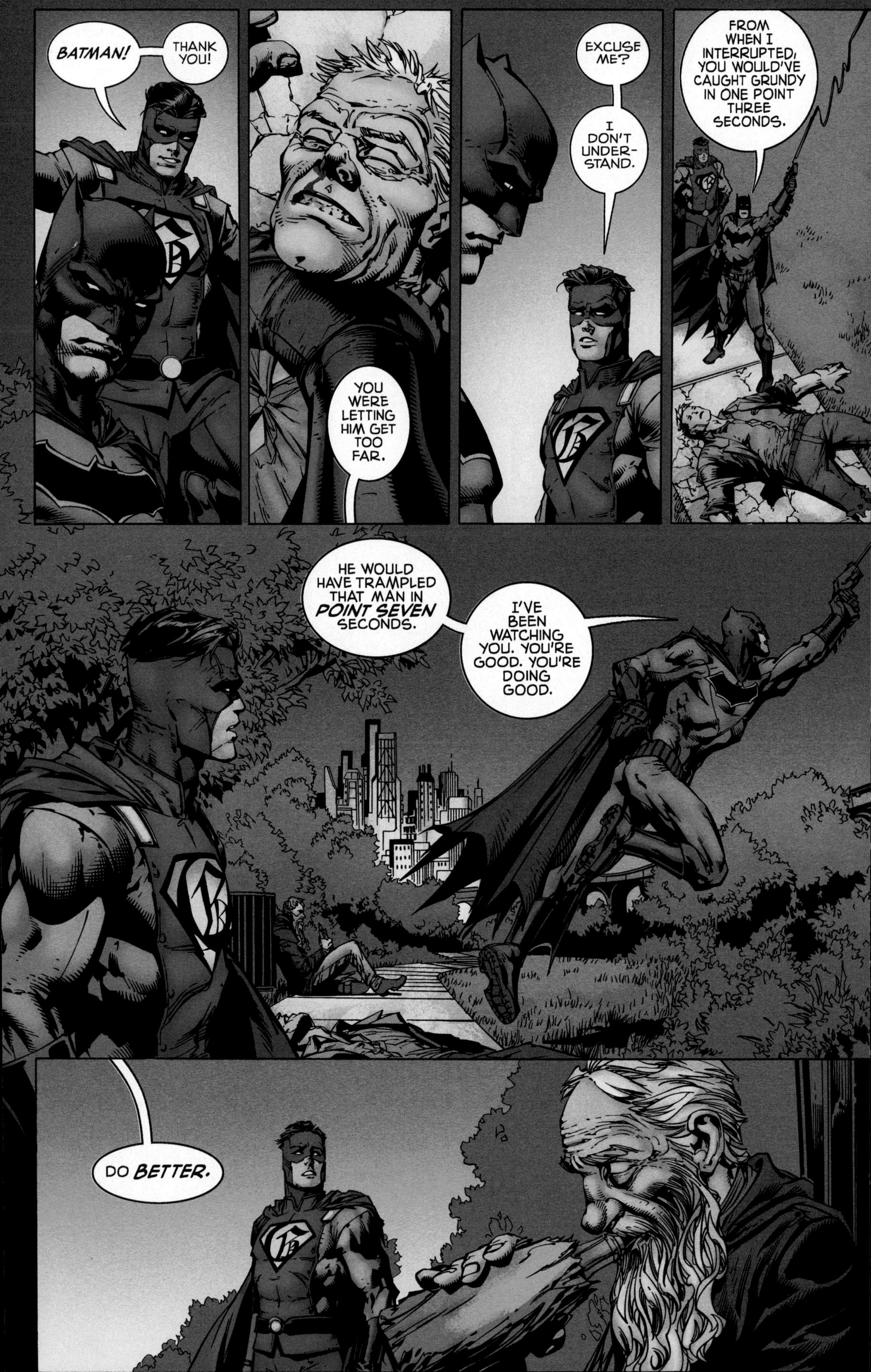
BATMAN!
THANK YOU!
YOU WERE LETTING HIM GET TOO FAR.
EXCUSE ME?
I DON'T UNDER-STAND.
FROM WHEN I INTERRUPTED, YOU WOULD'VE CAUGHT GRUNDY IN ONE POINT THREE SECONDS.
HE WOULD HAVE TRAMPLED THAT MAN IN POINT SEVEN SECONDS.
I'VE BEEN WATCHING YOU. YOU'RE GOOD. YOU'RE DOING GOOD.
DO BETTER.

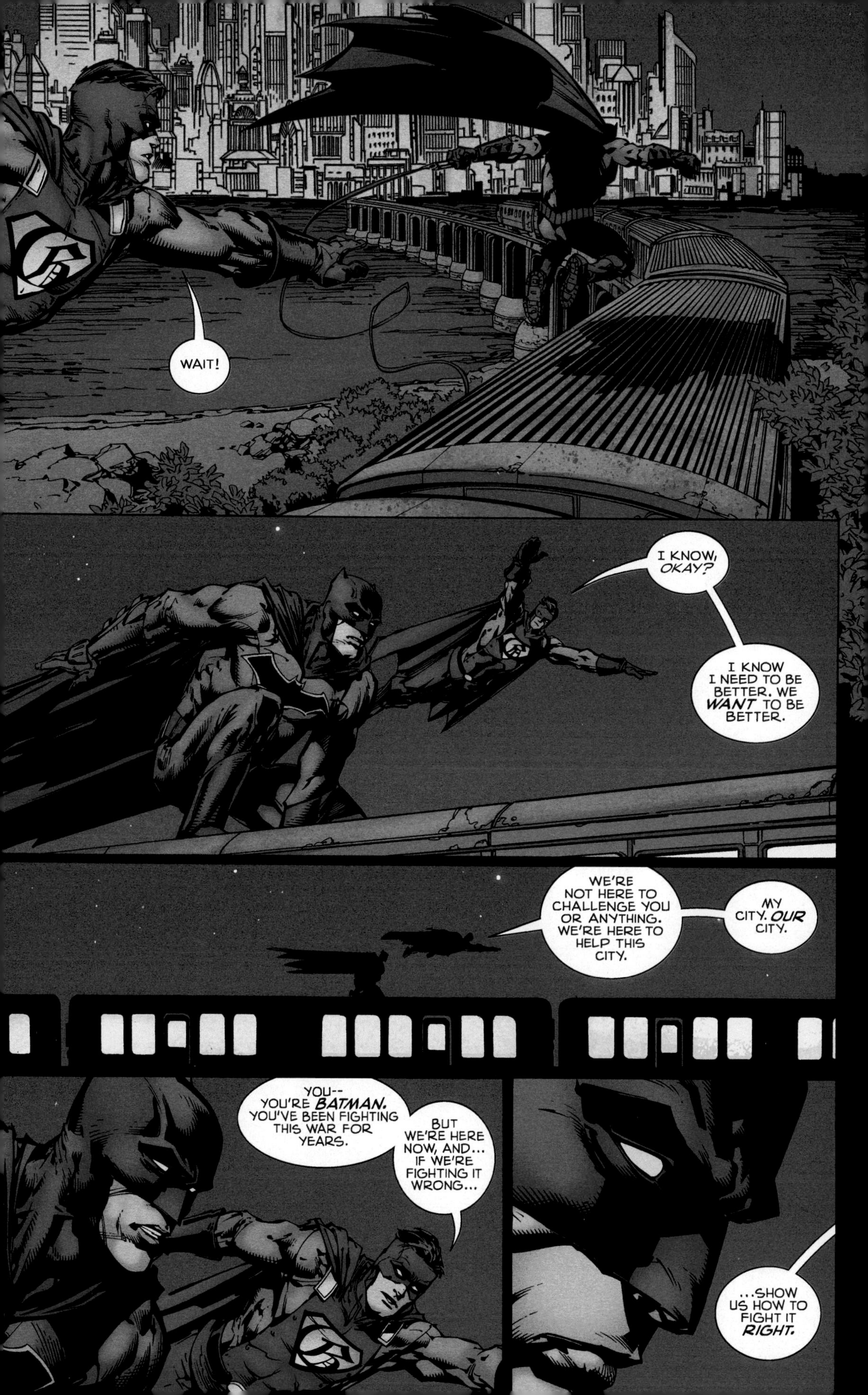
WAIT!
I KNOW, OKAY?
I KNOW I NEED TO BE BETTER. WE WANT TO BE BETTER.
WE'RE NOT HERE TO CHALLENGE YOU OR ANYTHING. WE'RE HERE TO HELP THIS CITY.
MY CITY. OUR CITY.
YOU-- YOU'RE BATMAN. YOU'VE BEEN FIGHTING THIS WAR FOR YEARS.
BUT WE'RE HERE NOW, AND... IF WE'RE FIGHTING IT WRONG...
...SHOW US HOW TO FIGHT IT RIGHT.

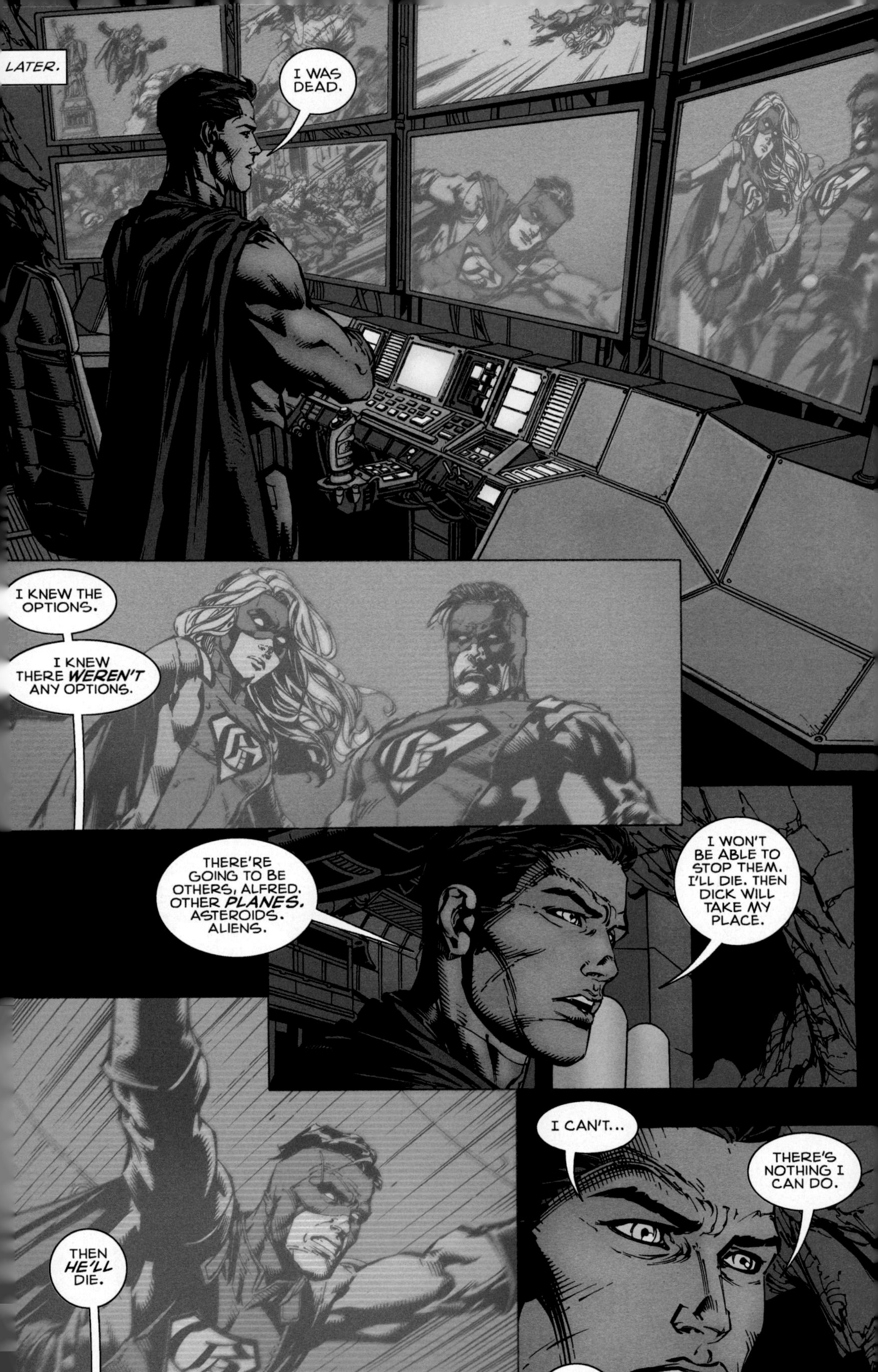
LATER.
I WAS DEAD.
I KNEW THE OPTIONS.
I KNEW THERE WEREN'T ANY OPTIONS.
THERE'RE GOING TO BE OTHERS, ALFRED. OTHER PLANES. ASTEROIDS. ALIENS.
I WON'T BE ABLE TO STOP THEM. I'LL DIE. THEN DICK WILL TAKE MY PLACE.
THEN HE'LL DIE.
I CAN'T...
THERE'S NOTHING I CAN DO.
WELL,

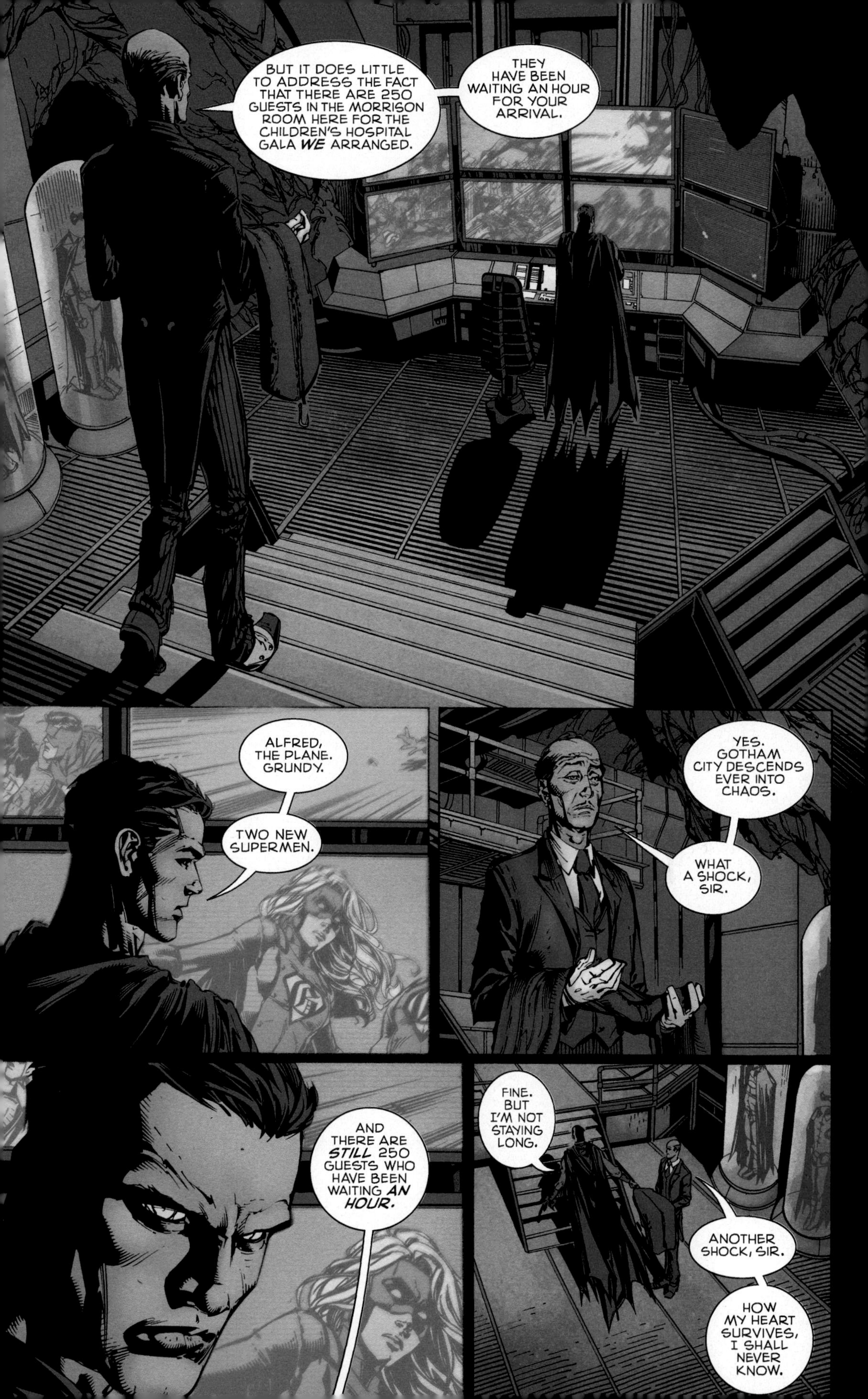
BUT IT DOES LITTLE TO ADDRESS THE FACT THAT THERE ARE 250 GUESTS IN THE MORRISON ROOM HERE FOR THE CHILDREN'S HOSPITAL GALA *WE* ARRANGED.
THEY HAVE BEEN WAITING AN HOUR FOR YOUR ARRIVAL.
ALFRED, THE PLANE. GRUNDY.
TWO NEW SUPERMEN.
YES. GOTHAM CITY DESCENDS EVER INTO CHAOS.
WHAT A SHOCK, SIR.
AND THERE ARE *STILL* 250 GUESTS WHO HAVE BEEN WAITING *AN HOUR.*
FINE. BUT I'M NOT STAYING LONG.
ANOTHER SHOCK, SIR.
HOW MY HEART SURVIVES, I SHALL NEVER KNOW.

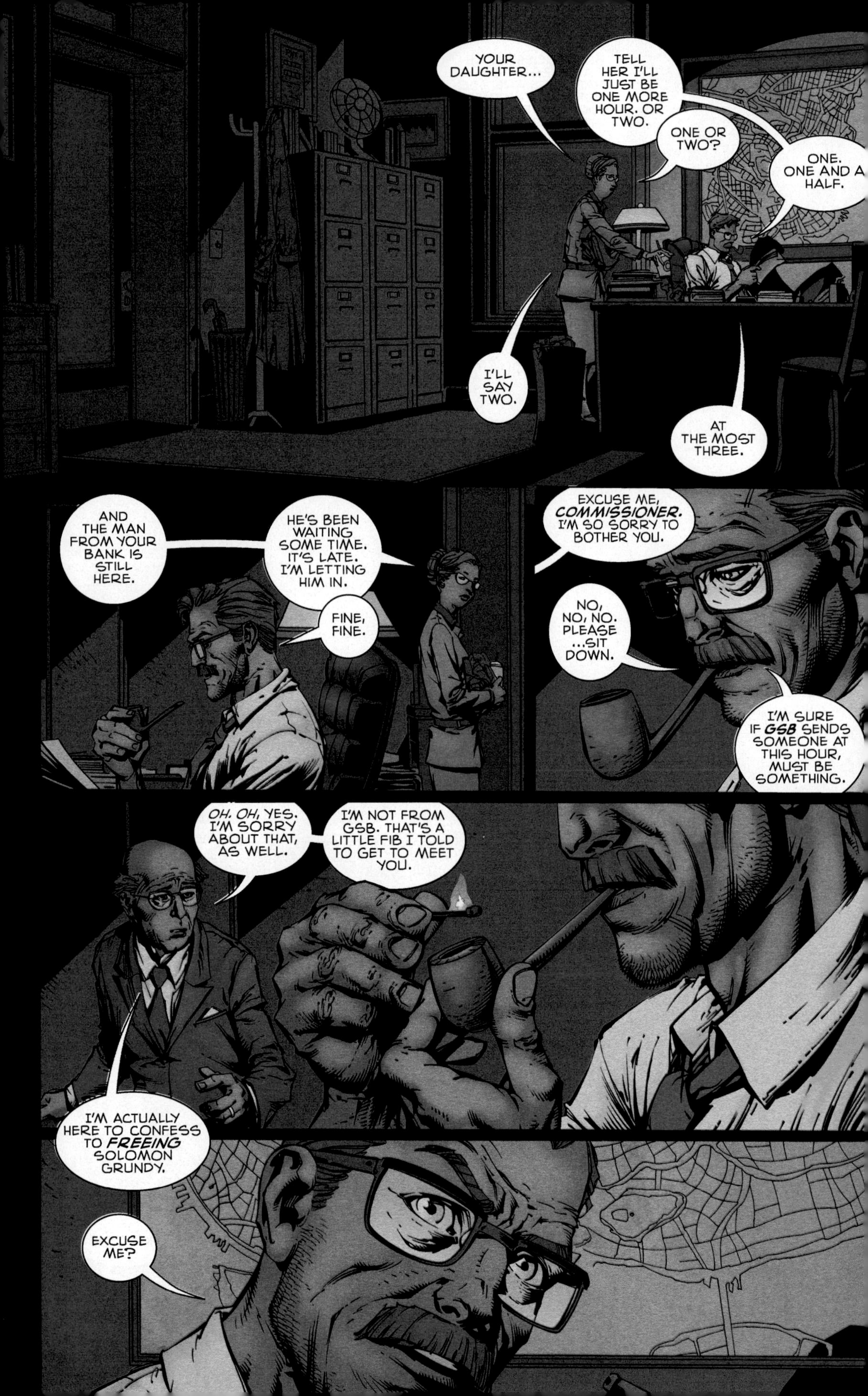

YOUR DAUGHTER...
TELL HER I'LL JUST BE ONE MORE HOUR. OR TWO.
ONE OR TWO?
ONE. ONE AND A HALF.
I'LL SAY TWO.
AT THE MOST THREE.
AND THE MAN FROM YOUR BANK IS STILL HERE.
HE'S BEEN WAITING SOME TIME. IT'S LATE. I'M LETTING HIM IN.
FINE, FINE.
EXCUSE ME, *COMMISSIONER.* I'M SO SORRY TO BOTHER YOU.
NO, NO, NO. PLEASE ...SIT DOWN.
I'M SURE IF **GSB** SENDS SOMEONE AT THIS HOUR, MUST BE SOMETHING.
OH. OH, YES. I'M SORRY ABOUT THAT, AS WELL.
I'M NOT FROM GSB. THAT'S A LITTLE FIB I TOLD TO GET TO MEET YOU.
I'M ACTUALLY HERE TO CONFESS TO ***FREEING*** SOLOMON GRUNDY.
EXCUSE ME?

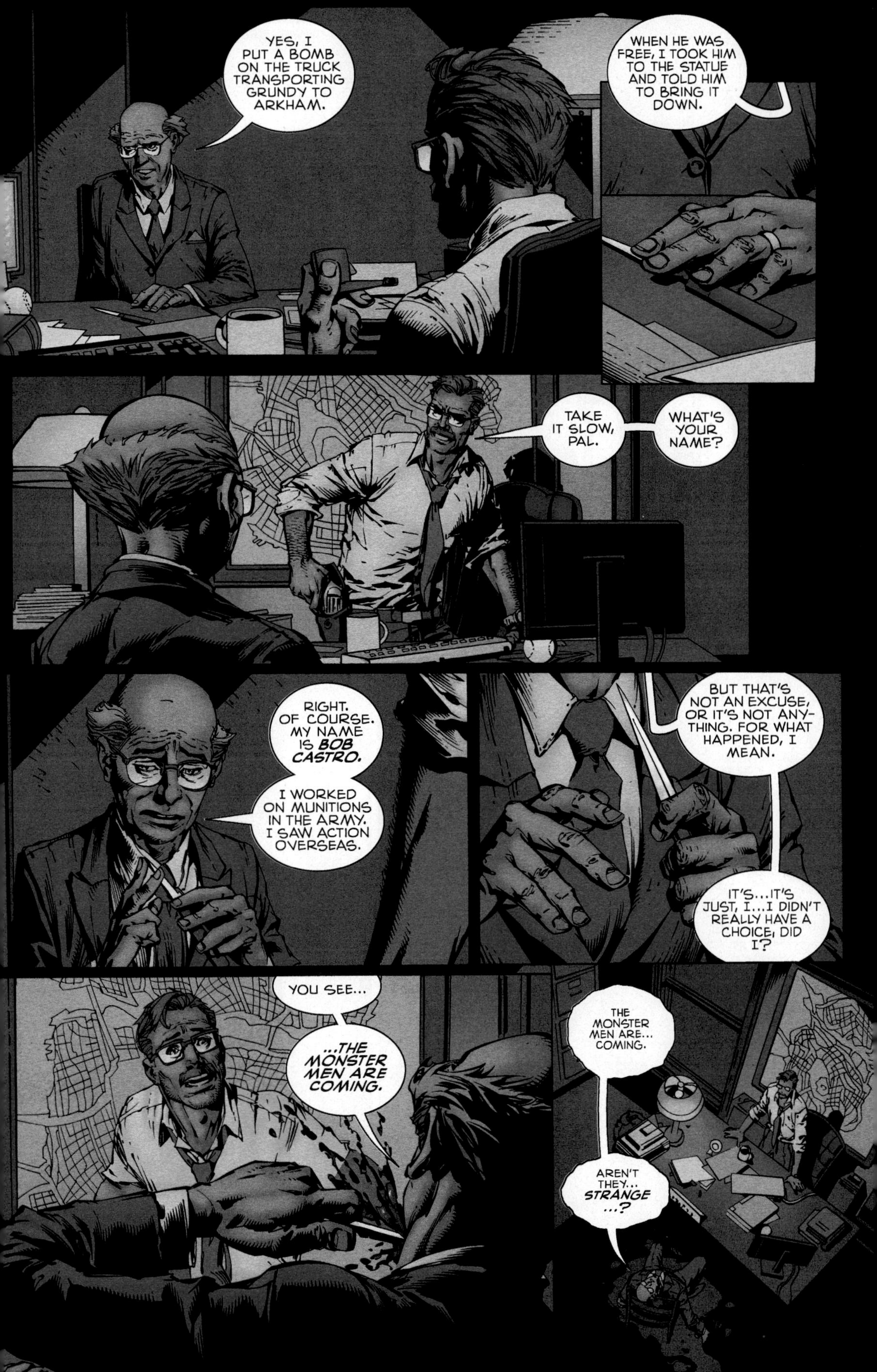
YES, I PUT A BOMB ON THE TRUCK TRANSPORTING GRUNDY TO ARKHAM.
WHEN HE WAS FREE, I TOOK HIM TO THE STATUE AND TOLD HIM TO BRING IT DOWN.
TAKE IT SLOW, PAL.
WHAT'S YOUR NAME?
RIGHT. OF COURSE. MY NAME IS *BOB CASTRO.*
I WORKED ON MUNITIONS IN THE ARMY. I SAW ACTION OVERSEAS.
BUT THAT'S NOT AN EXCUSE, OR IT'S NOT ANYTHING. FOR WHAT HAPPENED, I MEAN.
IT'S...IT'S JUST, I...I DIDN'T REALLY HAVE A CHOICE, DID I?
YOU SEE...
...THE MONSTER MEN ARE COMING.
THE MONSTER MEN ARE... COMING.
AREN'T THEY... *STRANGE* ...?

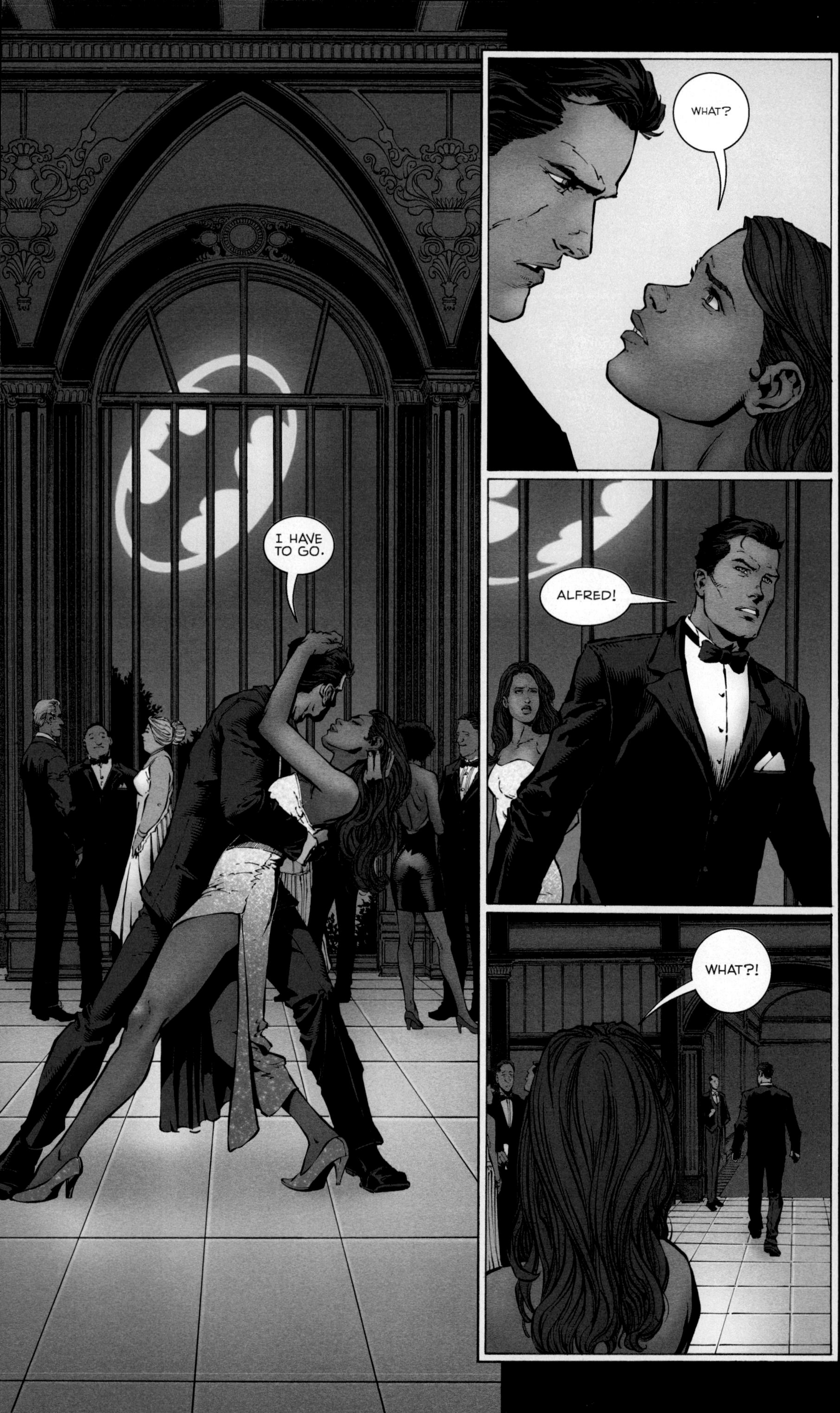
I HAVE TO GO.
WHAT?
ALFRED!
WHAT?!

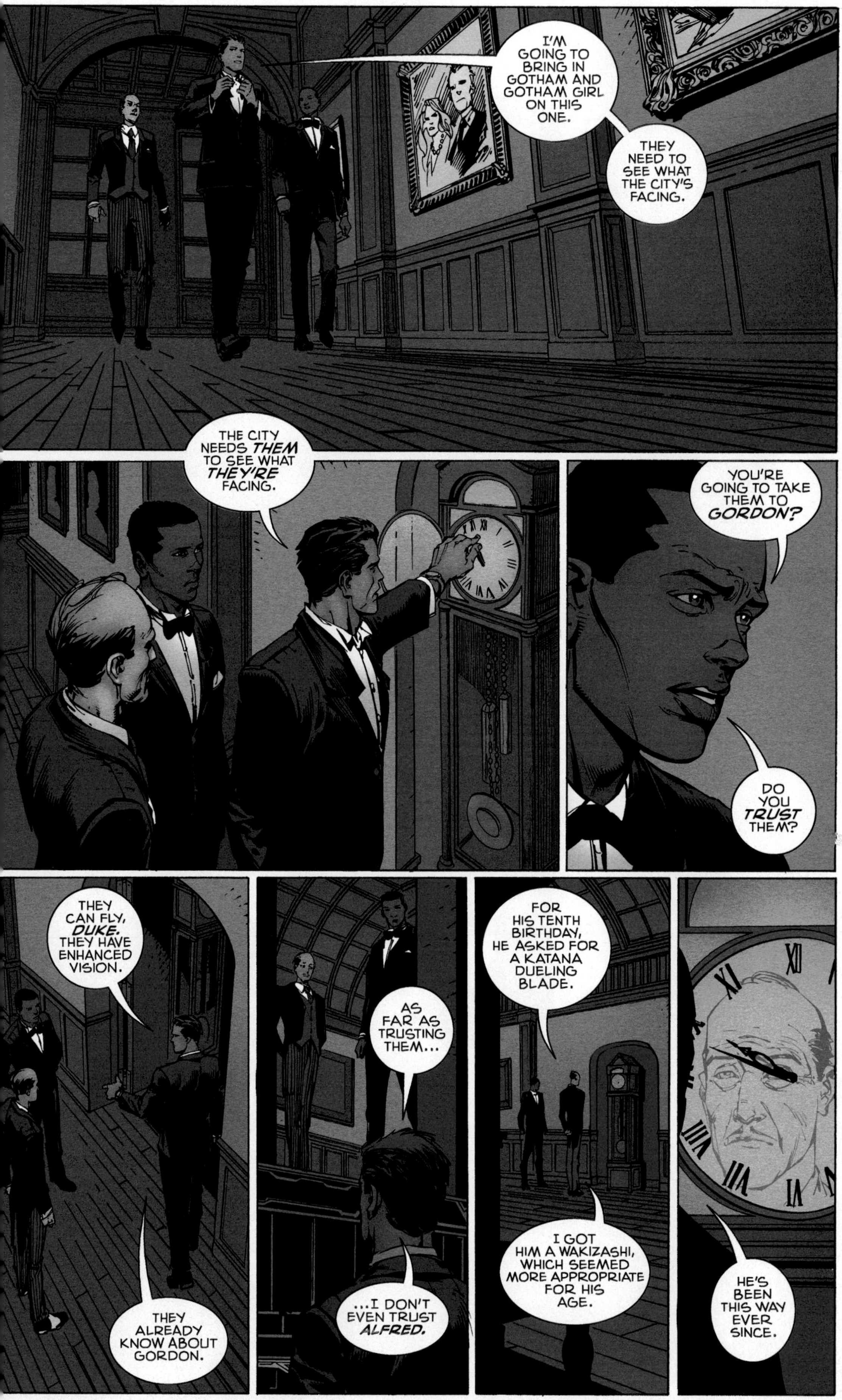
I'M GOING TO BRING IN GOTHAM AND GOTHAM GIRL ON THIS ONE.
THEY NEED TO SEE WHAT THE CITY'S FACING.
THE CITY NEEDS *THEM* TO SEE WHAT *THEY'RE* FACING.
YOU'RE GOING TO TAKE THEM TO *GORDON?*
DO YOU *TRUST* THEM?
THEY CAN FLY, *DUKE.* THEY HAVE ENHANCED VISION.
THEY ALREADY KNOW ABOUT GORDON.
AS FAR AS TRUSTING THEM...
...I DON'T EVEN TRUST *ALFRED.*
FOR HIS TENTH BIRTHDAY, HE ASKED FOR A KATANA DUELING BLADE.
I GOT HIM A WAKIZASHI, WHICH SEEMED MORE APPROPRIATE FOR HIS AGE.
HE'S BEEN THIS WAY EVER SINCE.

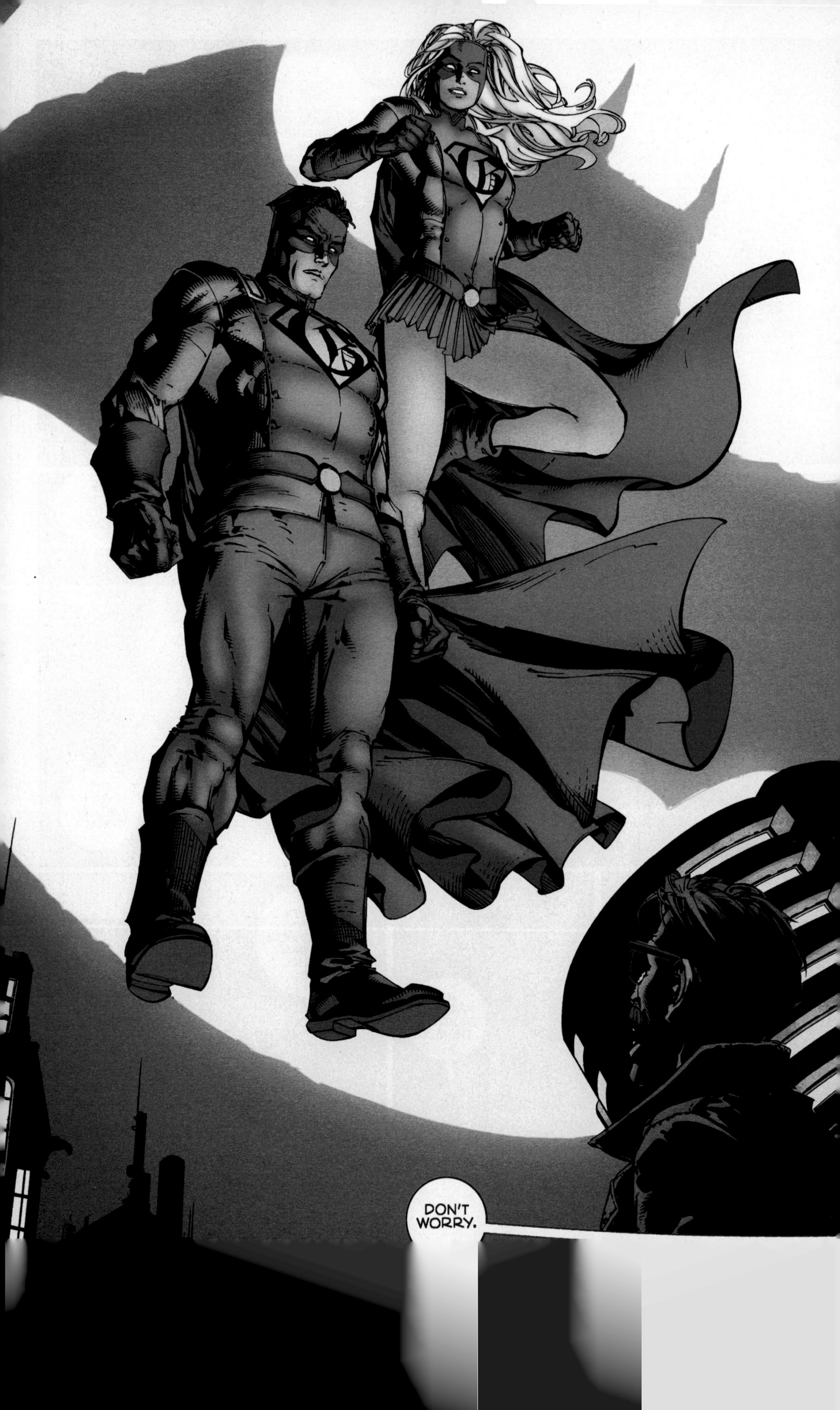
DON'T WORRY.

THEY'RE WITH ME, JIM.

SURE.

I WANT THEM TO HEAR THIS. THEY SAVED THE PLANE. THEY'VE SAVED OTHERS.

I'M SEEING IF THEY CAN DO MORE.

I AM GOTHAM. SHE IS GOTHAM GIRL.

IT'S AN HONOR TO MEET YOU, COMMISSIONER.

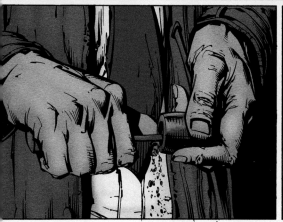

IS IT REALLY EASIER TO FIGHT CRIME WITH A MASK ON?

I'D THINK IT WOULD ITCH.

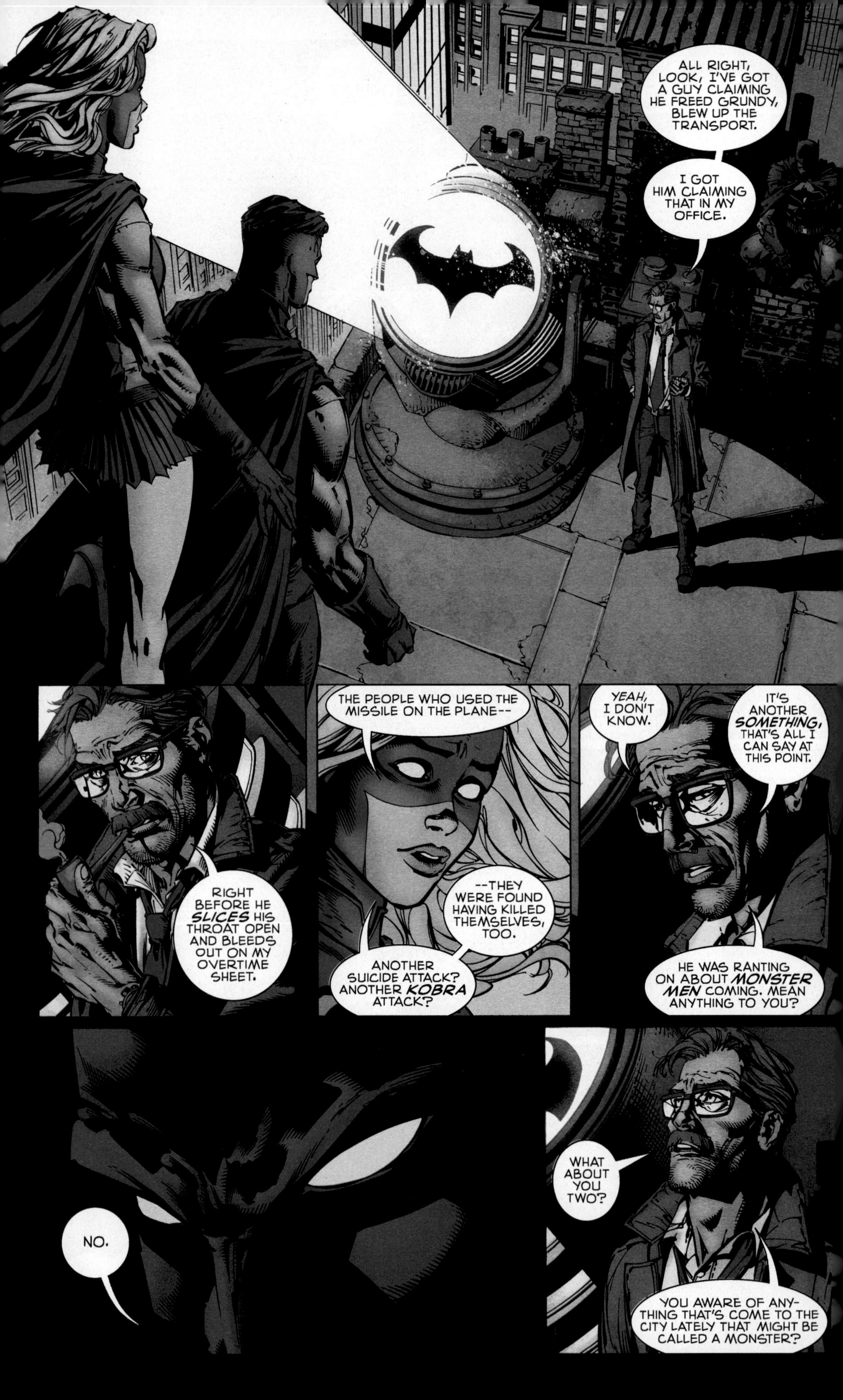
ALL RIGHT, LOOK, I'VE GOT A GUY CLAIMING HE FREED GRUNDY, BLEW UP THE TRANSPORT.
I GOT HIM CLAIMING THAT IN MY OFFICE.
RIGHT BEFORE HE *SLICES* HIS THROAT OPEN AND BLEEDS OUT ON MY OVERTIME SHEET.
THE PEOPLE WHO USED THE MISSILE ON THE PLANE--
--THEY WERE FOUND HAVING KILLED THEMSELVES, TOO.
ANOTHER SUICIDE ATTACK? ANOTHER *KOBRA* ATTACK?
YEAH, I DON'T KNOW.
IT'S ANOTHER *SOMETHING,* THAT'S ALL I CAN SAY AT THIS POINT.
HE WAS RANTING ON ABOUT *MONSTER MEN* COMING. MEAN ANYTHING TO YOU?
WHAT ABOUT YOU TWO?
NO.
YOU AWARE OF ANY-THING THAT'S COME TO THE CITY LATELY THAT MIGHT BE CALLED A MONSTER?

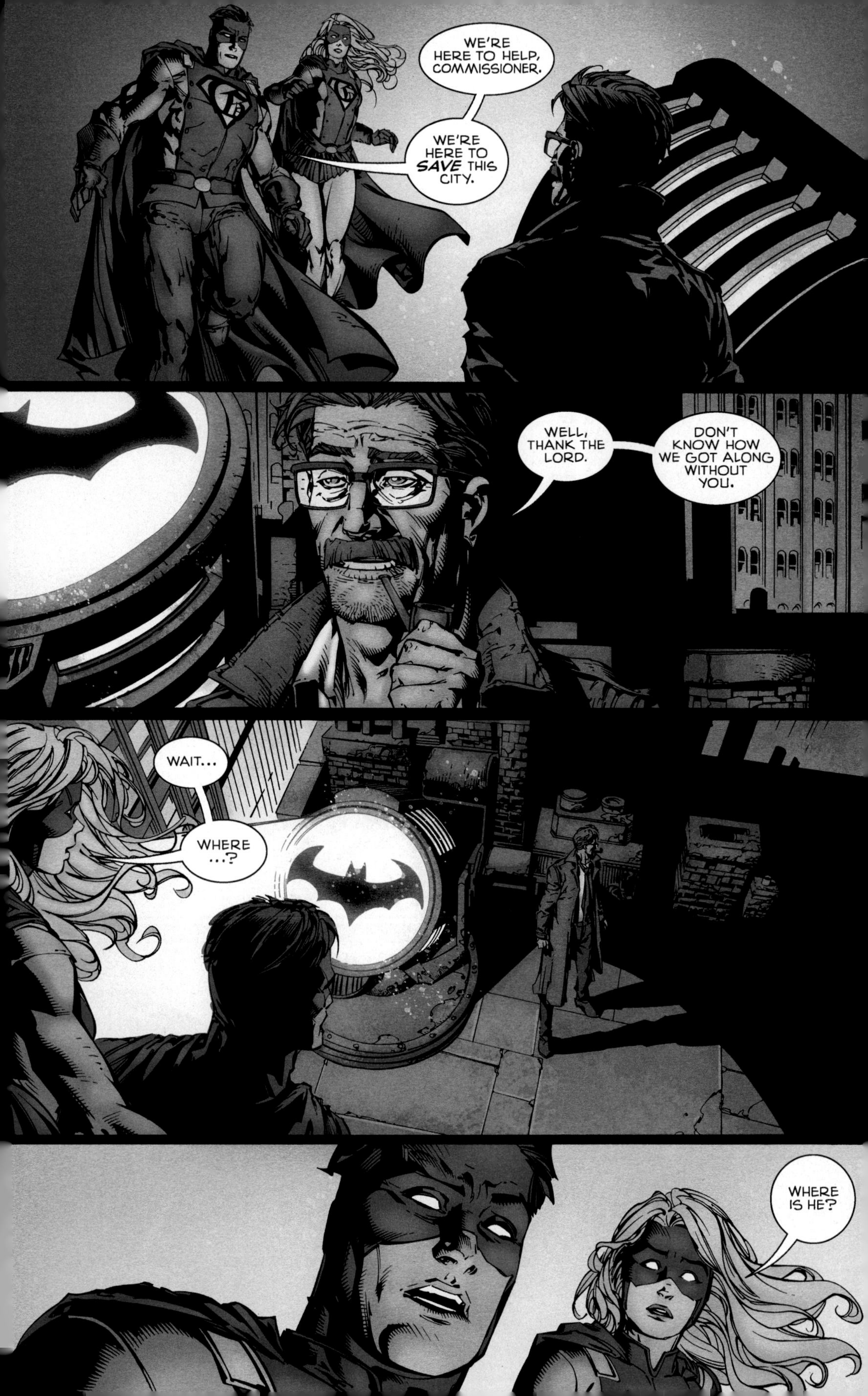
WE'RE HERE TO HELP, COMMISSIONER.
WE'RE HERE TO SAVE THIS CITY.
WELL, THANK THE LORD.
DON'T KNOW HOW WE GOT ALONG WITHOUT YOU.
WAIT...
WHERE ...?
WHERE IS HE?

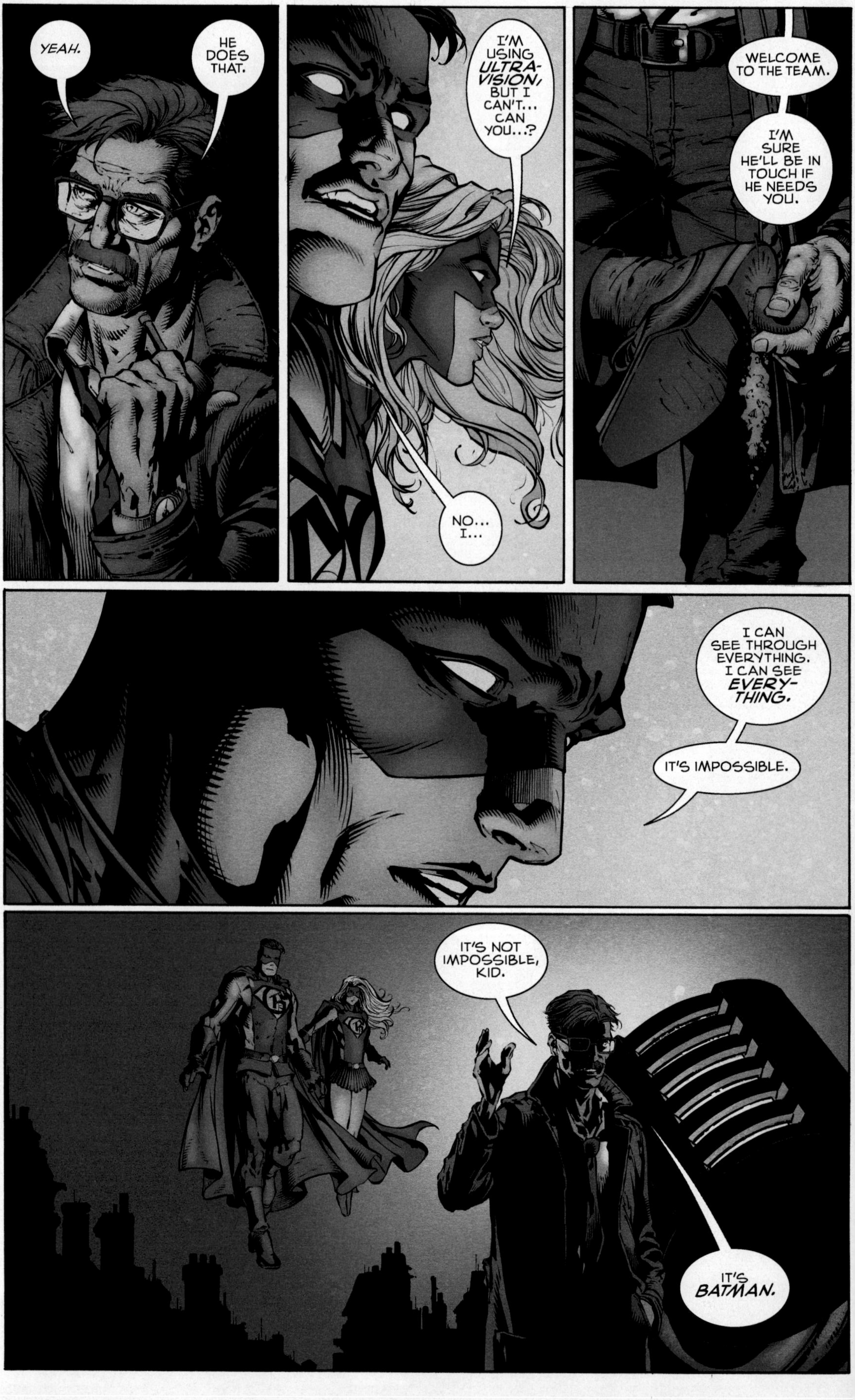
YEAH.
HE DOES THAT.
I'M USING *ULTRA-VISION,* BUT I CAN'T... CAN YOU...?
NO... I...
WELCOME TO THE TEAM.
I'M SURE HE'LL BE IN TOUCH IF HE NEEDS YOU.
I CAN SEE THROUGH EVERYTHING. I CAN SEE *EVERY-THING.*
IT'S IMPOSSIBLE.
IT'S NOT IMPOSSIBLE, KID.
IT'S *BATMAN.*

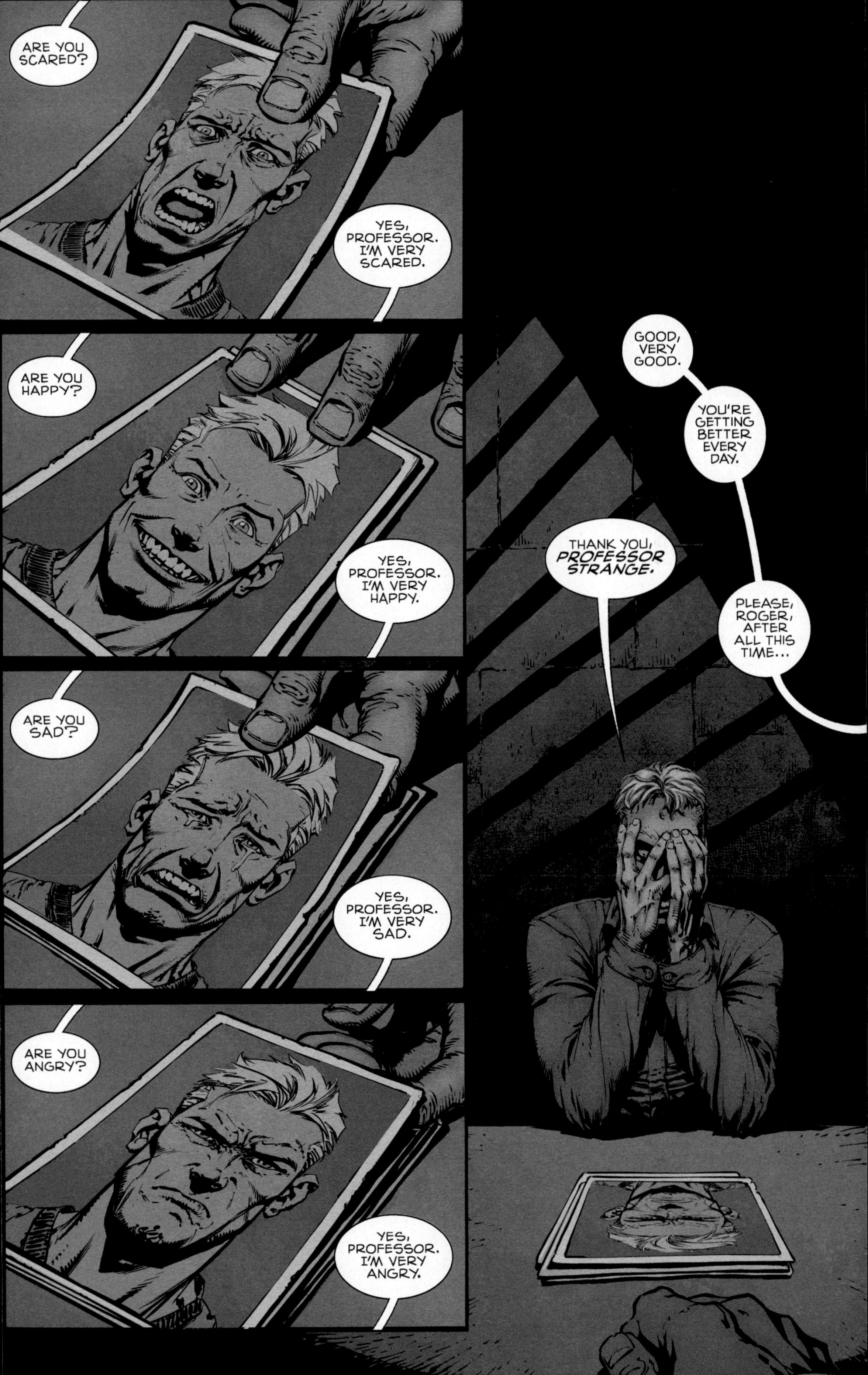
ARE YOU SCARED?
YES, PROFESSOR. I'M VERY SCARED.
ARE YOU HAPPY?
YES, PROFESSOR. I'M VERY HAPPY.
ARE YOU SAD?
YES, PROFESSOR. I'M VERY SAD.
ARE YOU ANGRY?
YES, PROFESSOR. I'M VERY ANGRY.
GOOD, VERY GOOD.
YOU'RE GETTING BETTER EVERY DAY.
THANK YOU, *PROFESSOR STRANGE.*
PLEASE, ROGER, AFTER ALL THIS TIME...

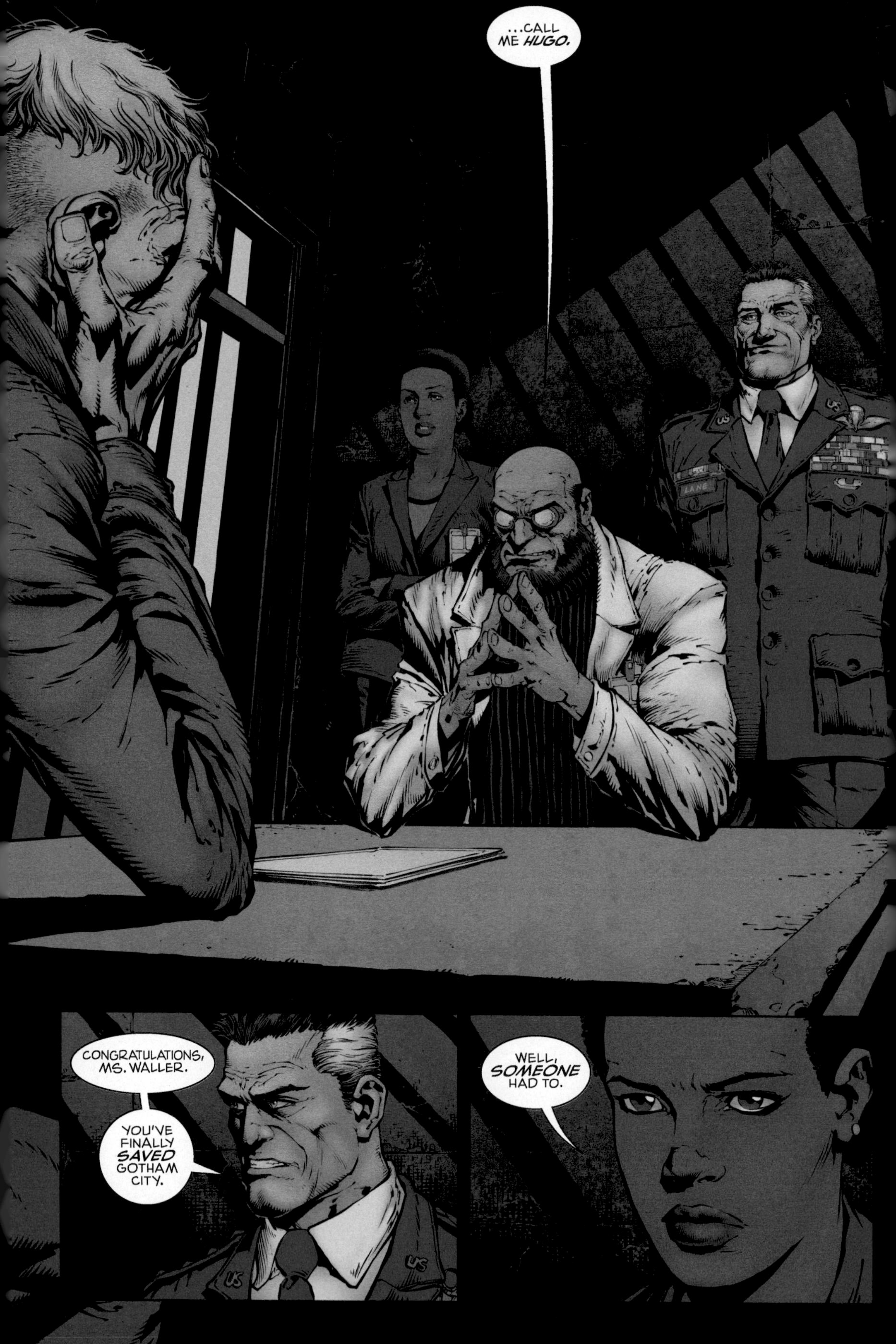
...CALL ME HUGO.
CONGRATULATIONS, MS. WALLER.
YOU'VE FINALLY SAVED GOTHAM CITY.
WELL, SOMEONE HAD TO.

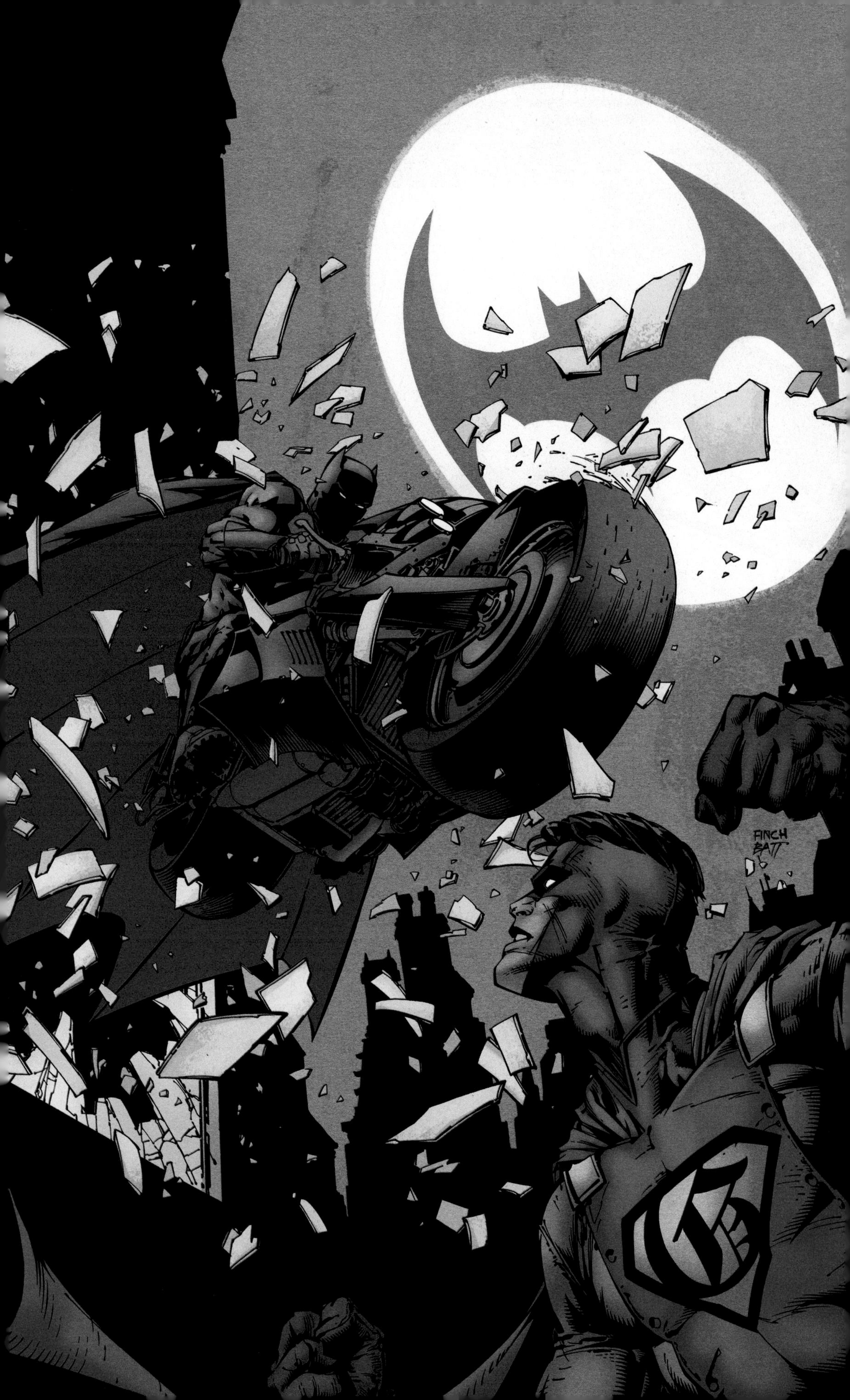
FINCH
BATT

I AM GOTHAM part three

TOM KING writer * DAVID FINCH penciller * DANNY MIKI inker * JORDIE BELLAIRE colorist
JOHN WORKMAN letterer * DAVID FINCH, MATT BANNING and JORDIE BELLAIRE cover artists

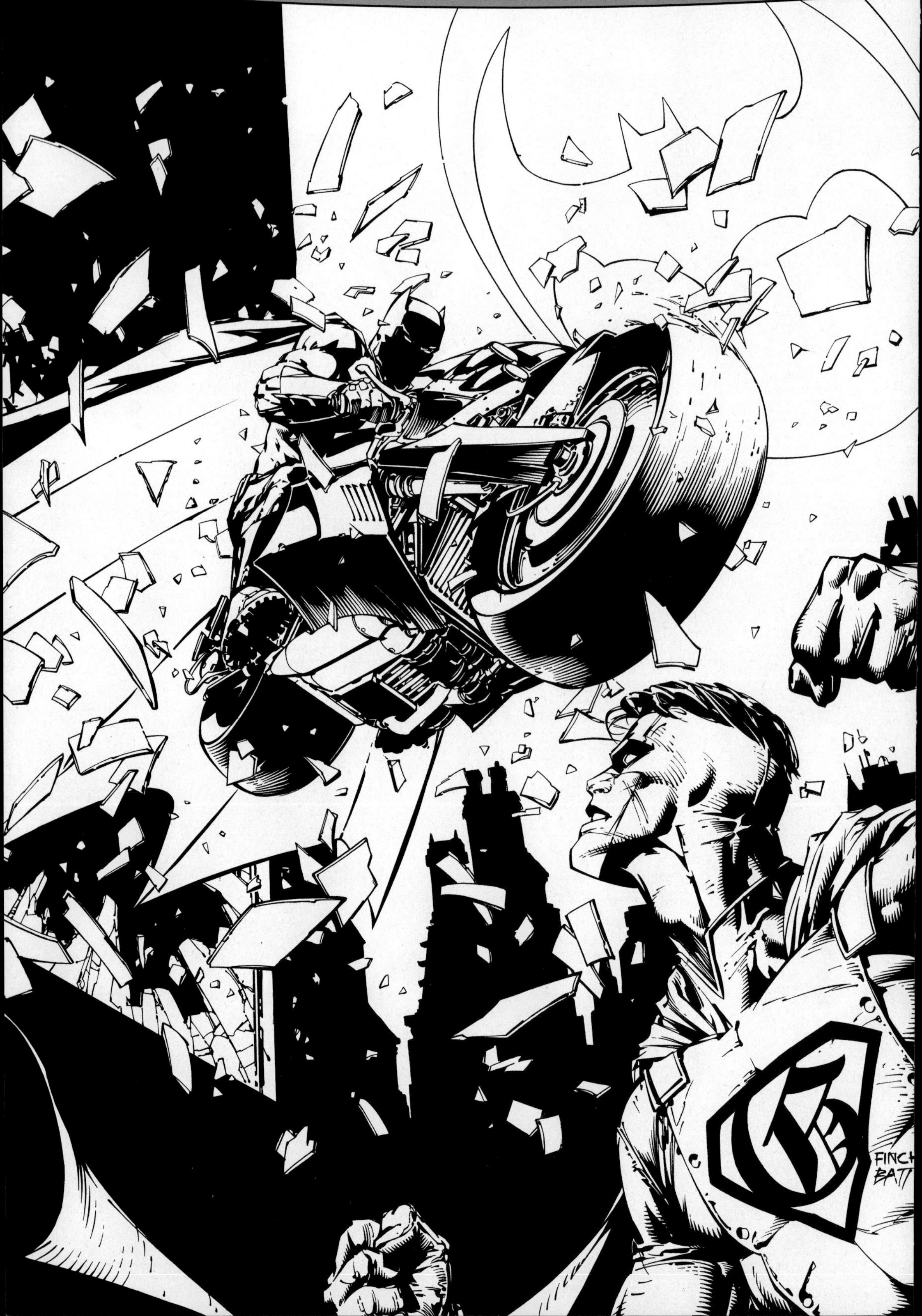
FINCH

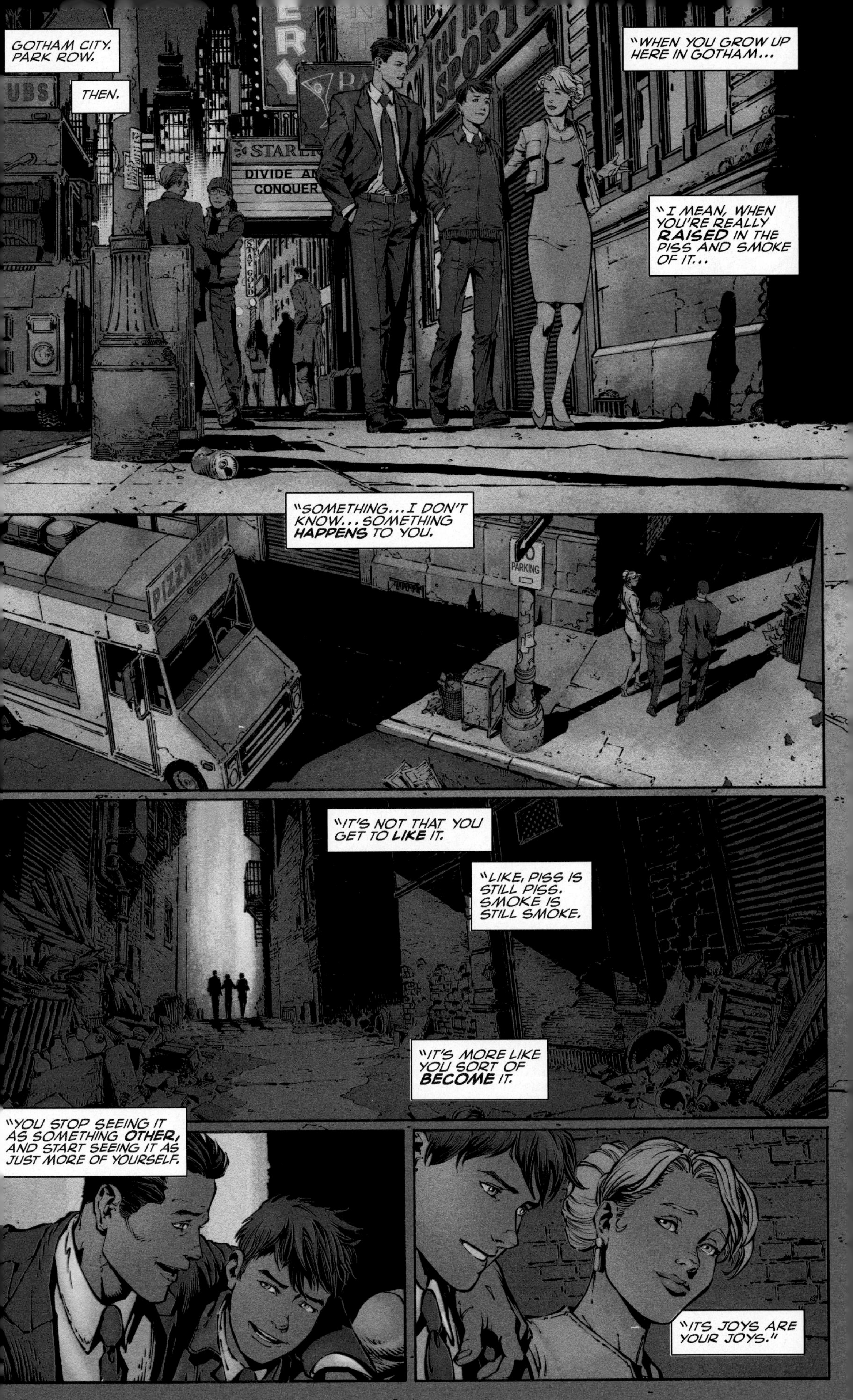
GOTHAM CITY. PARK ROW.
THEN.
"WHEN YOU GROW UP HERE IN GOTHAM...
"I MEAN, WHEN YOU'RE REALLY **RAISED** IN THE PISS AND SMOKE OF IT...
"SOMETHING...I DON'T KNOW...SOMETHING **HAPPENS** TO YOU.
"IT'S NOT THAT YOU GET TO **LIKE** IT.
"LIKE, PISS IS STILL PISS. SMOKE IS STILL SMOKE.
"IT'S MORE LIKE YOU SORT OF **BECOME** IT.
"YOU STOP SEEING IT AS SOMETHING **OTHER**, AND START SEEING IT AS JUST MORE OF YOURSELF.
"ITS JOYS ARE YOUR JOYS."

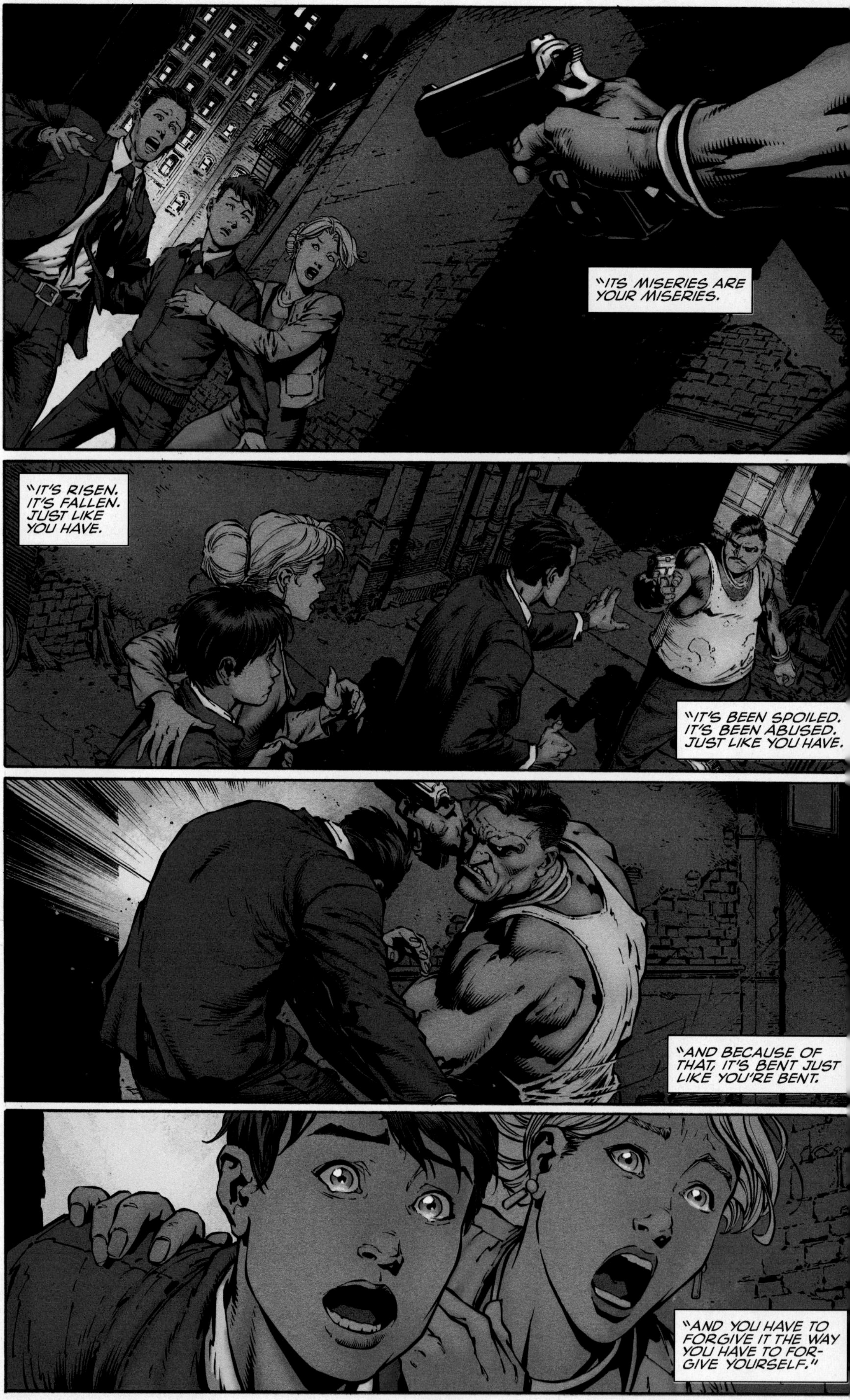
"ITS MISERIES ARE YOUR MISERIES.
"IT'S RISEN. IT'S FALLEN. JUST LIKE YOU HAVE.
"IT'S BEEN SPOILED. IT'S BEEN ABUSED. JUST LIKE YOU HAVE.
"AND BECAUSE OF THAT, IT'S BENT JUST LIKE YOU'RE BENT.
"AND YOU HAVE TO FORGIVE IT THE WAY YOU HAVE TO FOR-GIVE YOURSELF."

"SO THE PISS AND THE SMOKE, IT STILL GETS ME.

"I STILL FEEL LIKE RETCHING WHEN I GET A SMELL OF THE WORST OF IT.

"LIKE, I JUST NEED TO GET AWAY FROM IT, ANY WAY I CAN.

"BUT, BEING FROM HERE, I KNOW... SOMEHOW I KNOW WHERE THAT ALL COMES FROM.

"I UNDERSTAND ALL THAT'S IN ME, TOO.

"AND SOMEHOW, THAT--THAT MAKES IT BETTER.

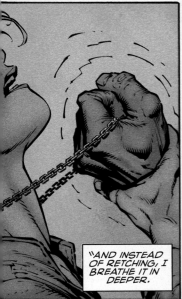

"AND INSTEAD OF RETCHING, I BREATHE IT IN DEEPER.

"AND I SMILE.

"AND I SHOUT IT. GOOD AND LOUD..."

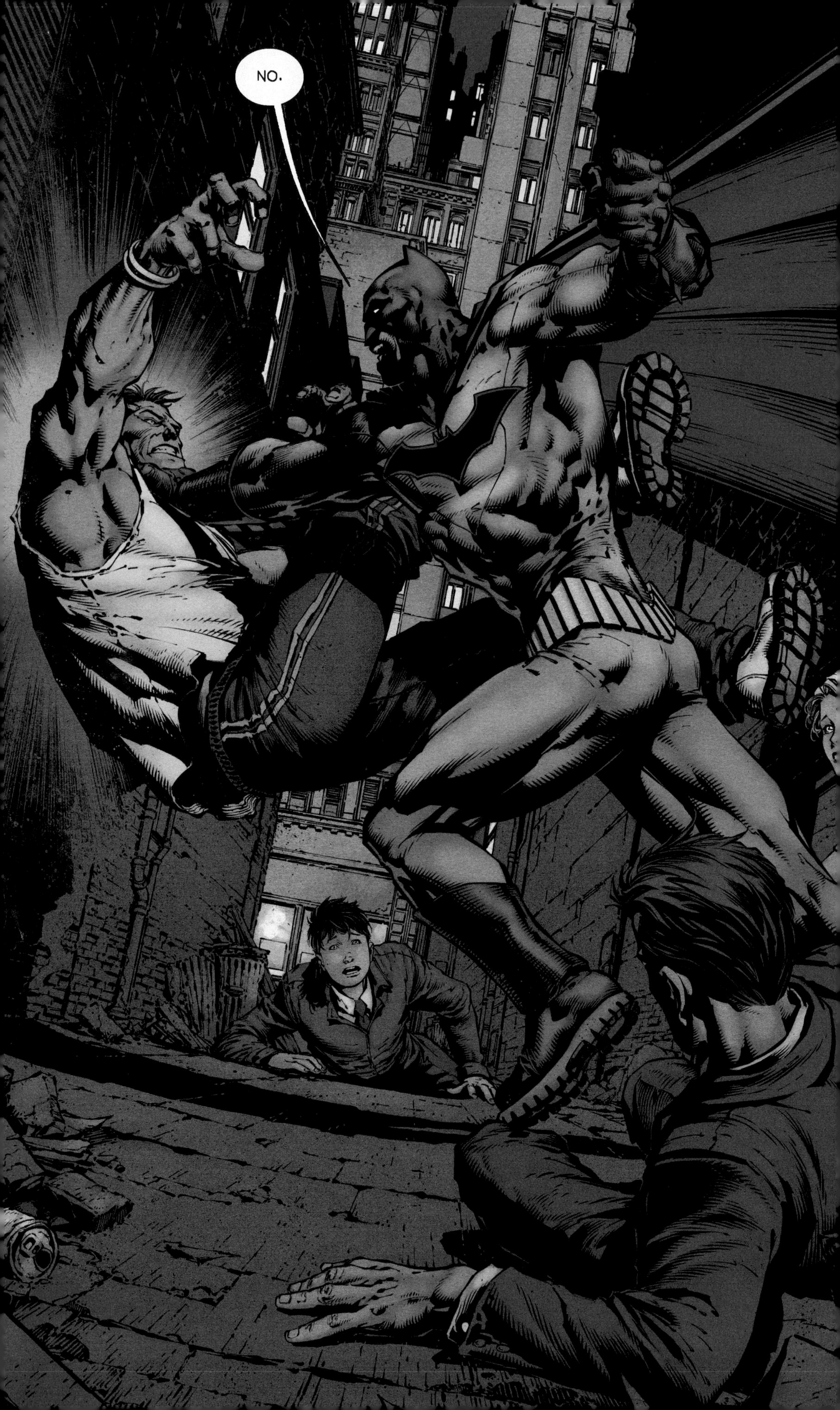
NO.

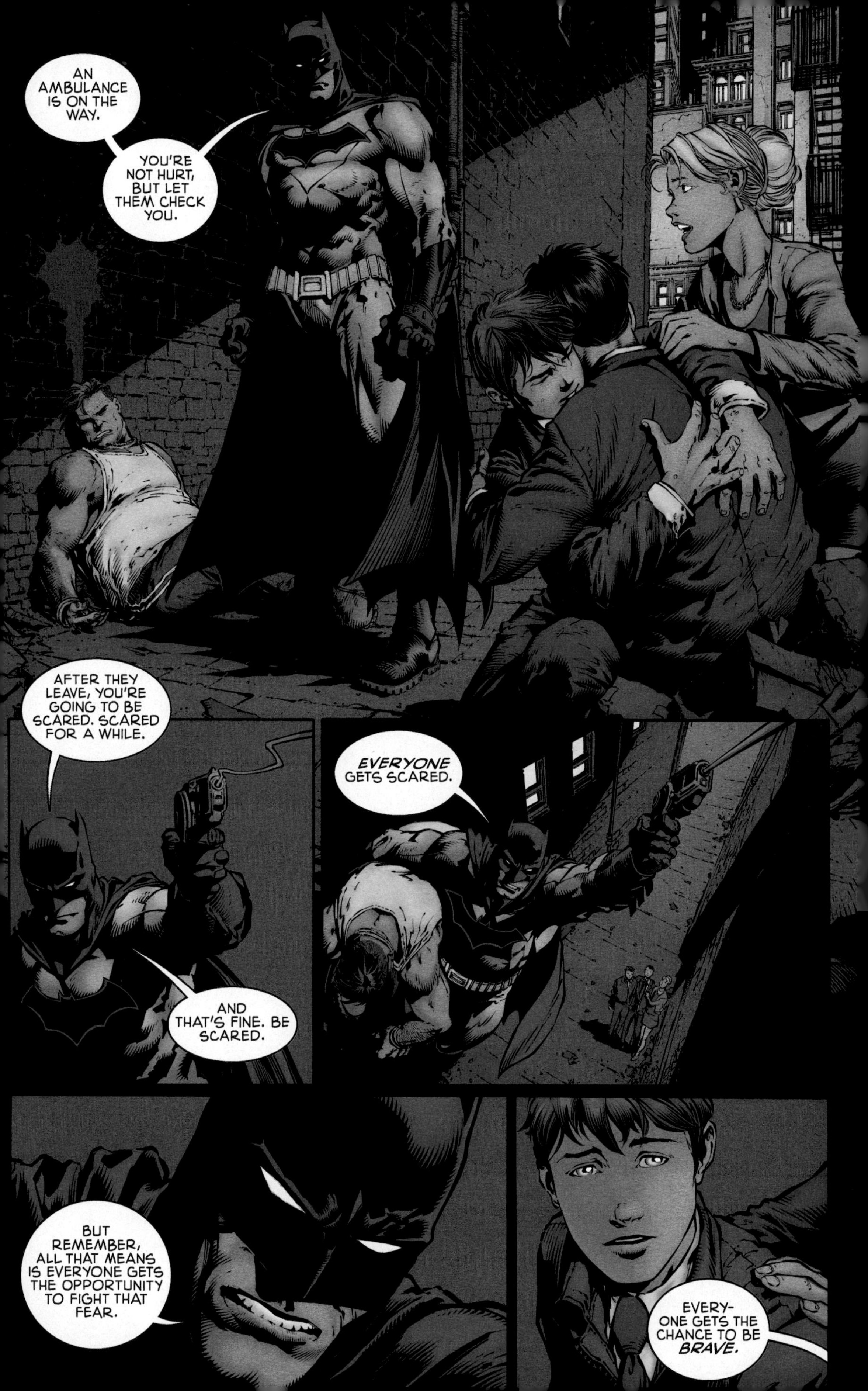
AN AMBULANCE IS ON THE WAY.
YOU'RE NOT HURT, BUT LET THEM CHECK YOU.
AFTER THEY LEAVE, YOU'RE GOING TO BE SCARED. SCARED FOR A WHILE.
AND THAT'S FINE. BE SCARED.
EVERYONE GETS SCARED.
BUT REMEMBER, ALL THAT MEANS IS EVERYONE GETS THE OPPORTUNITY TO FIGHT THAT FEAR.
EVERY-ONE GETS THE CHANCE TO BE BRAVE.

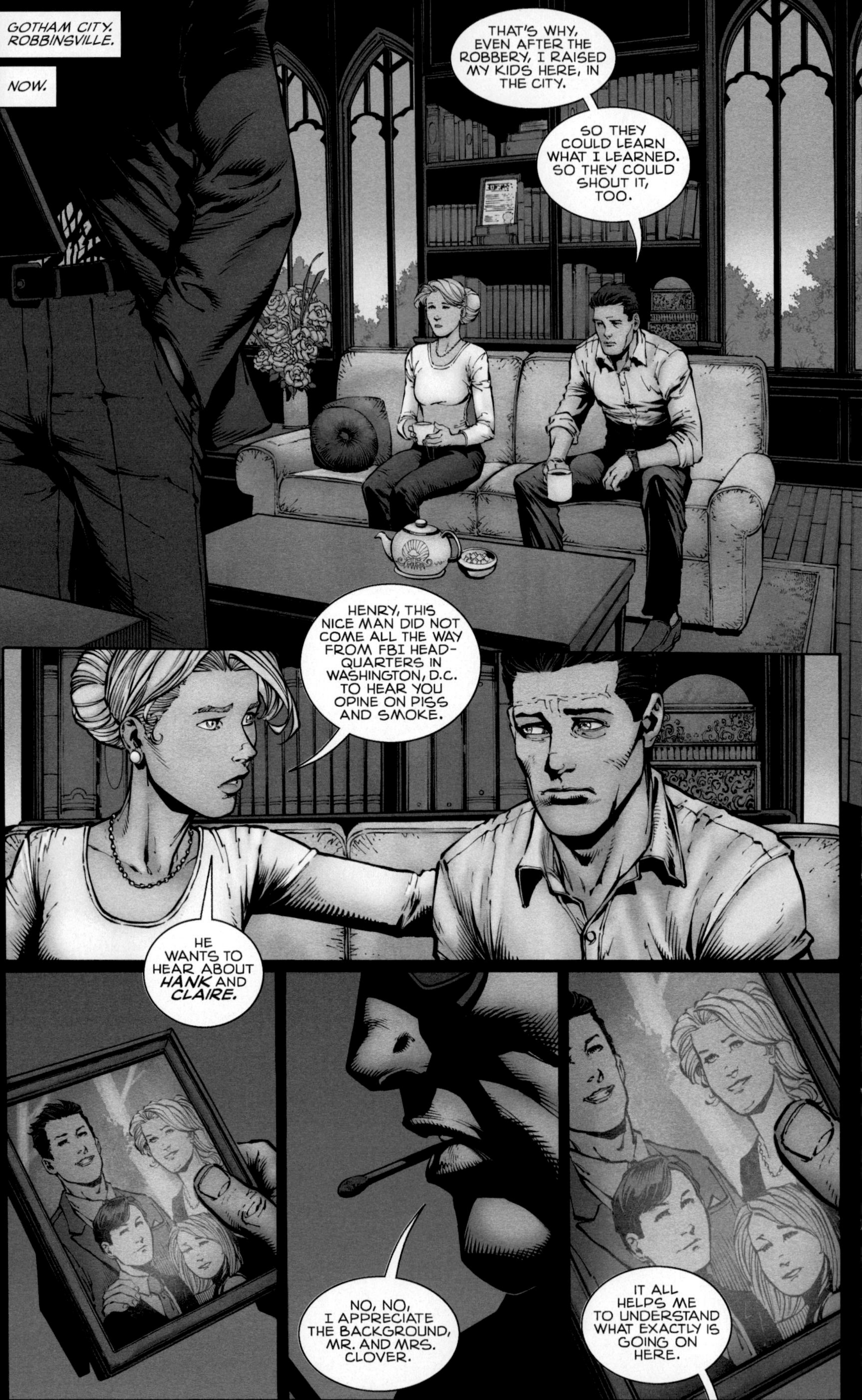
GOTHAM CITY. ROBBINSVILLE.
NOW.
THAT'S WHY, EVEN AFTER THE ROBBERY, I RAISED MY KIDS HERE, IN THE CITY.
SO THEY COULD LEARN WHAT I LEARNED. SO THEY COULD SHOUT IT, TOO.
HENRY, THIS NICE MAN DID NOT COME ALL THE WAY FROM FBI HEAD-QUARTERS IN WASHINGTON, D.C. TO HEAR YOU OPINE ON PISS AND SMOKE.
HE WANTS TO HEAR ABOUT *HANK* AND *CLAIRE.*
NO, NO, I APPRECIATE THE BACKGROUND, MR. AND MRS. CLOVER.
IT ALL HELPS ME TO UNDERSTAND WHAT EXACTLY IS GOING ON HERE.

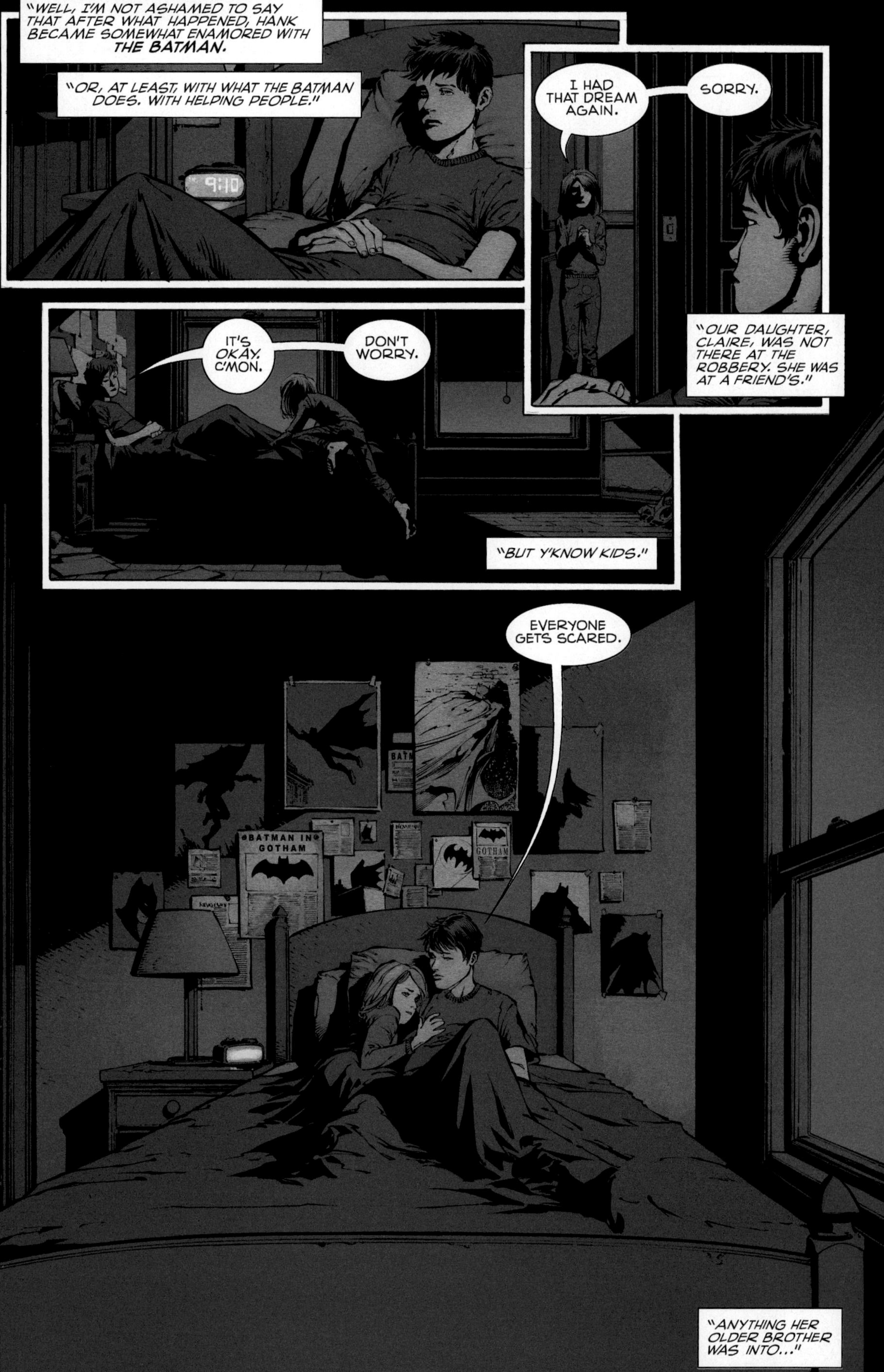
"WELL, I'M NOT ASHAMED TO SAY THAT AFTER WHAT HAPPENED, HANK BECAME SOMEWHAT ENAMORED WITH THE BATMAN.
"OR, AT LEAST, WITH WHAT THE BATMAN DOES. WITH HELPING PEOPLE."
9:10
I HAD THAT DREAM AGAIN.
SORRY.
"OUR DAUGHTER, CLAIRE, WAS NOT THERE AT THE ROBBERY. SHE WAS AT A FRIEND'S."
IT'S OKAY. C'MON.
DON'T WORRY.
"BUT Y'KNOW KIDS."
EVERYONE GETS SCARED.
BATMAN IN GOTHAM
GOTHAM
"ANYTHING HER OLDER BROTHER WAS INTO..."

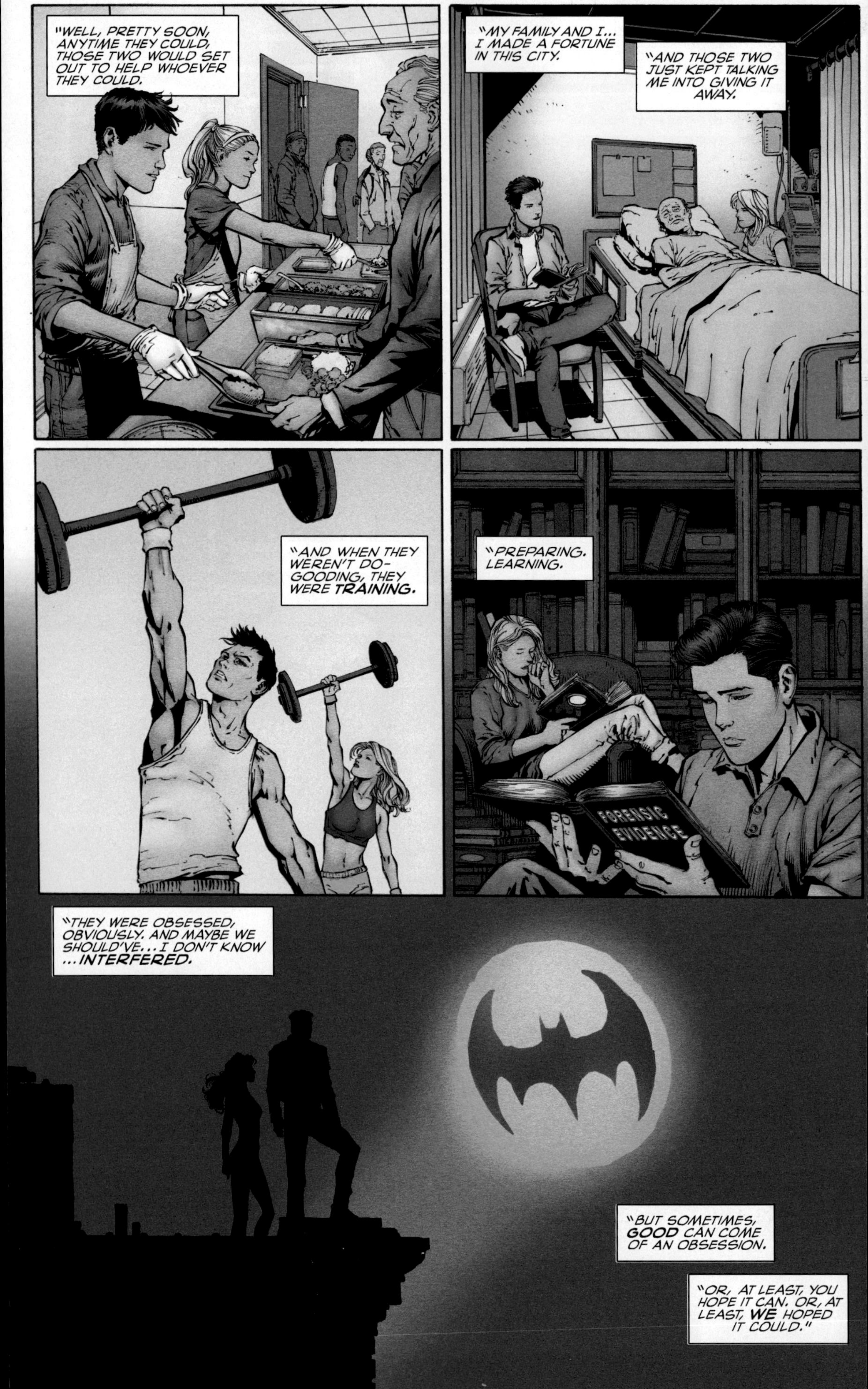
"WELL, PRETTY SOON, ANYTIME THEY COULD, THOSE TWO WOULD SET OUT TO HELP WHOEVER THEY COULD.
"MY FAMILY AND I... I MADE A FORTUNE IN THIS CITY.
"AND THOSE TWO JUST KEPT TALKING ME INTO GIVING IT AWAY.
"AND WHEN THEY WEREN'T DO-GOODING, THEY WERE TRAINING.
"PREPARING. LEARNING.
FORENSIC EVIDENCE
"THEY WERE OBSESSED, OBVIOUSLY. AND MAYBE WE SHOULD'VE... I DON'T KNOW ...INTERFERED.
"BUT SOMETIMES, GOOD CAN COME OF AN OBSESSION.
"OR, AT LEAST, YOU HOPE IT CAN. OR, AT LEAST, WE HOPED IT COULD."

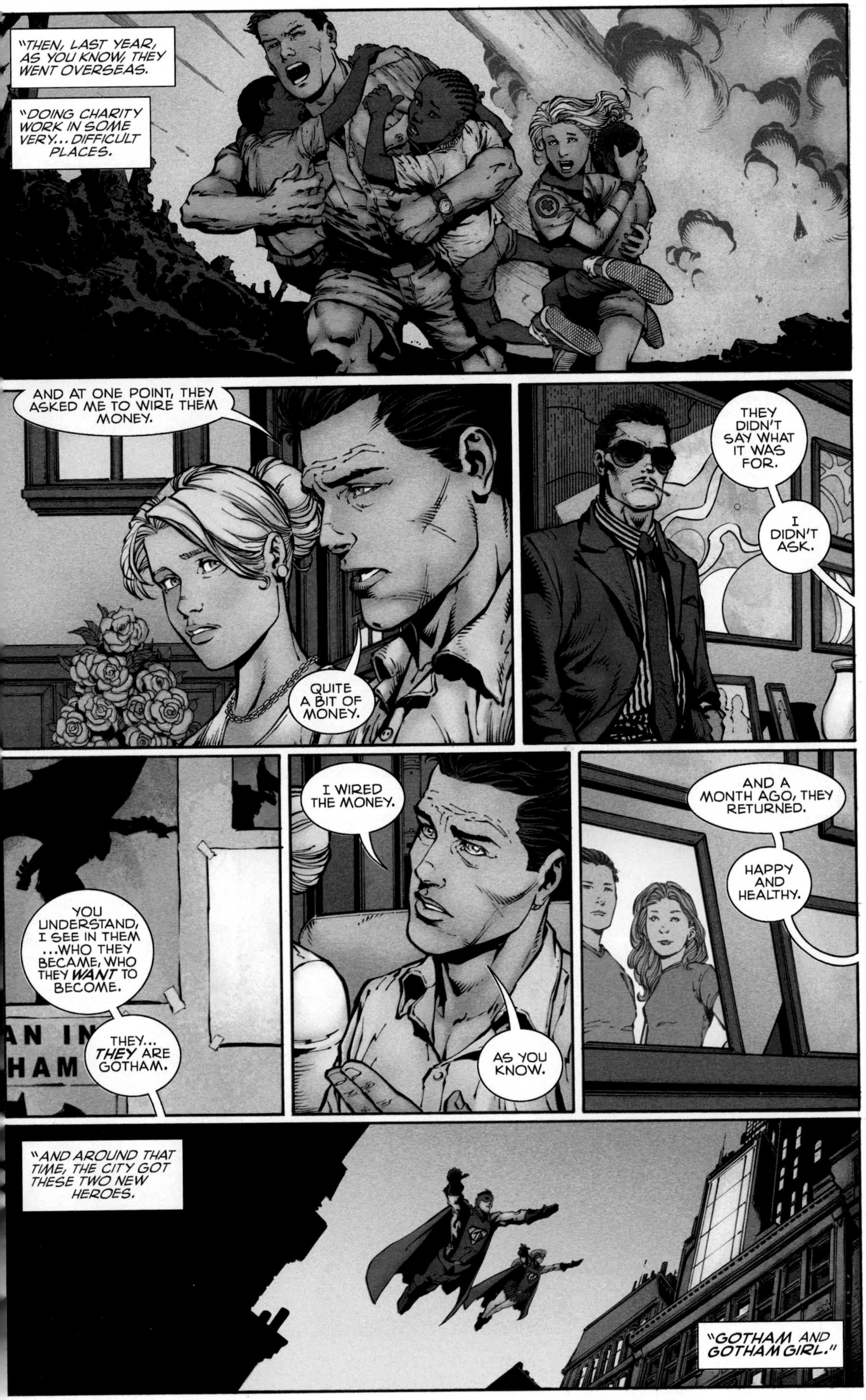
"THEN, LAST YEAR, AS YOU KNOW, THEY WENT OVERSEAS.
"DOING CHARITY WORK IN SOME VERY... DIFFICULT PLACES.
AND AT ONE POINT, THEY ASKED ME TO WIRE THEM MONEY.
QUITE A BIT OF MONEY.
THEY DIDN'T SAY WHAT IT WAS FOR.
I DIDN'T ASK.
YOU UNDERSTAND, I SEE IN THEM ...WHO THEY BECAME, WHO THEY WANT TO BECOME.
THEY... THEY ARE GOTHAM.
AN IN
HAM
I WIRED THE MONEY.
AS YOU KNOW.
AND A MONTH AGO, THEY RETURNED.
HAPPY AND HEALTHY.
"AND AROUND THAT TIME, THE CITY GOT THESE TWO NEW HEROES.
"GOTHAM AND GOTHAM GIRL."

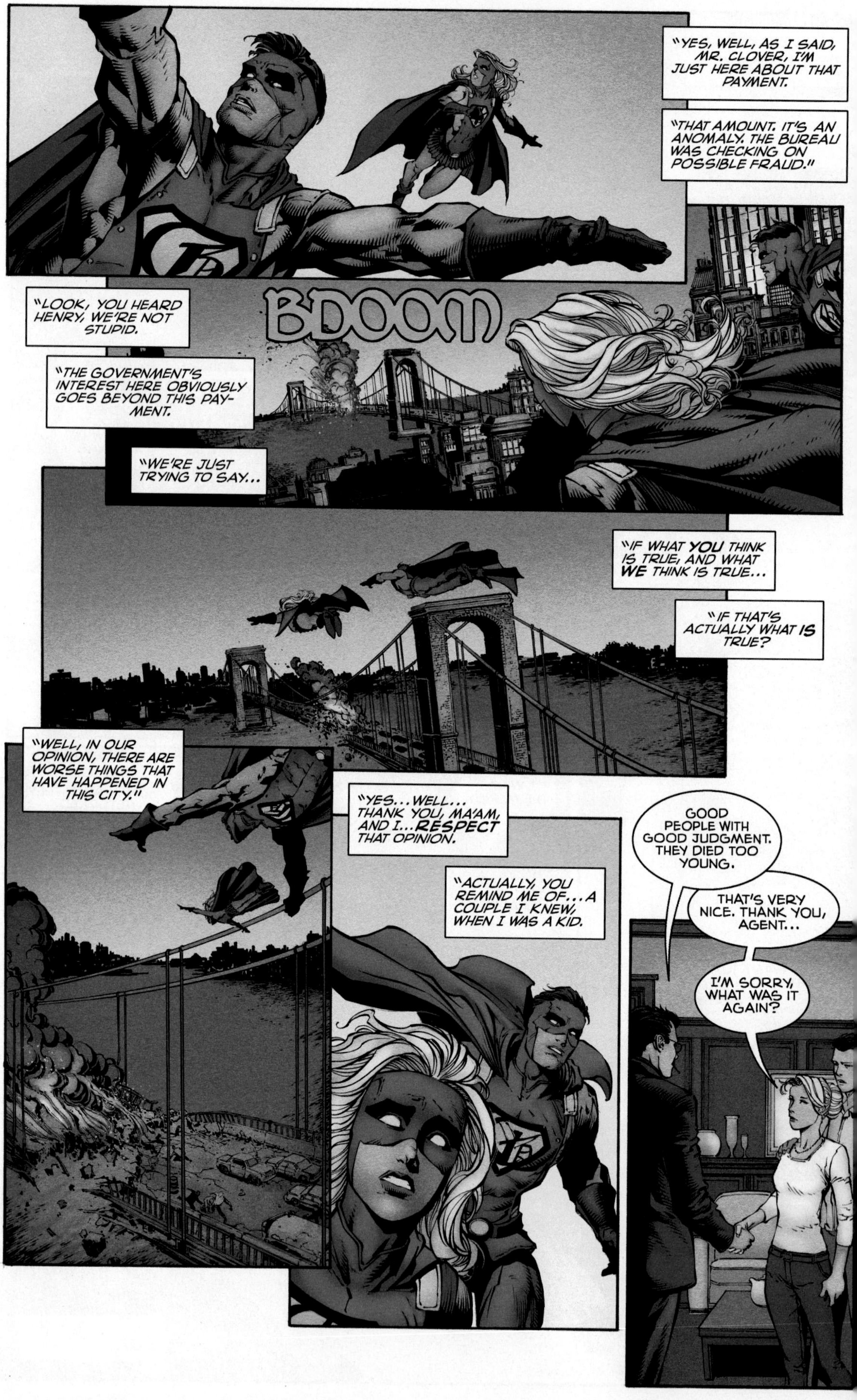
"YES, WELL, AS I SAID, MR. CLOVER, I'M JUST HERE ABOUT THAT PAYMENT.
"THAT AMOUNT. IT'S AN ANOMALY. THE BUREAU WAS CHECKING ON POSSIBLE FRAUD."
"LOOK, YOU HEARD HENRY, WE'RE NOT STUPID.
BDOOM
"THE GOVERNMENT'S INTEREST HERE OBVIOUSLY GOES BEYOND THIS PAYMENT.
"WE'RE JUST TRYING TO SAY...
"IF WHAT **YOU** THINK IS TRUE, AND WHAT **WE** THINK IS TRUE...
"IF THAT'S ACTUALLY WHAT **IS** TRUE?
"WELL, IN OUR OPINION, THERE ARE WORSE THINGS THAT HAVE HAPPENED IN THIS CITY."
"YES...WELL... THANK YOU, MA'AM, AND I...**RESPECT** THAT OPINION.
"ACTUALLY, YOU REMIND ME OF...A COUPLE I KNEW, WHEN I WAS A KID.
GOOD PEOPLE WITH GOOD JUDGMENT. THEY DIED TOO YOUNG.
THAT'S VERY NICE. THANK YOU, AGENT...
I'M SORRY, WHAT WAS IT AGAIN?

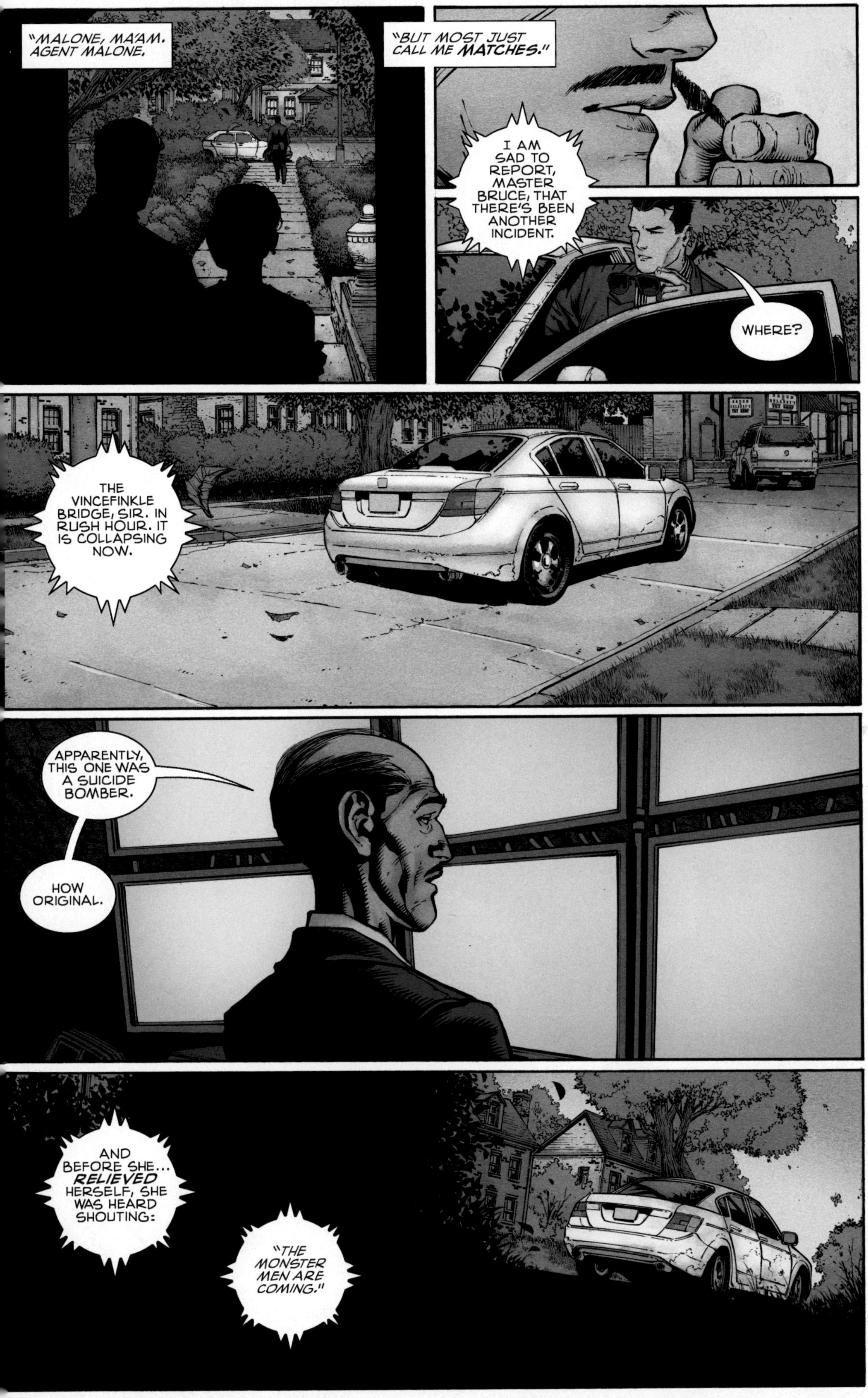
"MALONE, MA'AM. AGENT MALONE.
"BUT MOST JUST CALL ME MATCHES."
I AM SAD TO REPORT, MASTER BRUCE, THAT THERE'S BEEN ANOTHER INCIDENT.
WHERE?
THE VINCEFINKLE BRIDGE, SIR. IN RUSH HOUR. IT IS COLLAPSING NOW.
APPARENTLY, THIS ONE WAS A SUICIDE BOMBER.
HOW ORIGINAL.
AND BEFORE SHE... RELIEVED HERSELF, SHE WAS HEARD SHOUTING:
"THE MONSTER MEN ARE COMING."

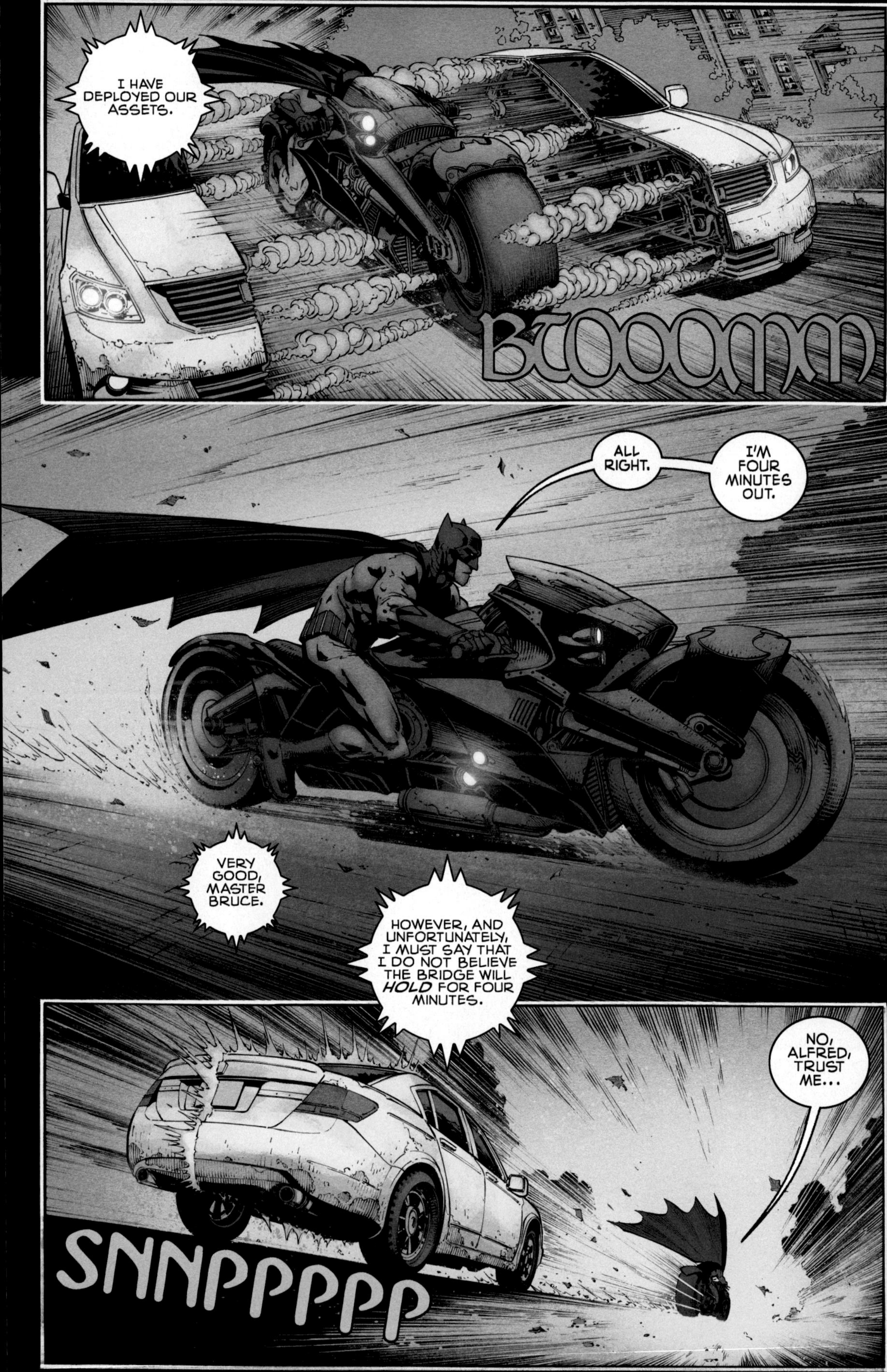
I HAVE DEPLOYED OUR ASSETS.
BTOOOMM
ALL RIGHT.
I'M FOUR MINUTES OUT.
VERY GOOD, MASTER BRUCE.
HOWEVER, AND UNFORTUNATELY, I MUST SAY THAT I DO NOT BELIEVE THE BRIDGE WILL *HOLD* FOR FOUR MINUTES.
NO, ALFRED, TRUST ME...
SNNPPPPP

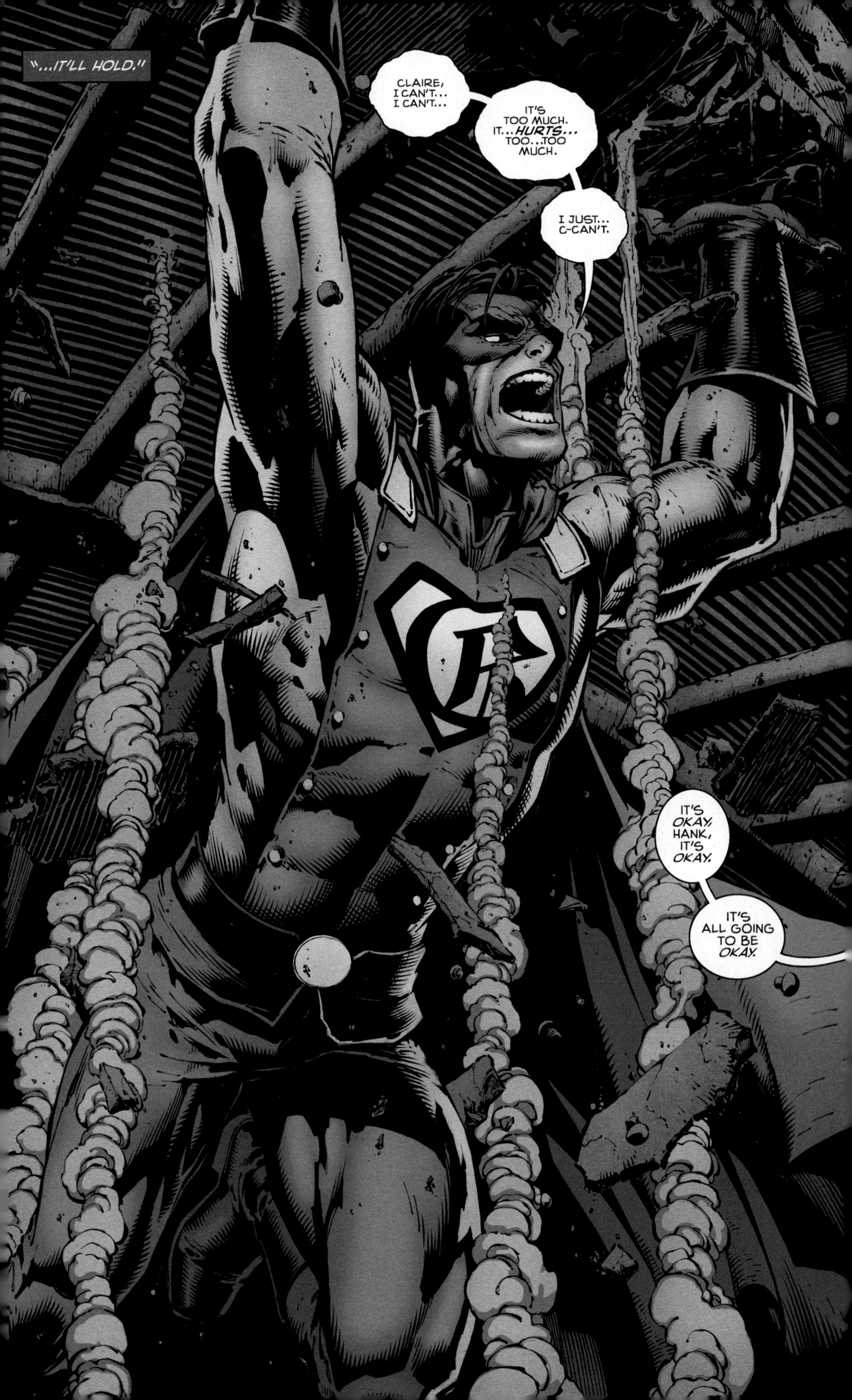
"...IT'LL HOLD."
CLAIRE, I CAN'T... I CAN'T...
IT'S TOO MUCH. IT...HURTS... TOO...TOO MUCH.
I JUST... C-CAN'T.
IT'S OKAY, HANK, IT'S OKAY.
IT'S ALL GOING TO BE OKAY.

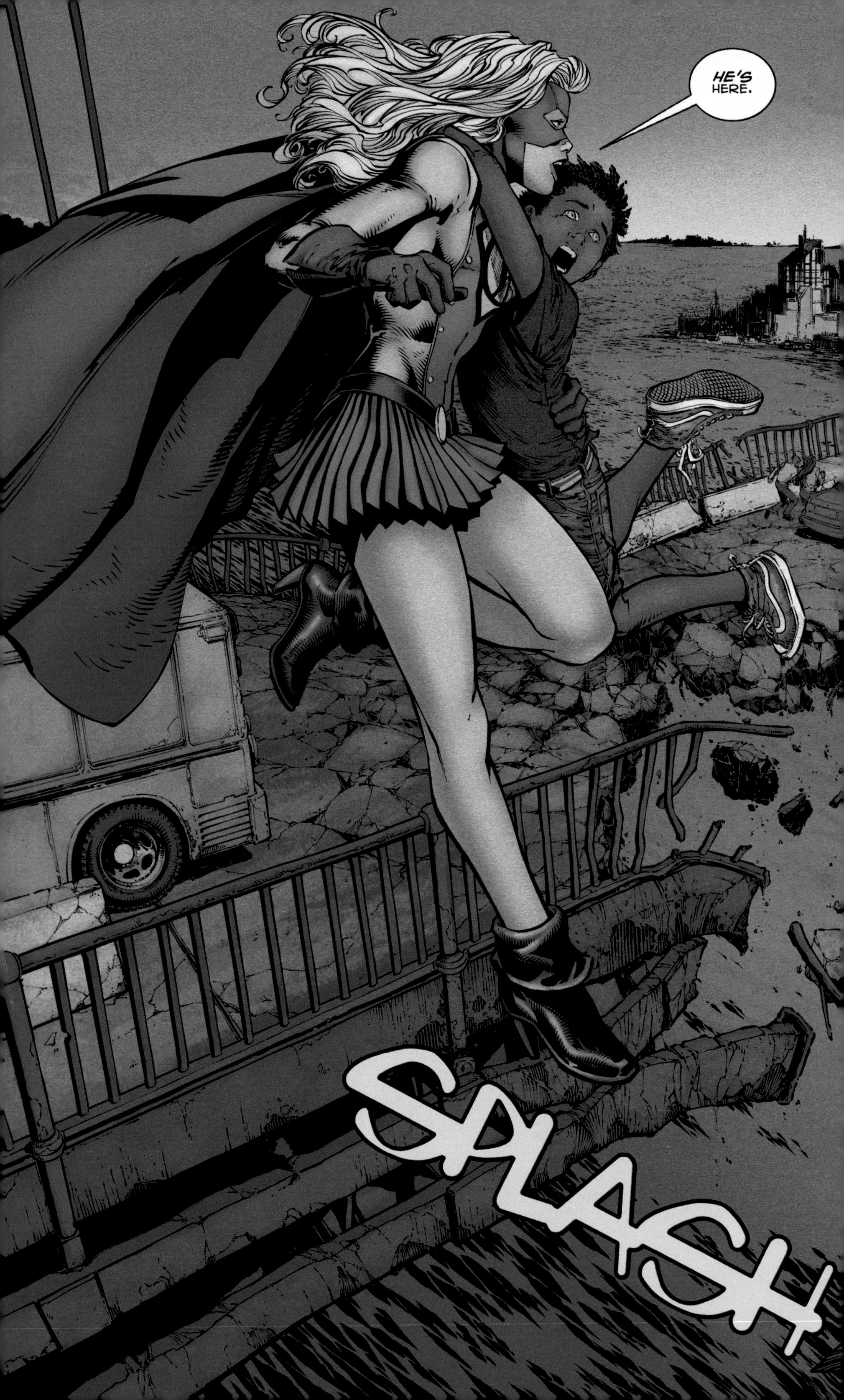
HE'S HERE.
SPLASH

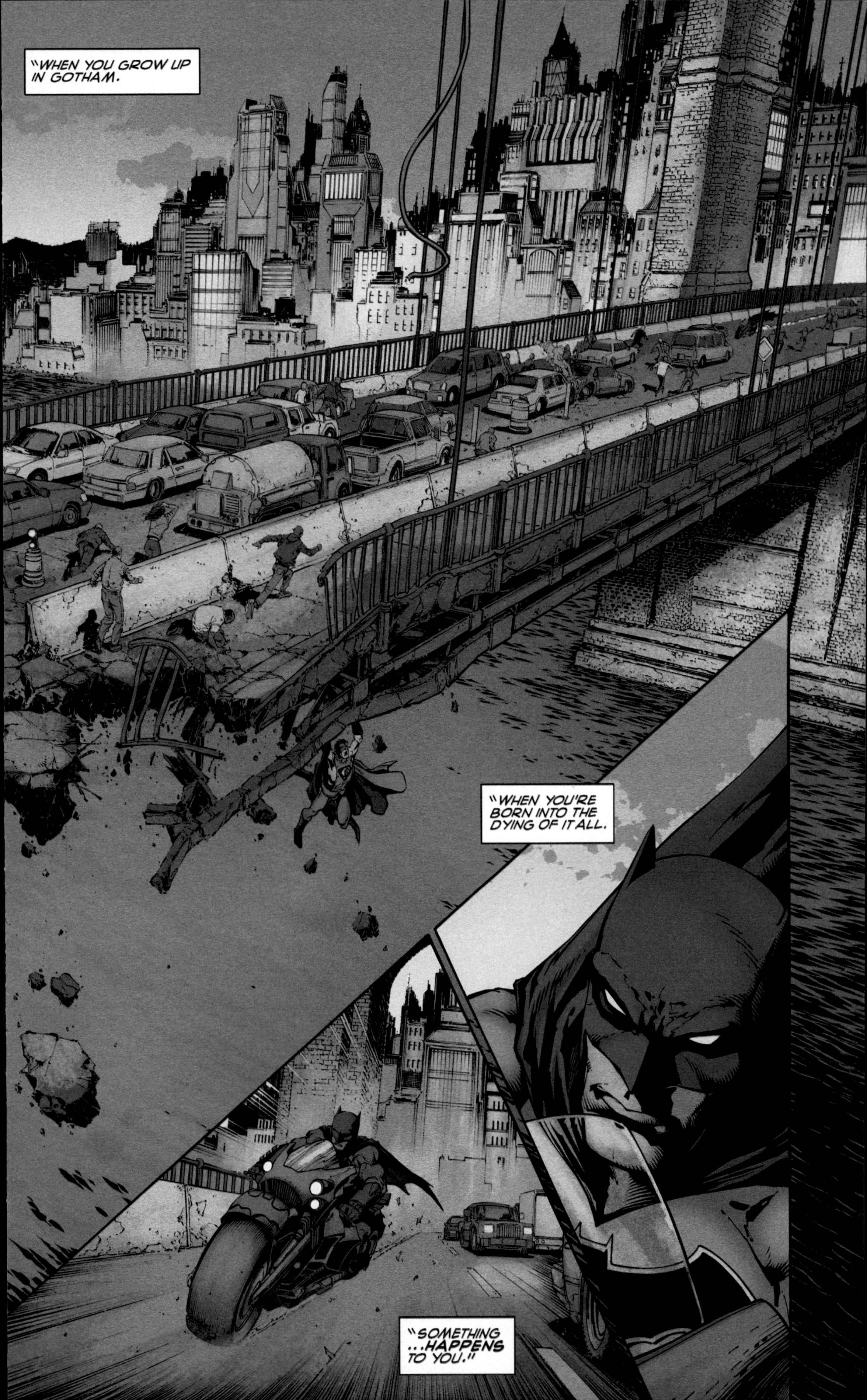
"WHEN YOU GROW UP IN GOTHAM.
"WHEN YOU'RE BORN INTO THE DYING OF IT ALL.
"SOMETHING ...HAPPENS TO YOU."

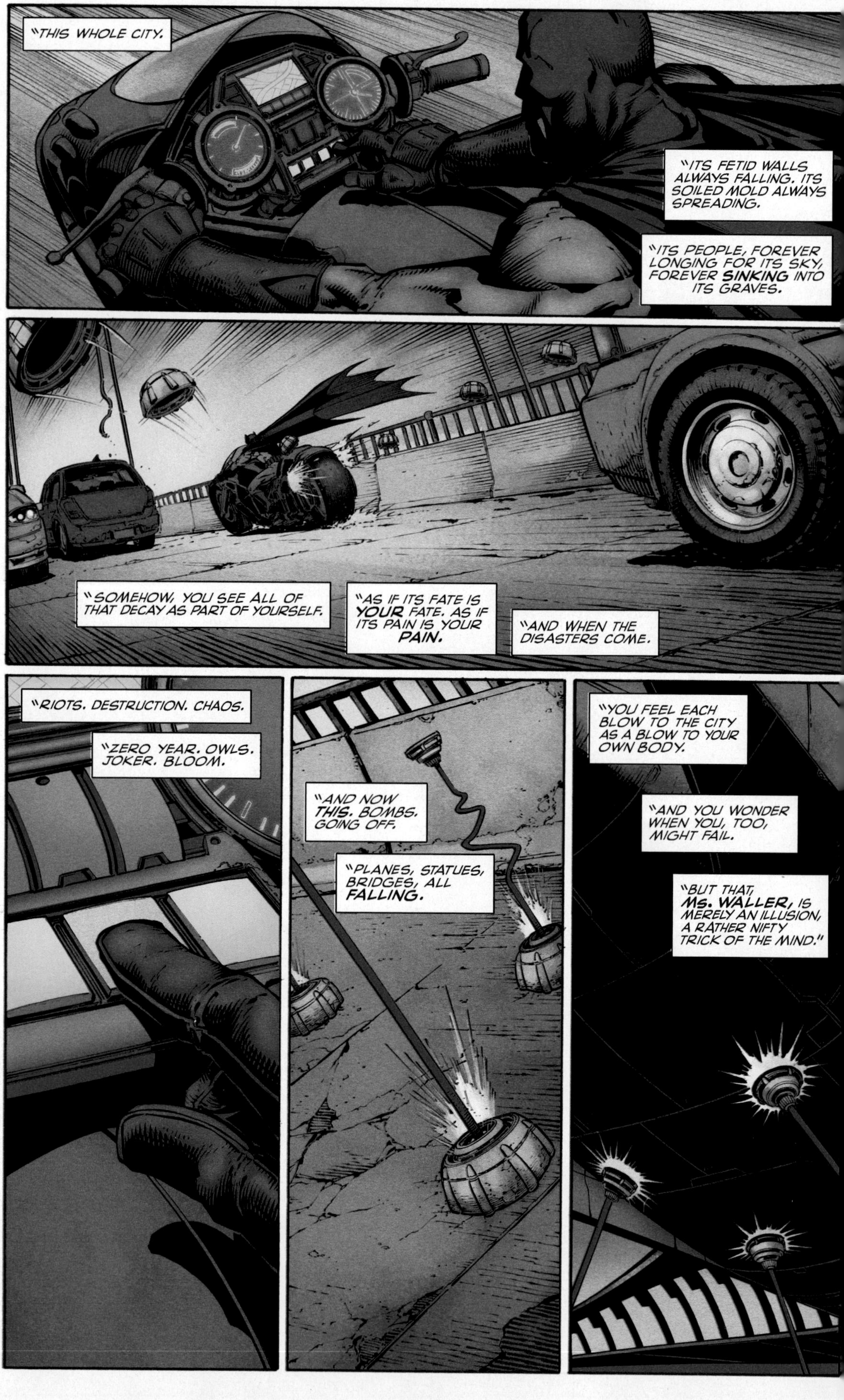
"THIS WHOLE CITY.
"ITS FETID WALLS ALWAYS FALLING. ITS SOILED MOLD ALWAYS SPREADING.
"ITS PEOPLE, FOREVER LONGING FOR ITS SKY, FOREVER SINKING INTO ITS GRAVES.
"SOMEHOW, YOU SEE ALL OF THAT DECAY AS PART OF YOURSELF.
"AS IF ITS FATE IS YOUR FATE. AS IF ITS PAIN IS YOUR PAIN.
"AND WHEN THE DISASTERS COME.
"RIOTS. DESTRUCTION. CHAOS.
"ZERO YEAR. OWLS. JOKER. BLOOM.
"AND NOW THIS. BOMBS. GOING OFF.
"PLANES, STATUES, BRIDGES, ALL FALLING.
"YOU FEEL EACH BLOW TO THE CITY AS A BLOW TO YOUR OWN BODY.
"AND YOU WONDER WHEN YOU, TOO, MIGHT FAIL.
"BUT THAT, MS. WALLER, IS MERELY AN ILLUSION, A RATHER NIFTY TRICK OF THE MIND."

"IT IS HOW THE PEOPLE OF THIS CITY ACCEPT WHAT THEY **CAN-NOT** ACCEPT.

"INDEED, WHAT THEY **SHOULD** NOT ACCEPT.

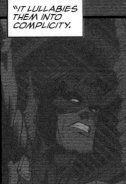

"IT LULLABIES THEM INTO COMPLICITY.

"TEACHES THEM TO IGNORE THE HORRORS.

"TO EMBRACE THE HORRORS.

"TO **BECOME** THE HORRORS.

"IT IS OUR GOAL, THEN, TO ELIMINATE THIS ILLUSION.

"TO FREE THE PEOPLE FROM THE PSYCHOSIS OF THE CITY.

"THEY WILL NOT RIOT! THEY WILL RESIST!

"THEY WILL NOT PANIC! THEY WILL PERSEVERE!

"VILLAINS WILL SURRENDER. HEROES WILL TRIUMPH.

"WITH MY COAXING AND ROGER'S GIFTS...

"...THEY WILL FINALLY SEPARATE THE LIFE OF THE MIND FROM THE ROT OF THE CITY.

"AND THEY WILL HAPPILY DECLARE...

...I AM **NOT** GOTHAM.

I AM **BETTER** THAN GOTHAM.

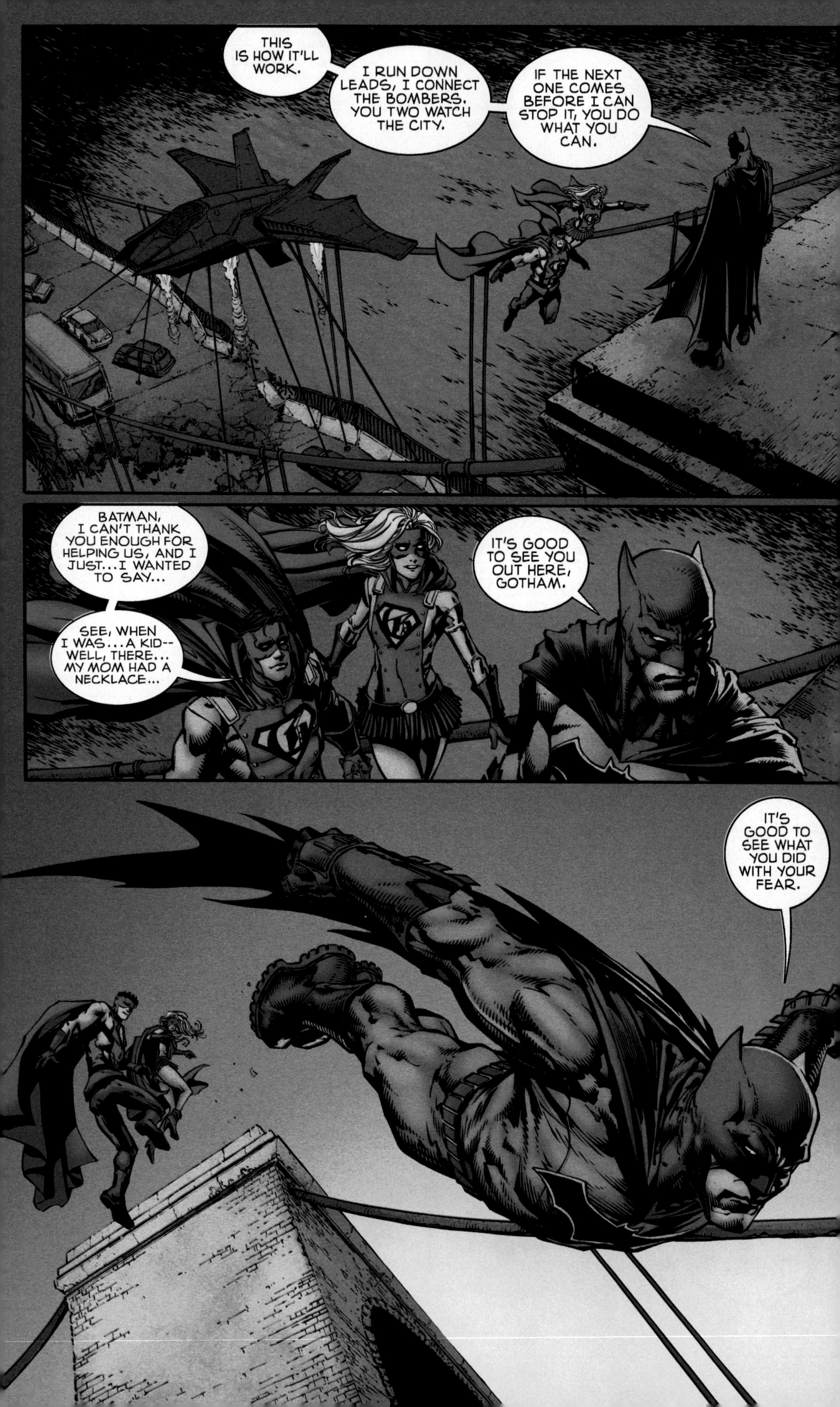

THIS IS HOW IT'LL WORK.
I RUN DOWN LEADS, I CONNECT THE BOMBERS. YOU TWO WATCH THE CITY.
IF THE NEXT ONE COMES BEFORE I CAN STOP IT, YOU DO WHAT YOU CAN.
BATMAN, I CAN'T THANK YOU ENOUGH FOR HELPING US, AND I JUST...I WANTED TO SAY...
SEE, WHEN I WAS...A KID-- WELL, THERE... MY MOM HAD A NECKLACE...
IT'S GOOD TO SEE YOU OUT HERE, GOTHAM.
IT'S GOOD TO SEE WHAT YOU DID WITH YOUR FEAR.

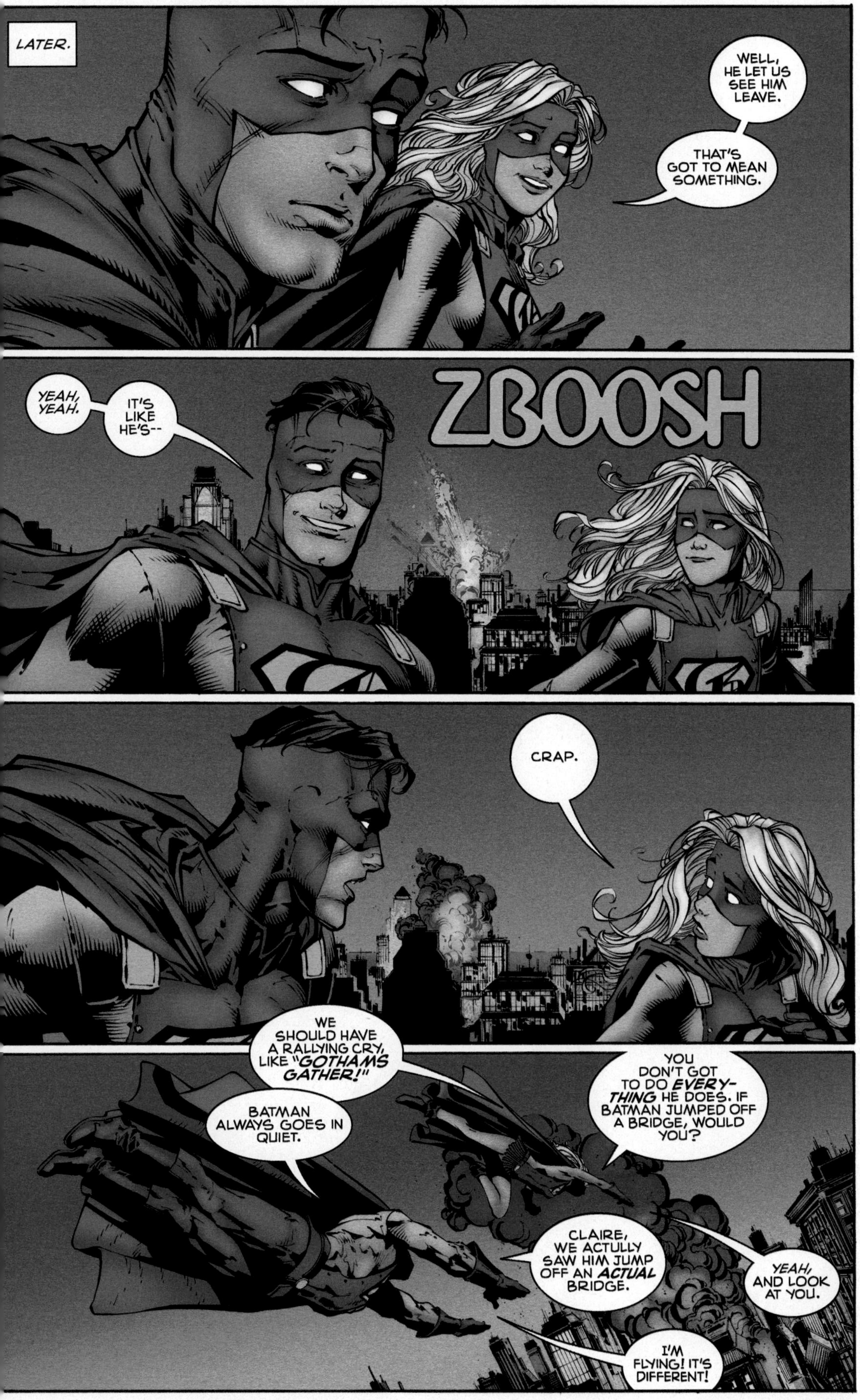
LATER.
WELL, HE LET US SEE HIM LEAVE.
THAT'S GOT TO MEAN SOMETHING.
ZBOOSH
YEAH, YEAH.
IT'S LIKE HE'S--
CRAP.
WE SHOULD HAVE A RALLYING CRY, LIKE "GOTHAMS GATHER!"
BATMAN ALWAYS GOES IN QUIET.
YOU DON'T GOT TO DO EVERY-THING HE DOES. IF BATMAN JUMPED OFF A BRIDGE, WOULD YOU?
CLAIRE, WE ACTULLY SAW HIM JUMP OFF AN ACTUAL BRIDGE.
YEAH, AND LOOK AT YOU.
I'M FLYING! IT'S DIFFERENT!

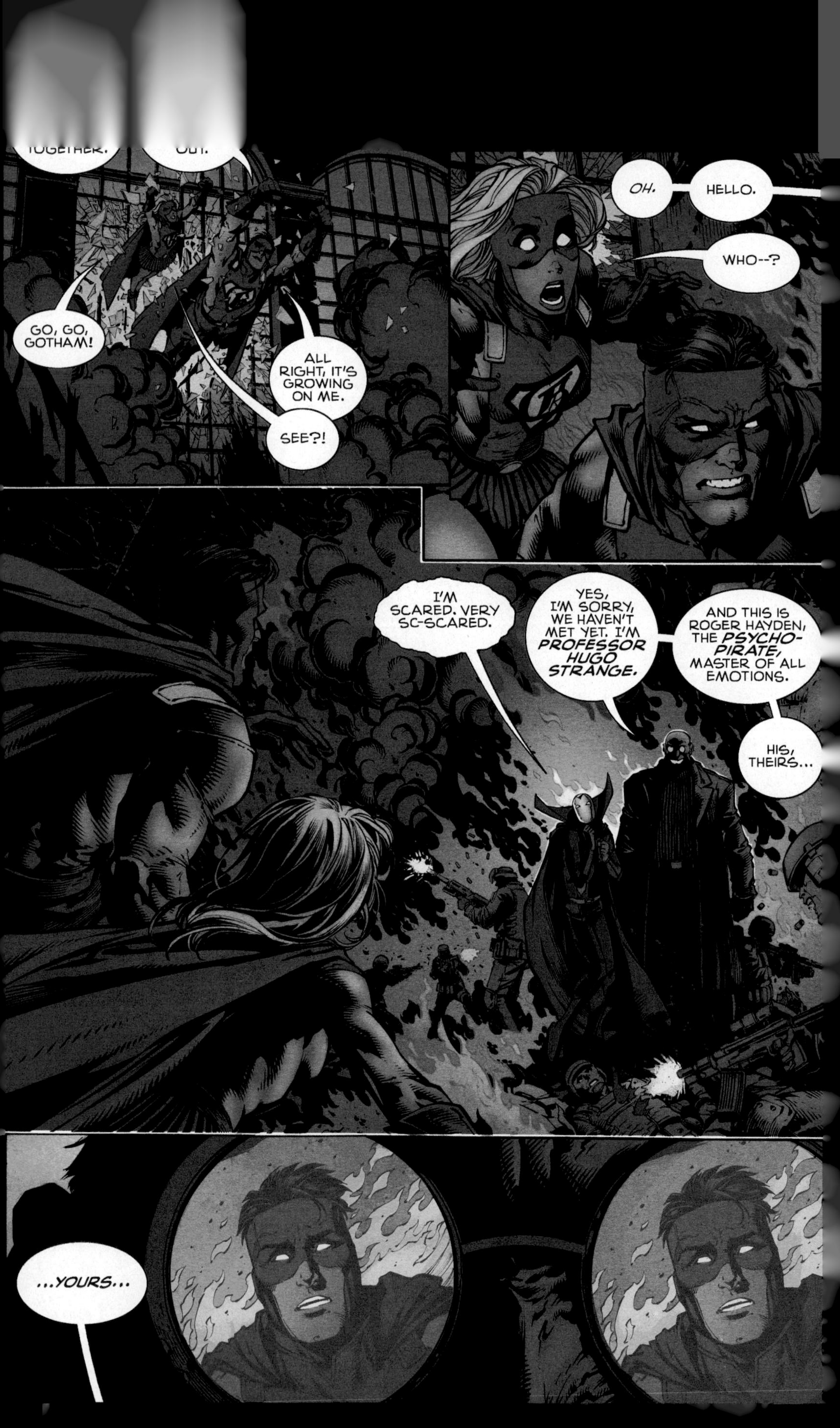

TOGETHER.
OUT.
GO, GO, GOTHAM!
ALL RIGHT, IT'S GROWING ON ME.
SEE?!
OH.
HELLO.
WHO--?
I'M SCARED. VERY SC-SCARED.
YES, I'M SORRY, WE HAVEN'T MET YET. I'M PROFESSOR HUGO STRANGE.
AND THIS IS ROGER HAYDEN, THE PSYCHO-PIRATE, MASTER OF ALL EMOTIONS.
HIS, THEIRS...
...YOURS...

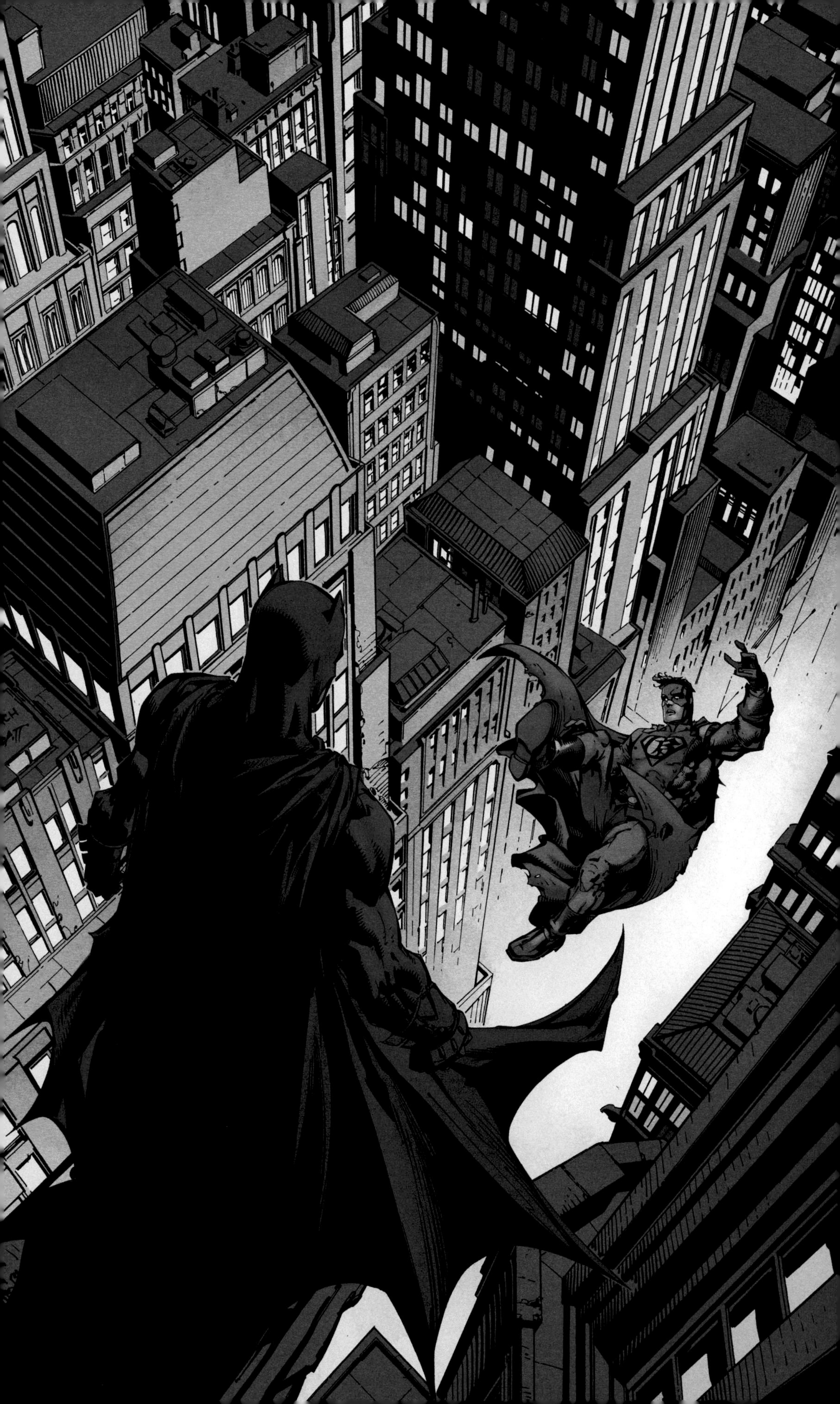

TOM KING writer * DAVID FINCH penciller * SANDRA HOPE and MATT B [illegible] JORDIE BELLAIRE colorist
JOHN WORKMAN letterer * DAVID FINCH, MATT BANNING and JORDIE BELLAIRE cover artists

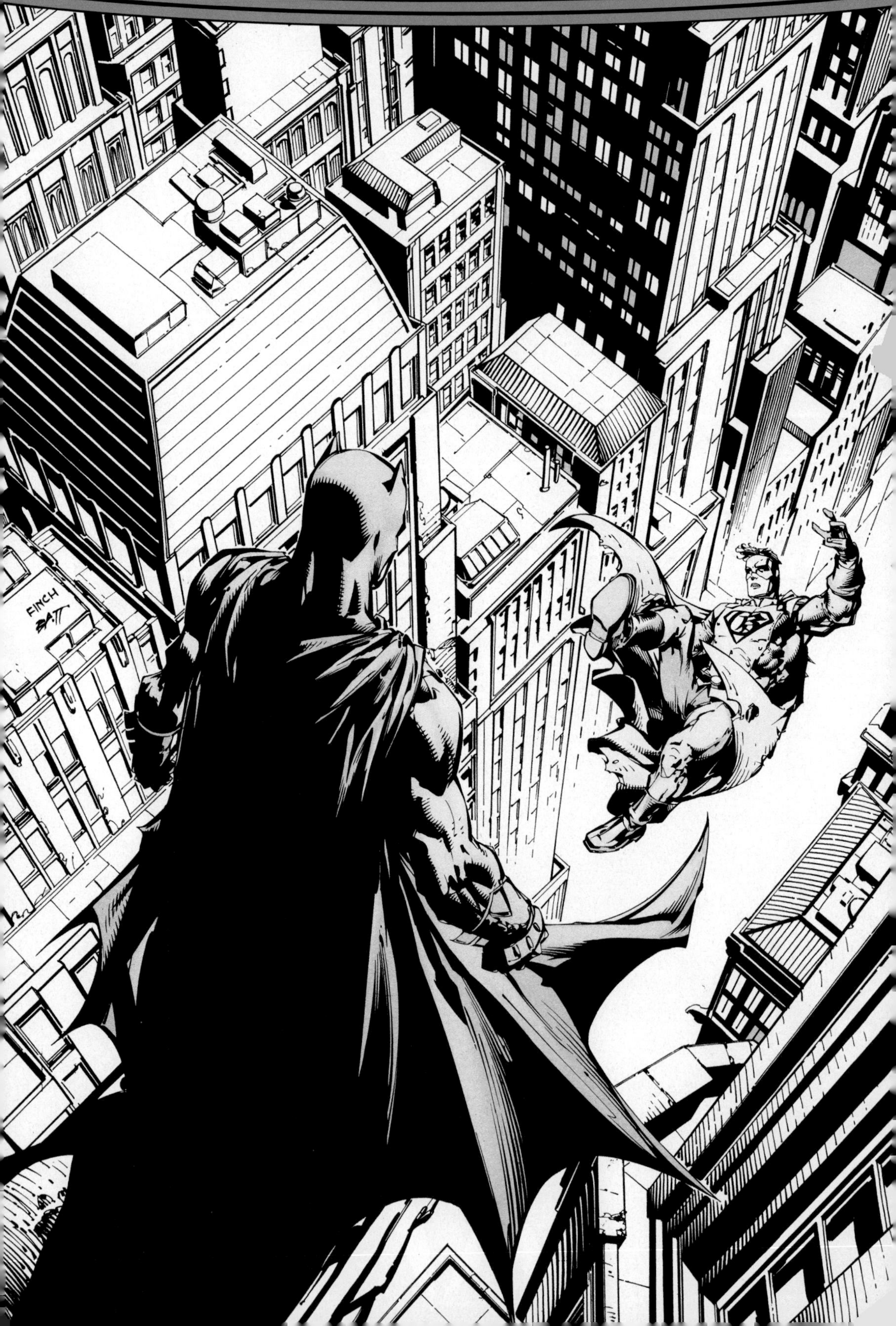
FINCH

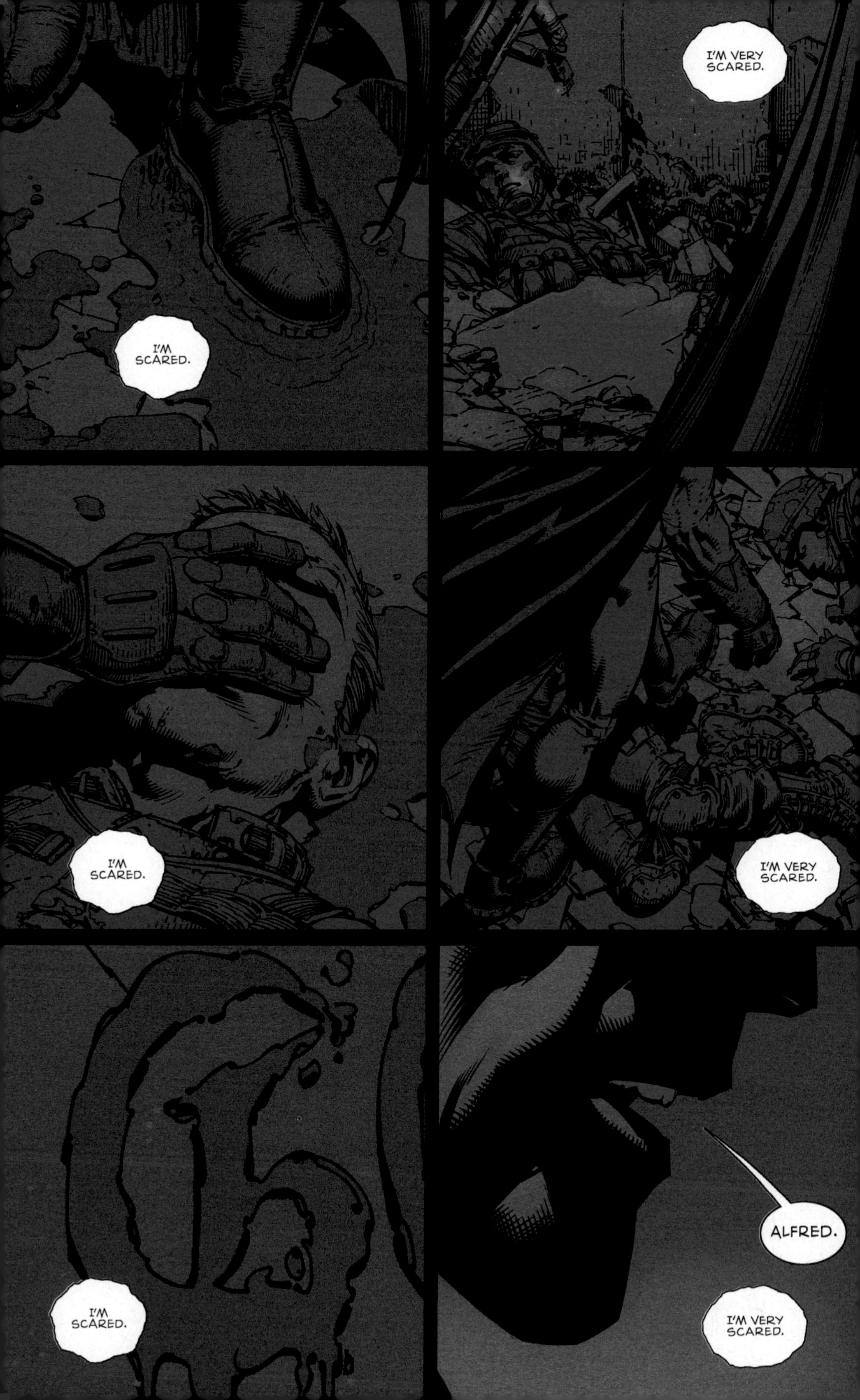
I'M SCARED.
I'M VERY SCARED.
I'M SCARED.
I'M VERY SCARED.
I'M SCARED.
ALFRED.
I'M VERY SCARED.

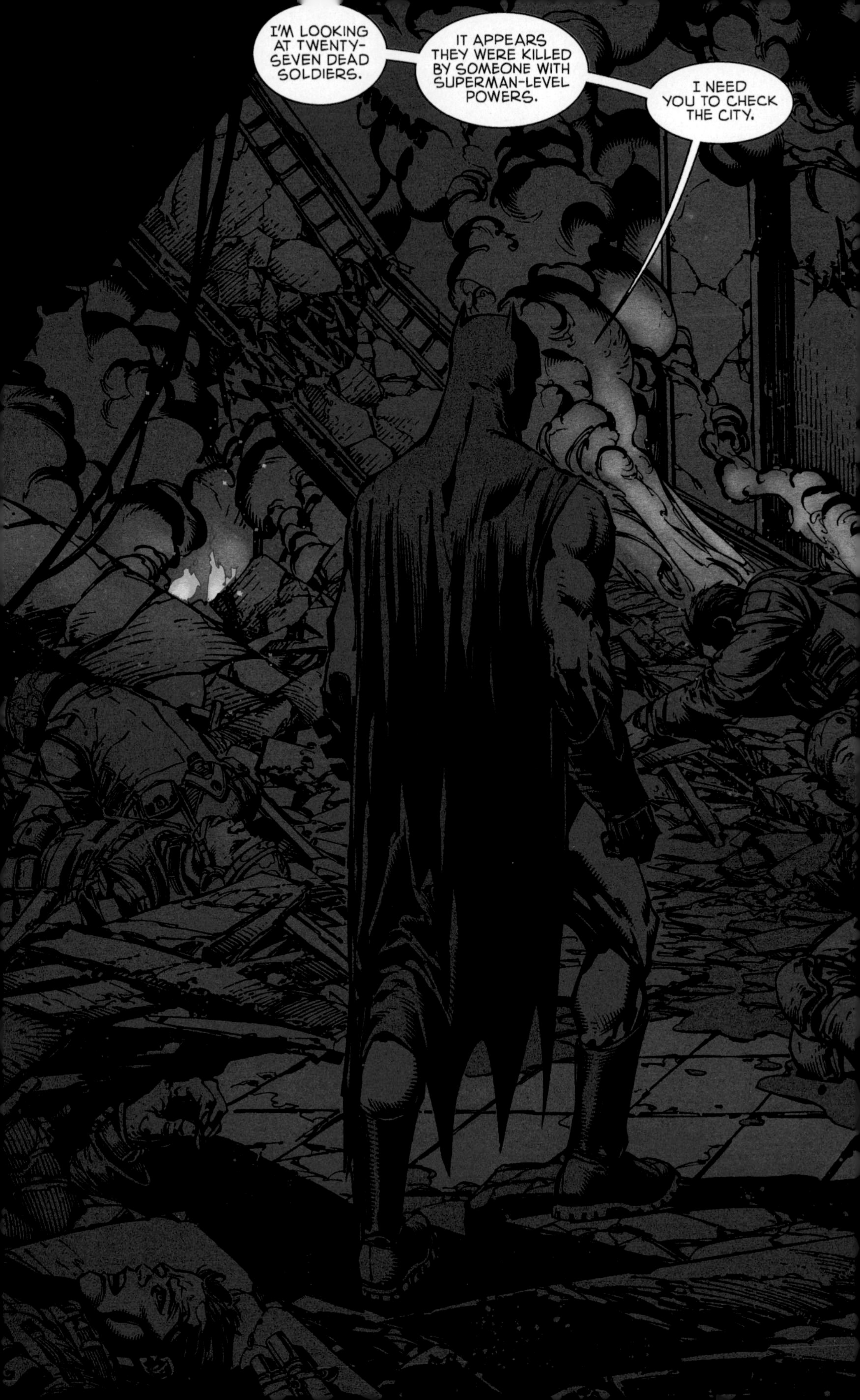
I'M LOOKING AT TWENTY-SEVEN DEAD SOLDIERS.
IT APPEARS THEY WERE KILLED BY SOMEONE WITH SUPERMAN-LEVEL POWERS.
I NEED YOU TO CHECK THE CITY.

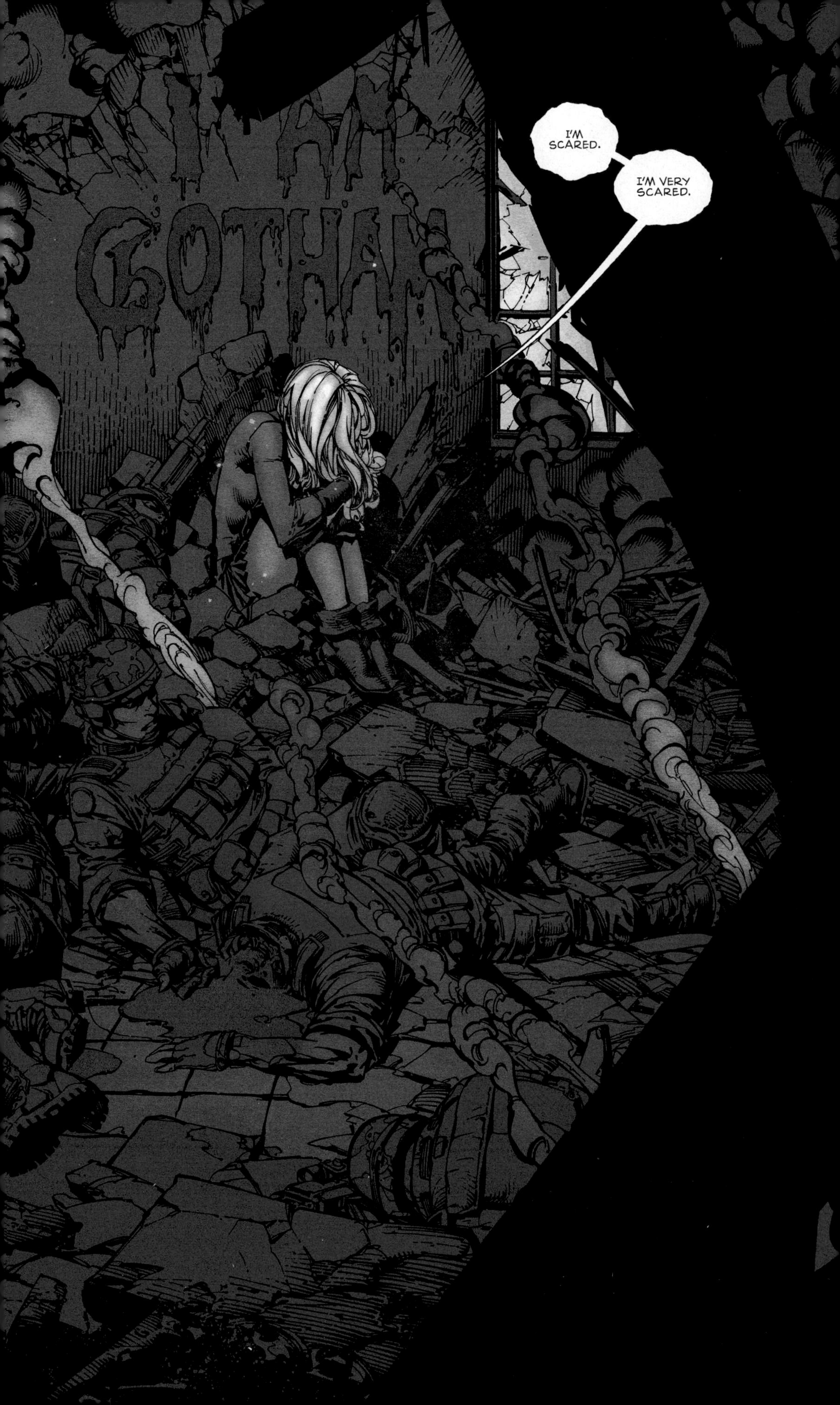

I AM GOTHAM
I'M SCARED.
I'M VERY SCARED.

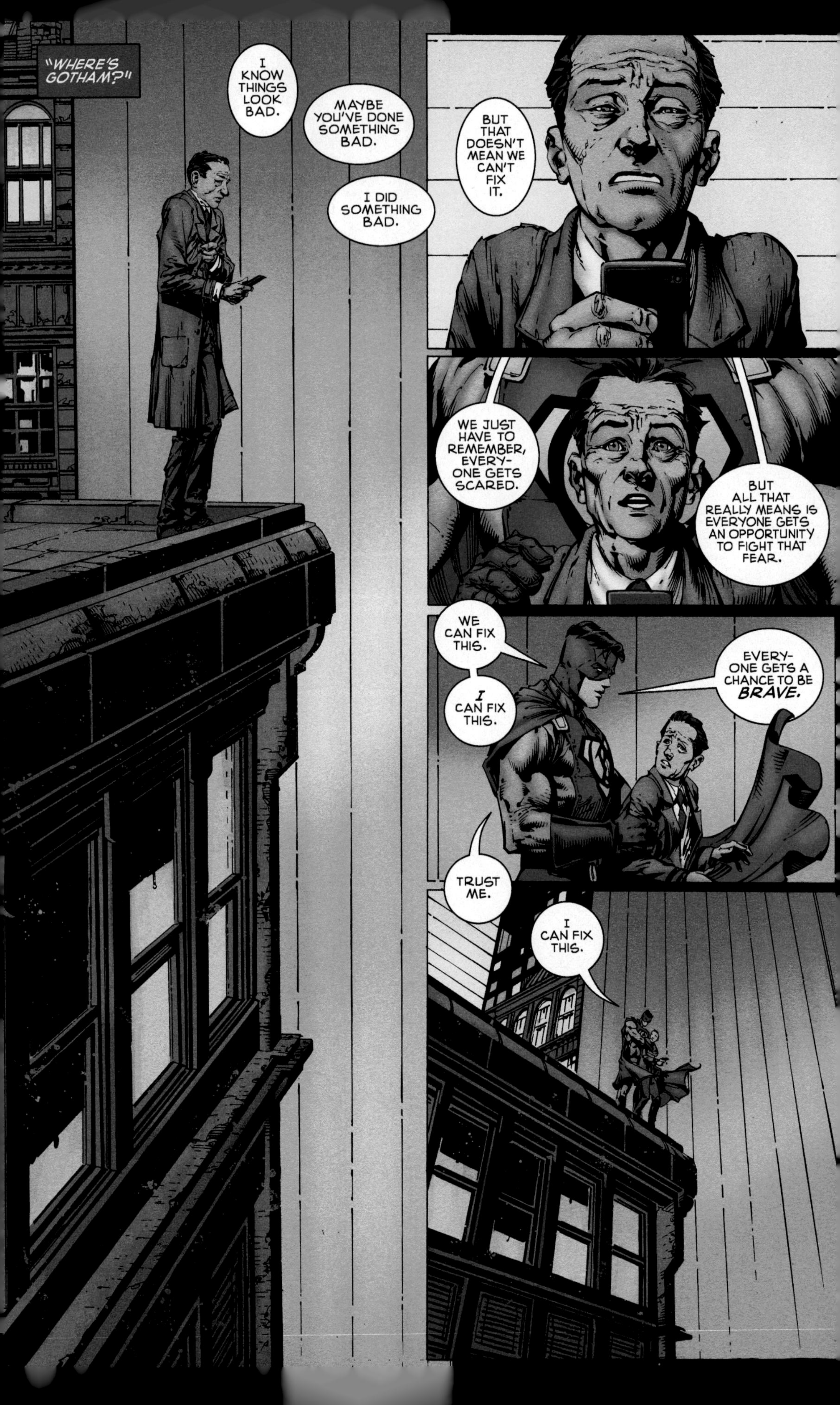
"WHERE'S GOTHAM?"
I KNOW THINGS LOOK BAD.
MAYBE YOU'VE DONE SOMETHING BAD.
I DID SOMETHING BAD.
BUT THAT DOESN'T MEAN WE CAN'T FIX IT.
WE JUST HAVE TO REMEMBER, EVERY-ONE GETS SCARED.
BUT ALL THAT REALLY MEANS IS EVERYONE GETS AN OPPORTUNITY TO FIGHT THAT FEAR.
WE CAN FIX THIS.
I CAN FIX THIS.
EVERY-ONE GETS A CHANCE TO BE BRAVE.
TRUST ME.
I CAN FIX THIS.

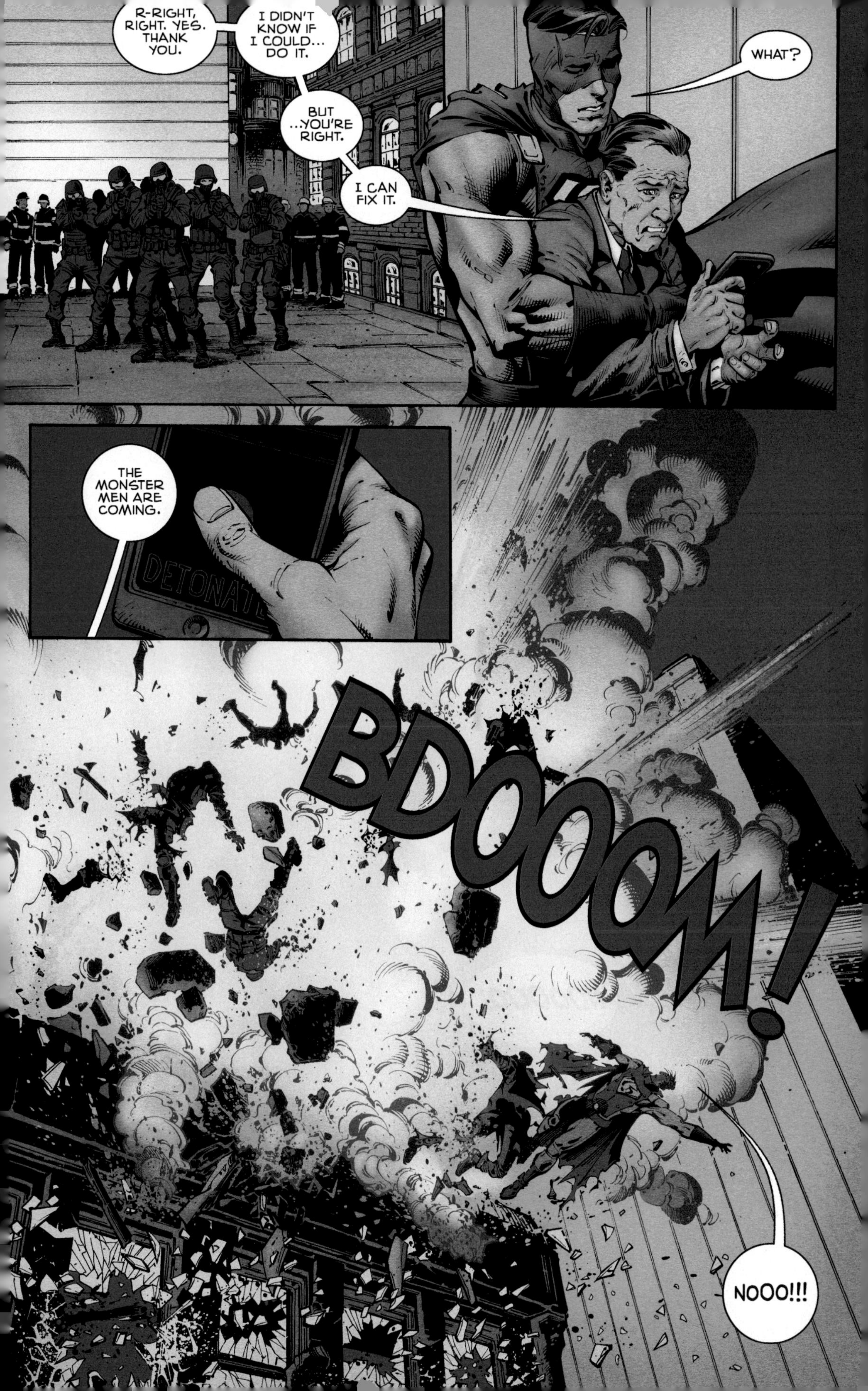
R-RIGHT, RIGHT. YES. THANK YOU.
I DIDN'T KNOW IF I COULD... DO IT.
BUT ...YOU'RE RIGHT.
I CAN FIX IT.
WHAT?
THE MONSTER MEN ARE COMING.
DETONATE
BDOOOM!
NOOO!!!

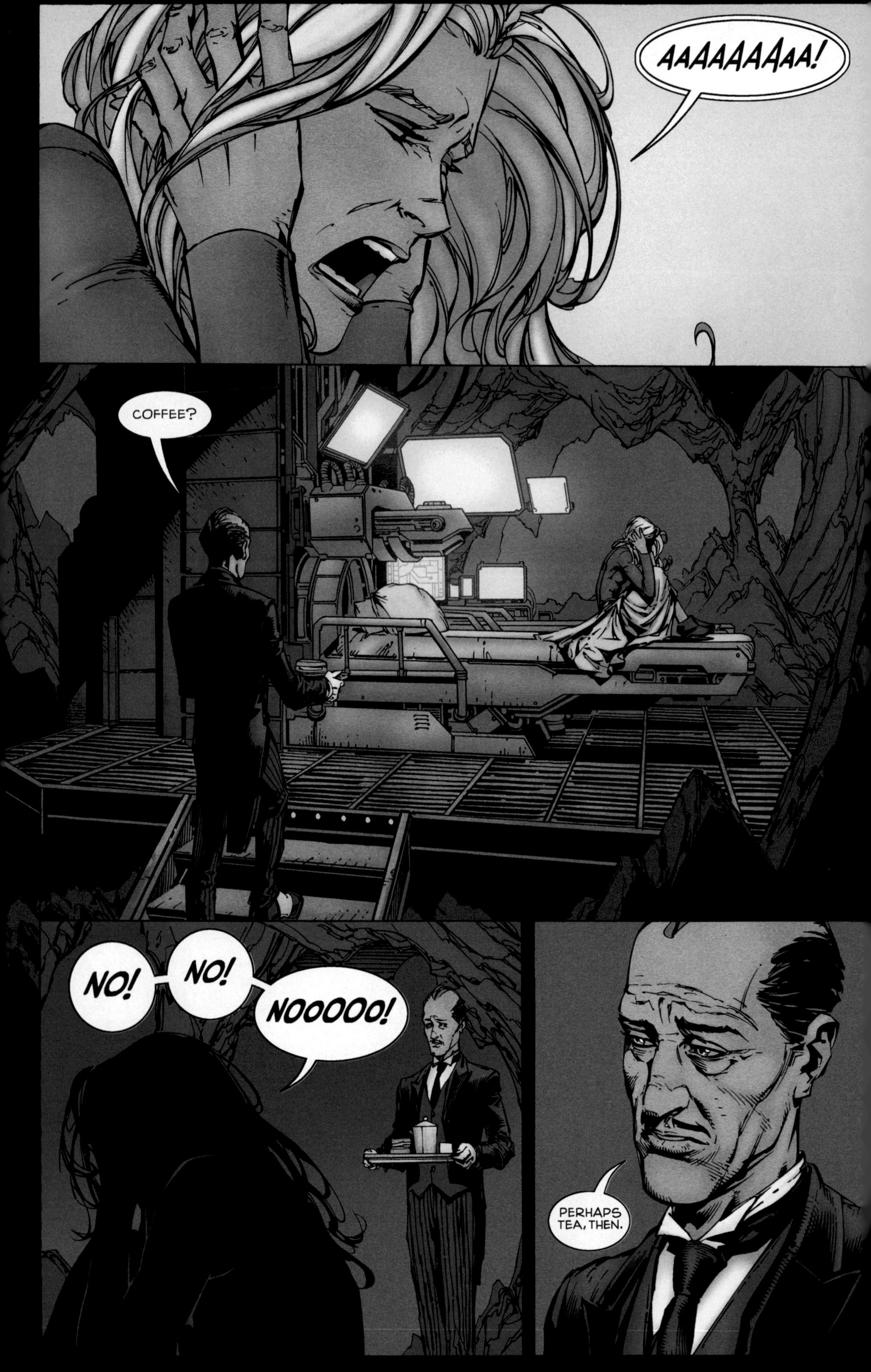
AAAAAAAAA!
COFFEE?
NO!
NO!
NOOOOO!
PERHAPS TEA, THEN.

HERE, I...*UHM*... I'VE GOT THIS.

IF IT'LL HELP.

I'M VERY SCARED.

YEAH, WELL...

I'M, LIKE, *VERY* CLOSE TO A SEMI-POSSESSED SUPER-PERSON WHO COULD RIP MY HEAD OFF.

SO, Y'KNOW, ME, TOO.

I'M SCARED.

OKAY. OKAY.

THEN MAYBE WE CAN BE SCARED TOGETHER?

MR. THOMAS.

SORRY, BATMAN... I'M...

I'M ON IT...I JUST...

MR. THOMAS, I HAVE EYES ON GOTHAM.

HAVE YOU COMPLETED YOUR ANALYSIS OF THE CRIME SCENE?

I NEED THAT ANALYSIS *NOW.*

WE GO, MASTER DUKE, WHERE WE ARE NEEDED MOST.

YEAH, YEAH.

OKAY.

JAIMIE KNOWLES 26911; CHRIS TAYLOR 174624; CONER FLANAGAN 085812; JOSH RICHARDS 990123; GIL SAIZ 743505; CHRIS HENRY 43

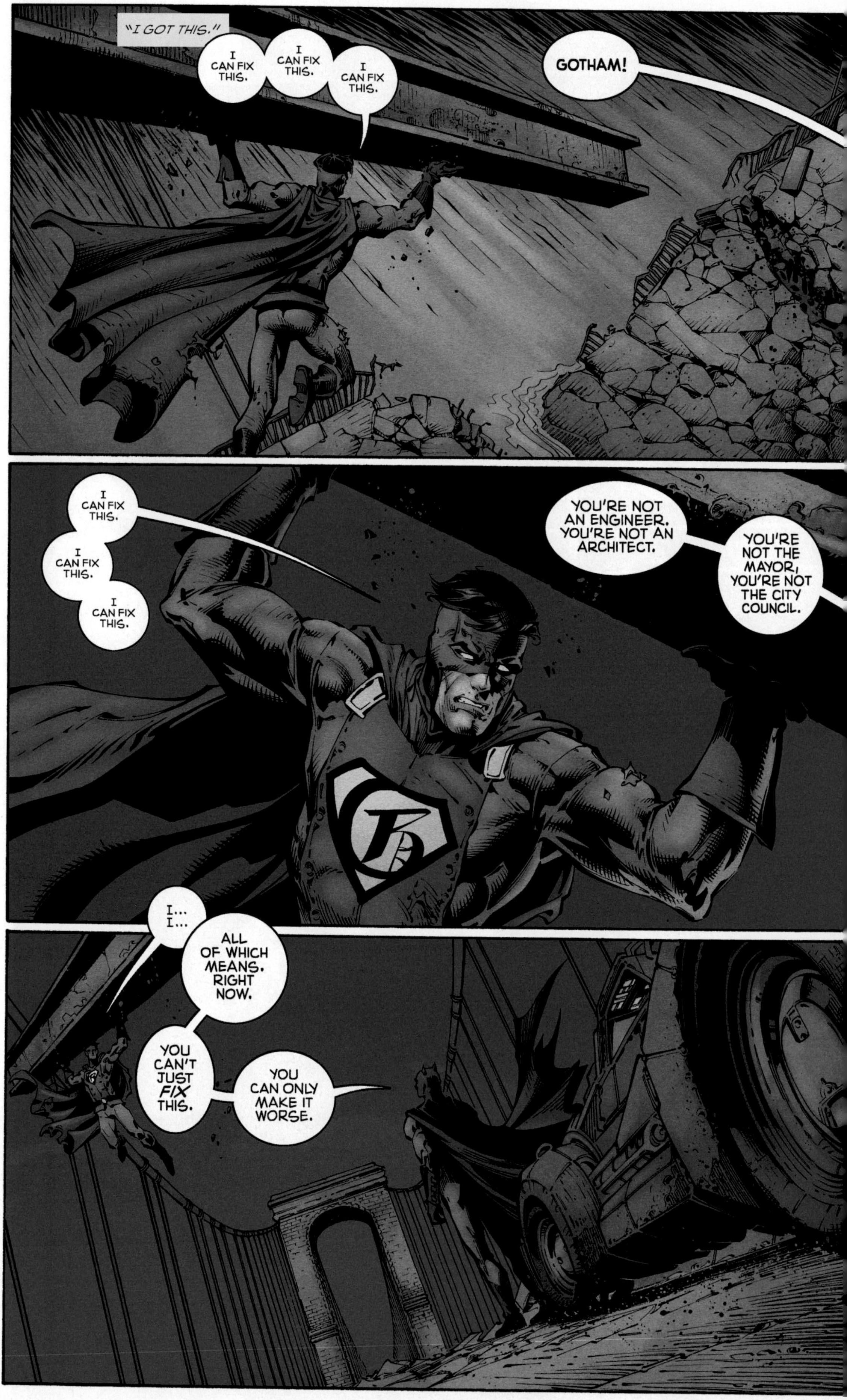
"I GOT THIS."
I CAN FIX THIS.
I CAN FIX THIS.
I CAN FIX THIS.
GOTHAM!
I CAN FIX THIS.
I CAN FIX THIS.
I CAN FIX THIS.
YOU'RE NOT AN ENGINEER. YOU'RE NOT AN ARCHITECT.
YOU'RE NOT THE MAYOR, YOU'RE NOT THE CITY COUNCIL.
I... I...
ALL OF WHICH MEANS. RIGHT NOW.
YOU CAN'T JUST *FIX* THIS.
YOU CAN ONLY MAKE IT WORSE.

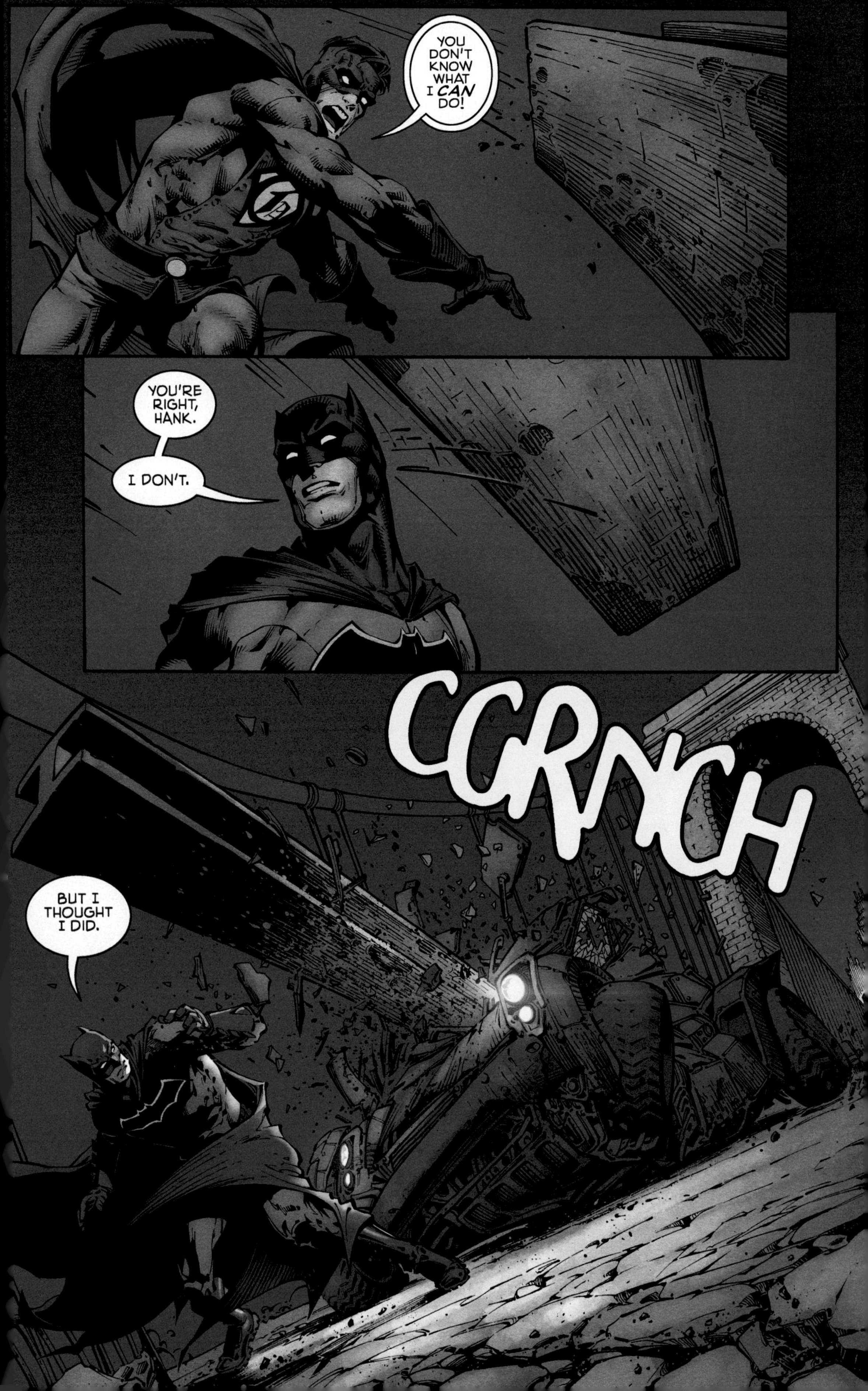

YOU DON'T KNOW WHAT I CAN DO!
YOU'RE RIGHT, HANK.
I DON'T.
CCRNCH
BUT I THOUGHT I DID.

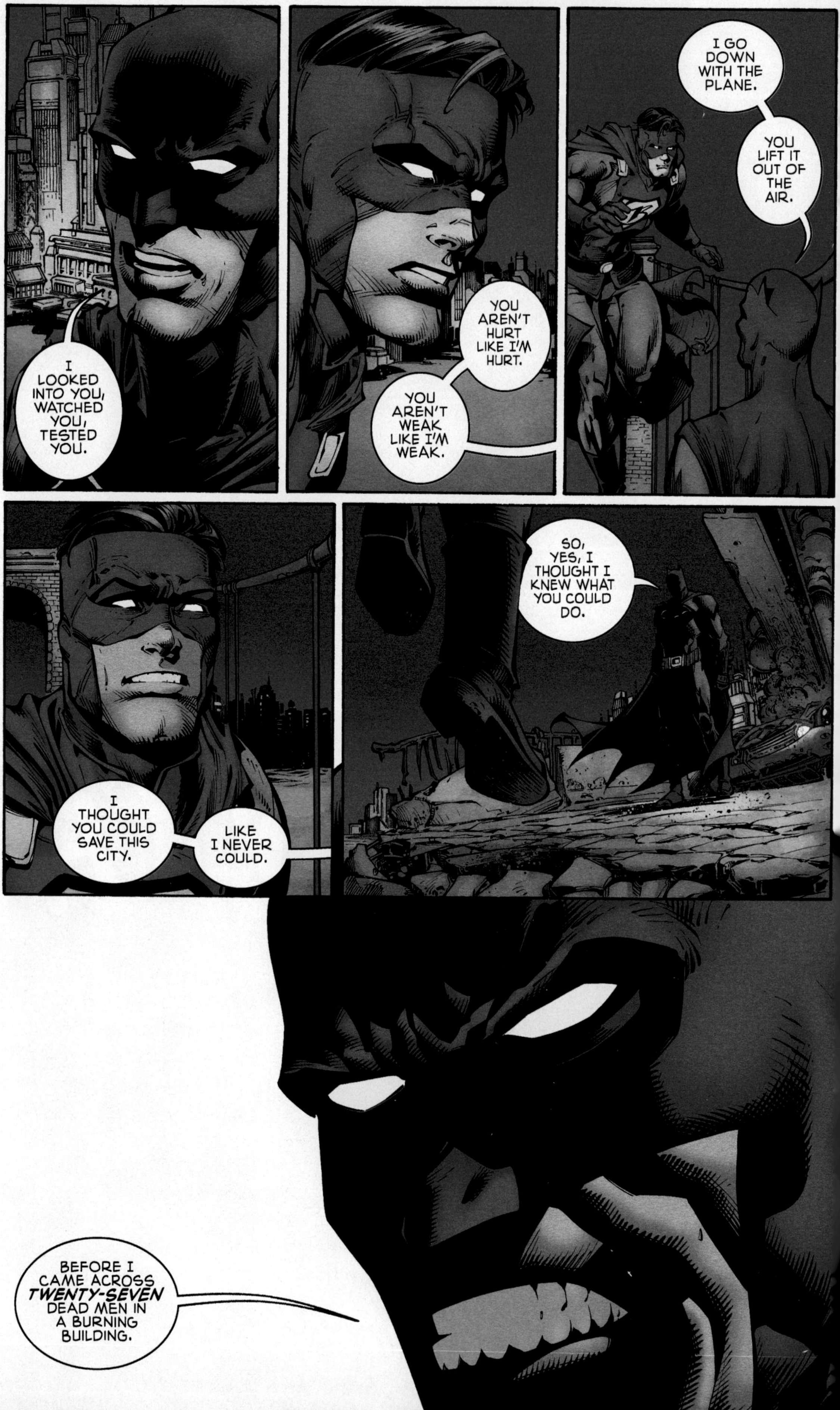
I LOOKED INTO YOU, WATCHED YOU, TESTED YOU.
YOU AREN'T HURT LIKE I'M HURT.
YOU AREN'T WEAK LIKE I'M WEAK.
I GO DOWN WITH THE PLANE.
YOU LIFT IT OUT OF THE AIR.
I THOUGHT YOU COULD SAVE THIS CITY.
LIKE I NEVER COULD.
SO, YES, I THOUGHT I KNEW WHAT YOU COULD DO.
BEFORE I CAME ACROSS *TWENTY-SEVEN* DEAD MEN IN A BURNING BUILDING.

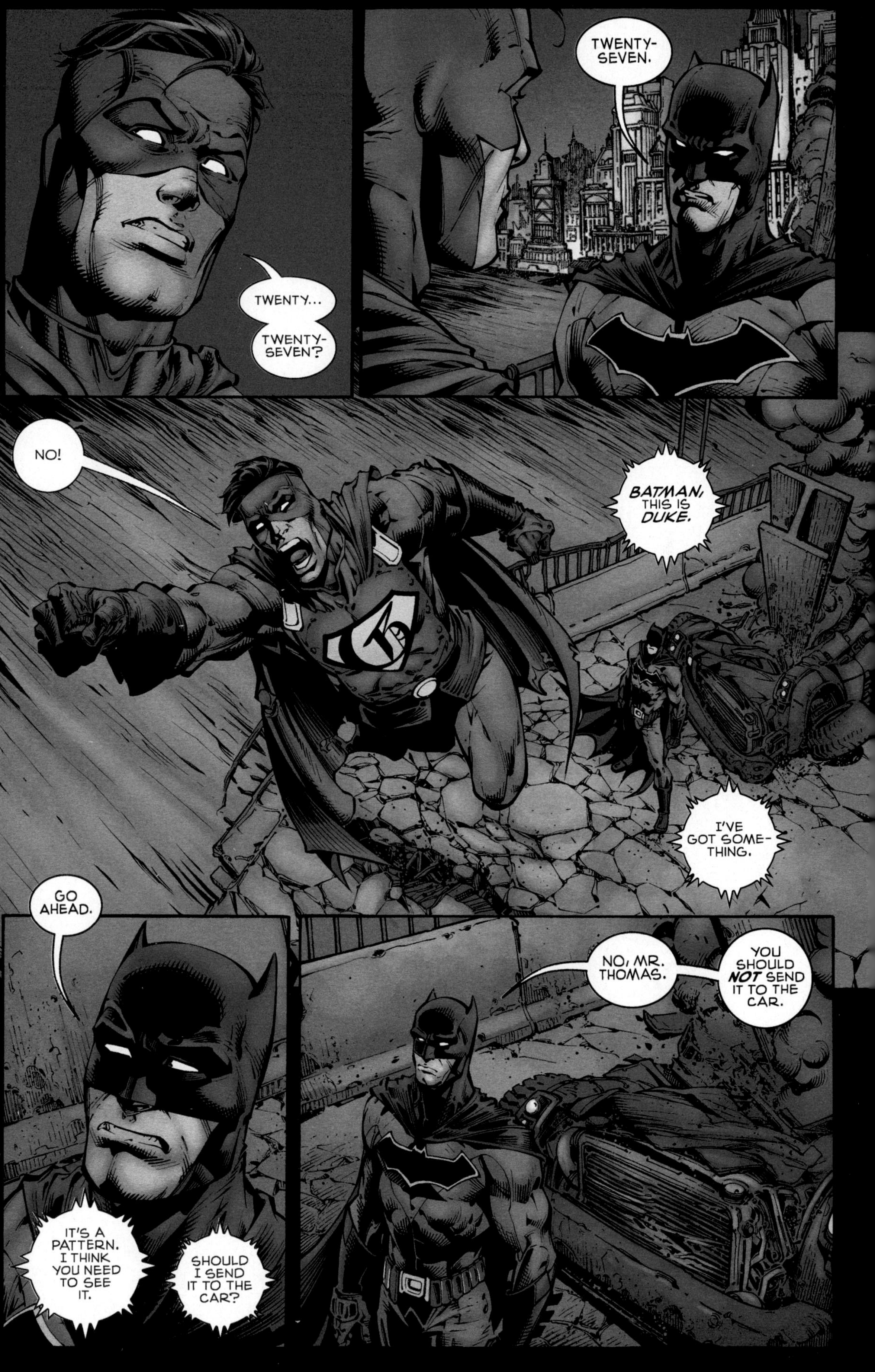
TWENTY...
TWENTY-SEVEN?
TWENTY-SEVEN.
NO!
BATMAN, THIS IS DUKE.
I'VE GOT SOME-THING.
GO AHEAD.
IT'S A PATTERN. I THINK YOU NEED TO SEE IT.
SHOULD I SEND IT TO THE CAR?
NO, MR. THOMAS.
YOU SHOULD NOT SEND IT TO THE CAR.

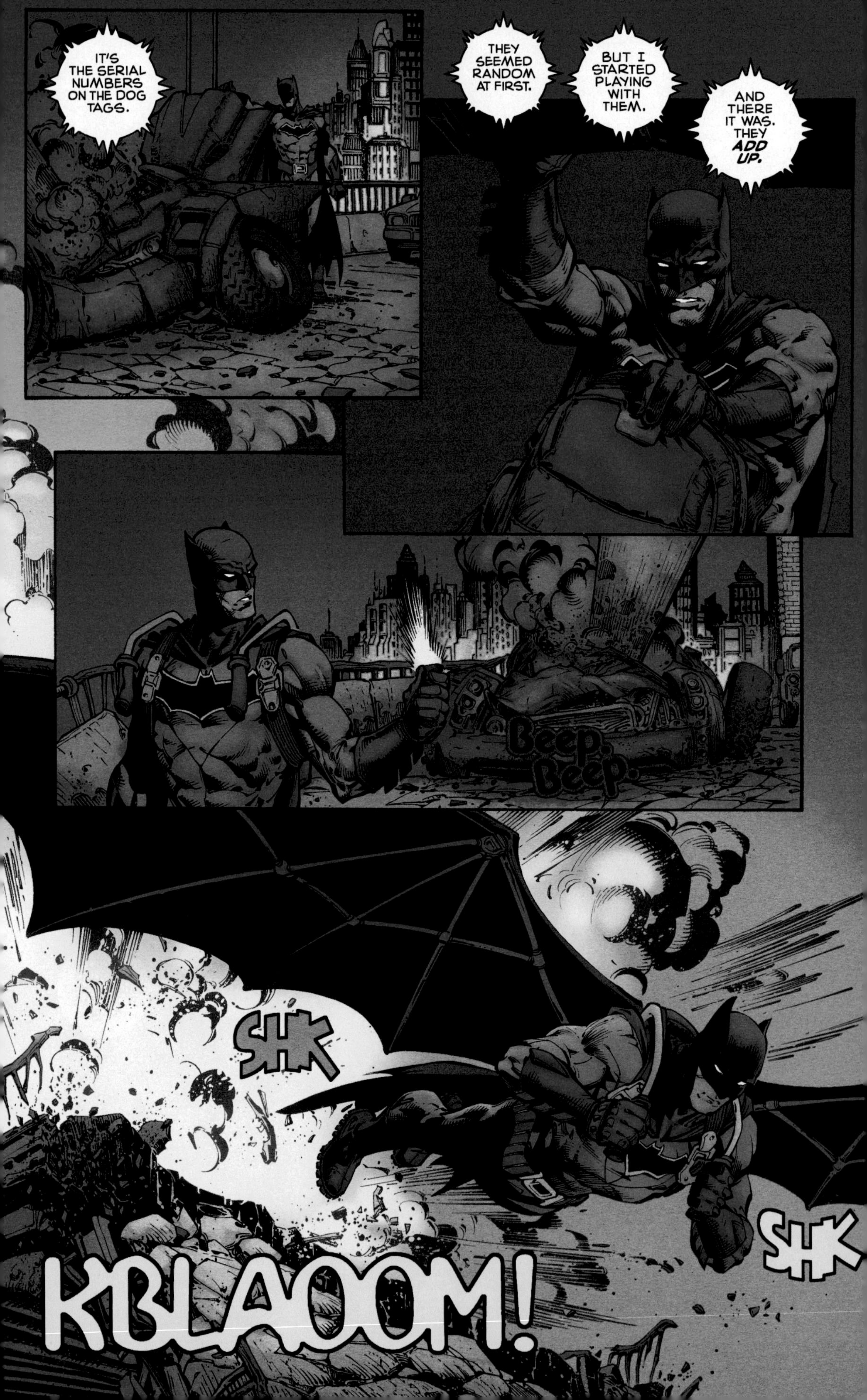
IT'S THE SERIAL NUMBERS ON THE DOG TAGS.
THEY SEEMED RANDOM AT FIRST.
BUT I STARTED PLAYING WITH THEM.
AND THERE IT WAS. THEY *ADD UP.*
Beep. Beep.
SHK
SHK
KBLAOOM!

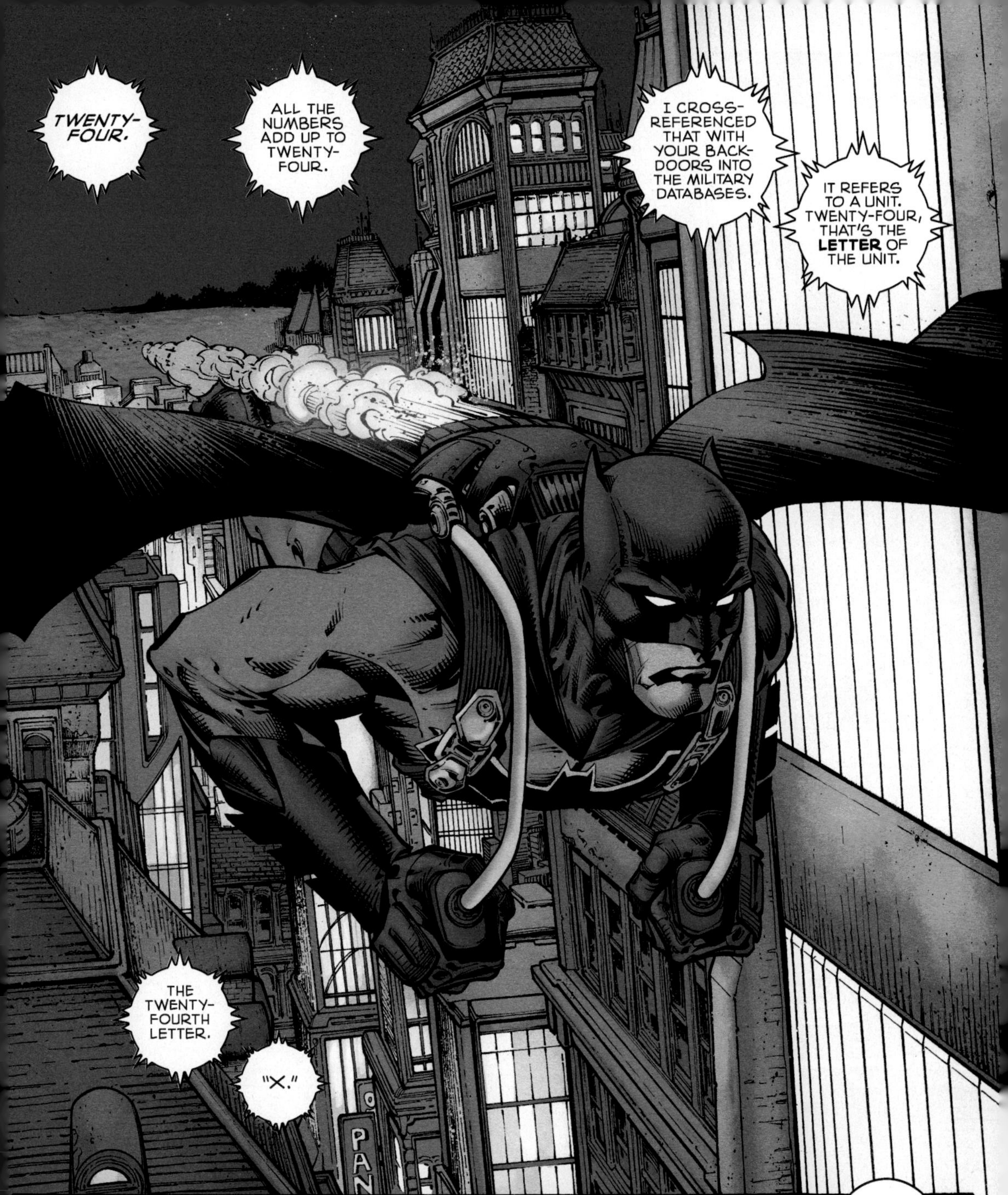

TWENTY-FOUR.
ALL THE NUMBERS ADD UP TO TWENTY-FOUR.
I CROSS-REFERENCED THAT WITH YOUR BACK-DOORS INTO THE MILITARY DATABASES.
IT REFERS TO A UNIT. TWENTY-FOUR, THAT'S THE **LETTER** OF THE UNIT.
THE TWENTY-FOURTH LETTER.
"X."

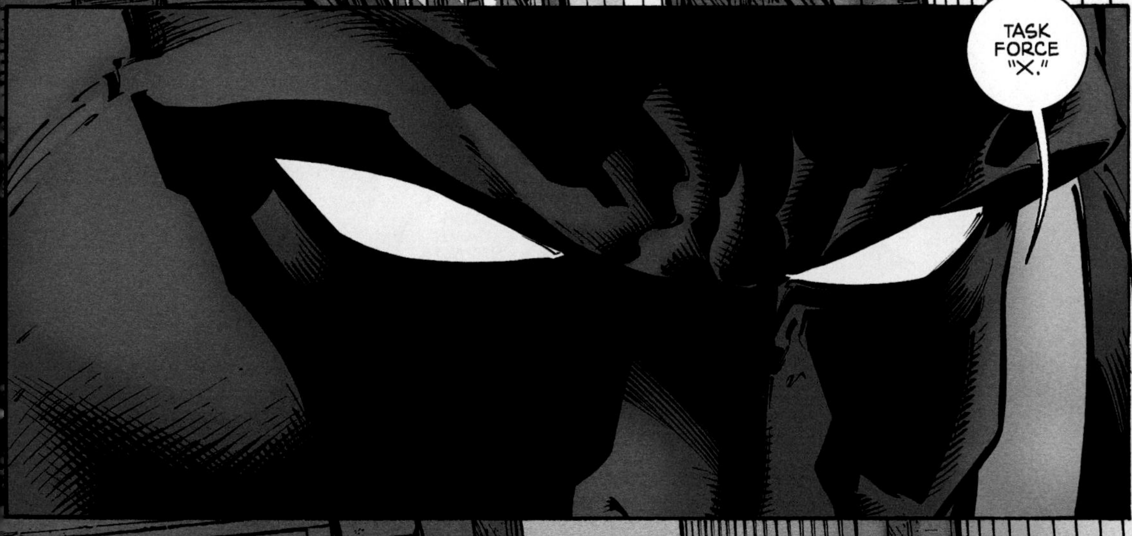

TASK FORCE "X."

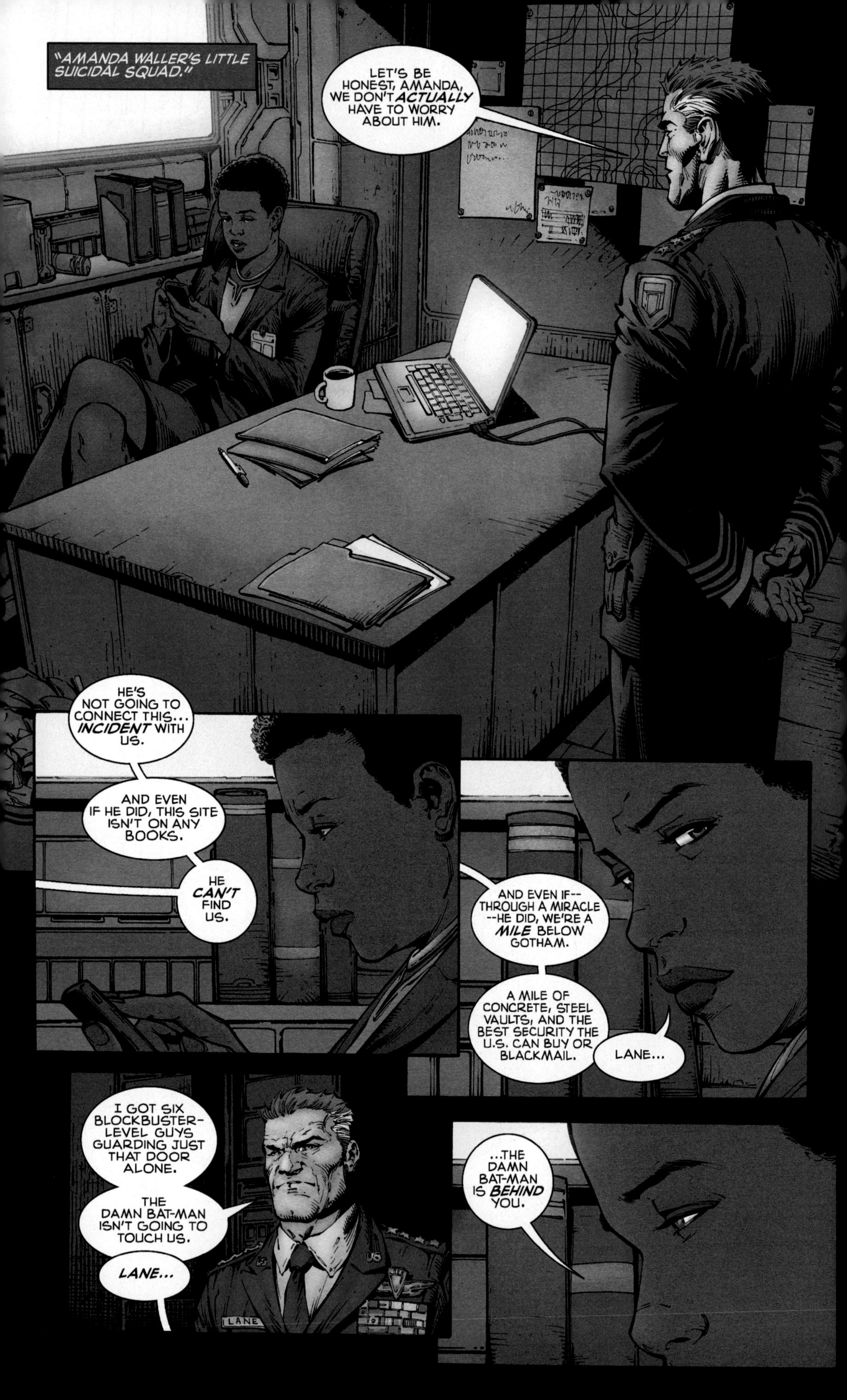
"AMANDA WALLER'S LITTLE SUICIDAL SQUAD."
LET'S BE HONEST, AMANDA, WE DON'T ACTUALLY HAVE TO WORRY ABOUT HIM.
HE'S NOT GOING TO CONNECT THIS... INCIDENT WITH US.
AND EVEN IF HE DID, THIS SITE ISN'T ON ANY BOOKS.
HE CAN'T FIND US.
AND EVEN IF-- THROUGH A MIRACLE --HE DID, WE'RE A MILE BELOW GOTHAM.
A MILE OF CONCRETE, STEEL VAULTS, AND THE BEST SECURITY THE U.S. CAN BUY OR BLACKMAIL.
LANE...
I GOT SIX BLOCKBUSTER-LEVEL GUYS GUARDING JUST THAT DOOR ALONE.
THE DAMN BAT-MAN ISN'T GOING TO TOUCH US.
LANE...
...THE DAMN BAT-MAN IS BEHIND YOU.
LANE

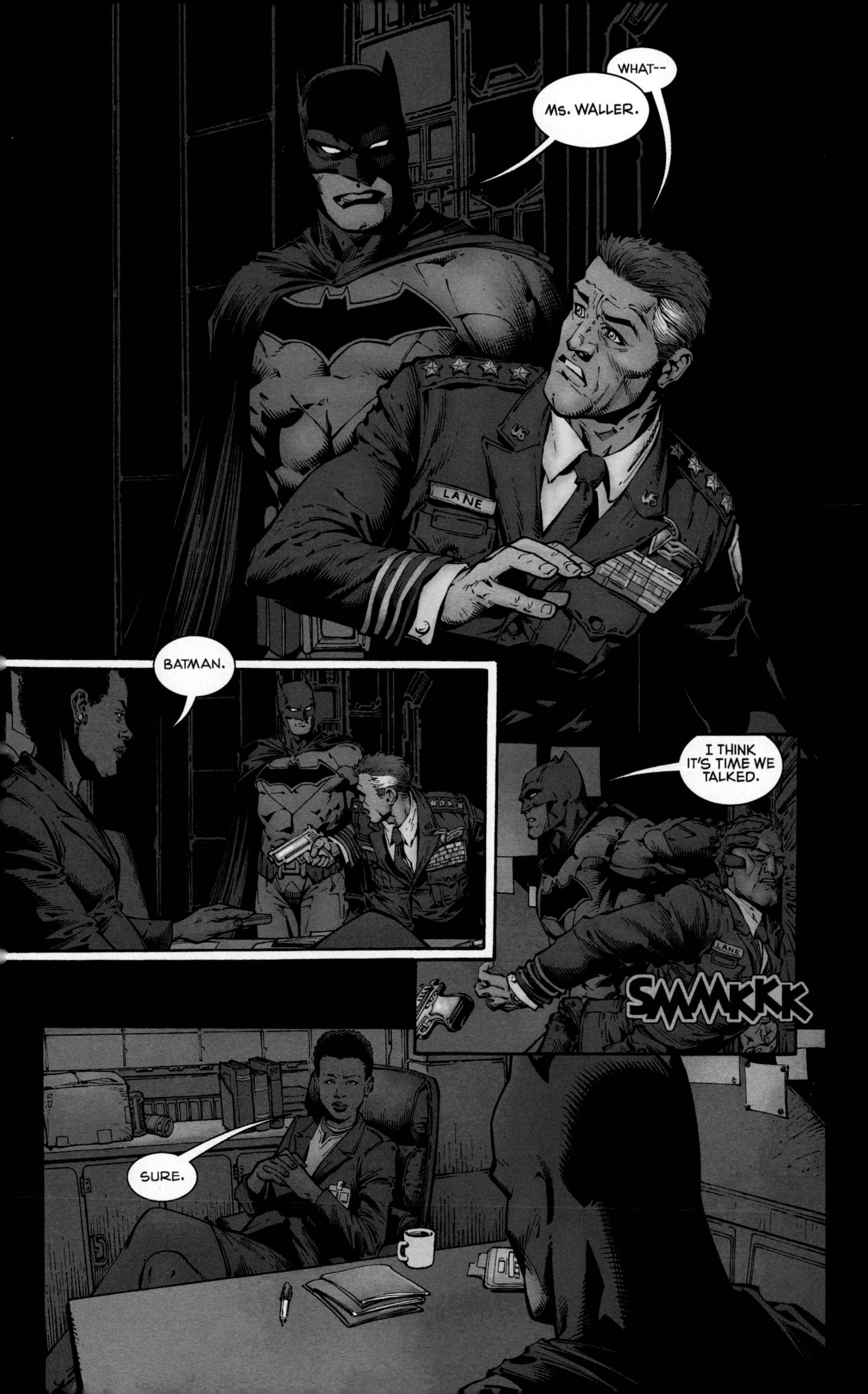
WHAT--
MS. WALLER.
BATMAN.
I THINK IT'S TIME WE TALKED.
SMMKKK
SURE.

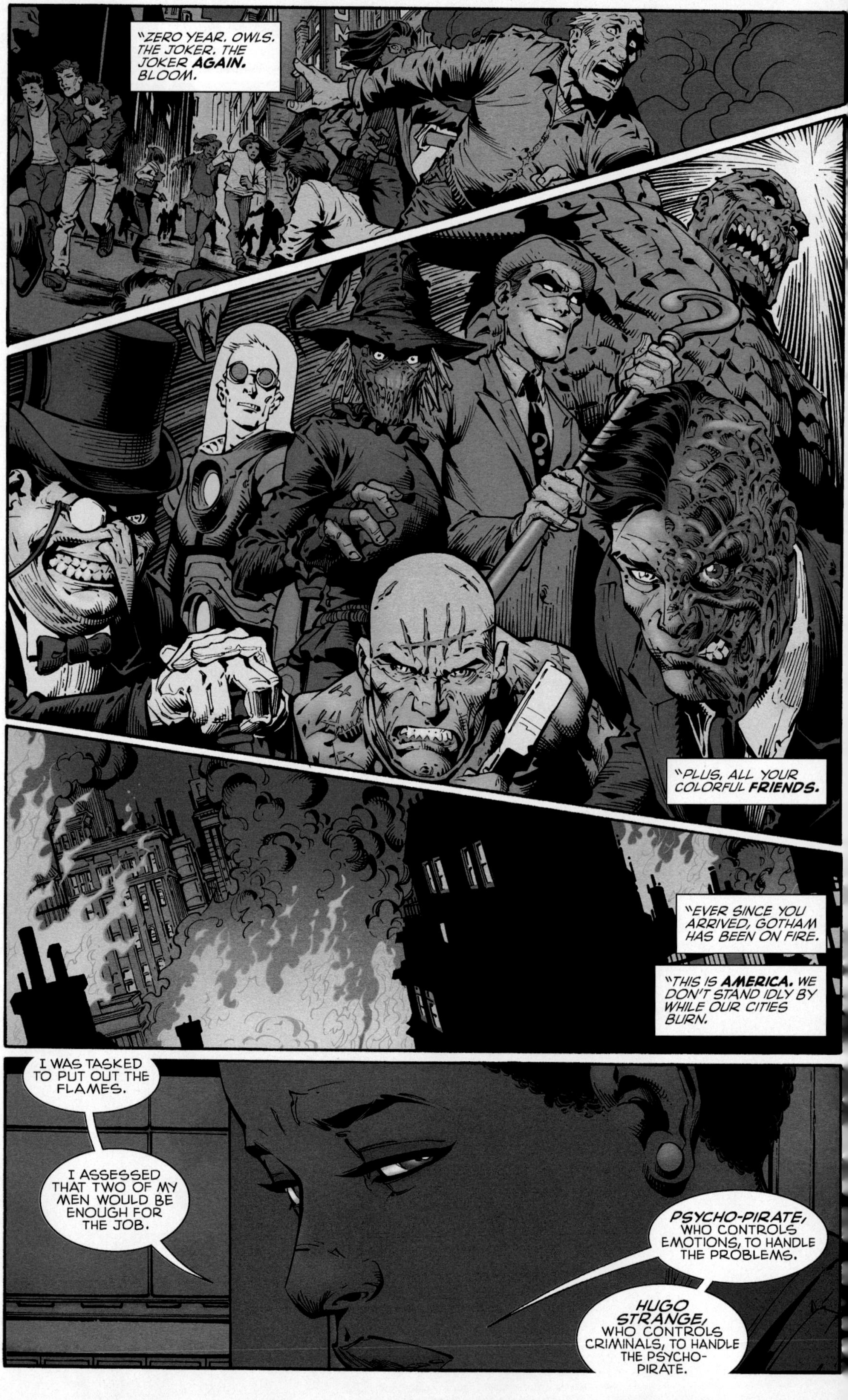
"ZERO YEAR. OWLS. THE JOKER. THE JOKER **AGAIN.** BLOOM.
"PLUS, ALL YOUR COLORFUL **FRIENDS.**
"EVER SINCE YOU ARRIVED, GOTHAM HAS BEEN ON FIRE.
"THIS IS **AMERICA.** WE DON'T STAND IDLY BY WHILE OUR CITIES BURN.
I WAS TASKED TO PUT OUT THE FLAMES.
I ASSESSED THAT TWO OF MY MEN WOULD BE ENOUGH FOR THE JOB.
PSYCHO-PIRATE, WHO CONTROLS EMOTIONS, TO HANDLE THE PROBLEMS.
HUGO STRANGE, WHO CONTROLS CRIMINALS, TO HANDLE THE PSYCHO-PIRATE.

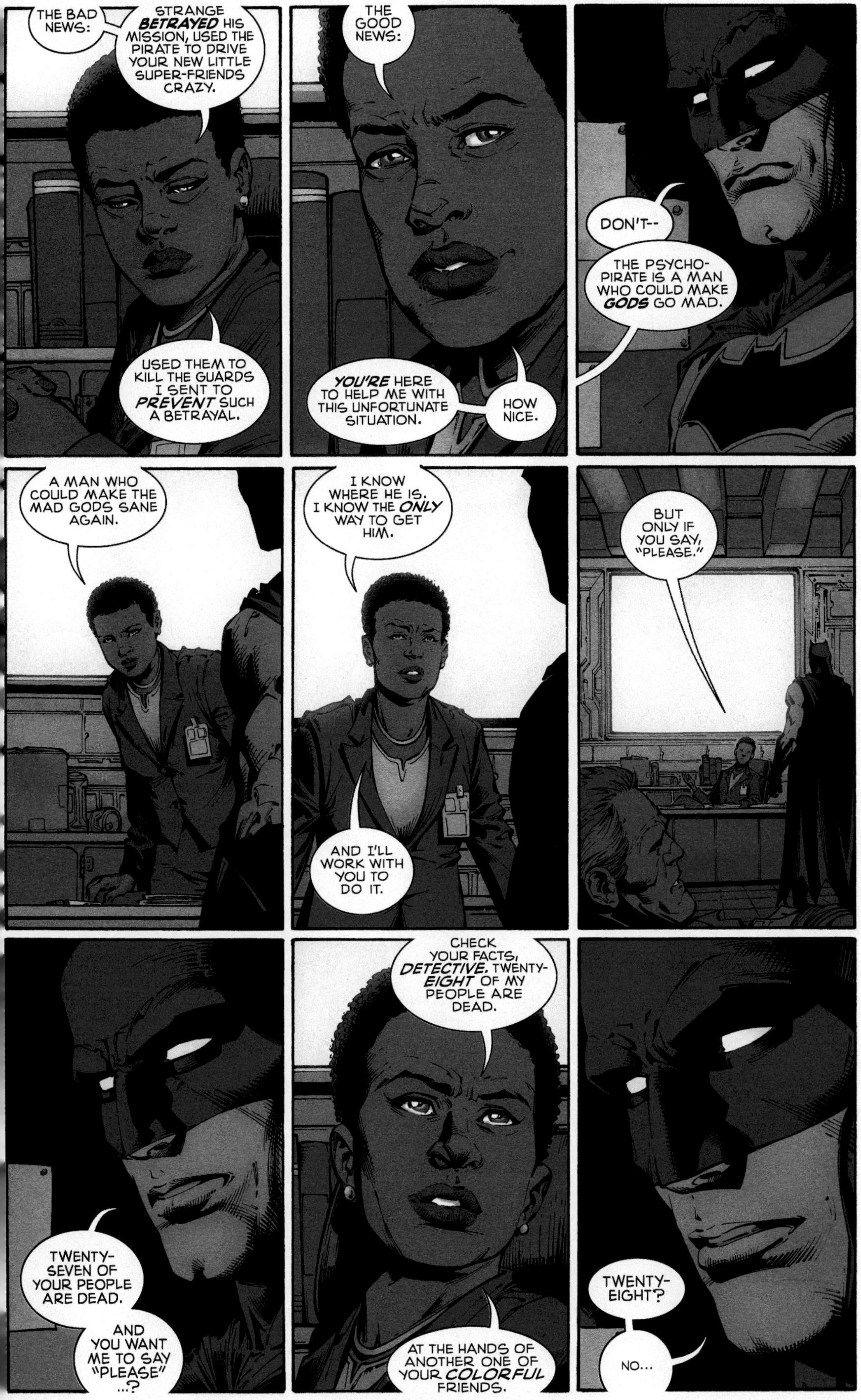
THE BAD NEWS:
STRANGE BETRAYED HIS MISSION, USED THE PIRATE TO DRIVE YOUR NEW LITTLE SUPER-FRIENDS CRAZY.
USED THEM TO KILL THE GUARDS I SENT TO PREVENT SUCH A BETRAYAL.
THE GOOD NEWS:
YOU'RE HERE TO HELP ME WITH THIS UNFORTUNATE SITUATION.
HOW NICE.
DON'T--
THE PSYCHO-PIRATE IS A MAN WHO COULD MAKE GODS GO MAD.
A MAN WHO COULD MAKE THE MAD GODS SANE AGAIN.
I KNOW WHERE HE IS. I KNOW THE ONLY WAY TO GET HIM.
AND I'LL WORK WITH YOU TO DO IT.
BUT ONLY IF YOU SAY, "PLEASE."
TWENTY-SEVEN OF YOUR PEOPLE ARE DEAD.
AND YOU WANT ME TO SAY "PLEASE" ...?
CHECK YOUR FACTS, DETECTIVE. TWENTY-EIGHT OF MY PEOPLE ARE DEAD.
AT THE HANDS OF ANOTHER ONE OF YOUR COLORFUL FRIENDS.
TWENTY-EIGHT?
NO...

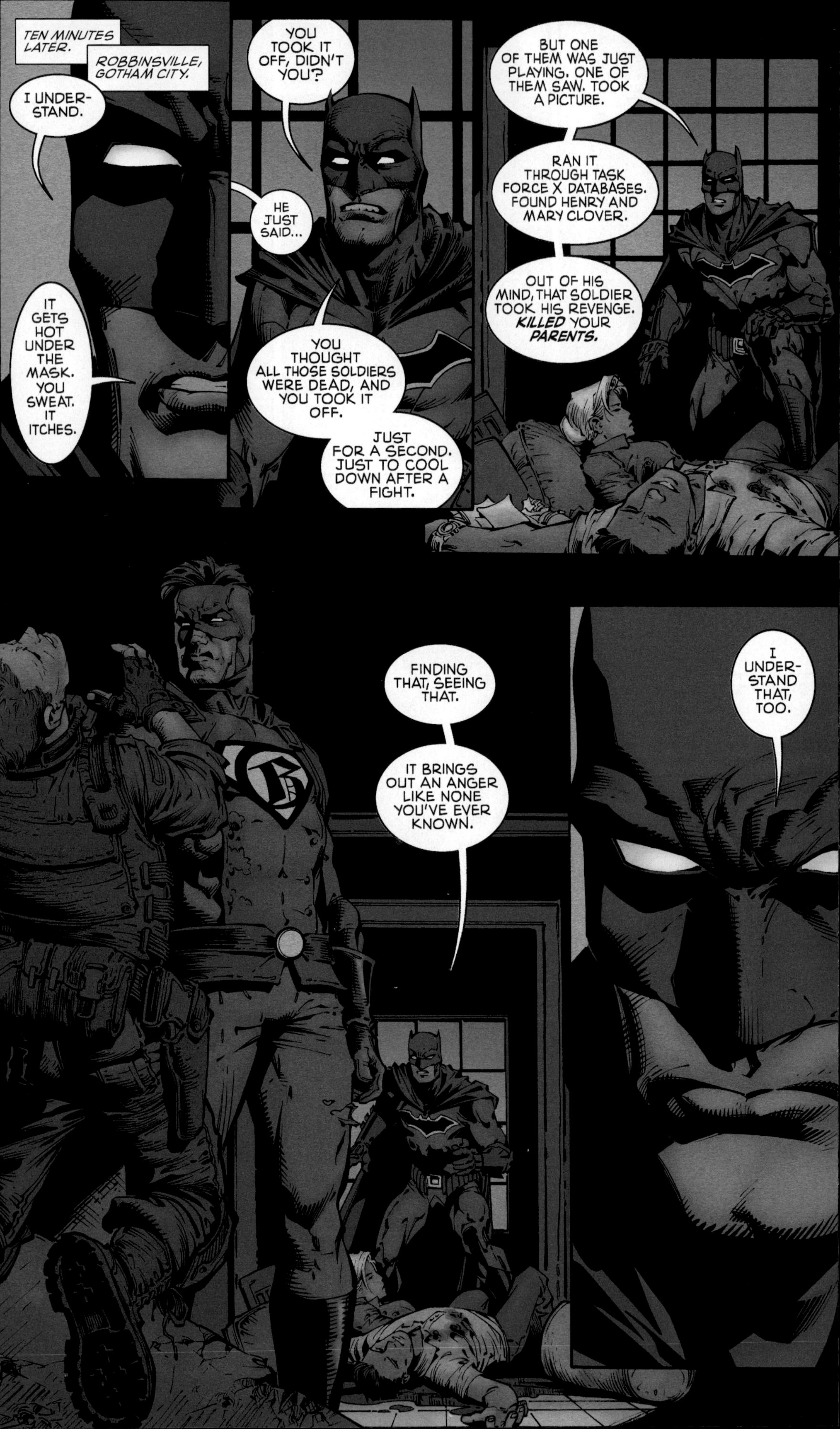
TEN MINUTES LATER.
ROBBINSVILLE, GOTHAM CITY.
I UNDERSTAND.
IT GETS HOT UNDER THE MASK. YOU SWEAT. IT ITCHES.
YOU TOOK IT OFF, DIDN'T YOU?
HE JUST SAID...
YOU THOUGHT ALL THOSE SOLDIERS WERE DEAD, AND YOU TOOK IT OFF.
JUST FOR A SECOND. JUST TO COOL DOWN AFTER A FIGHT.
BUT ONE OF THEM WAS JUST PLAYING. ONE OF THEM SAW. TOOK A PICTURE.
RAN IT THROUGH TASK FORCE X DATABASES. FOUND HENRY AND MARY CLOVER.
OUT OF HIS MIND, THAT SOLDIER TOOK HIS REVENGE. *KILLED* YOUR *PARENTS.*
FINDING THAT, SEEING THAT.
IT BRINGS OUT AN ANGER LIKE NONE YOU'VE EVER KNOWN.
I UNDERSTAND THAT, TOO.

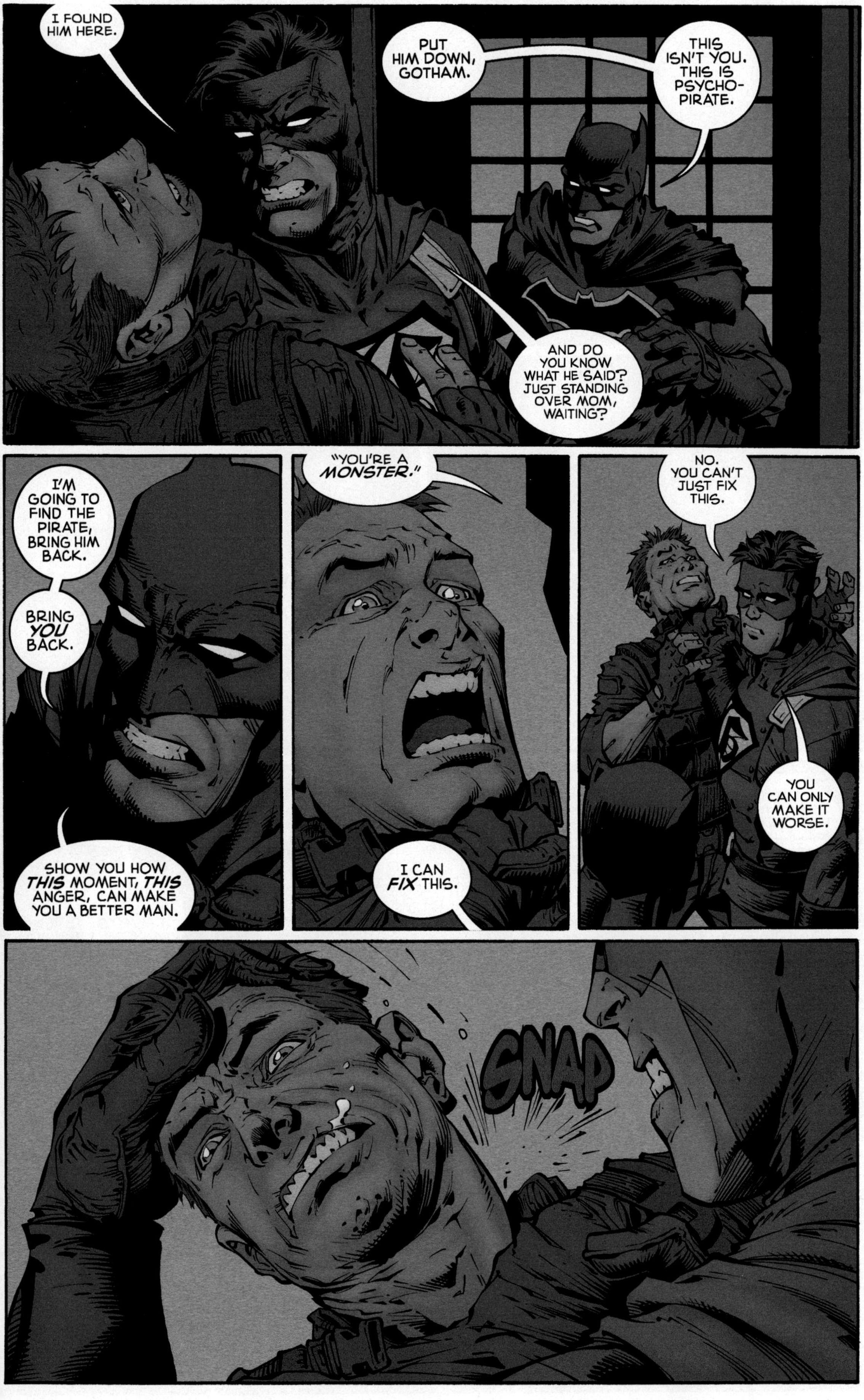
I FOUND HIM HERE.
PUT HIM DOWN, GOTHAM.
THIS ISN'T YOU. THIS IS PSYCHO-PIRATE.
AND DO YOU KNOW WHAT HE SAID? JUST STANDING OVER MOM, WAITING?
"YOU'RE A MONSTER."
I'M GOING TO FIND THE PIRATE, BRING HIM BACK.
BRING YOU BACK.
SHOW YOU HOW THIS MOMENT, THIS ANGER, CAN MAKE YOU A BETTER MAN.
I CAN FIX THIS.
NO. YOU CAN'T JUST FIX THIS.
YOU CAN ONLY MAKE IT WORSE.
SNAP

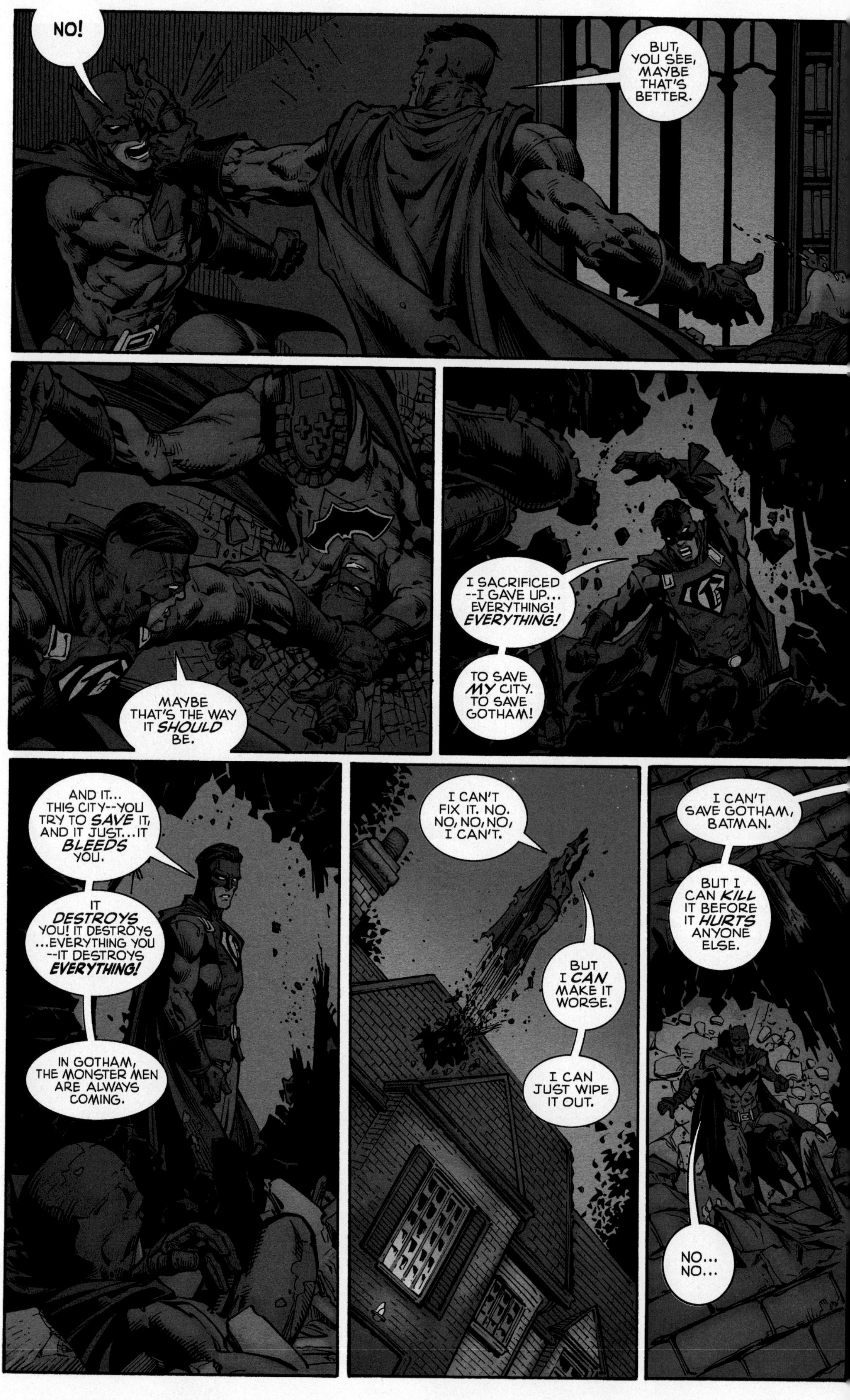
NO!
BUT, YOU SEE, MAYBE THAT'S BETTER.
MAYBE THAT'S THE WAY IT SHOULD BE.
I SACRIFICED --I GAVE UP... EVERYTHING! EVERYTHING!
TO SAVE MY CITY. TO SAVE GOTHAM!
AND IT... THIS CITY--YOU TRY TO SAVE IT, AND IT JUST...IT BLEEDS YOU.
IT DESTROYS YOU! IT DESTROYS ...EVERYTHING YOU --IT DESTROYS EVERYTHING!
IN GOTHAM, THE MONSTER MEN ARE ALWAYS COMING.
I CAN'T FIX IT. NO. NO, NO, NO, I CAN'T.
BUT I CAN MAKE IT WORSE.
I CAN JUST WIPE IT OUT.
I CAN'T SAVE GOTHAM, BATMAN.
BUT I CAN KILL IT BEFORE IT HURTS ANYONE ELSE.
NO... NO...

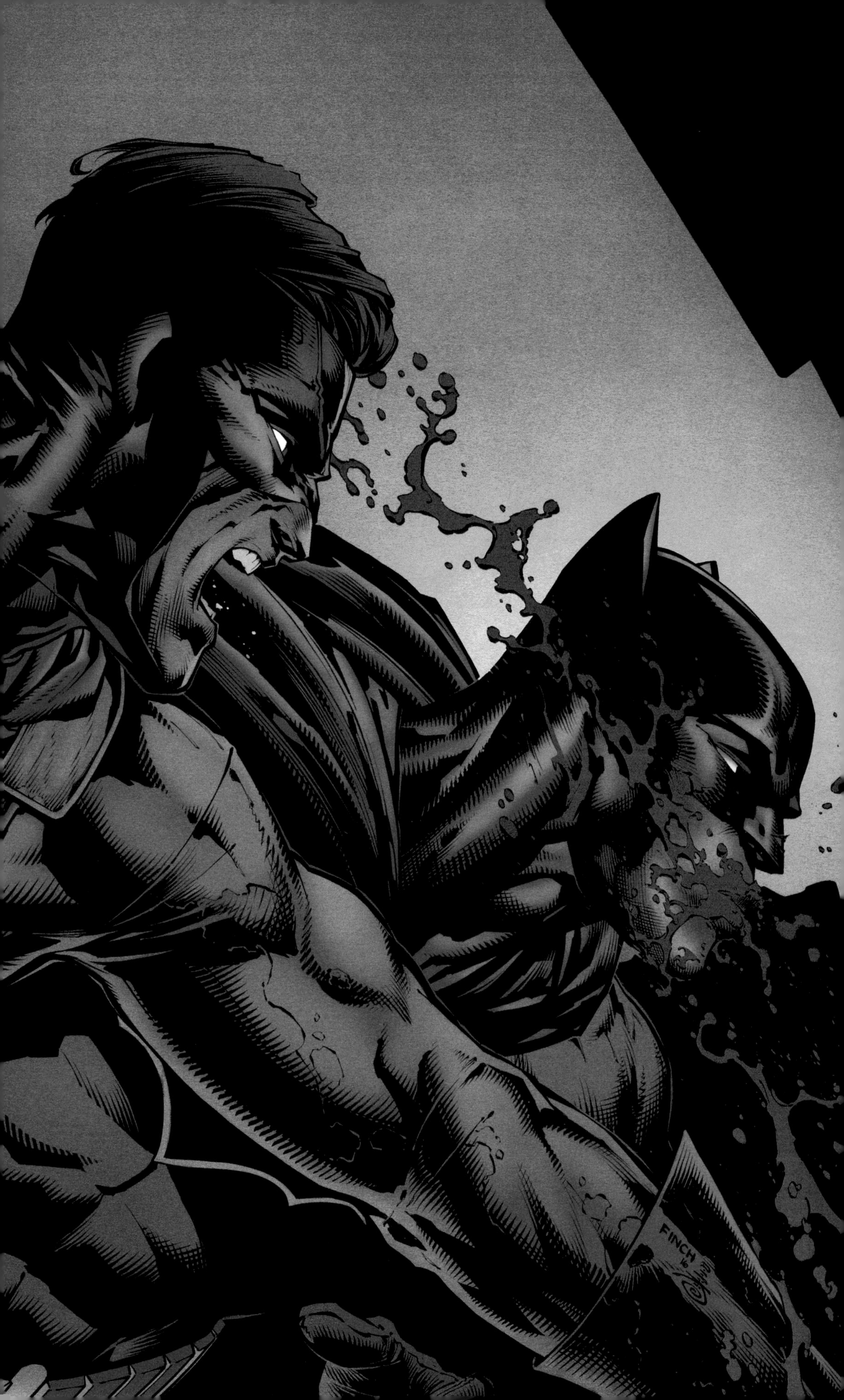

I AM GOTHAM part five

TOM KING writer * DAVID FINCH penciller * DAVID FINCH, SANDRA HOPE, MATT BANNING and SCOTT HANNA inkers
JORDIE BELLAIRE colorist * JOHN WORKMAN letterer * DAVID FINCH, DANNY MIKI and JORDIE BELLAIRE cover artists

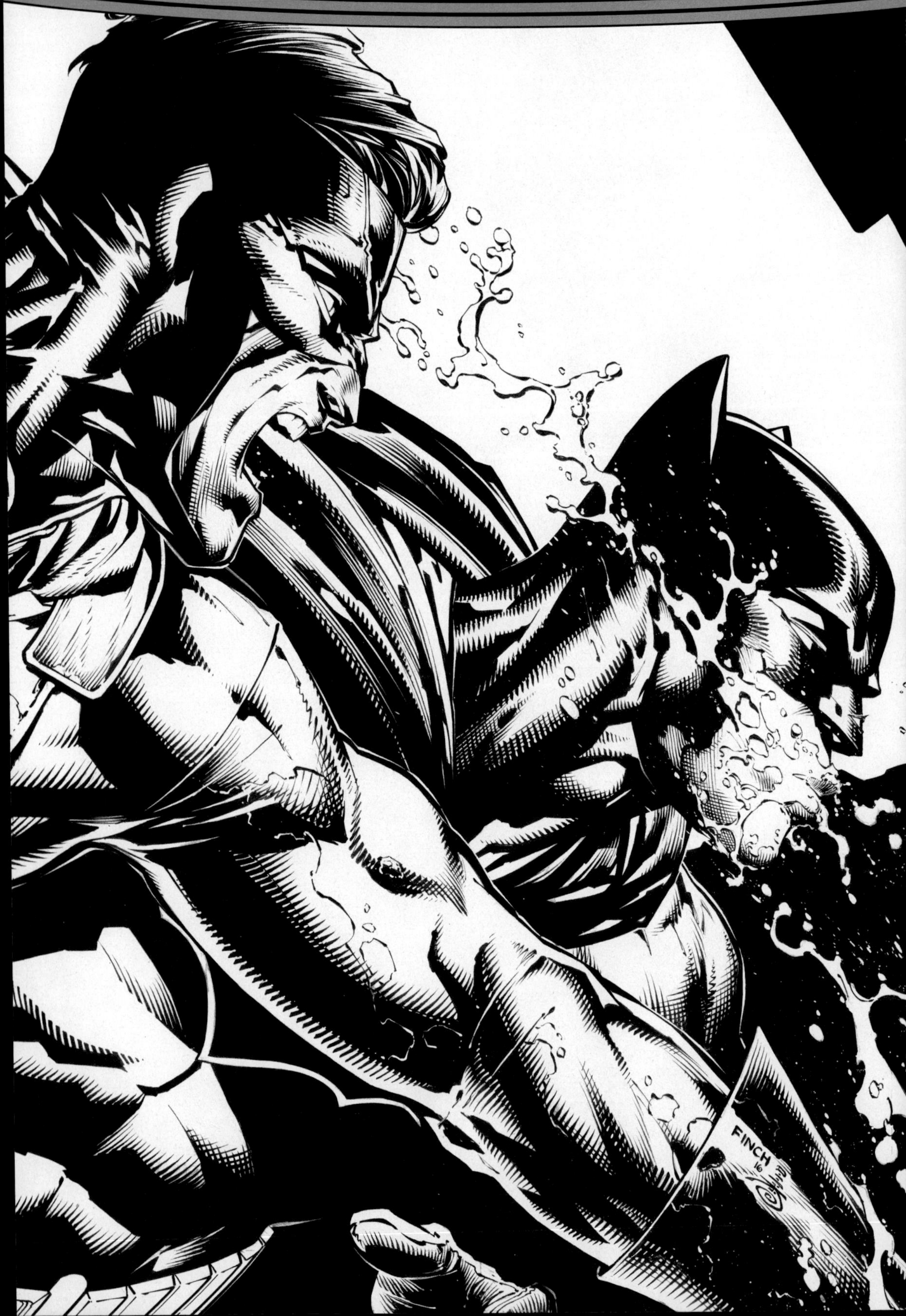
FINCH

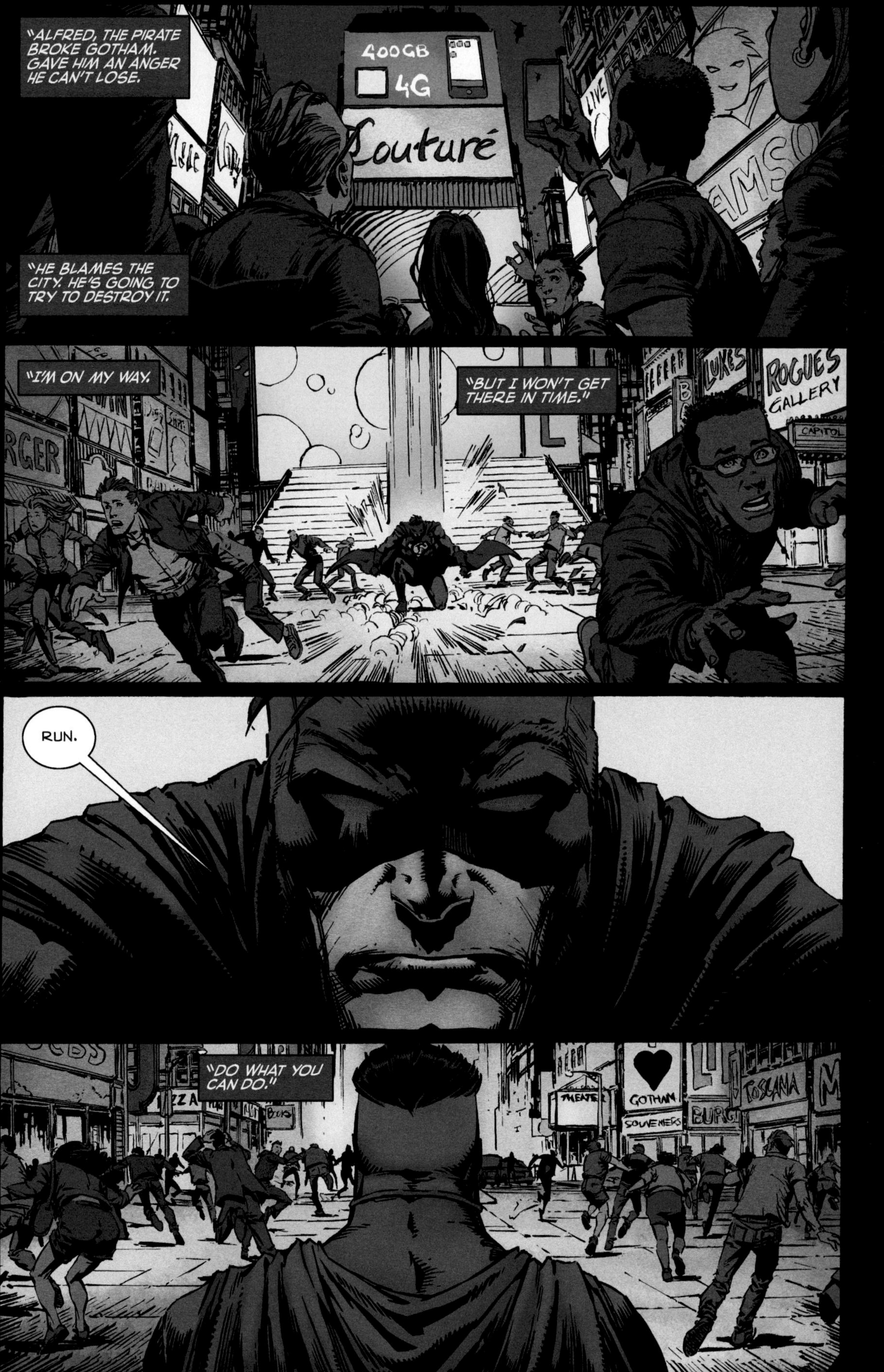
"ALFRED, THE PIRATE BROKE GOTHAM. GAVE HIM AN ANGER HE CAN'T LOSE.
400GB
4G
Couturé
"HE BLAMES THE CITY. HE'S GOING TO TRY TO DESTROY IT.
"I'M ON MY WAY.
"BUT I WON'T GET THERE IN TIME."
ROGUES GALLERY
CAPITOL
RUN.
"DO WHAT YOU CAN DO."
THEATER
GOTHAM
SOUVENIRS
TOSCANA

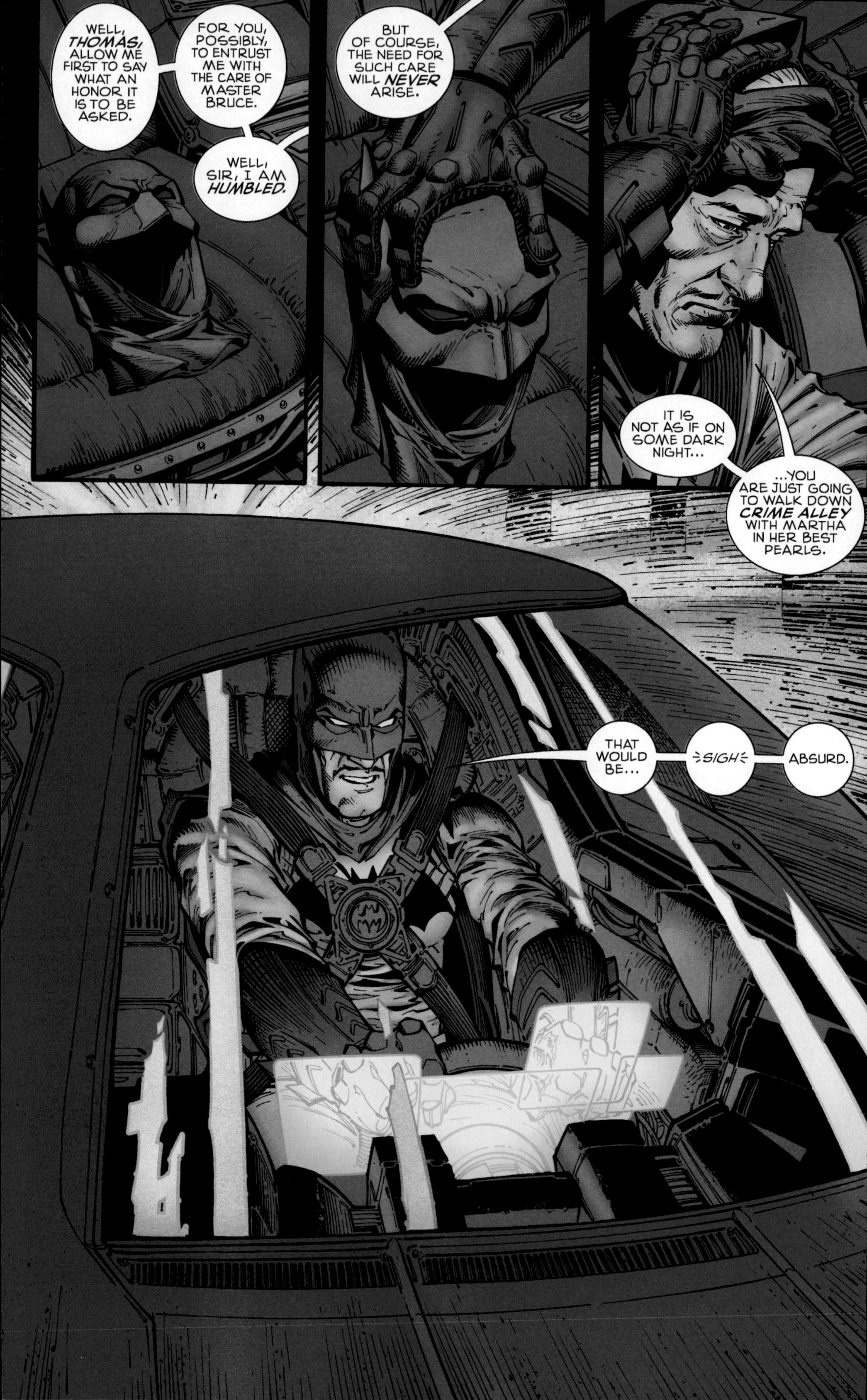
WELL, *THOMAS,* ALLOW ME FIRST TO SAY WHAT AN HONOR IT IS TO BE ASKED.
FOR YOU, POSSIBLY, TO ENTRUST ME WITH THE CARE OF MASTER BRUCE.
WELL, SIR, I AM *HUMBLED.*
BUT OF COURSE, THE NEED FOR SUCH CARE WILL *NEVER* ARISE.
IT IS NOT AS IF ON SOME DARK NIGHT...
...YOU ARE JUST GOING TO WALK DOWN *CRIME ALLEY* WITH MARTHA IN HER BEST PEARLS.
THAT WOULD BE...
SIGH
ABSURD.

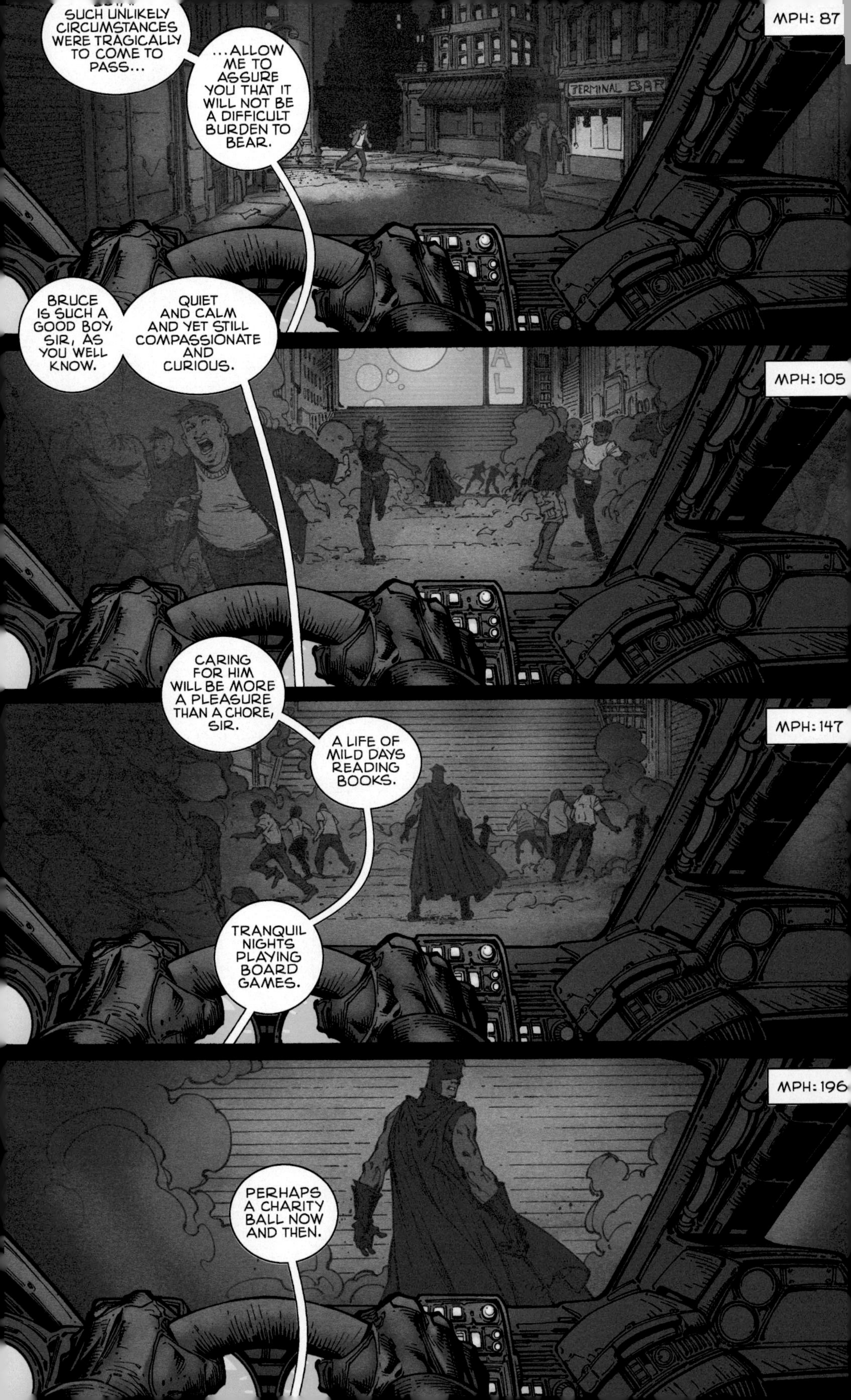
MPH: 87
SUCH UNLIKELY CIRCUMSTANCES WERE TRAGICALLY TO COME TO PASS...
...ALLOW ME TO ASSURE YOU THAT IT WILL NOT BE A DIFFICULT BURDEN TO BEAR.
TERMINAL BAR
BRUCE IS SUCH A GOOD BOY, SIR, AS YOU WELL KNOW.
QUIET AND CALM AND YET STILL COMPASSIONATE AND CURIOUS.
MPH: 105
CARING FOR HIM WILL BE MORE A PLEASURE THAN A CHORE, SIR.
MPH: 147
A LIFE OF MILD DAYS READING BOOKS.
TRANQUIL NIGHTS PLAYING BOARD GAMES.
MPH: 196
PERHAPS A CHARITY BALL NOW AND THEN.

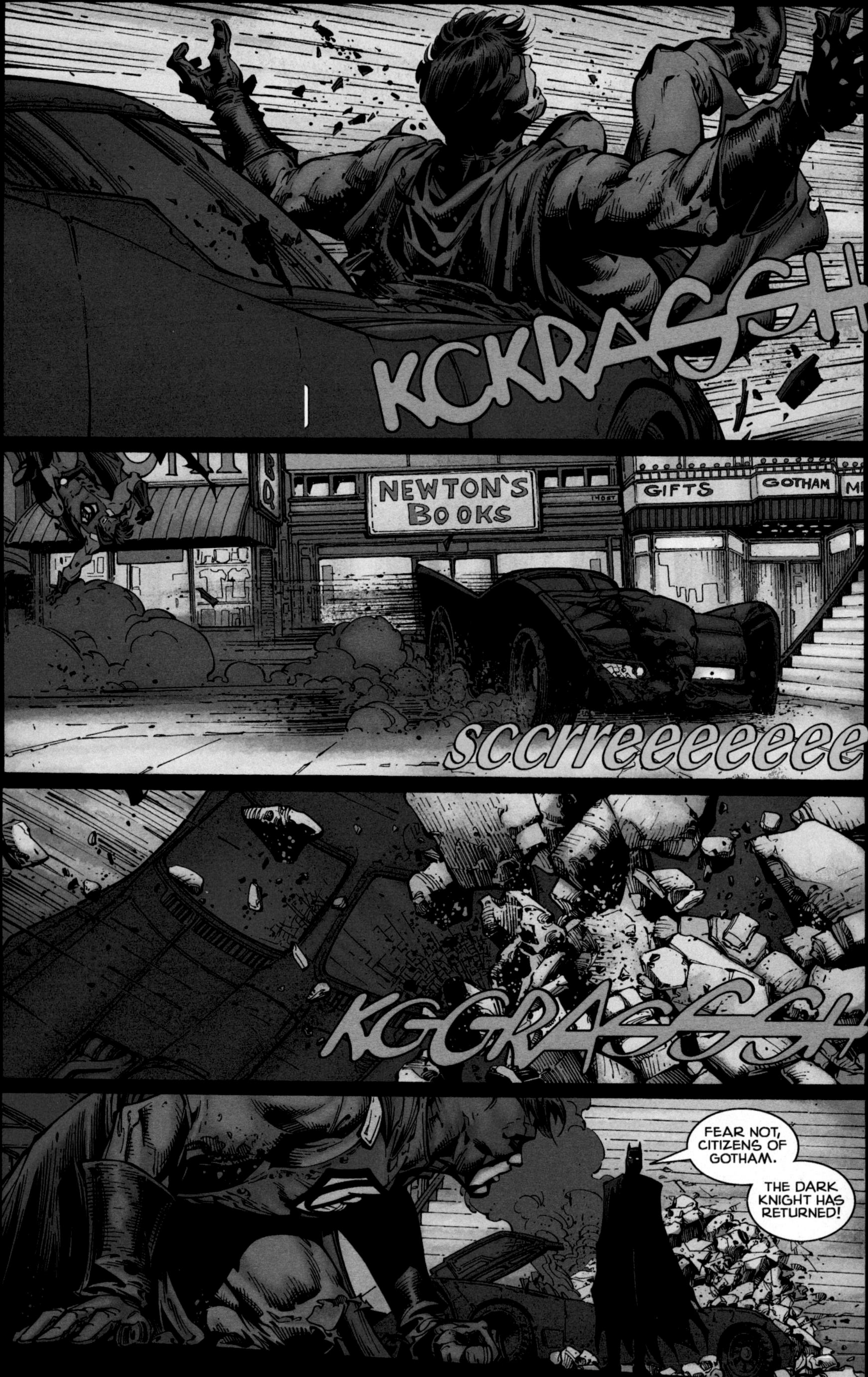
KCKRASSH
NEWTON'S BOOKS
GIFTS
GOTHAM
sccrreeeeeeee
KGGRASSH
FEAR NOT, CITIZENS OF GOTHAM.
THE DARK KNIGHT HAS RETURNED!

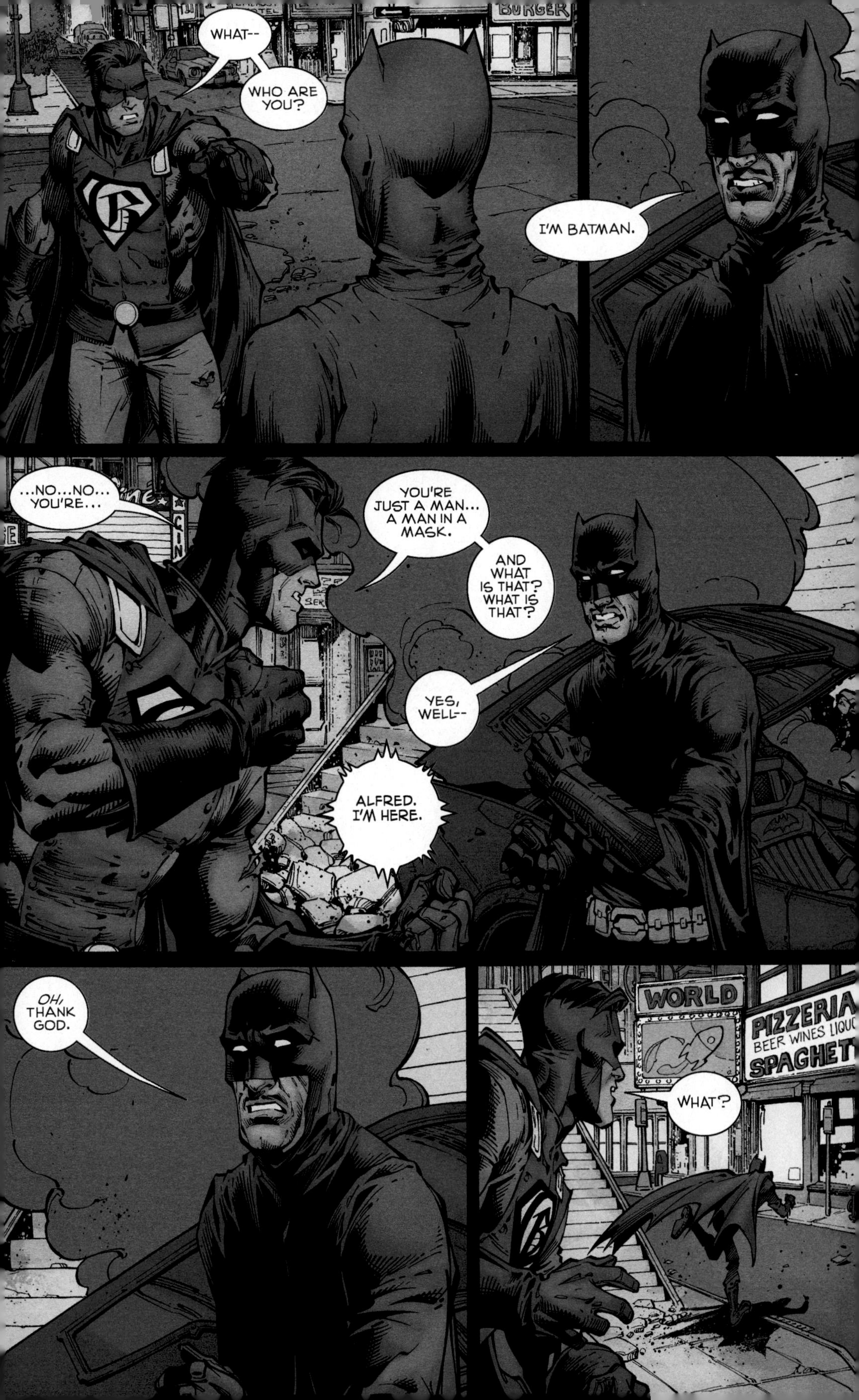

WHAT--
WHO ARE YOU?
I'M BATMAN.
...NO...NO... YOU'RE...
YOU'RE JUST A MAN... A MAN IN A MASK.
AND WHAT IS THAT? WHAT IS THAT?
YES, WELL--
ALFRED. I'M HERE.
OH, THANK GOD.
WHAT?
WORLD
PIZZERIA
BEER WINES LIQU
SPAGHET

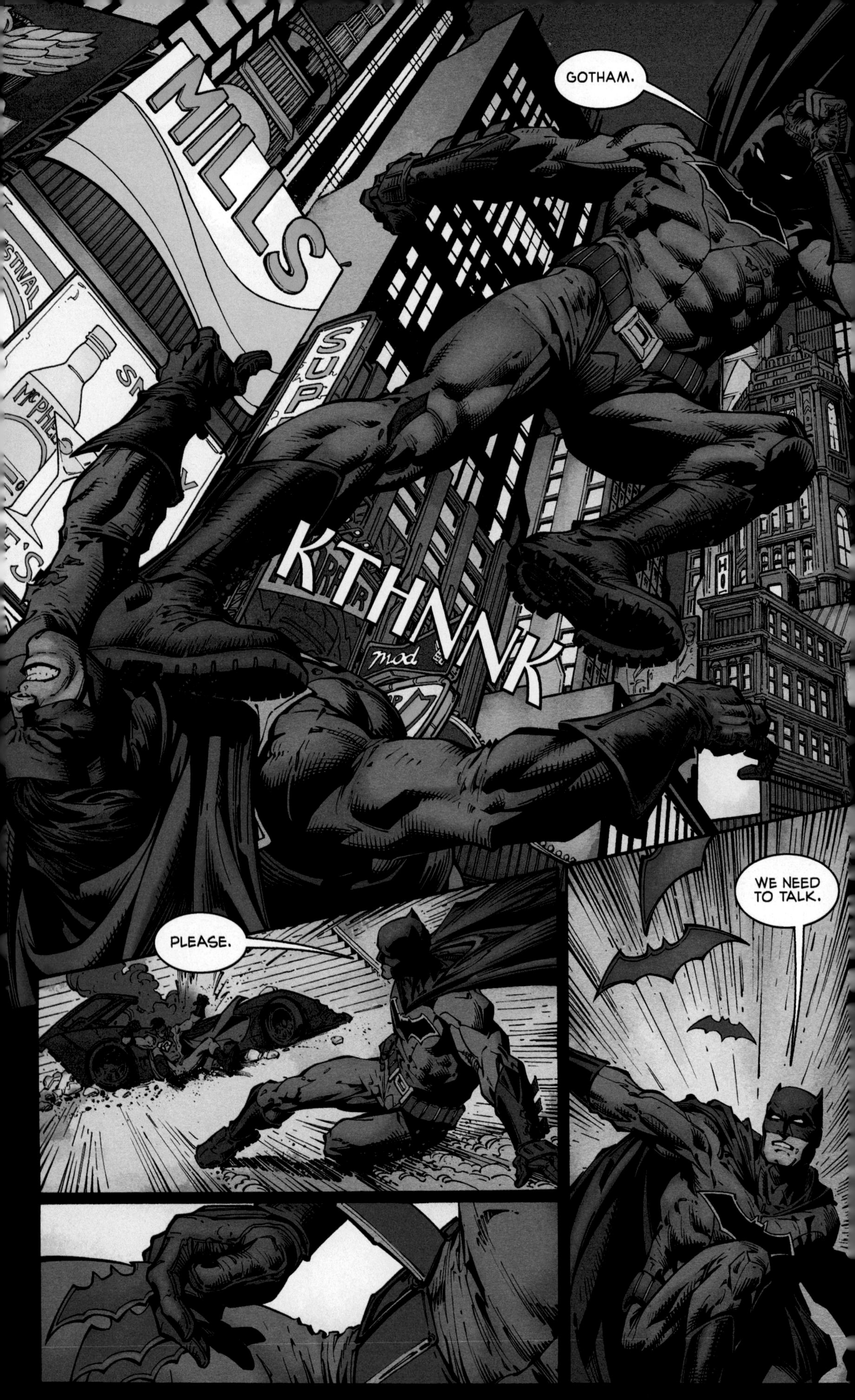
GOTHAM.
MILLS
SUP
KTHNNNK
PLEASE.
WE NEED TO TALK.

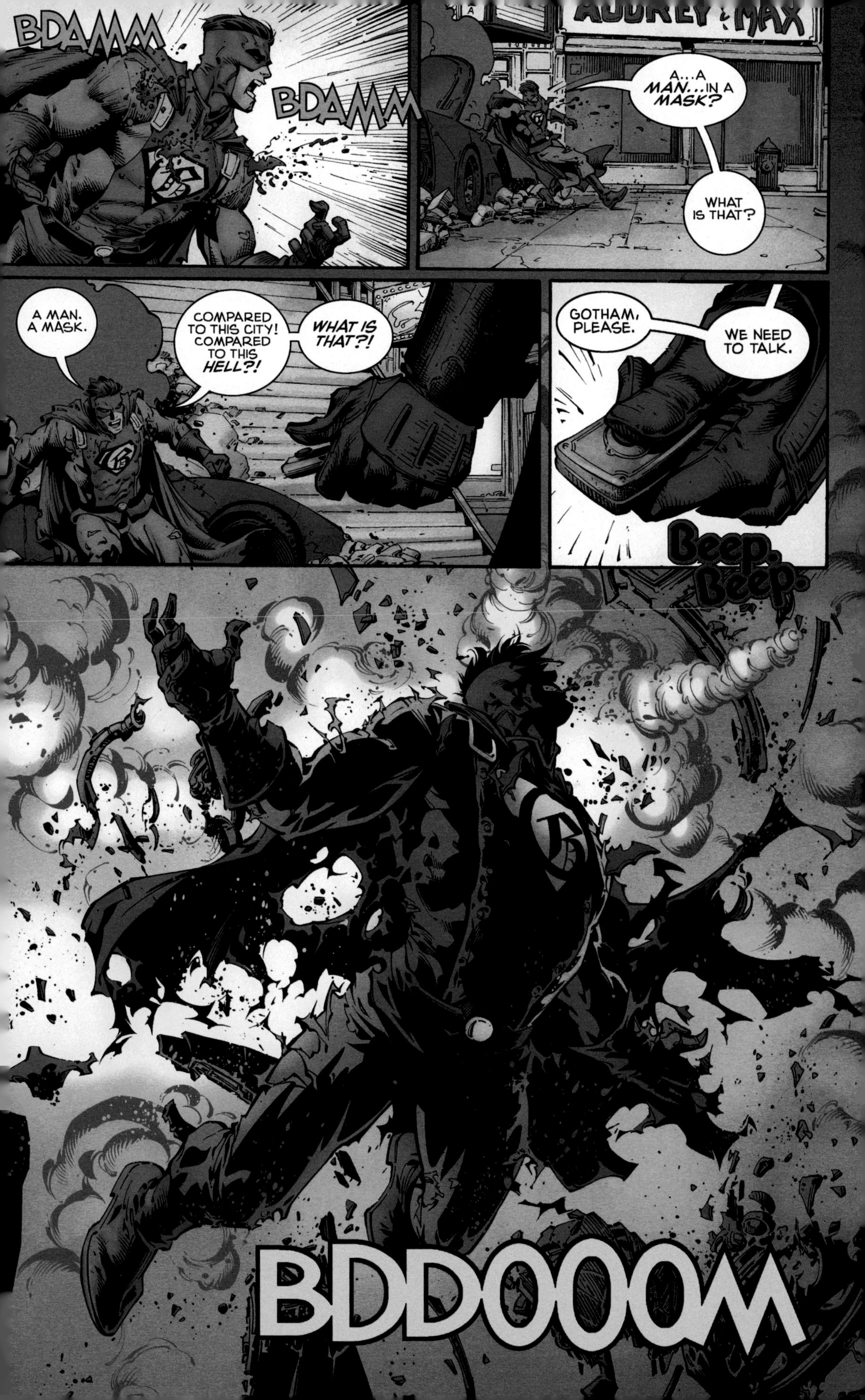
BDAMM
BDAMM
AUDREY : MAX
A...A MAN...IN A MASK?
WHAT IS THAT?
A MAN. A MASK.
COMPARED TO THIS CITY! COMPARED TO THIS HELL?!
WHAT IS THAT?!
GOTHAM, PLEASE.
WE NEED TO TALK.
Beep. Beep.
BDDOOOM

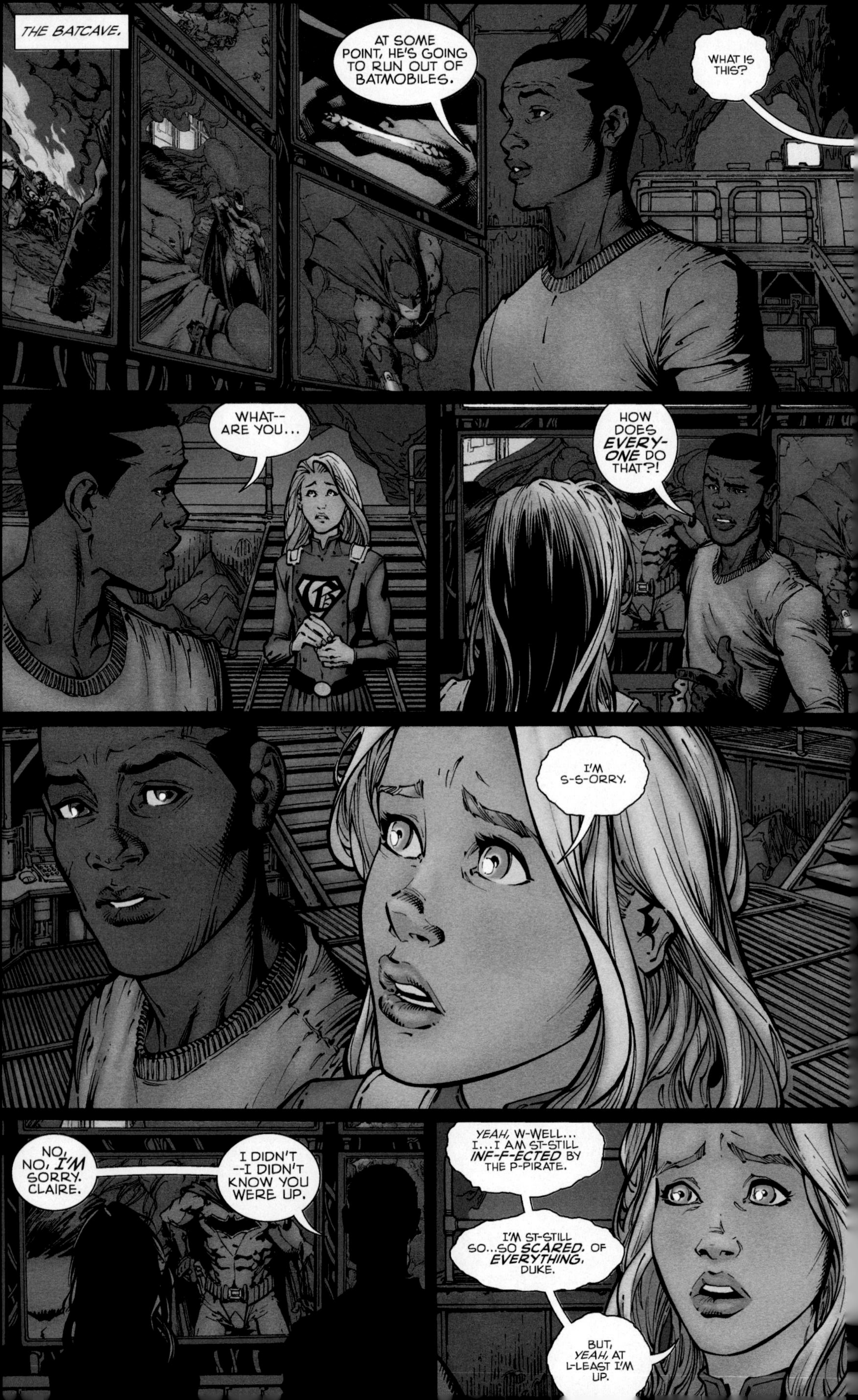
THE BATCAVE.
AT SOME POINT, HE'S GOING TO RUN OUT OF BATMOBILES.
WHAT IS THIS?
WHAT-- ARE YOU...
HOW DOES EVERY-ONE DO THAT?!
I'M S-S-ORRY.
NO, NO, I'M SORRY. CLAIRE.
I DIDN'T --I DIDN'T KNOW YOU WERE UP.
YEAH, W-WELL... I...I AM ST-STILL INF-F-ECTED BY THE P-PIRATE.
I'M ST-STILL SO...SO SCARED. OF EVERYTHING, DUKE.
BUT, YEAH, AT L-LEAST I'M UP.

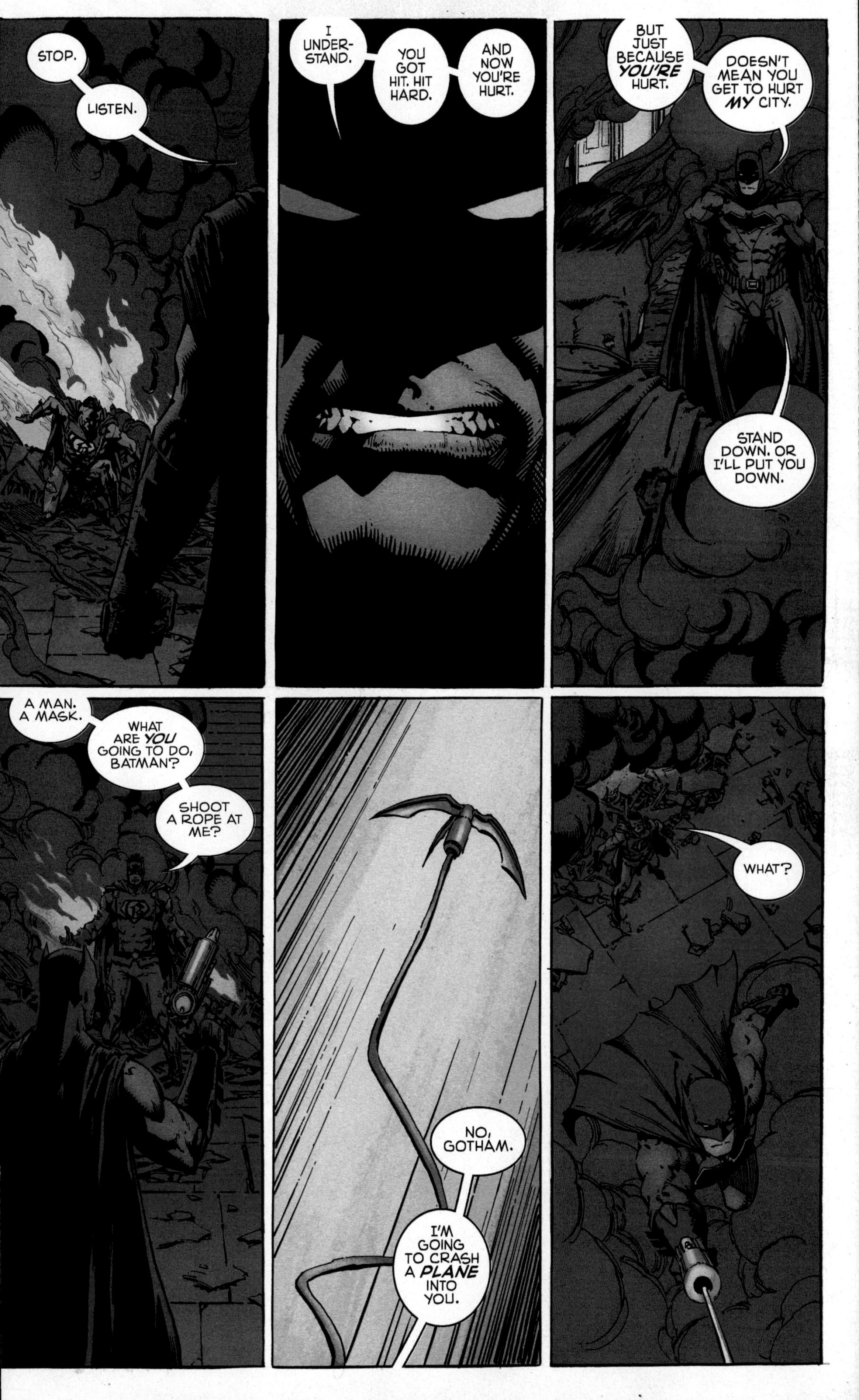

STOP.
LISTEN.
I UNDER-STAND.
YOU GOT HIT. HIT HARD.
AND NOW YOU'RE HURT.
BUT JUST BECAUSE *YOU'RE* HURT.
DOESN'T MEAN YOU GET TO HURT *MY* CITY.
STAND DOWN. OR I'LL PUT YOU DOWN.
A MAN. A MASK.
WHAT ARE *YOU* GOING TO DO, BATMAN?
SHOOT A ROPE AT ME?
NO, GOTHAM.
I'M GOING TO CRASH A *PLANE* INTO YOU.
WHAT?

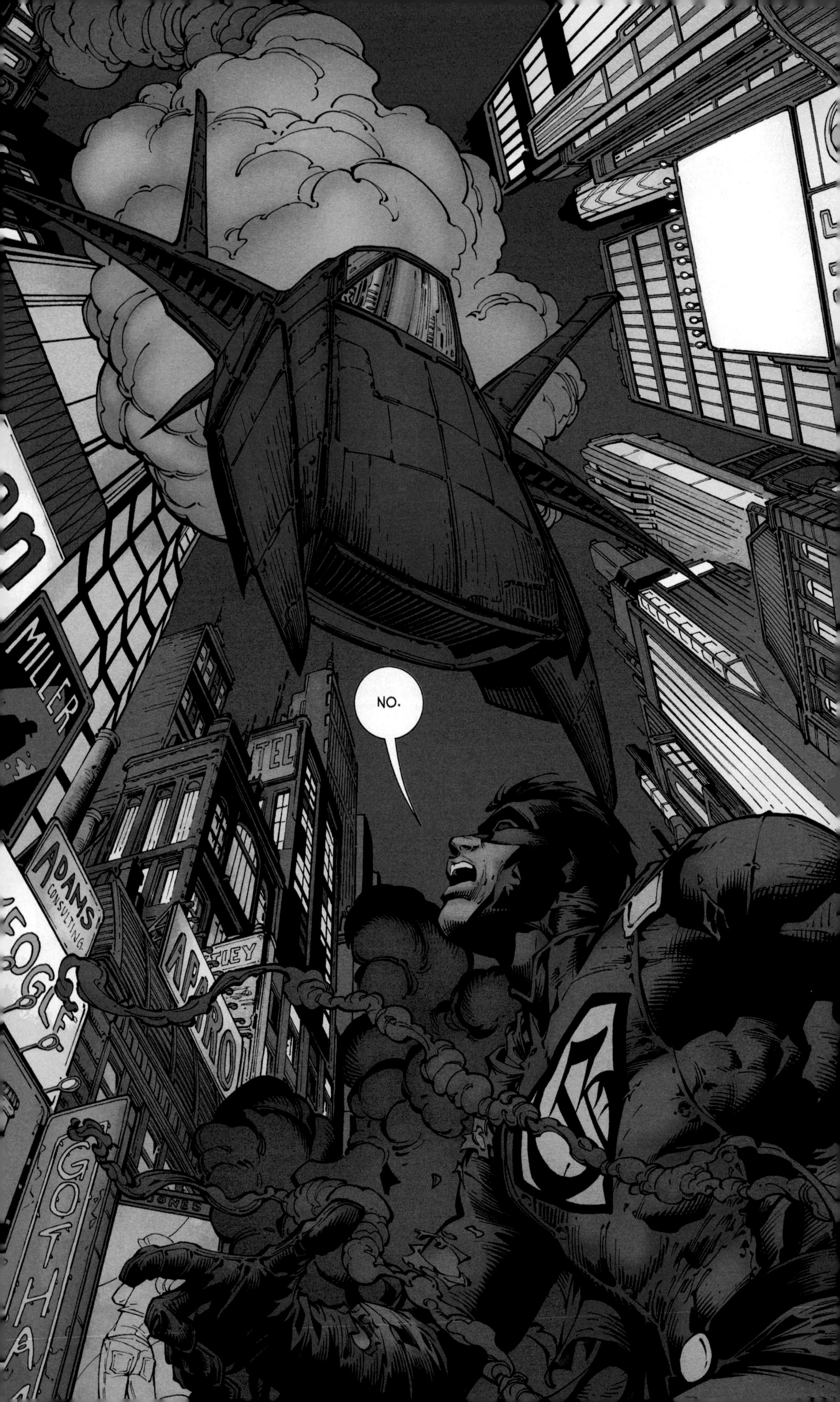

NO.
MILLER
ADAMS CONSULTING
GOTHAM

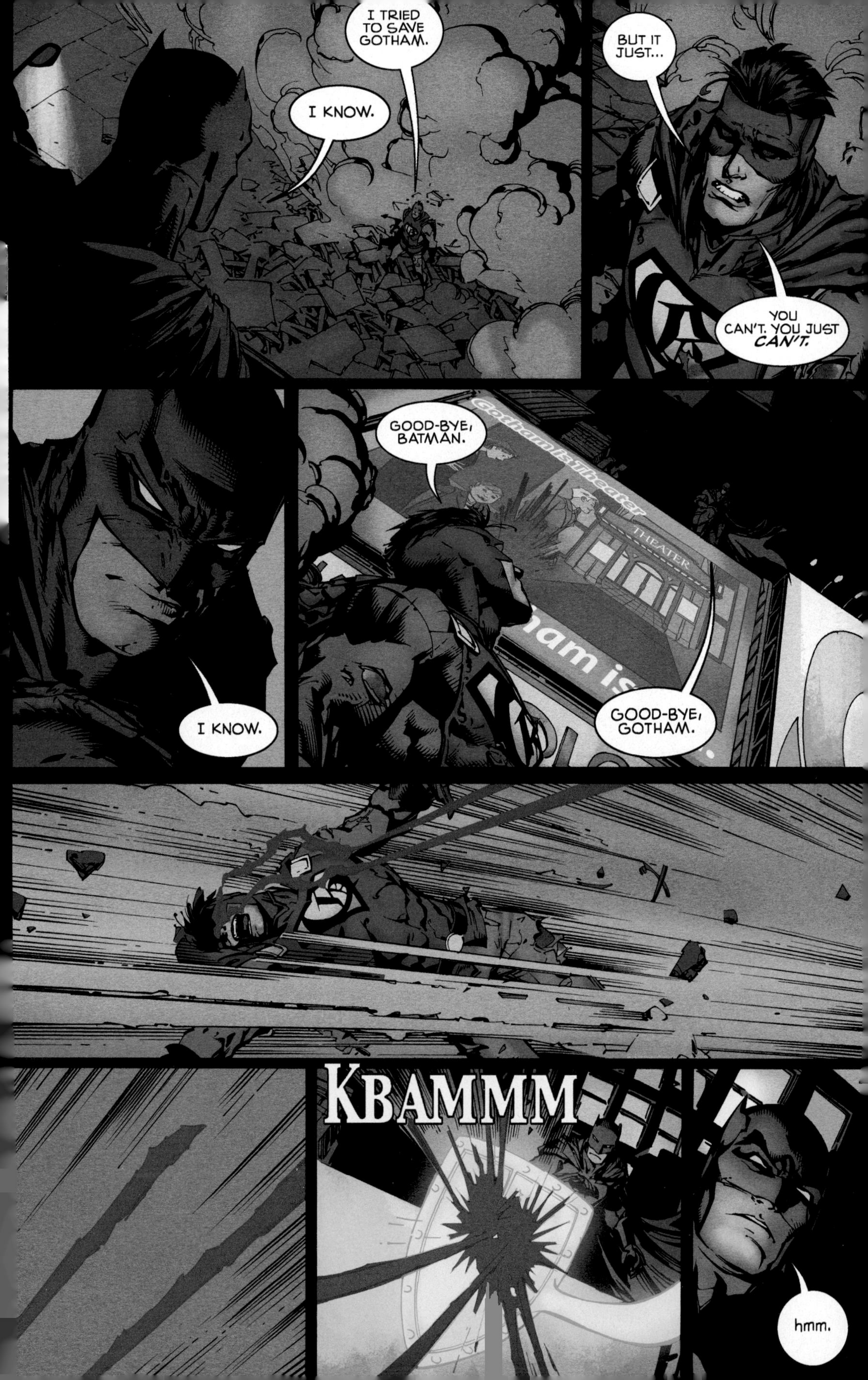
I TRIED TO SAVE GOTHAM.
I KNOW.
BUT IT JUST...
YOU CAN'T. YOU JUST *CAN'T.*
I KNOW.
GOOD-BYE, BATMAN.
Gotham is Theater
THEATER
GOOD-BYE, GOTHAM.
KBAMMM
hmm.

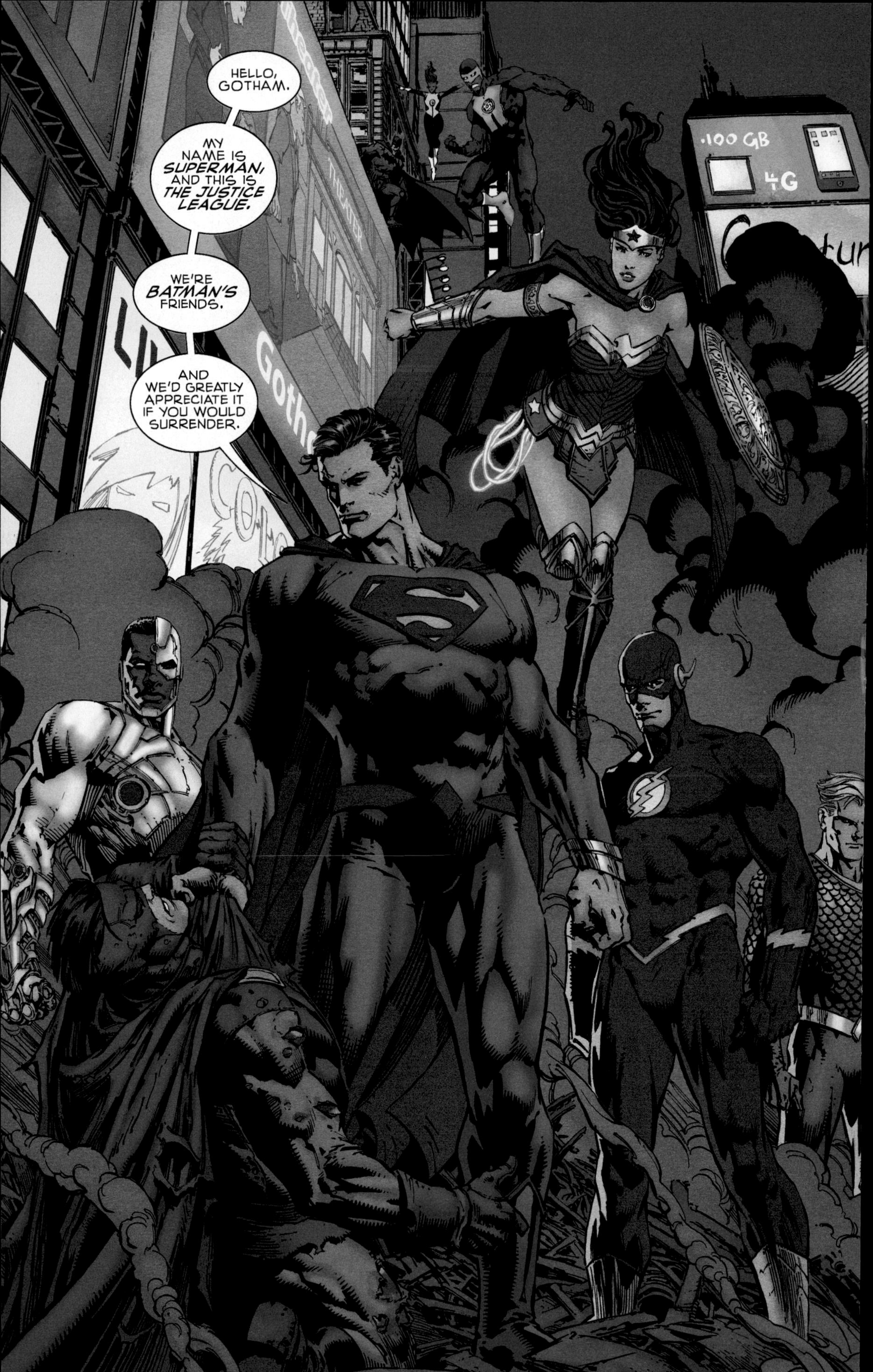
HELLO, GOTHAM.
MY NAME IS SUPERMAN, AND THIS IS THE JUSTICE LEAGUE.
WE'RE BATMAN'S FRIENDS.
AND WE'D GREATLY APPRECIATE IT IF YOU WOULD SURRENDER.

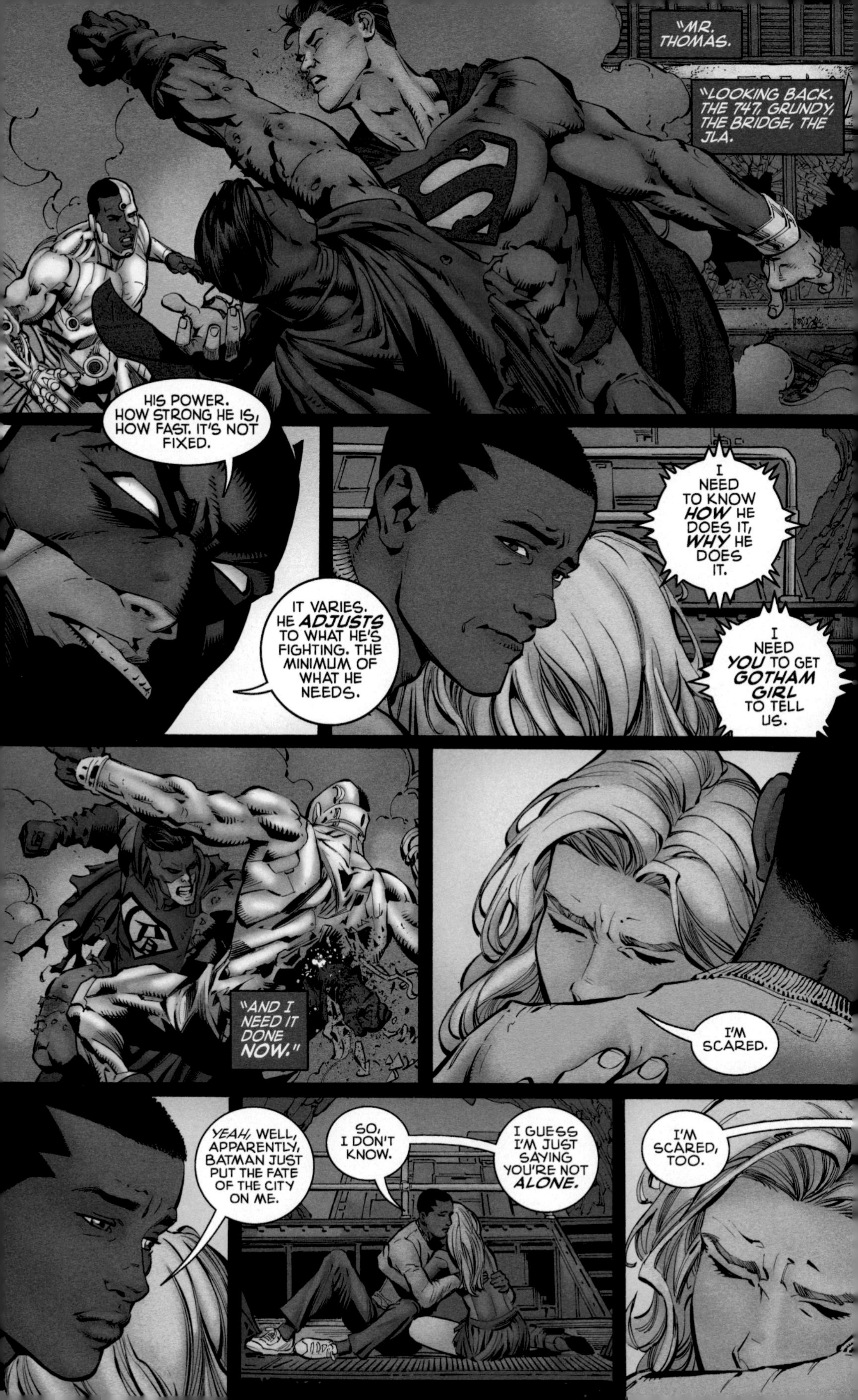
"MR. THOMAS.
"LOOKING BACK. THE 747, GRUNDY, THE BRIDGE, THE JLA.
HIS POWER. HOW STRONG HE IS, HOW FAST. IT'S NOT FIXED.
IT VARIES. HE ADJUSTS TO WHAT HE'S FIGHTING. THE MINIMUM OF WHAT HE NEEDS.
I NEED TO KNOW HOW HE DOES IT, WHY HE DOES IT.
I NEED YOU TO GET GOTHAM GIRL TO TELL US.
"AND I NEED IT DONE NOW."
I'M SCARED.
YEAH, WELL, APPARENTLY, BATMAN JUST PUT THE FATE OF THE CITY ON ME.
SO, I DON'T KNOW.
I GUESS I'M JUST SAYING YOU'RE NOT ALONE.
I'M SCARED, TOO.

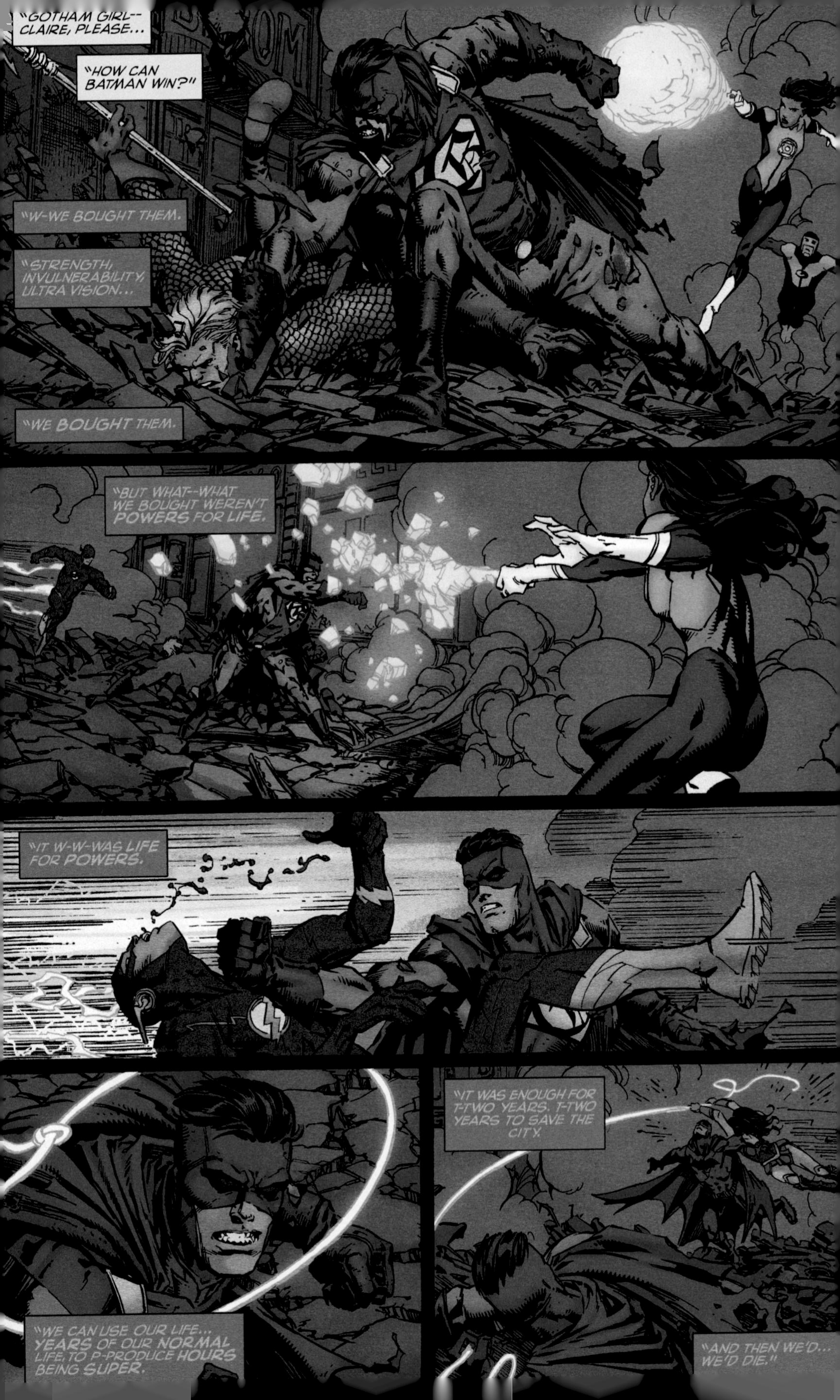
"GOTHAM GIRL--
CLAIRE, PLEASE...
"HOW CAN
BATMAN WIN?"
"W-WE BOUGHT THEM.
"STRENGTH,
INVULNERABILITY,
ULTRA VISION...
"WE BOUGHT THEM.
"BUT WHAT--WHAT
WE BOUGHT WEREN'T
POWERS FOR LIFE.
"IT W-W-WAS LIFE
FOR POWERS.
"WE CAN USE OUR LIFE...
YEARS OF OUR NORMAL
LIFE, TO P-PRODUCE HOURS
BEING SUPER.
"IT WAS ENOUGH FOR
T-TWO YEARS. T-TWO
YEARS TO SAVE THE
CITY.
"AND THEN WE'D...
WE'D DIE."

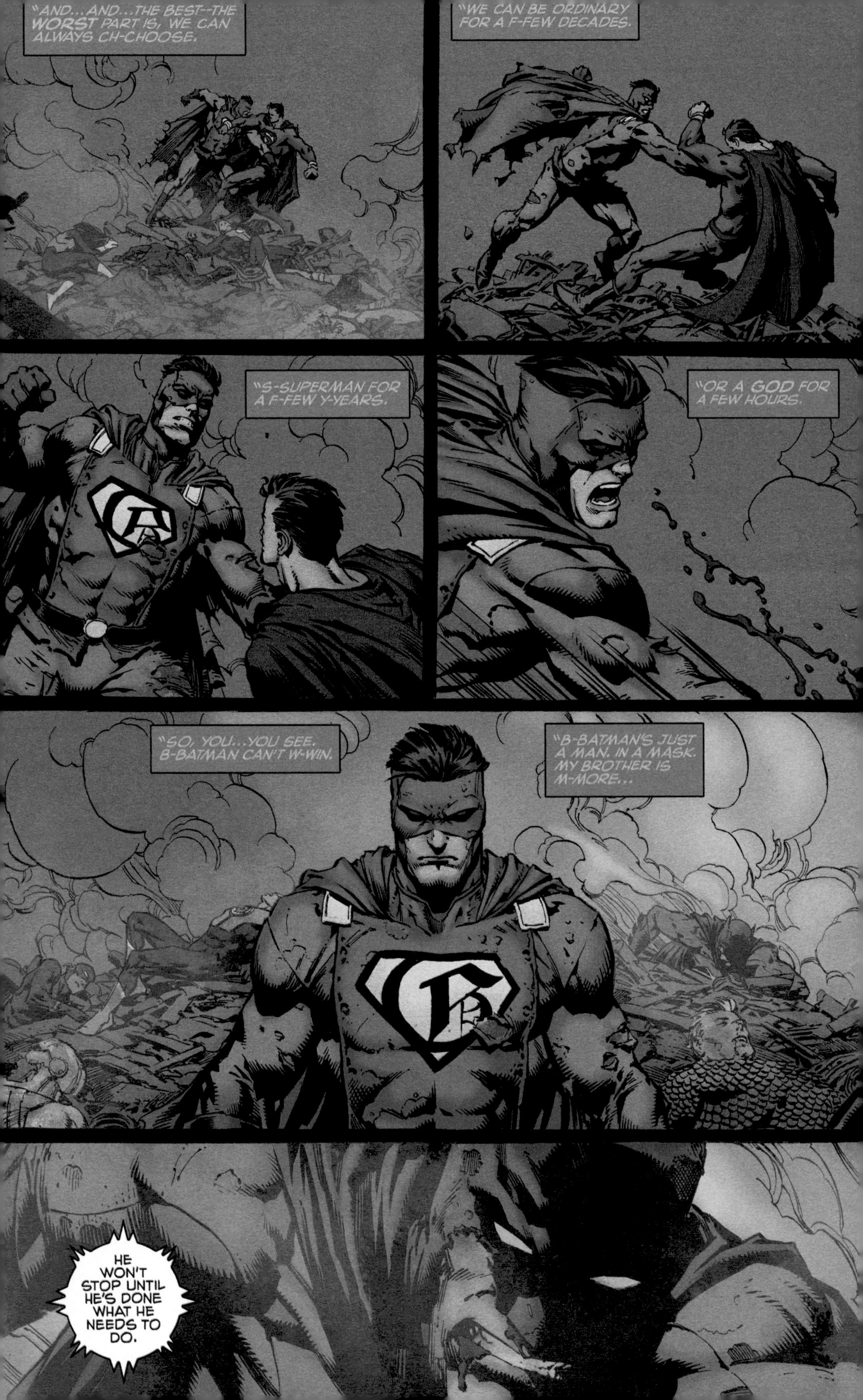
"AND...AND...THE BEST--THE WORST PART IS, WE CAN ALWAYS CH-CHOOSE.
"WE CAN BE ORDINARY FOR A F-FEW DECADES.
"S-SUPERMAN FOR A F-FEW Y-YEARS.
"OR A GOD FOR A FEW HOURS.
"SO, YOU...YOU SEE. B-BATMAN CAN'T W-WIN.
"B-BATMAN'S JUST A MAN. IN A MASK. MY BROTHER IS M-MORE...
HE WON'T STOP UNTIL HE'S DONE WHAT HE NEEDS TO DO.

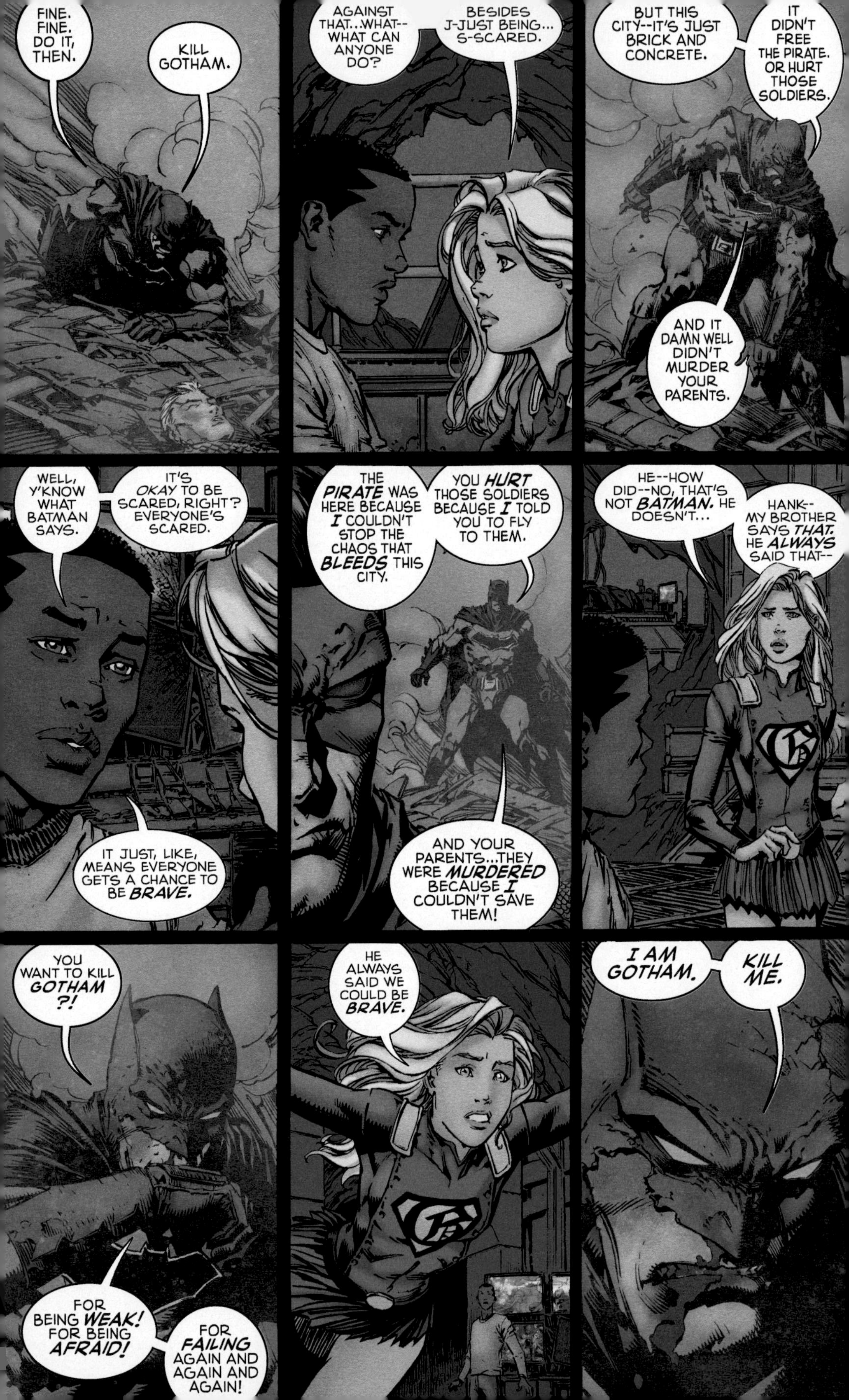
FINE. FINE. DO IT, THEN.
KILL GOTHAM.
AGAINST THAT...WHAT--WHAT CAN ANYONE DO?
BESIDES J-JUST BEING... S-SCARED.
BUT THIS CITY--IT'S JUST BRICK AND CONCRETE.
IT DIDN'T FREE THE PIRATE. OR HURT THOSE SOLDIERS.
AND IT DAMN WELL DIDN'T MURDER YOUR PARENTS.
WELL, Y'KNOW WHAT BATMAN SAYS.
IT'S OKAY TO BE SCARED, RIGHT? EVERYONE'S SCARED.
IT JUST, LIKE, MEANS EVERYONE GETS A CHANCE TO BE BRAVE.
THE PIRATE WAS HERE BECAUSE I COULDN'T STOP THE CHAOS THAT BLEEDS THIS CITY.
YOU HURT THOSE SOLDIERS BECAUSE I TOLD YOU TO FLY TO THEM.
AND YOUR PARENTS...THEY WERE MURDERED BECAUSE I COULDN'T SAVE THEM!
HE--HOW DID--NO, THAT'S NOT BATMAN. HE DOESN'T...
HANK-- MY BROTHER SAYS THAT. HE ALWAYS SAID THAT--
YOU WANT TO KILL GOTHAM ?!
FOR BEING WEAK! FOR BEING AFRAID!
FOR FAILING AGAIN AND AGAIN AND AGAIN!
HE ALWAYS SAID WE COULD BE BRAVE.
I AM GOTHAM.
KILL ME.

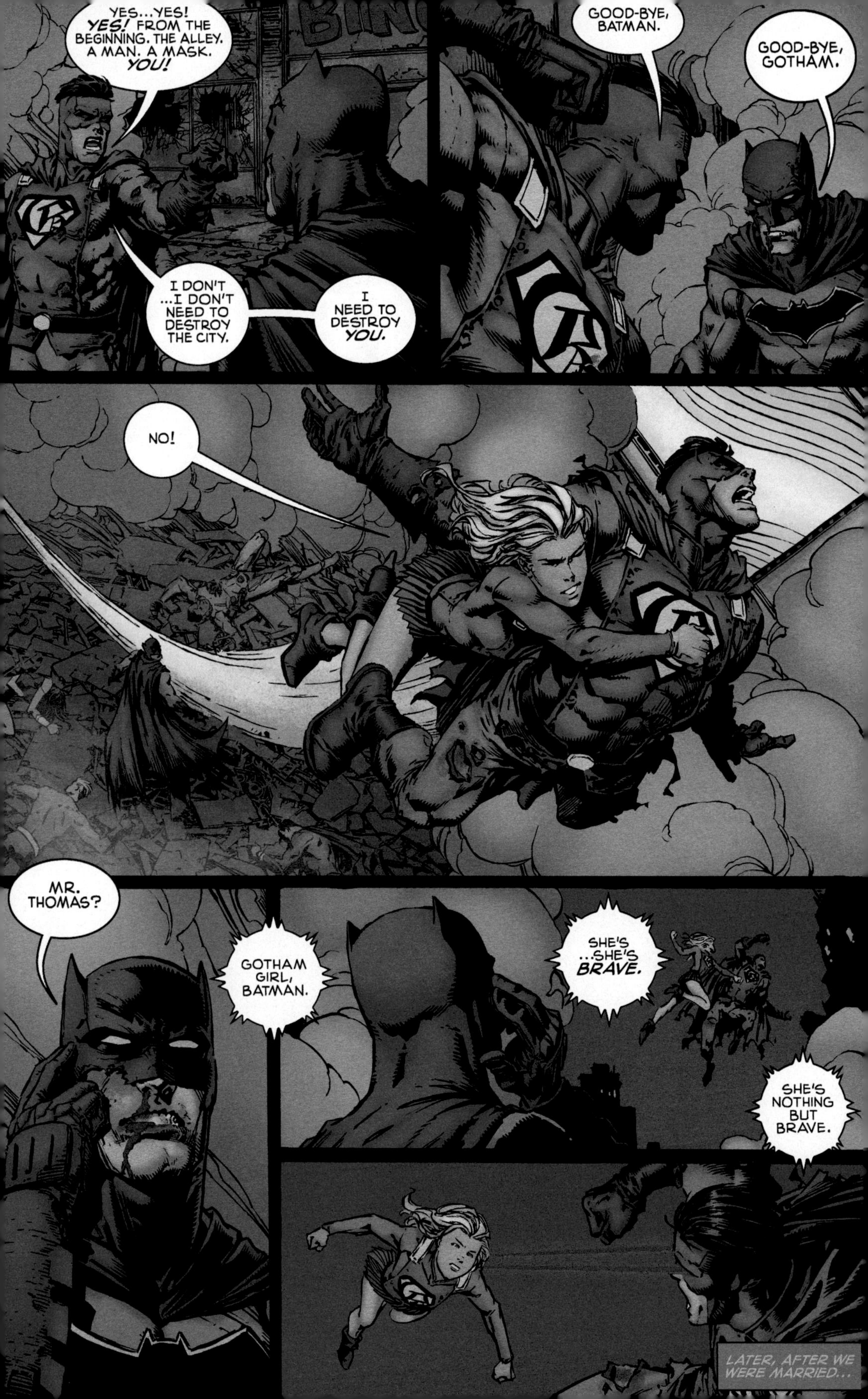

YES...YES! YES! FROM THE BEGINNING. THE ALLEY. A MAN. A MASK. YOU!
I DON'T ...I DON'T NEED TO DESTROY THE CITY.
I NEED TO DESTROY YOU.
GOOD-BYE, BATMAN.
GOOD-BYE, GOTHAM.
NO!
MR. THOMAS?
GOTHAM GIRL, BATMAN.
SHE'S ...SHE'S BRAVE.
SHE'S NOTHING BUT BRAVE.
LATER, AFTER WE WERE MARRIED...

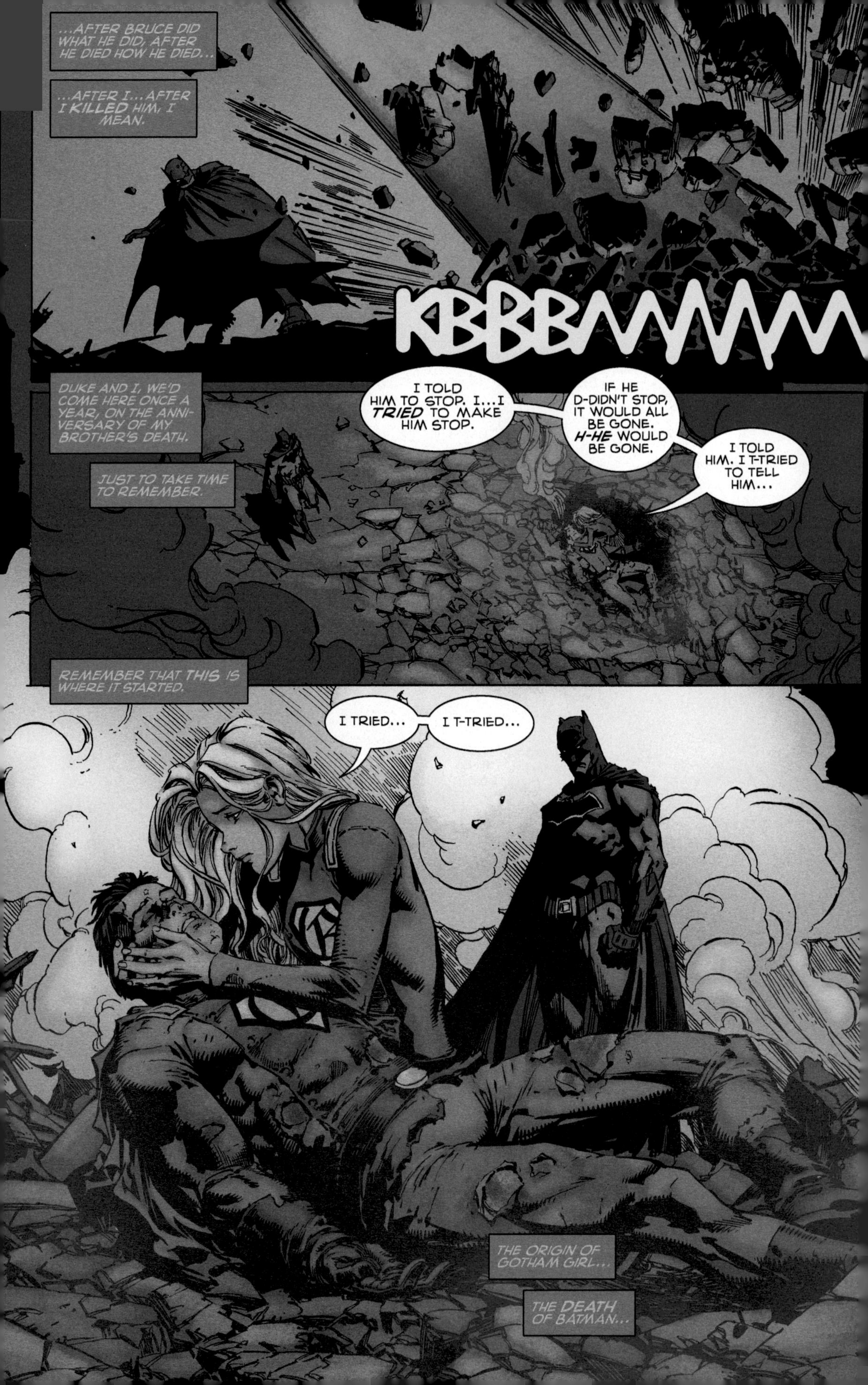
...AFTER BRUCE DID WHAT HE DID, AFTER HE DIED HOW HE DIED...
...AFTER I...AFTER I KILLED HIM, I MEAN.
KBBBAAAAAM
DUKE AND I, WE'D COME HERE ONCE A YEAR, ON THE ANNIVERSARY OF MY BROTHER'S DEATH.
JUST TO TAKE TIME TO REMEMBER.
I TOLD HIM TO STOP. I...I TRIED TO MAKE HIM STOP.
IF HE D-DIDN'T STOP, IT WOULD ALL BE GONE. H-HE WOULD BE GONE.
I TOLD HIM. I T-TRIED TO TELL HIM...
REMEMBER THAT THIS IS WHERE IT STARTED.
I TRIED...
I T-TRIED...
THE ORIGIN OF GOTHAM GIRL...
THE DEATH OF BATMAN...

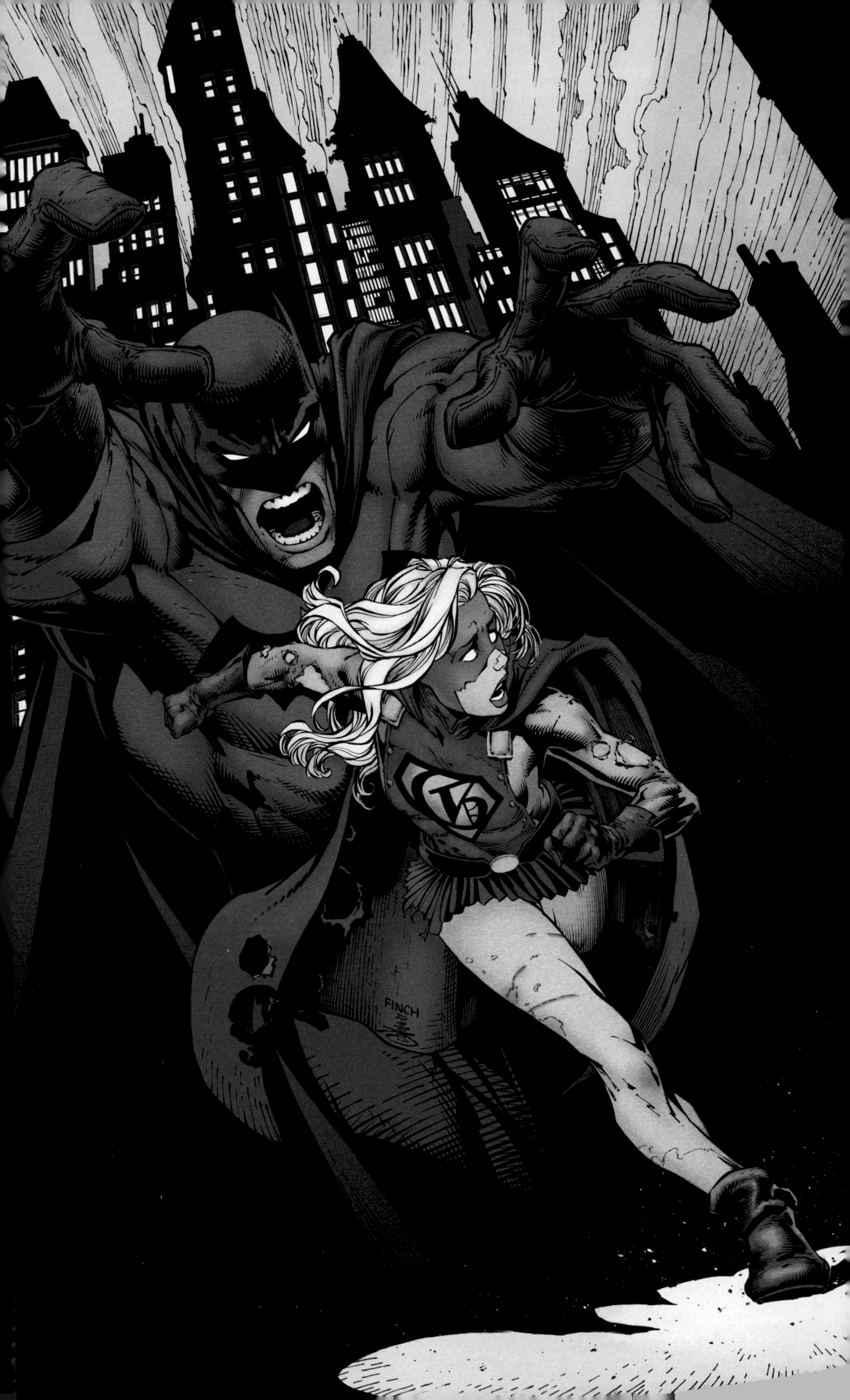
FINCH

I AM GOTHAM epilogue

TOM KING writer * IVAN REIS penciller * JOE PRADO, OCLAIR ALBERT and SCOTT HANNA inkers
MARCELO MAIOLO colorist * DERON BENNETT letterer * DAVID FINCH, DANNY MIKI and JORDIE BELLAIRE cover artists

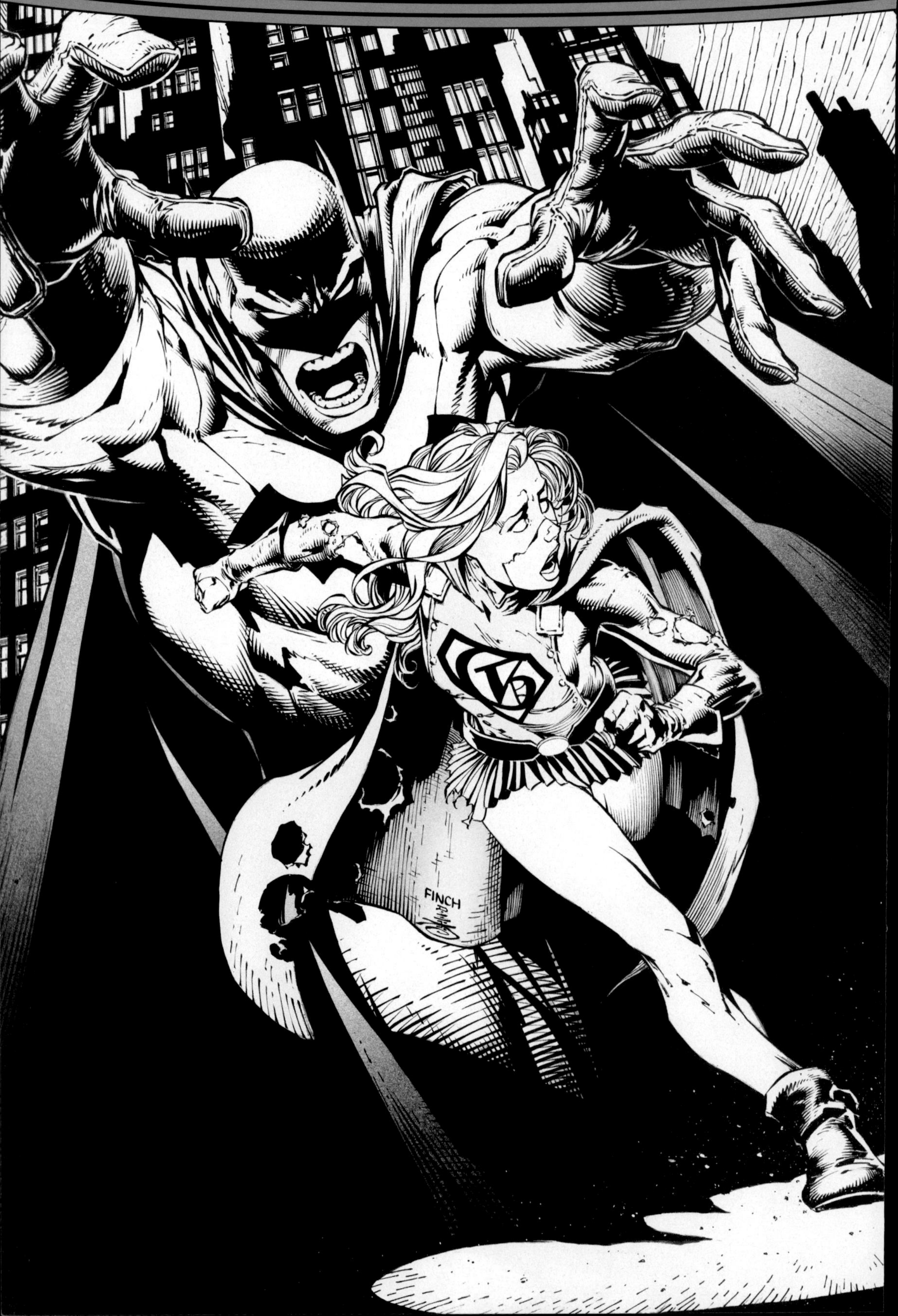
FINCH

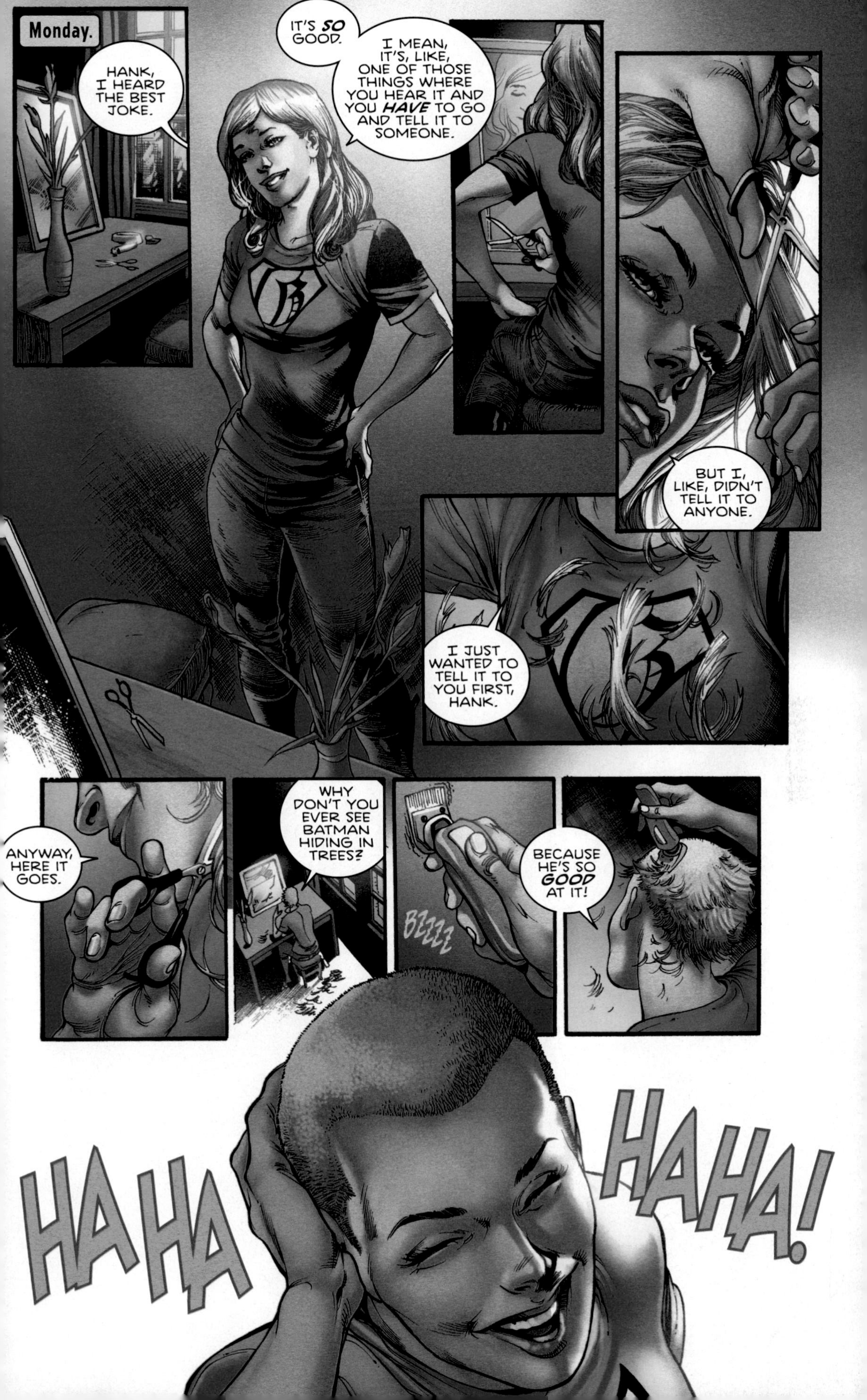
Monday.
HANK, I HEARD THE BEST JOKE.
IT'S SO GOOD.
I MEAN, IT'S, LIKE, ONE OF THOSE THINGS WHERE YOU HEAR IT AND YOU HAVE TO GO AND TELL IT TO SOMEONE.
BUT I, LIKE, DIDN'T TELL IT TO ANYONE.
I JUST WANTED TO TELL IT TO YOU FIRST, HANK.
ANYWAY, HERE IT GOES.
WHY DON'T YOU EVER SEE BATMAN HIDING IN TREES?
BZZZZ
BECAUSE HE'S SO GOOD AT IT!
HAHA
HAHA!

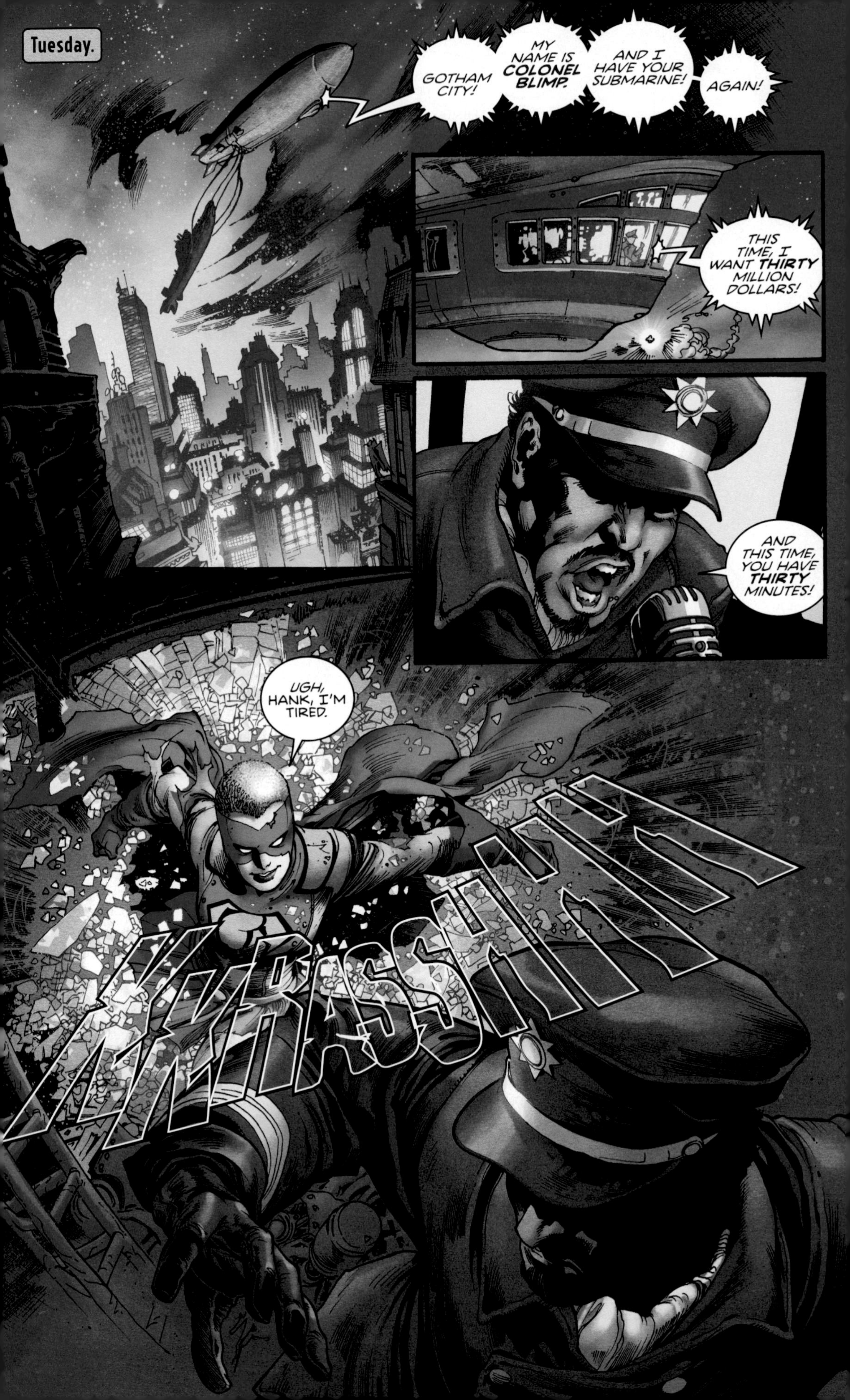
Tuesday.
GOTHAM CITY!
MY NAME IS COLONEL BLIMP.
AND I HAVE YOUR SUBMARINE!
AGAIN!
THIS TIME, I WANT THIRTY MILLION DOLLARS!
AND THIS TIME, YOU HAVE THIRTY MINUTES!
UGH, HANK, I'M TIRED.
KKRASSHH

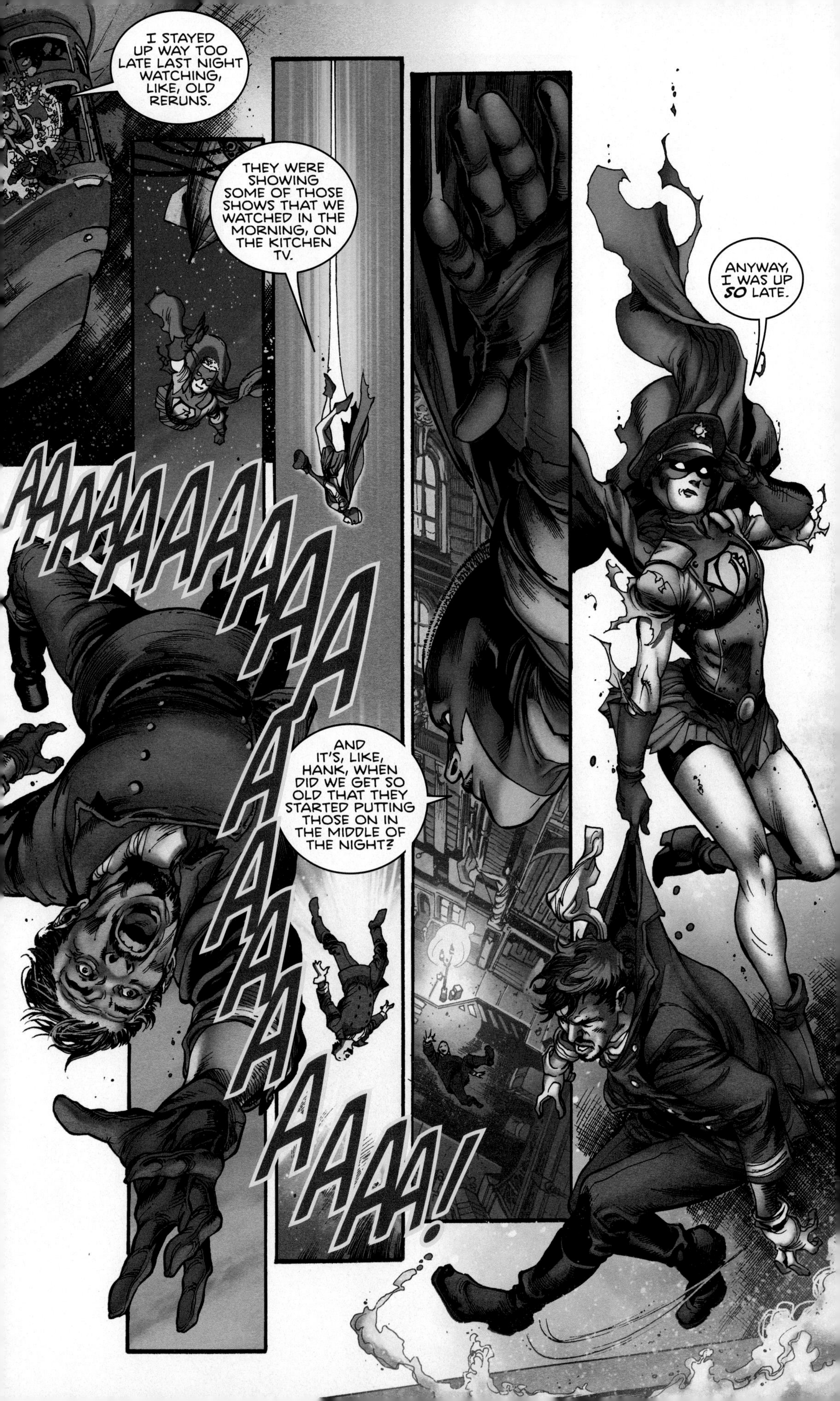

I STAYED UP WAY TOO LATE LAST NIGHT WATCHING, LIKE, OLD RERUNS.
THEY WERE SHOWING SOME OF THOSE SHOWS THAT WE WATCHED IN THE MORNING, ON THE KITCHEN TV.
ANYWAY, I WAS UP *SO* LATE.
AAAAAAAAAAAAAAAAAAAAAAAAAAA!
AND IT'S, LIKE, HANK, WHEN DID WE GET SO OLD THAT THEY STARTED PUTTING THOSE ON IN THE MIDDLE OF THE NIGHT?

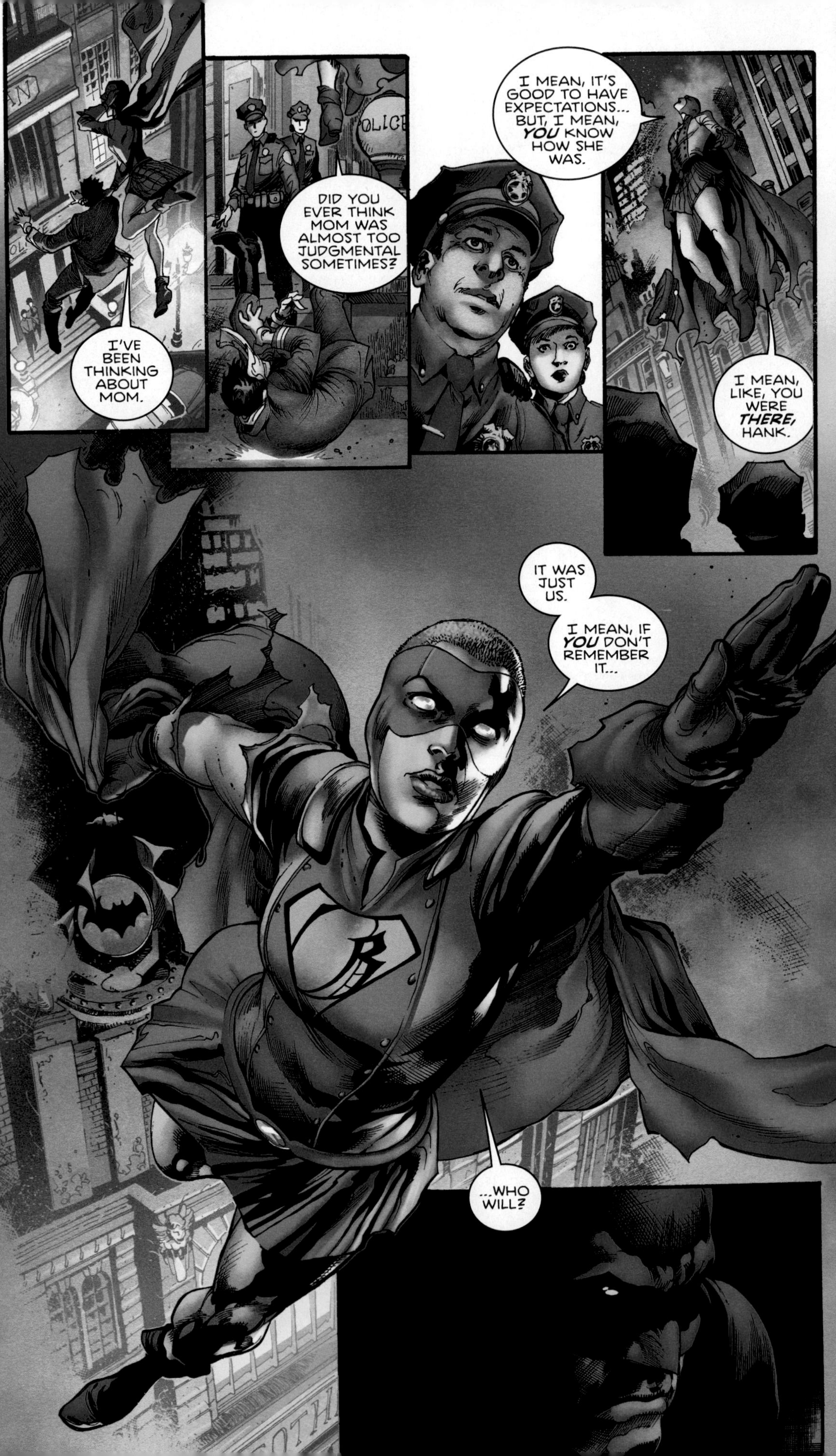

I'VE BEEN THINKING ABOUT MOM.
DID YOU EVER THINK MOM WAS ALMOST TOO JUDGMENTAL SOMETIMES?
I MEAN, IT'S GOOD TO HAVE EXPECTATIONS... BUT, I MEAN, YOU KNOW HOW SHE WAS.
I MEAN, LIKE, YOU WERE THERE, HANK.
IT WAS JUST US.
I MEAN, IF YOU DON'T REMEMBER IT...
...WHO WILL?

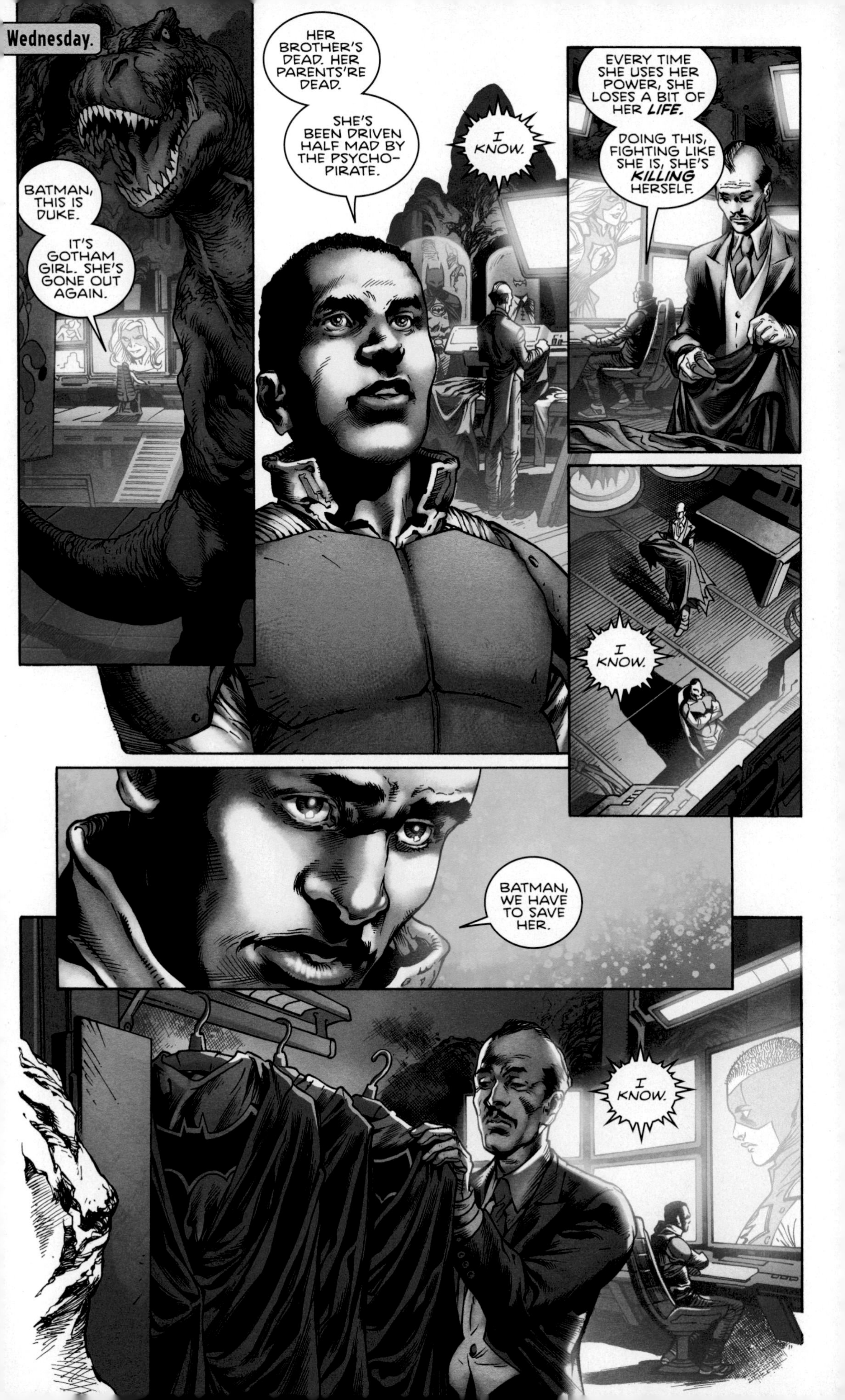
Wednesday.
BATMAN, THIS IS DUKE.
IT'S GOTHAM GIRL. SHE'S GONE OUT AGAIN.
HER BROTHER'S DEAD. HER PARENTS'RE DEAD.
SHE'S BEEN DRIVEN HALF MAD BY THE PSYCHO-PIRATE.
I KNOW.
EVERY TIME SHE USES HER POWER, SHE LOSES A BIT OF HER LIFE.
DOING THIS, FIGHTING LIKE SHE IS, SHE'S KILLING HERSELF.
I KNOW.
BATMAN, WE HAVE TO SAVE HER.
I KNOW.

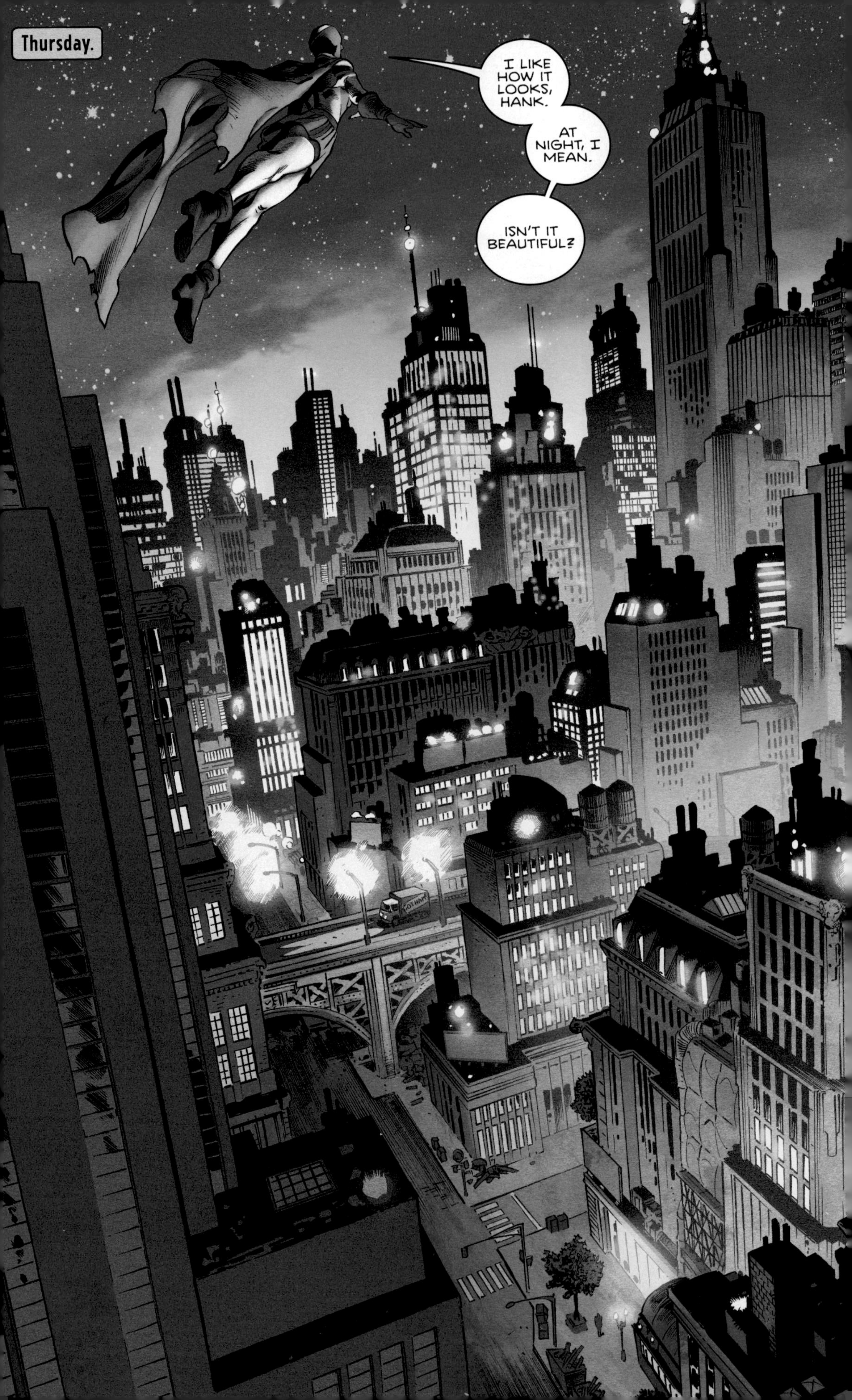
Thursday.
I LIKE HOW IT LOOKS, HANK.
AT NIGHT, I MEAN.
ISN'T IT BEAUTIFUL?

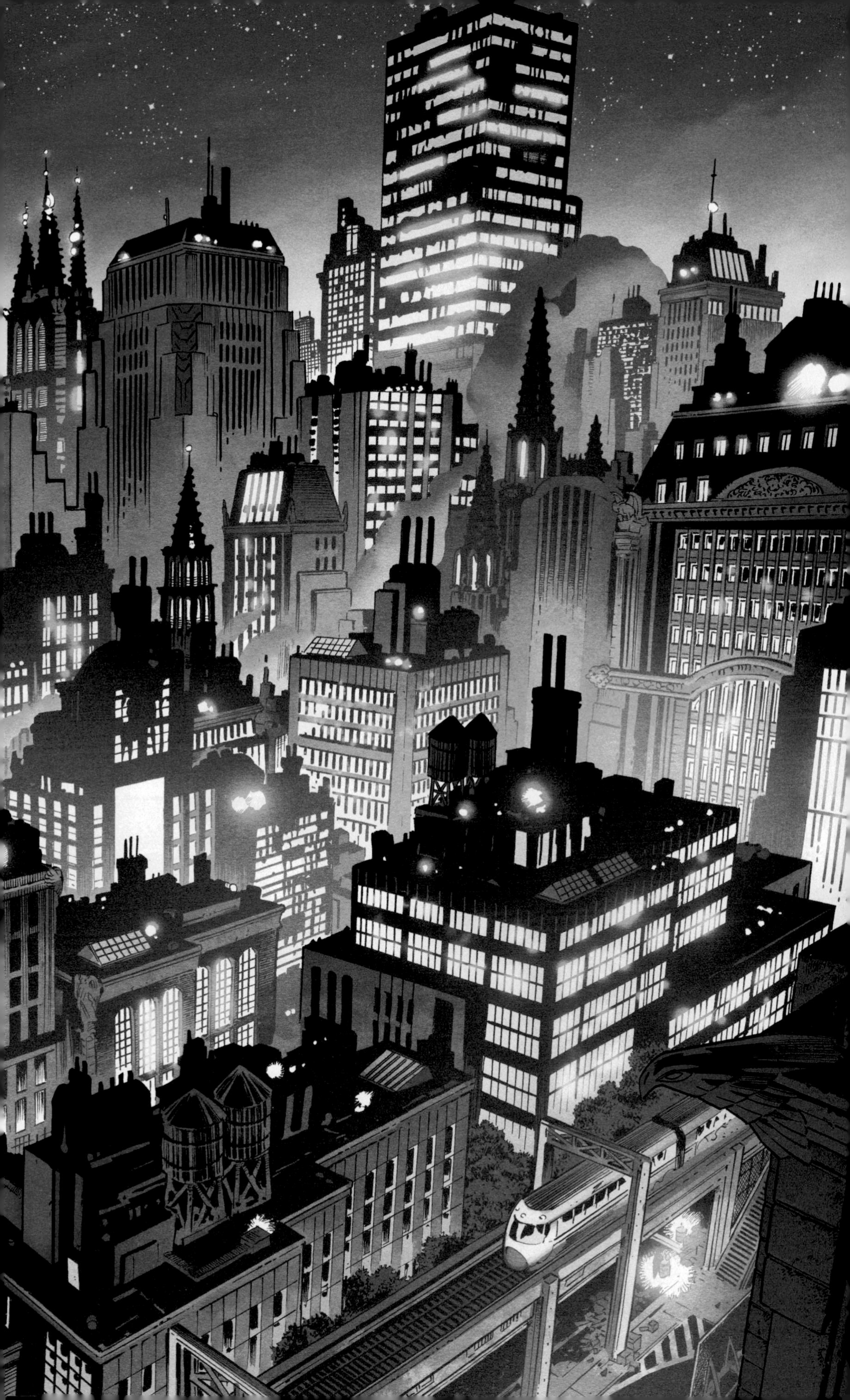

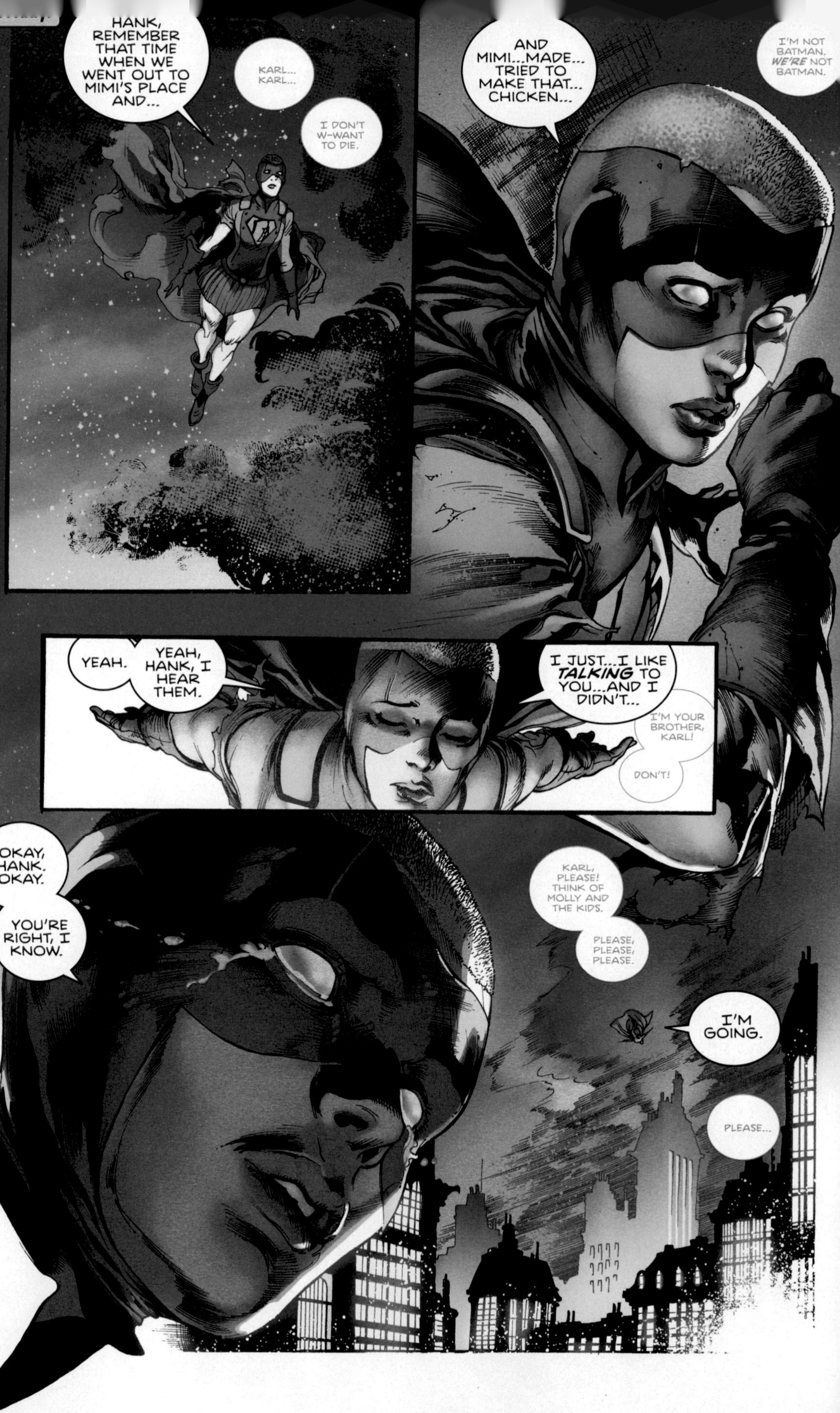
HANK, REMEMBER THAT TIME WHEN WE WENT OUT TO MIMI'S PLACE AND...
KARL... KARL...
I DON'T W-WANT TO DIE.
AND MIMI...MADE... TRIED TO MAKE THAT... CHICKEN...
I'M NOT BATMAN. WE'RE NOT BATMAN.
YEAH.
YEAH, HANK, I HEAR THEM.
I JUST...I LIKE TALKING TO YOU...AND I DIDN'T...
I'M YOUR BROTHER, KARL!
DON'T!
OKAY, HANK. OKAY.
YOU'RE RIGHT, I KNOW.
KARL, PLEASE! THINK OF MOLLY AND THE KIDS.
PLEASE, PLEASE, PLEASE.
I'M GOING.
PLEASE...

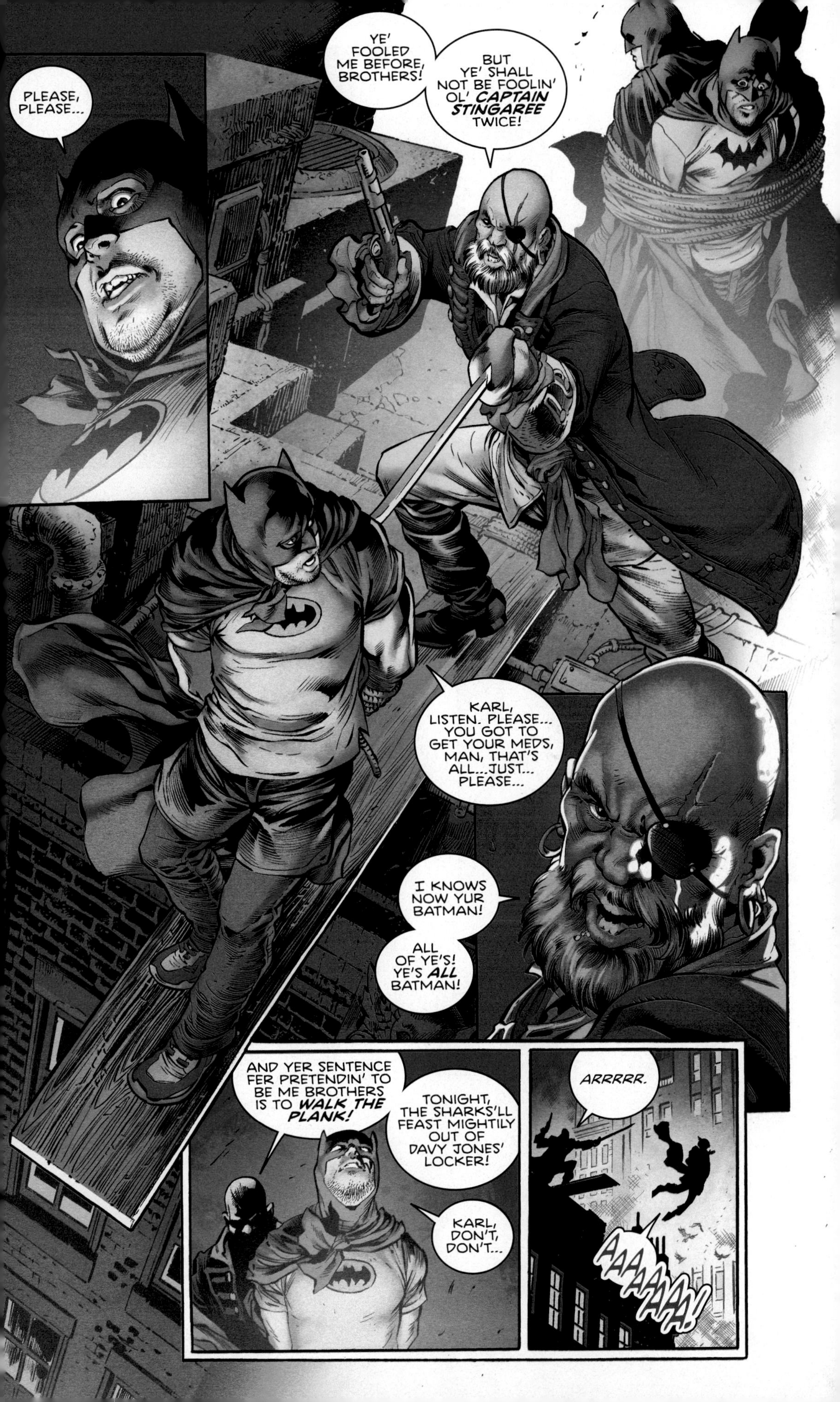
PLEASE, PLEASE...
YE' FOOLED ME BEFORE, BROTHERS!
BUT YE' SHALL NOT BE FOOLIN' OL' CAPTAIN STINGAREE TWICE!
KARL, LISTEN. PLEASE... YOU GOT TO GET YOUR MEDS, MAN, THAT'S ALL...JUST... PLEASE...
I KNOWS NOW YUR BATMAN!
ALL OF YE'S! YE'S ALL BATMAN!
AND YER SENTENCE FER PRETENDIN' TO BE ME BROTHERS IS TO WALK THE PLANK!
TONIGHT, THE SHARKS'LL FEAST MIGHTILY OUT OF DAVY JONES' LOCKER!
KARL, DON'T, DON'T...
ARRRRR.
AAAAAAAA!

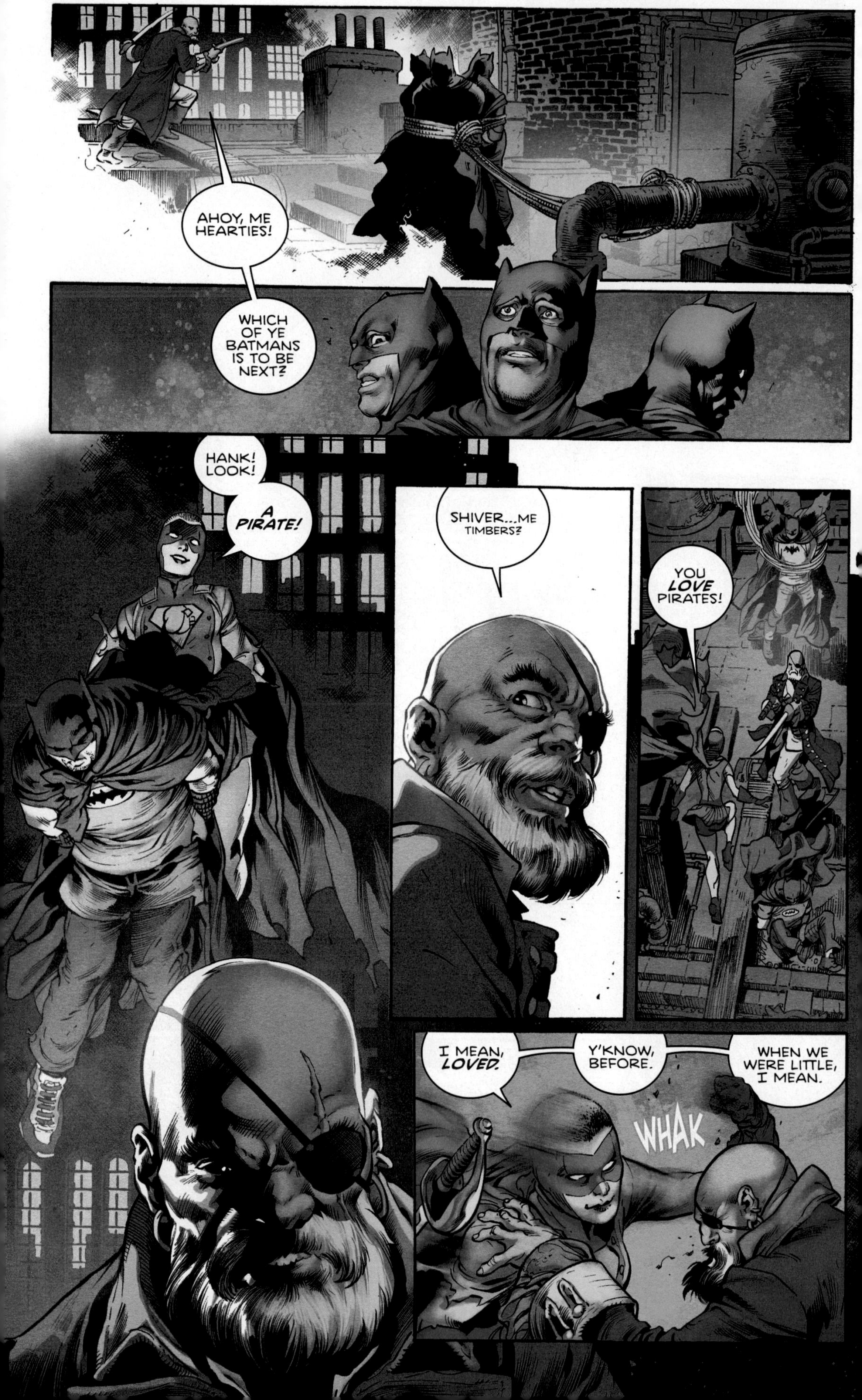

AHOY, ME HEARTIES!
WHICH OF YE BATMANS IS TO BE NEXT?
HANK! LOOK!
A PIRATE!
SHIVER...ME TIMBERS?
YOU LOVE PIRATES!
I MEAN, LOVED.
Y'KNOW, BEFORE.
WHEN WE WERE LITTLE, I MEAN.
WHAK

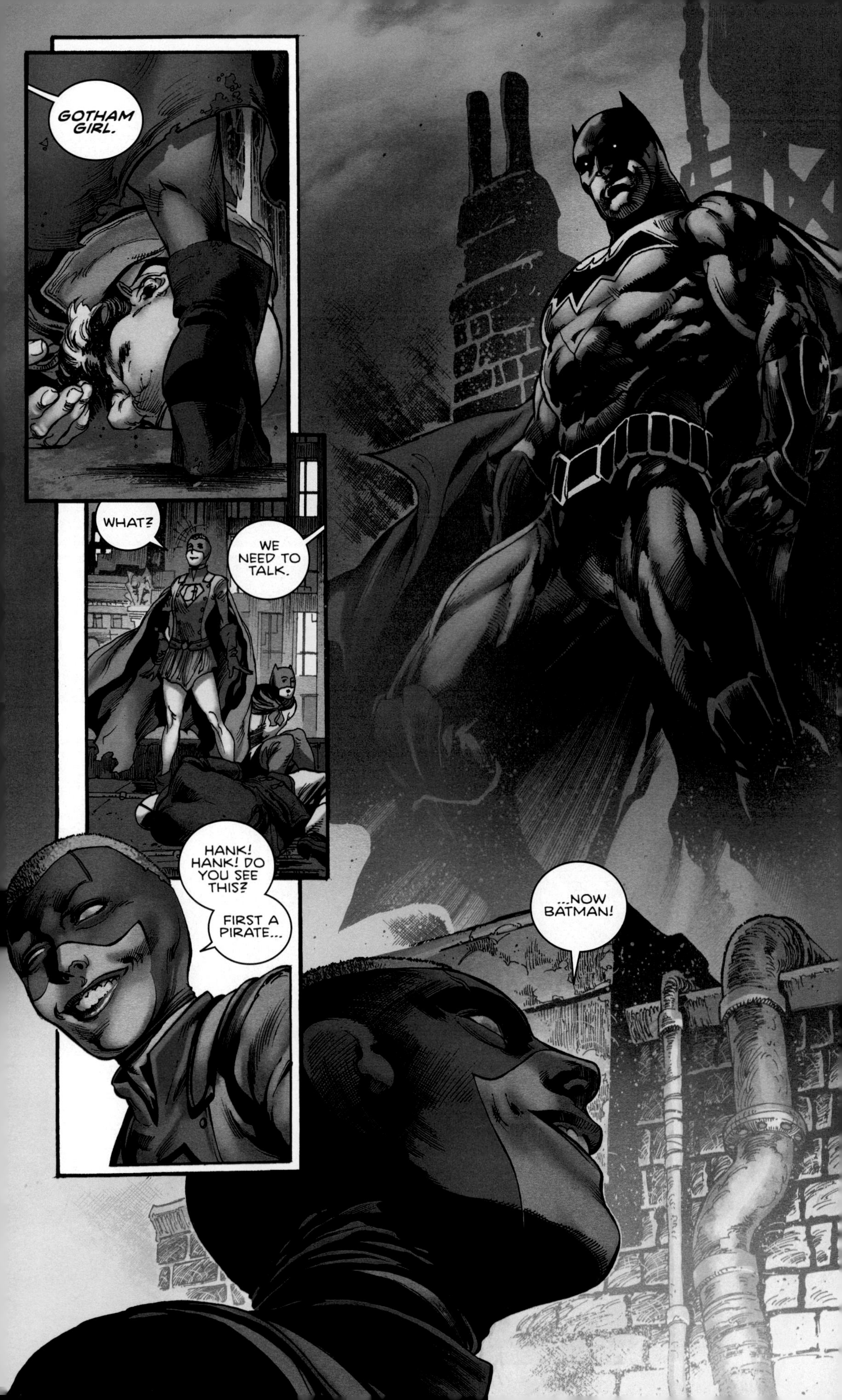
GOTHAM GIRL.
WHAT?
WE NEED TO TALK.
HANK! HANK! DO YOU SEE THIS?
FIRST A PIRATE...
...NOW BATMAN!

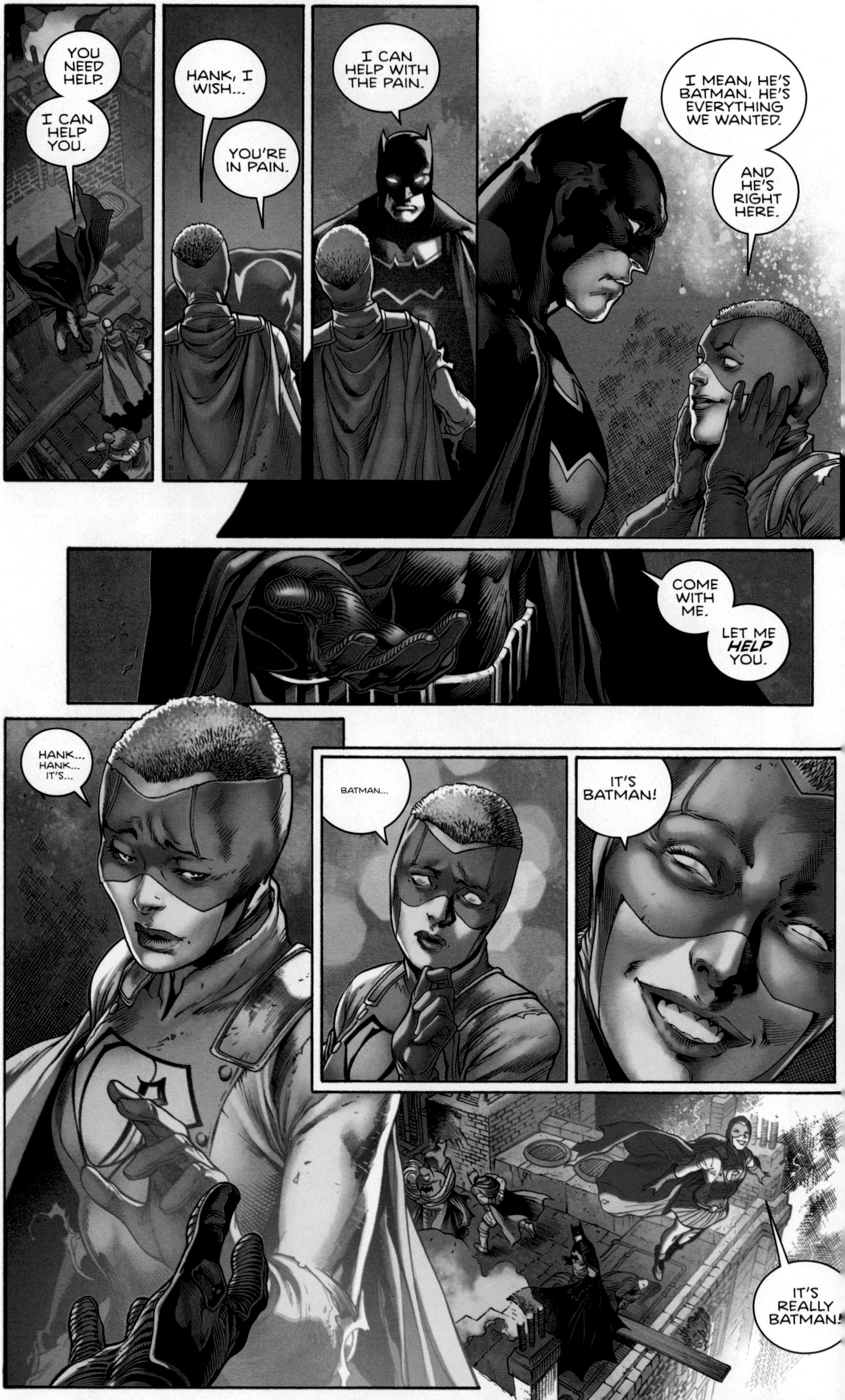
YOU NEED HELP.
I CAN HELP YOU.
HANK, I WISH...
YOU'RE IN PAIN.
I CAN HELP WITH THE PAIN.
I MEAN, HE'S BATMAN. HE'S EVERYTHING WE WANTED.
AND HE'S RIGHT HERE.
COME WITH ME.
LET ME HELP YOU.
HANK... HANK... IT'S...
BATMAN...
IT'S BATMAN!
IT'S REALLY BATMAN!

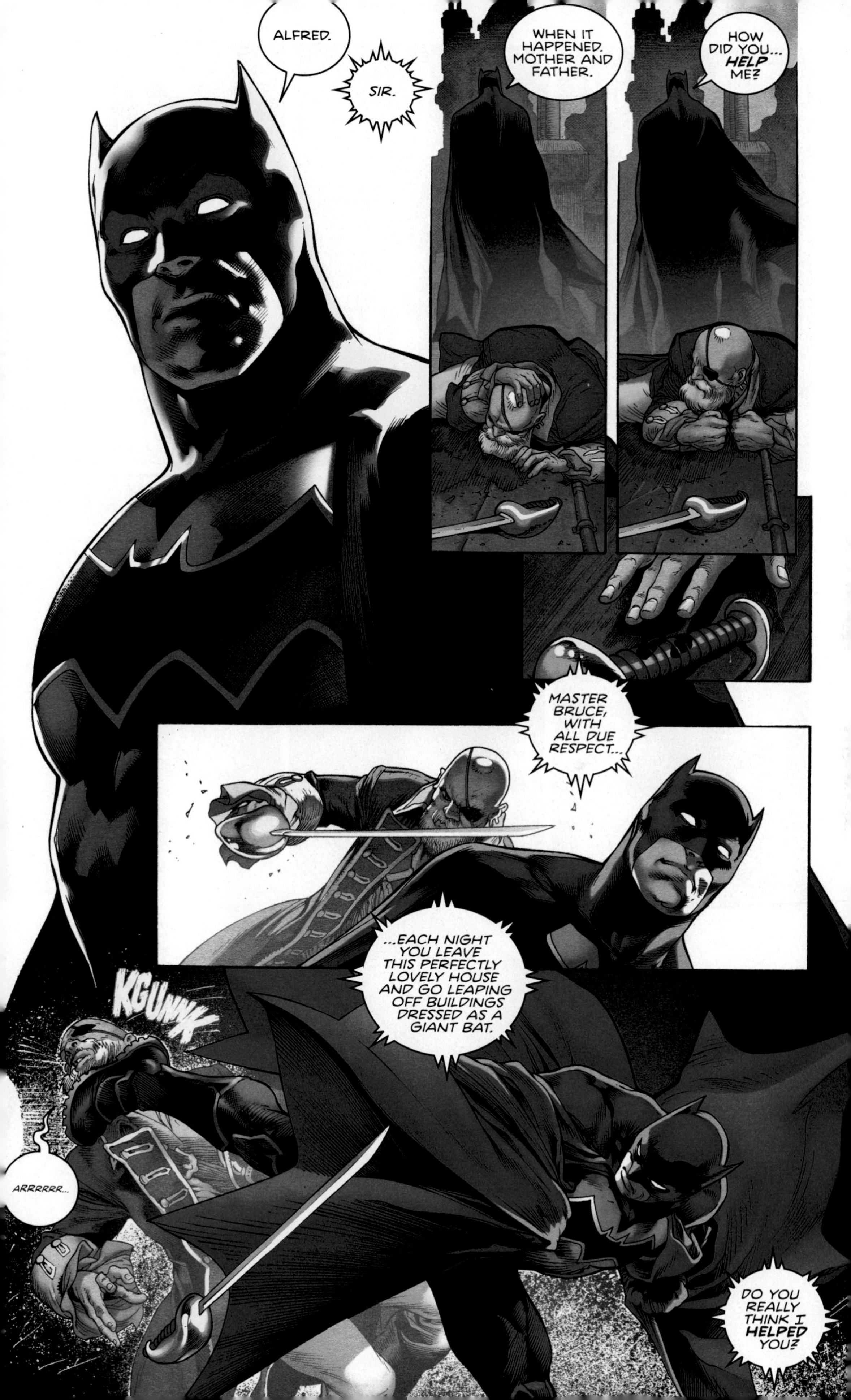
ALFRED.
SIR.
WHEN IT HAPPENED. MOTHER AND FATHER.
HOW DID YOU... HELP ME?
MASTER BRUCE, WITH ALL DUE RESPECT...
...EACH NIGHT YOU LEAVE THIS PERFECTLY LOVELY HOUSE AND GO LEAPING OFF BUILDINGS DRESSED AS A GIANT BAT.
KGUNNK
ARRRRRR...
DO YOU REALLY THINK I HELPED YOU?

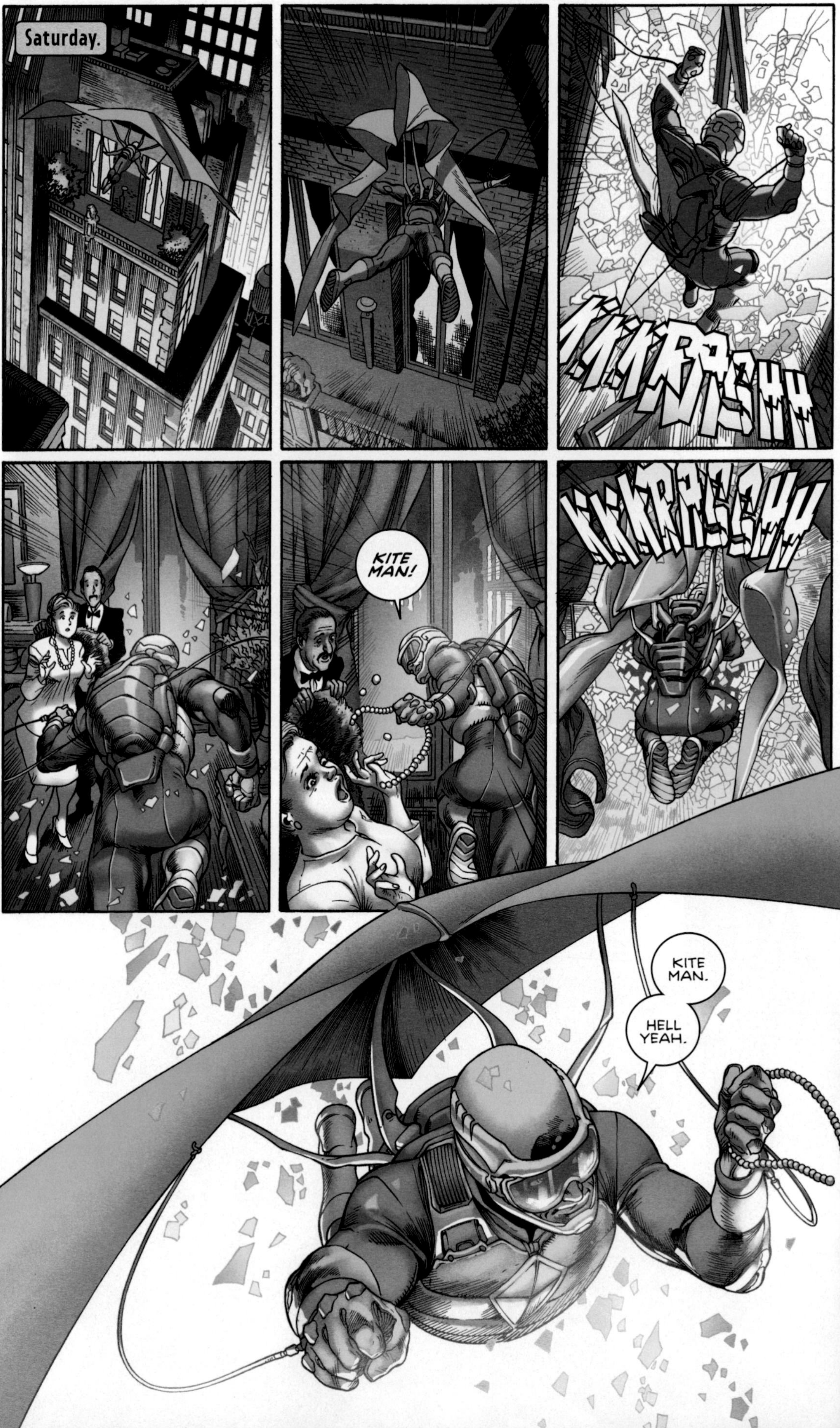
Saturday.
KITE MAN!
KITE MAN.
HELL YEAH.

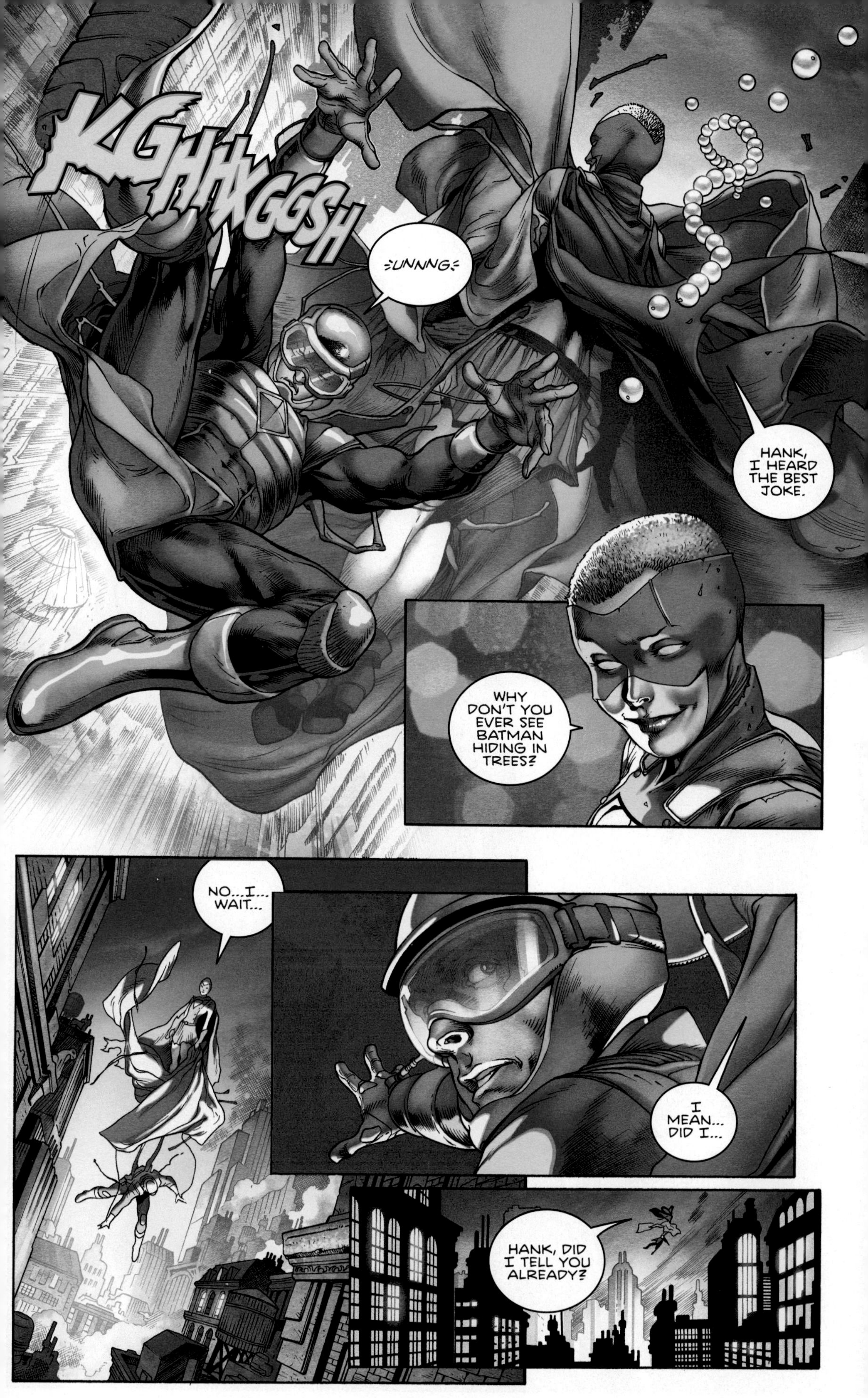
KGHHKGGSH
UNNNG
HANK, I HEARD THE BEST JOKE.
WHY DON'T YOU EVER SEE BATMAN HIDING IN TREES?
NO... I... WAIT...
I MEAN... DID I...
HANK, DID I TELL YOU ALREADY?

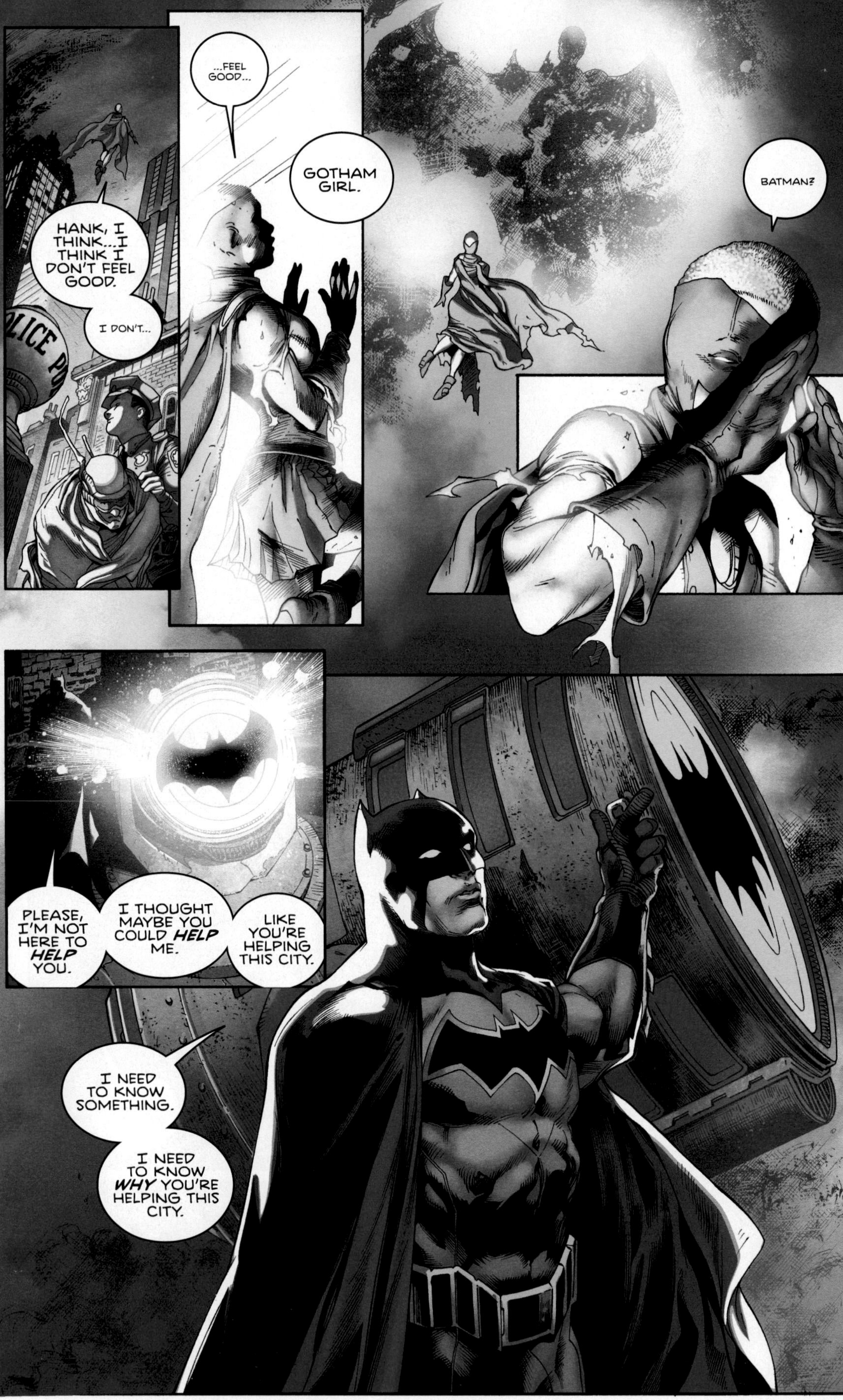
HANK, I THINK...I THINK I DON'T FEEL GOOD.
I DON'T...
...FEEL GOOD...
GOTHAM GIRL.
BATMAN?
PLEASE, I'M NOT HERE TO HELP YOU.
I THOUGHT MAYBE YOU COULD HELP ME.
LIKE YOU'RE HELPING THIS CITY.
I NEED TO KNOW SOMETHING.
I NEED TO KNOW WHY YOU'RE HELPING THIS CITY.

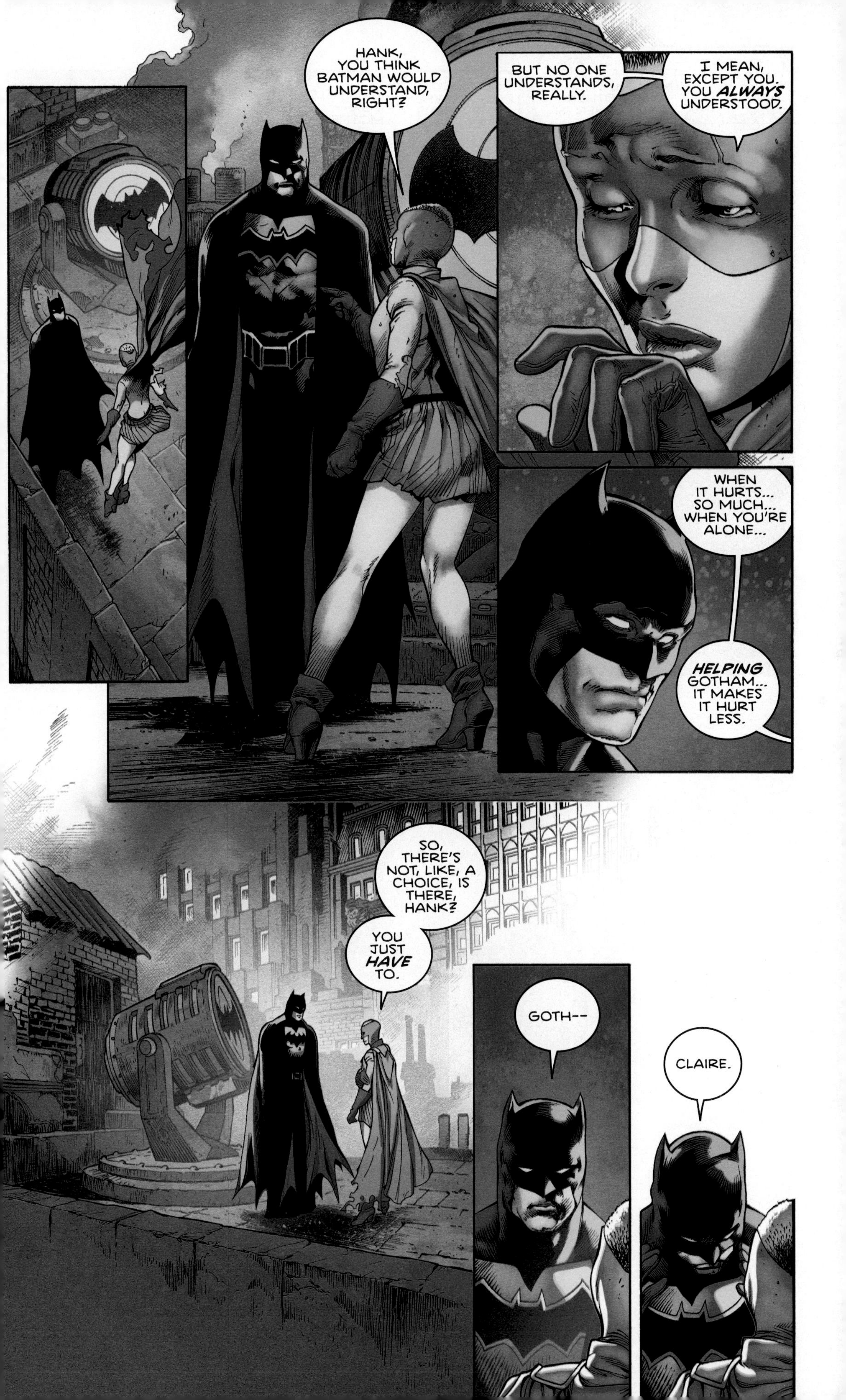
HANK, YOU THINK BATMAN WOULD UNDERSTAND, RIGHT?
BUT NO ONE UNDERSTANDS, REALLY.
I MEAN, EXCEPT YOU. YOU *ALWAYS* UNDERSTOOD.
WHEN IT HURTS... SO MUCH... WHEN YOU'RE ALONE...
HELPING GOTHAM... IT MAKES IT HURT LESS.
SO, THERE'S NOT, LIKE, A CHOICE, IS THERE, HANK?
YOU JUST *HAVE* TO.
GOTH--
CLAIRE.

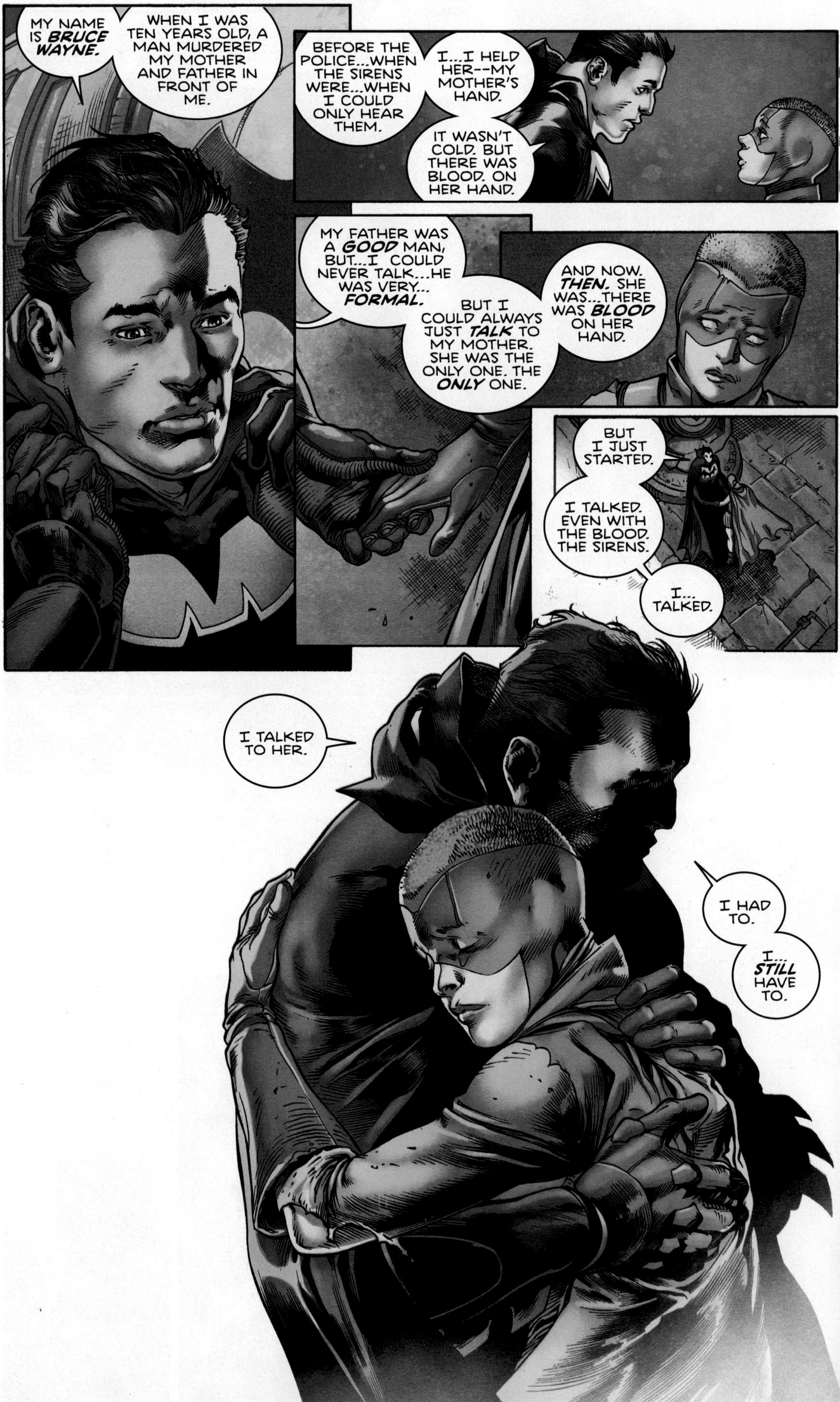

MY NAME IS ***BRUCE WAYNE.***
WHEN I WAS TEN YEARS OLD, A MAN MURDERED MY MOTHER AND FATHER IN FRONT OF ME.
BEFORE THE POLICE...WHEN THE SIRENS WERE...WHEN I COULD ONLY HEAR THEM.
I...I HELD HER--MY MOTHER'S HAND.
IT WASN'T COLD. BUT THERE WAS BLOOD. ON HER HAND.
MY FATHER WAS A ***GOOD*** MAN, BUT...I COULD NEVER TALK...HE WAS VERY... ***FORMAL.***
BUT I COULD ALWAYS JUST ***TALK*** TO MY MOTHER. SHE WAS THE ONLY ONE. THE ***ONLY*** ONE.
AND NOW. ***THEN.*** SHE WAS...THERE WAS ***BLOOD*** ON HER HAND.
BUT I JUST STARTED.
I TALKED. EVEN WITH THE BLOOD. THE SIRENS.
I... TALKED.
I TALKED TO HER.
I HAD TO.
I... ***STILL*** HAVE TO.

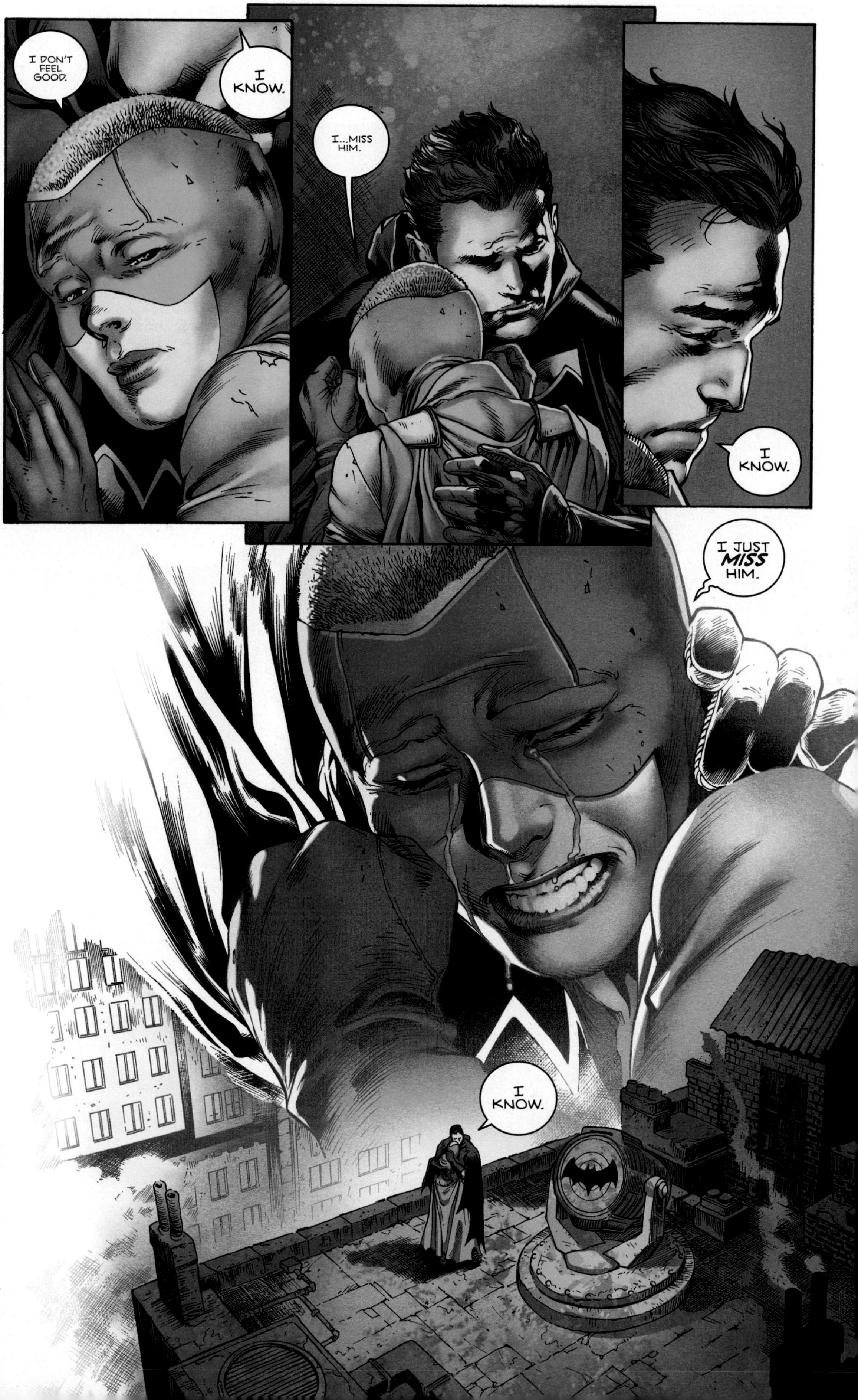
I DON'T FEEL GOOD.
I KNOW.
I...MISS HIM.
I KNOW.
I JUST MISS HIM.
I KNOW.

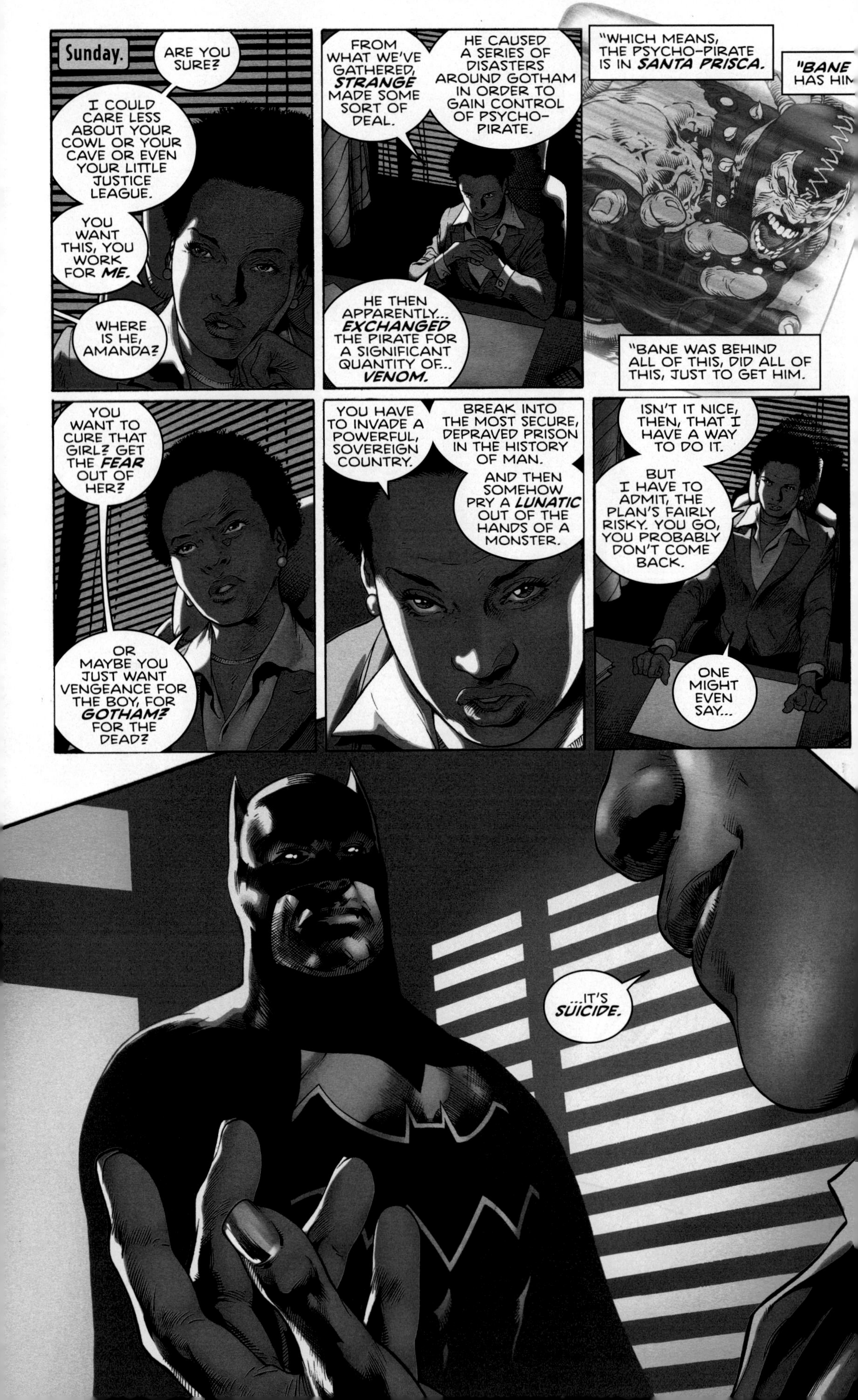
Sunday.
ARE YOU SURE?
I COULD CARE LESS ABOUT YOUR COWL OR YOUR CAVE OR EVEN YOUR LITTLE JUSTICE LEAGUE.
YOU WANT THIS, YOU WORK FOR *ME.*
WHERE IS HE, AMANDA?
FROM WHAT WE'VE GATHERED, *STRANGE* MADE SOME SORT OF DEAL.
HE CAUSED A SERIES OF DISASTERS AROUND GOTHAM IN ORDER TO GAIN CONTROL OF PSYCHO-PIRATE.
HE THEN APPARENTLY... *EXCHANGED* THE PIRATE FOR A SIGNIFICANT QUANTITY OF... *VENOM.*
"WHICH MEANS, THE PSYCHO-PIRATE IS IN *SANTA PRISCA.*
"*BANE* HAS HIM
"BANE WAS BEHIND ALL OF THIS, DID ALL OF THIS, JUST TO GET HIM.
YOU WANT TO CURE THAT GIRL? GET THE *FEAR* OUT OF HER?
OR MAYBE YOU JUST WANT VENGEANCE FOR THE BOY, FOR *GOTHAM?* FOR THE DEAD?
YOU HAVE TO INVADE A POWERFUL, SOVEREIGN COUNTRY.
BREAK INTO THE MOST SECURE, DEPRAVED PRISON IN THE HISTORY OF MAN.
AND THEN SOMEHOW PRY A *LUNATIC* OUT OF THE HANDS OF A MONSTER.
ISN'T IT NICE, THEN, THAT I HAVE A WAY TO DO IT.
BUT I HAVE TO ADMIT, THE PLAN'S FAIRLY RISKY. YOU GO, YOU PROBABLY DON'T COME BACK.
ONE MIGHT EVEN SAY...
...IT'S *SUICIDE.*

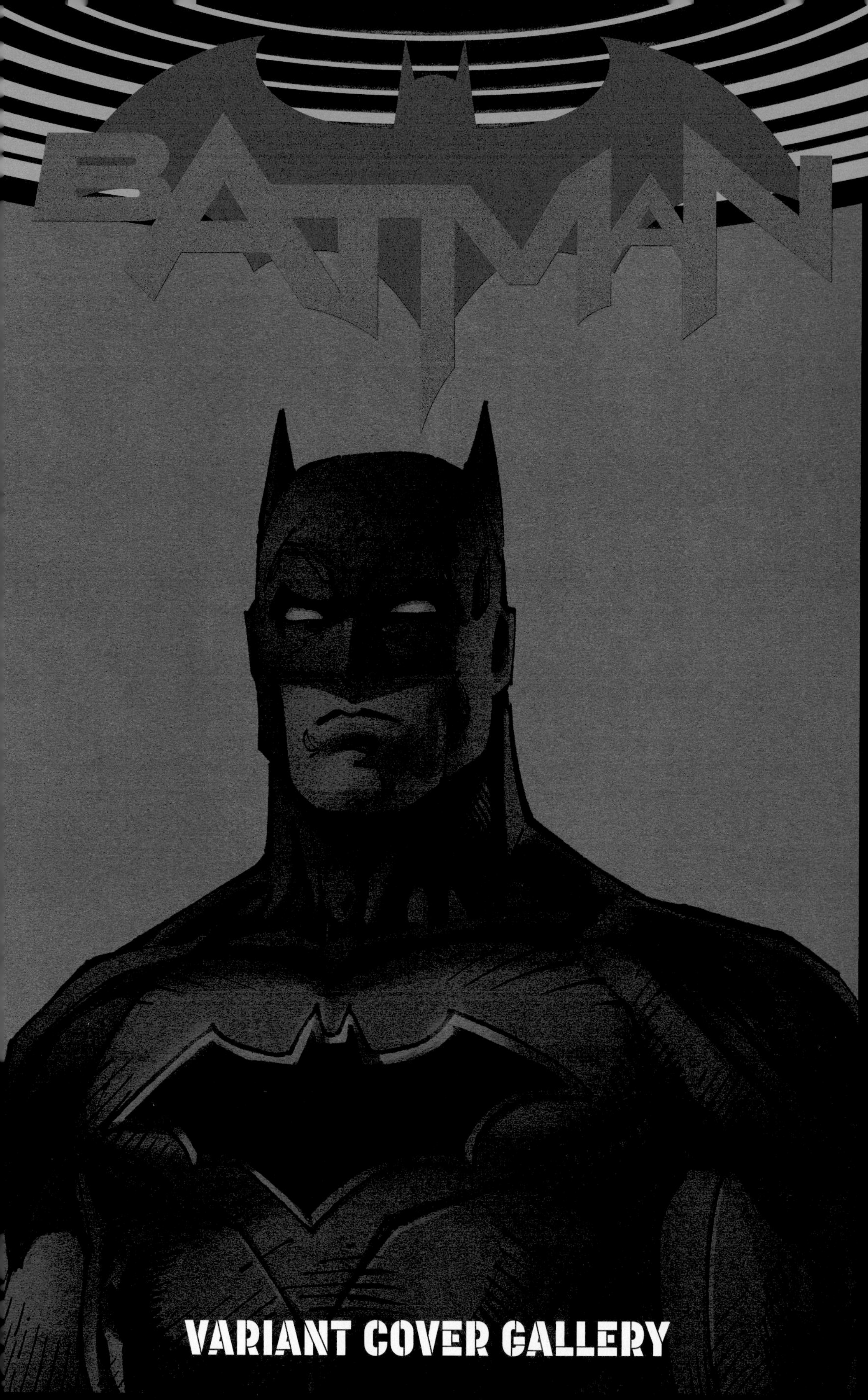
BATMAN

VARIANT COVER GALLERY

BATMAN: REBIRTH #1 variant cover by HOWARD PORTER with HI-FI

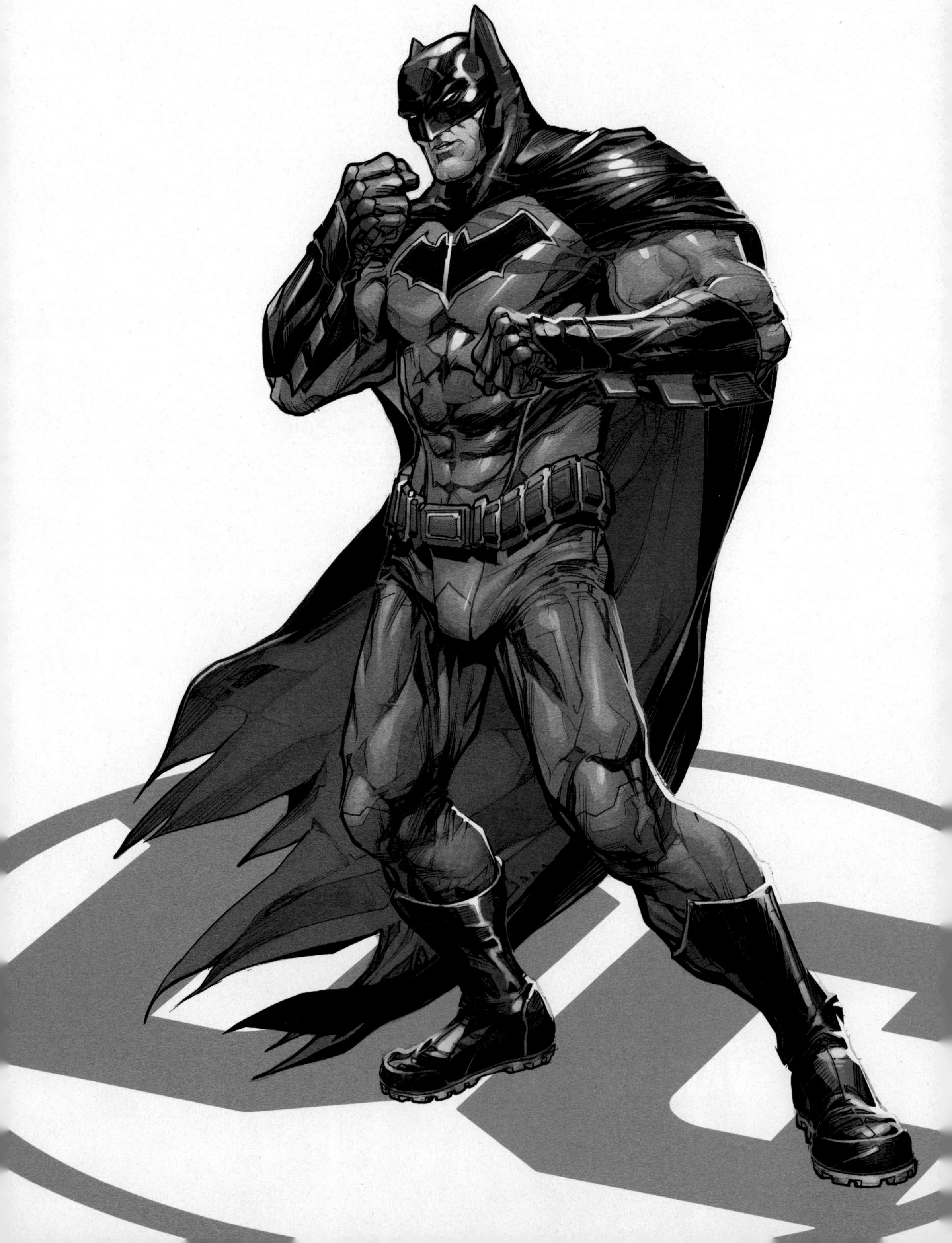

BATMAN #1 variant cover by JIM LEE

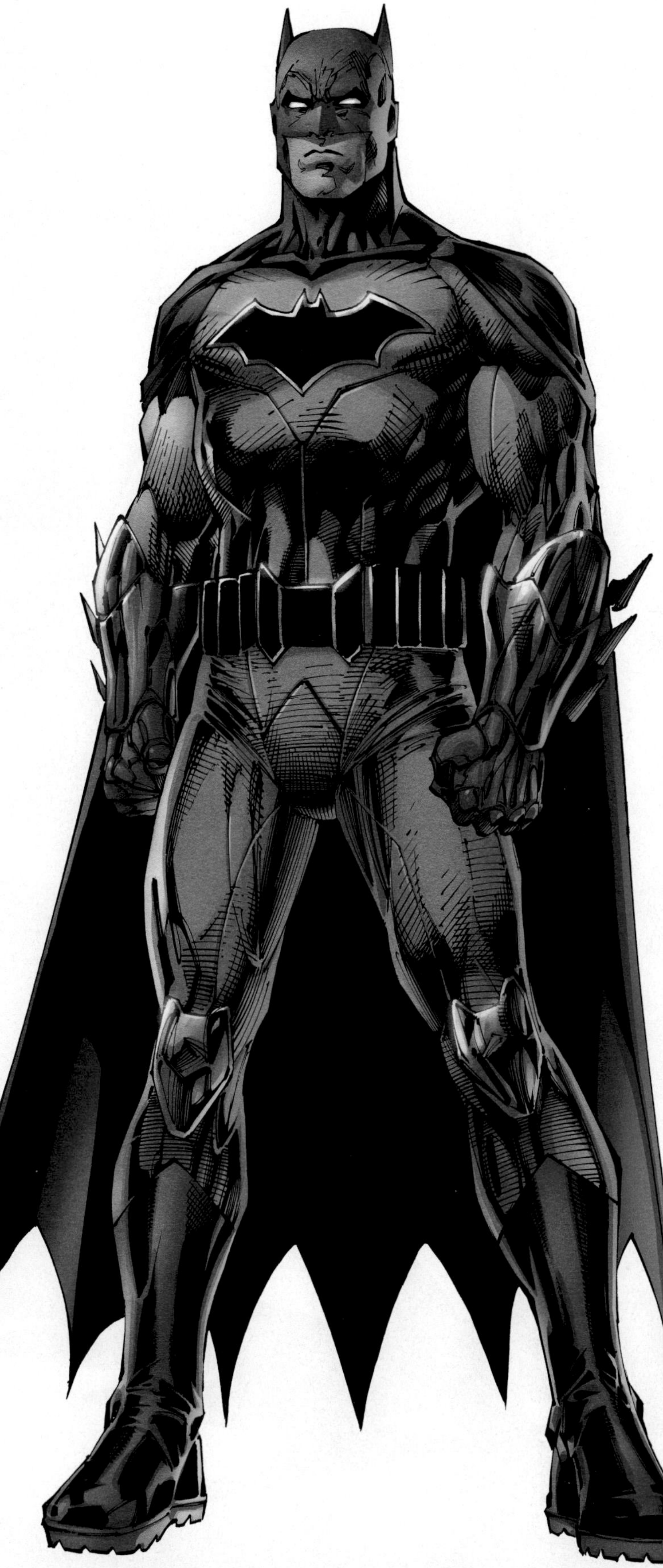

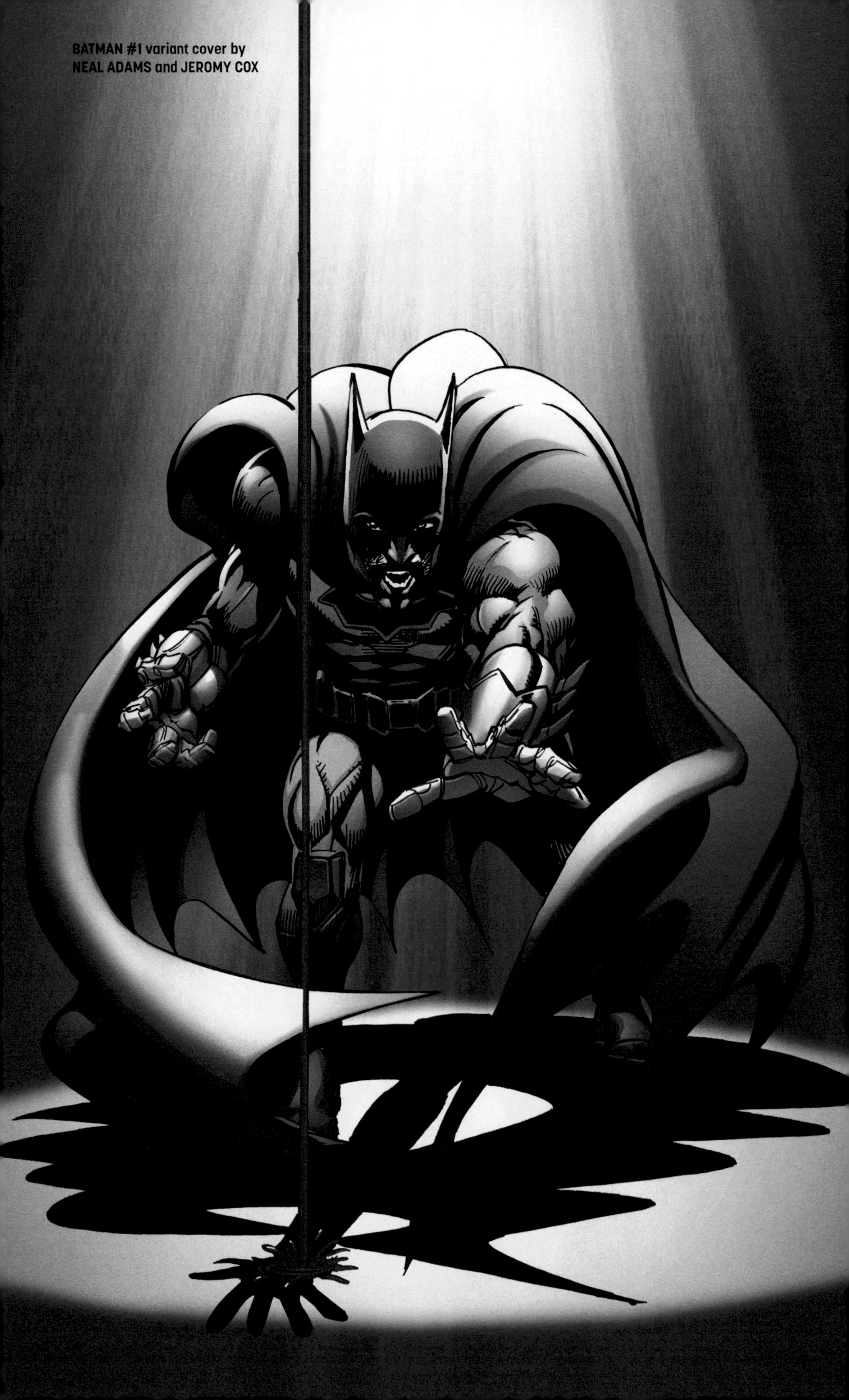

BATMAN #1 variant cover by
NEAL ADAMS and JEROMY COX

BATMAN #1 variant cover by RAFAEL ALBUQUERQUE

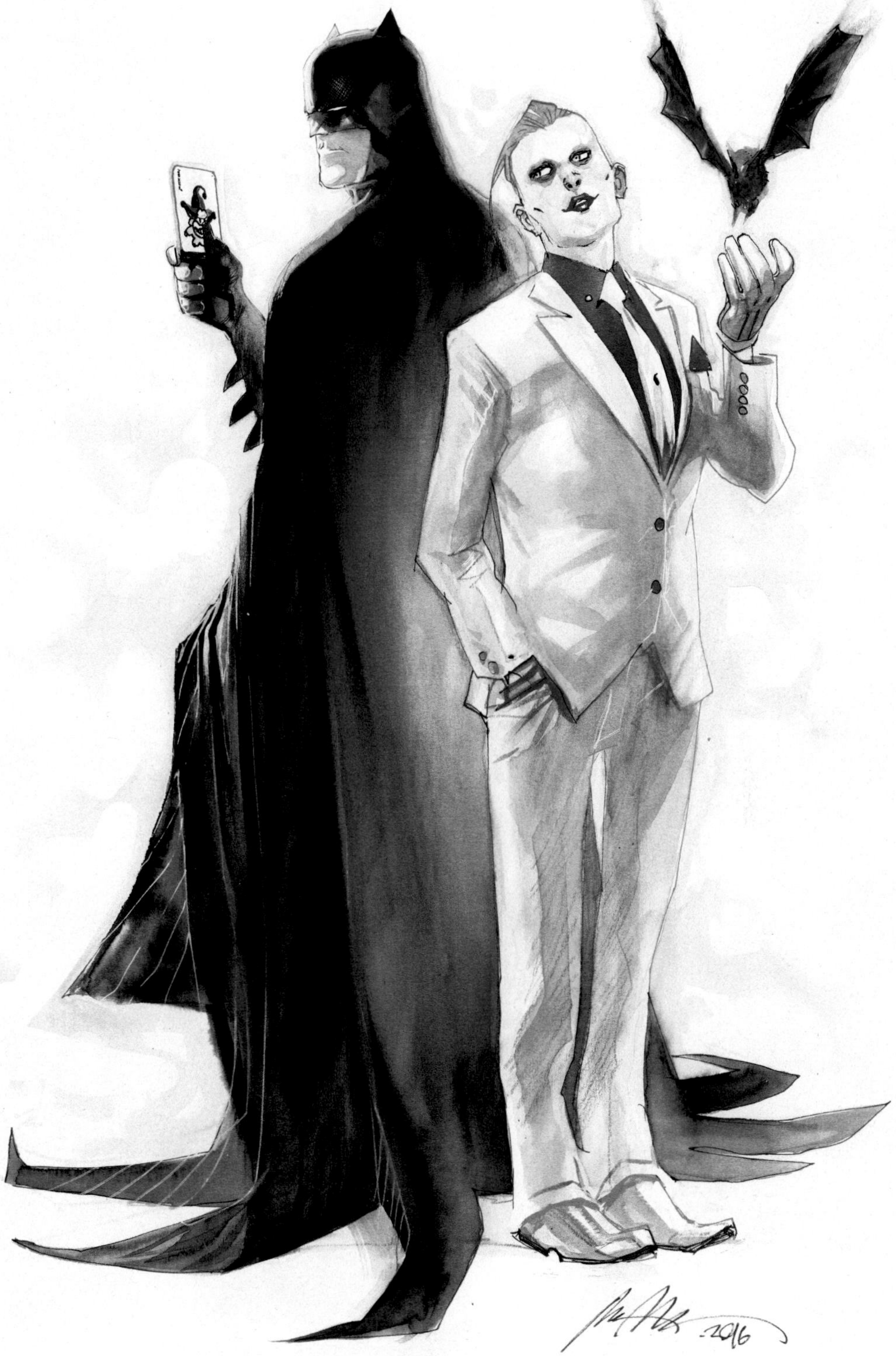
2016

BATMAN #1 variant cover by ED BENES and FCO PLASCENCIA

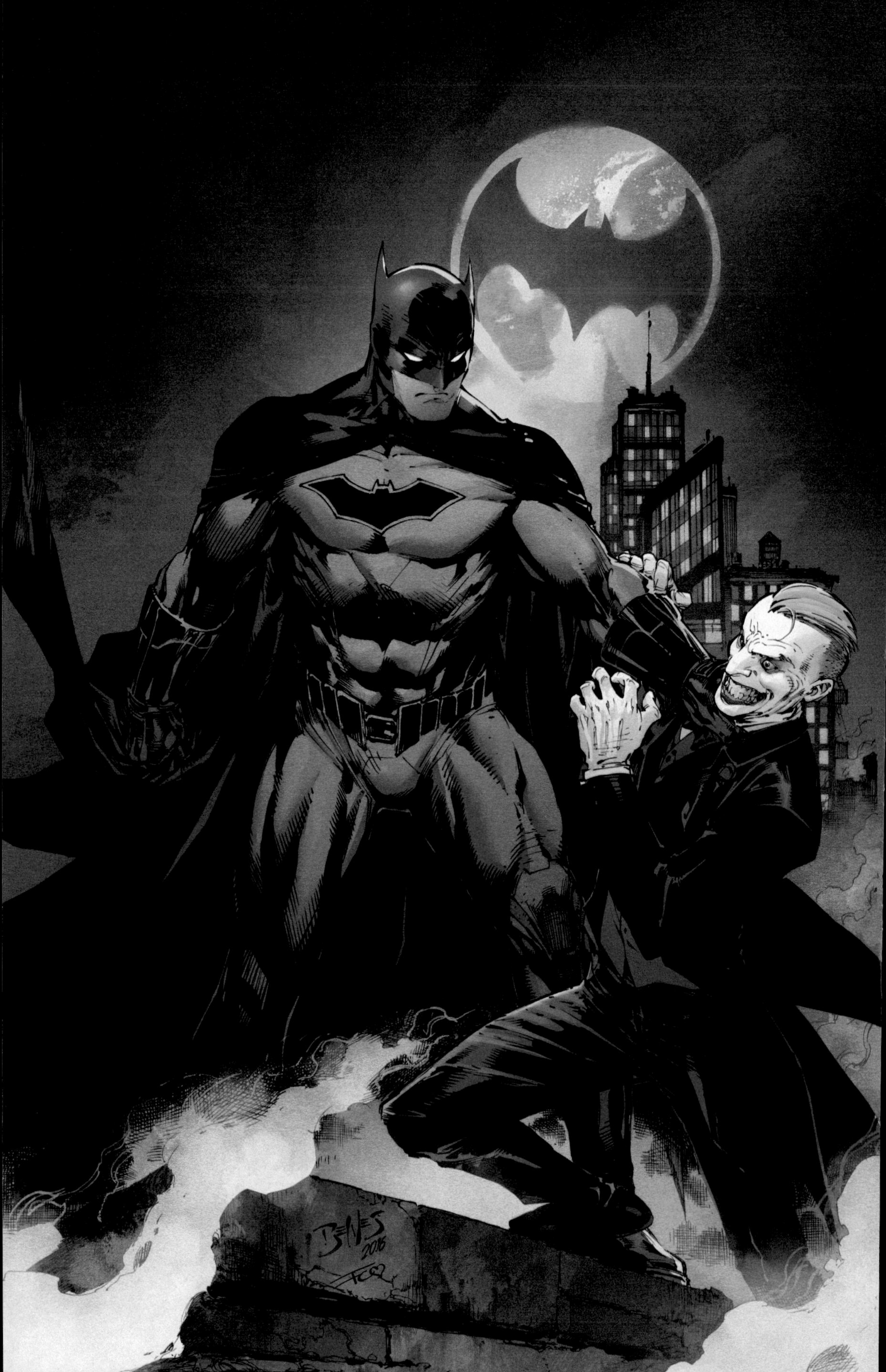

BATMAN #1 variant cover by LEE BERMEJO

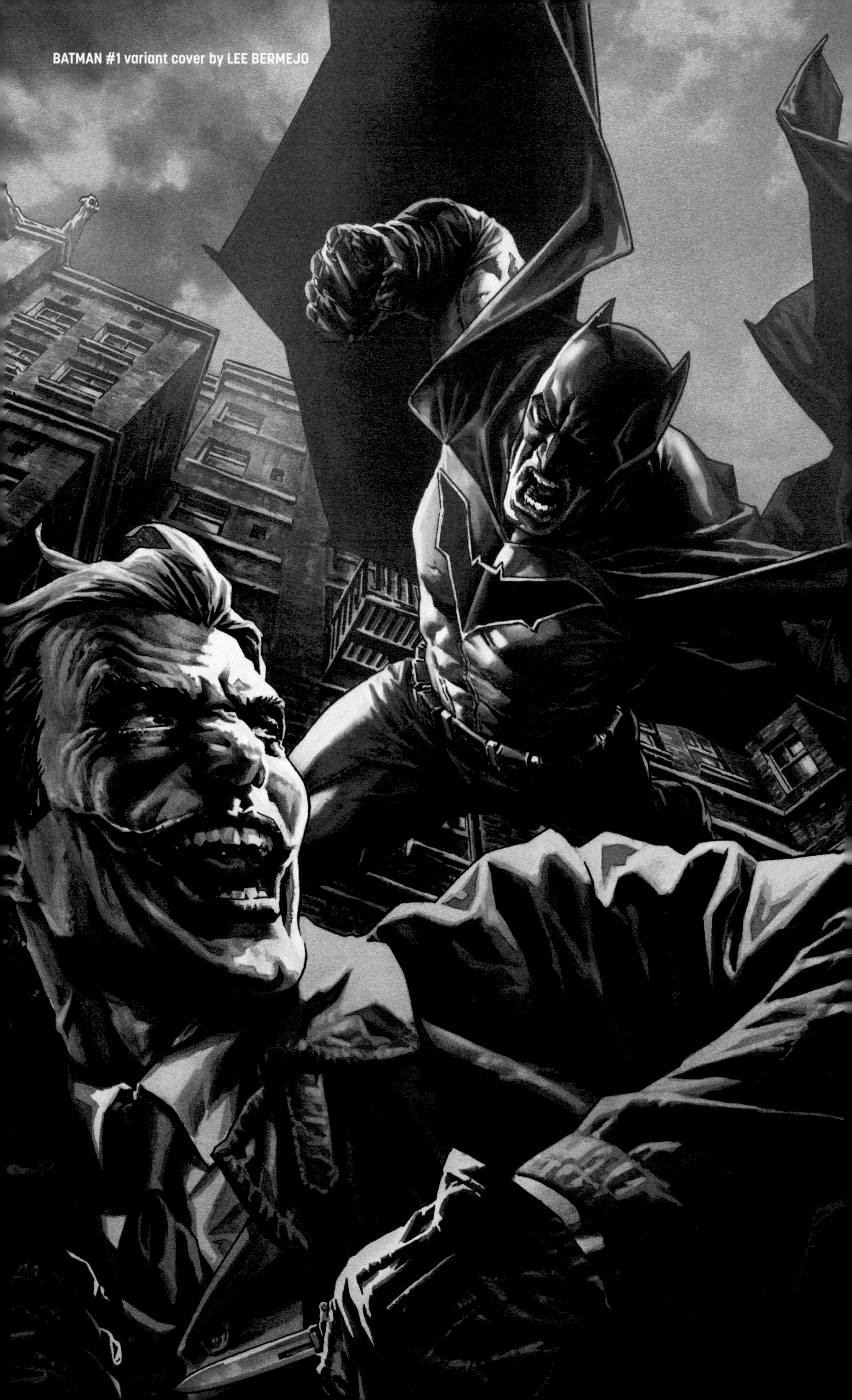

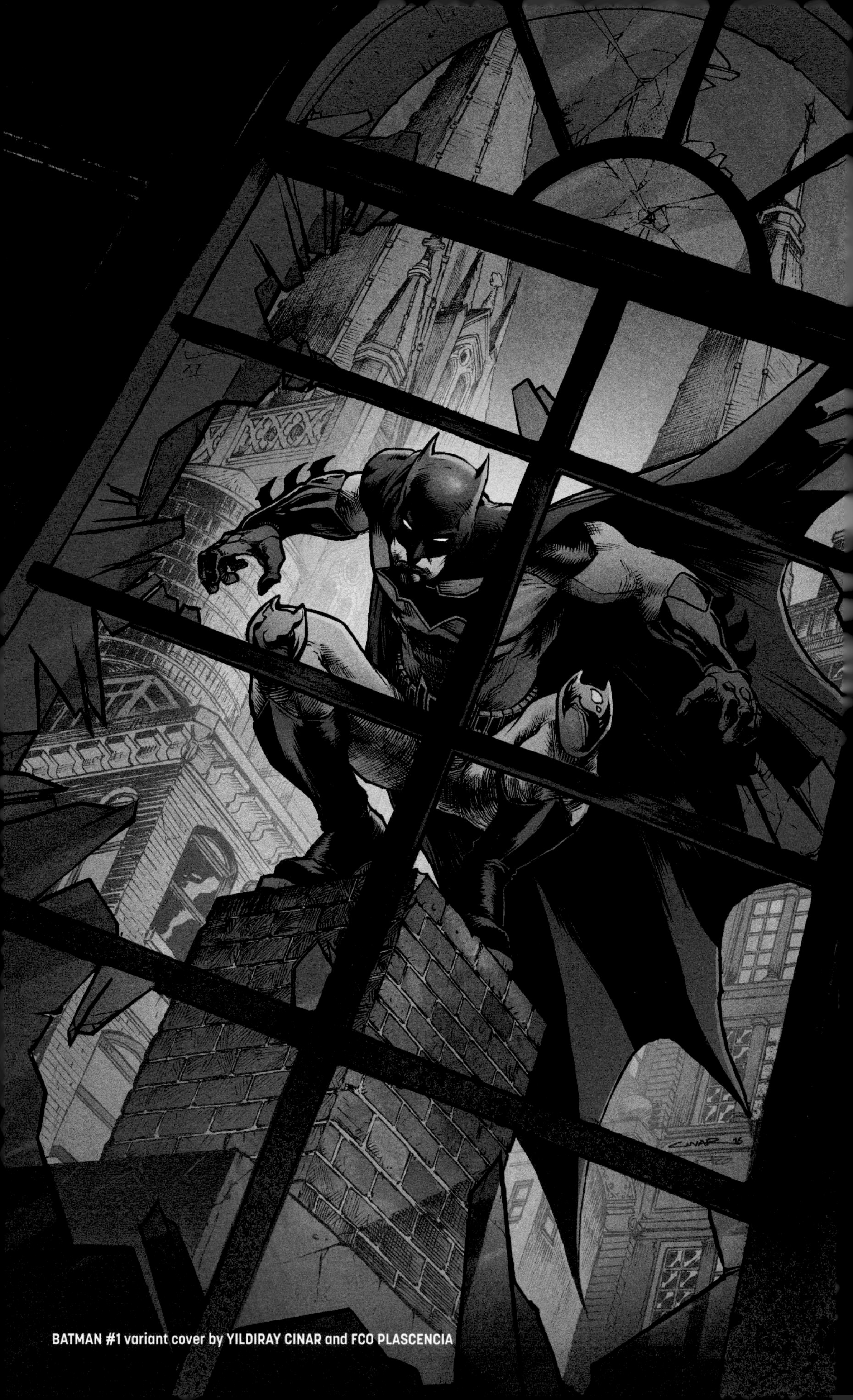

BATMAN #1 variant cover by YILDIRAY CINAR and FCO PLASCENCIA

BATMAN #1 variant cover by TONY S. DANIEL, SANDU FLOREA and TOMEU MOREY

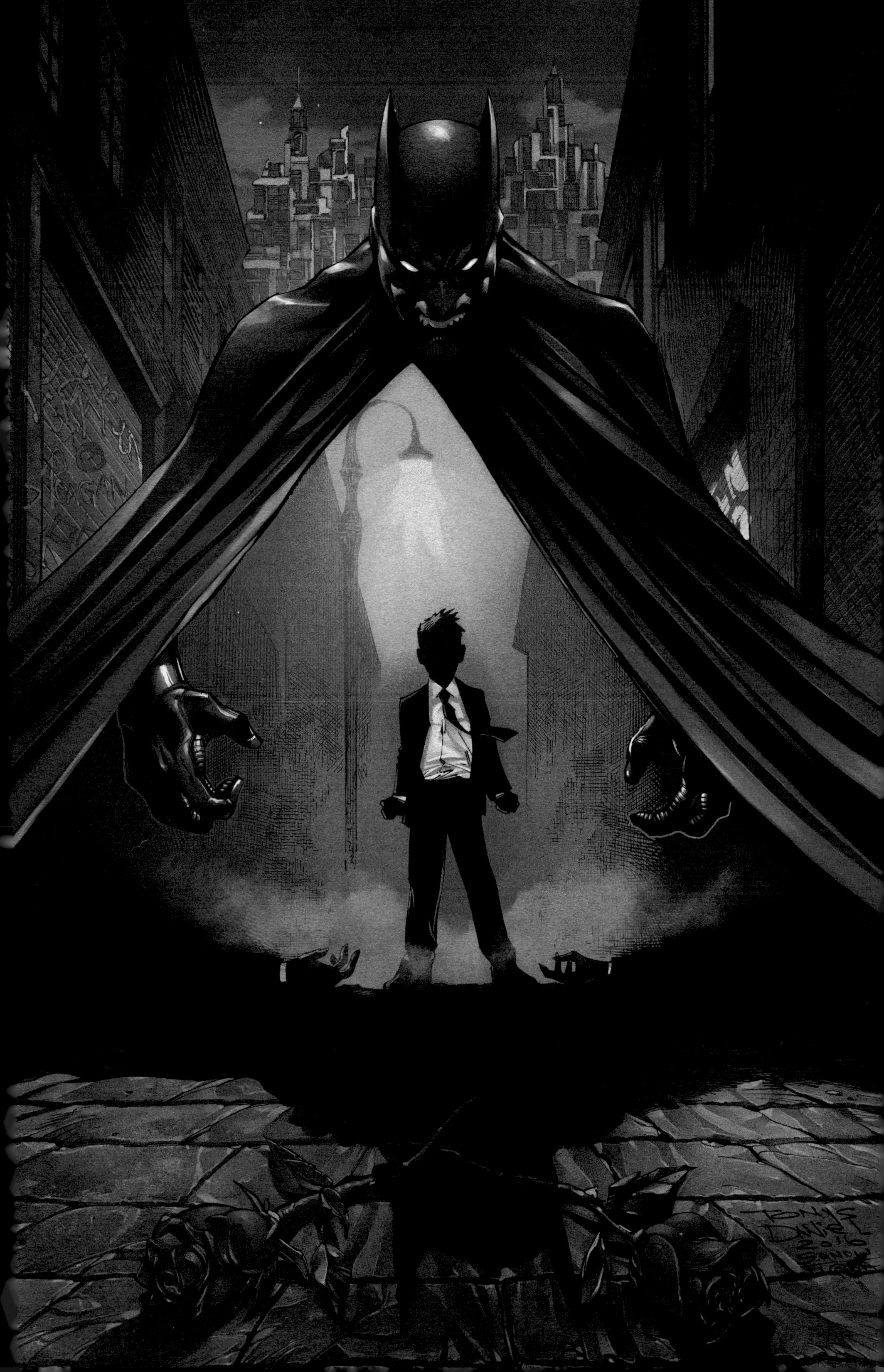

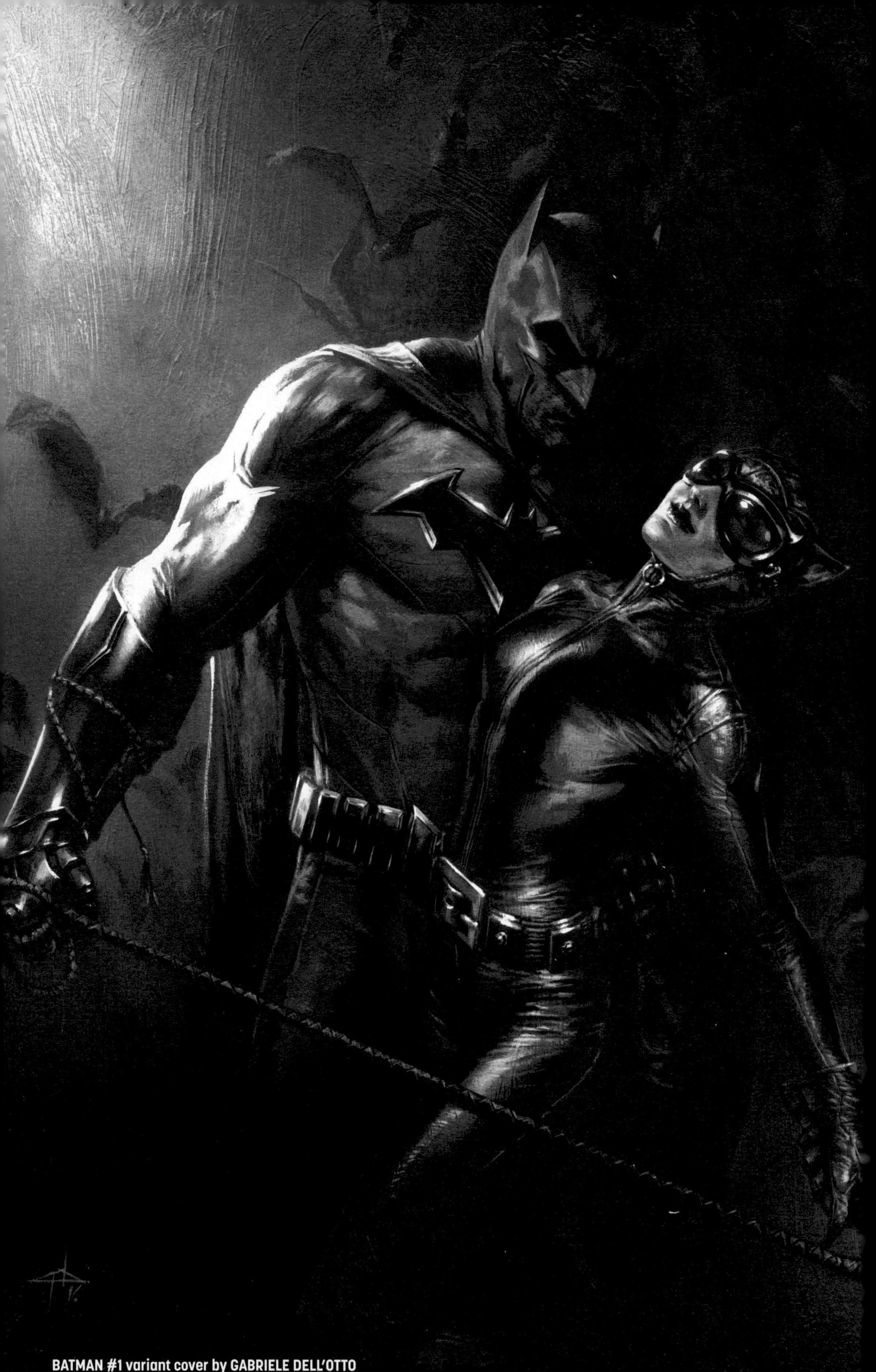

BATMAN #1 variant cover by GABRIELE DELL'OTTO

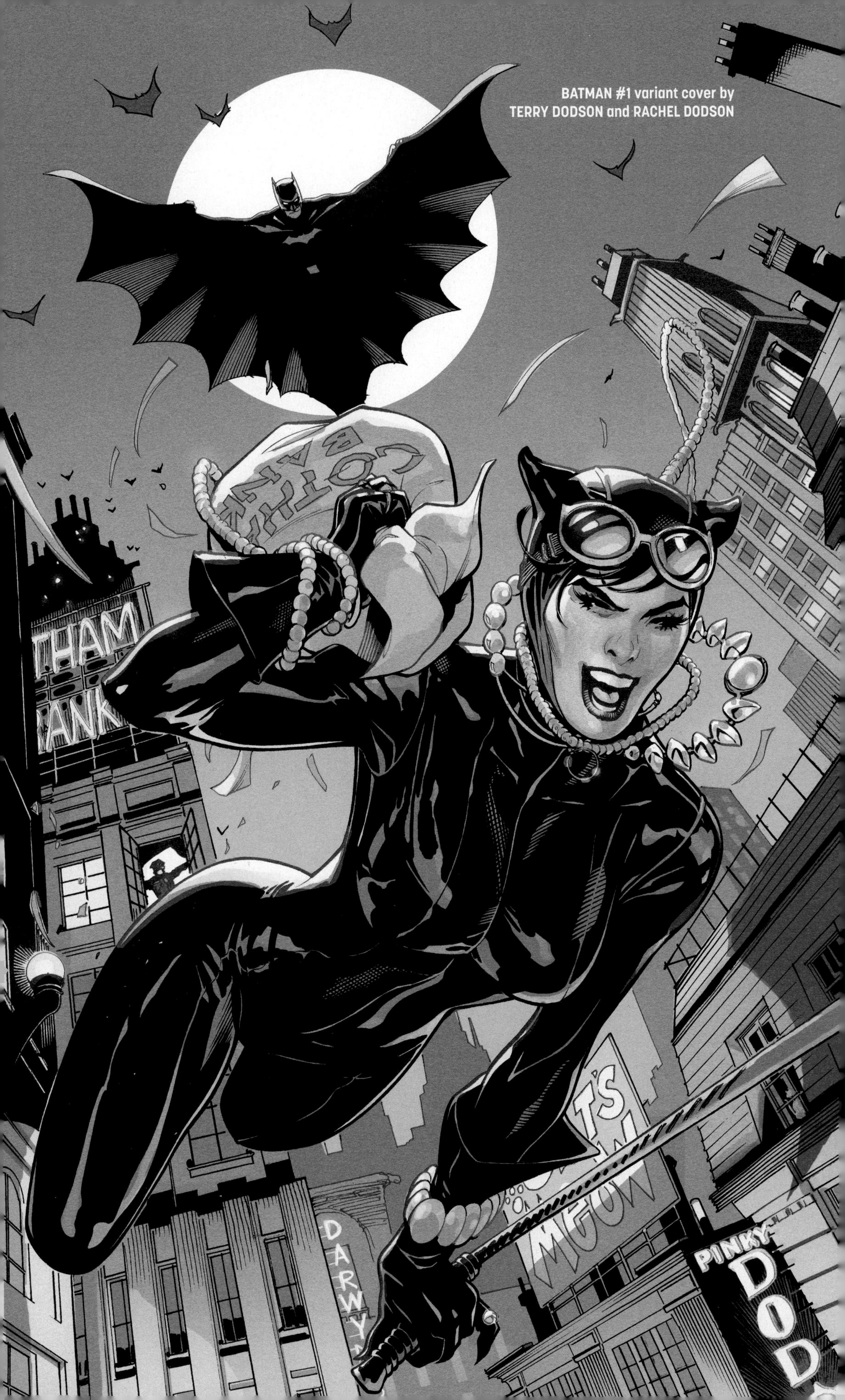
THAM
ANK
DARWY
PINKY
DOD

BATMAN #1 variant cover by
TERRY DODSON and RACHEL DODSON

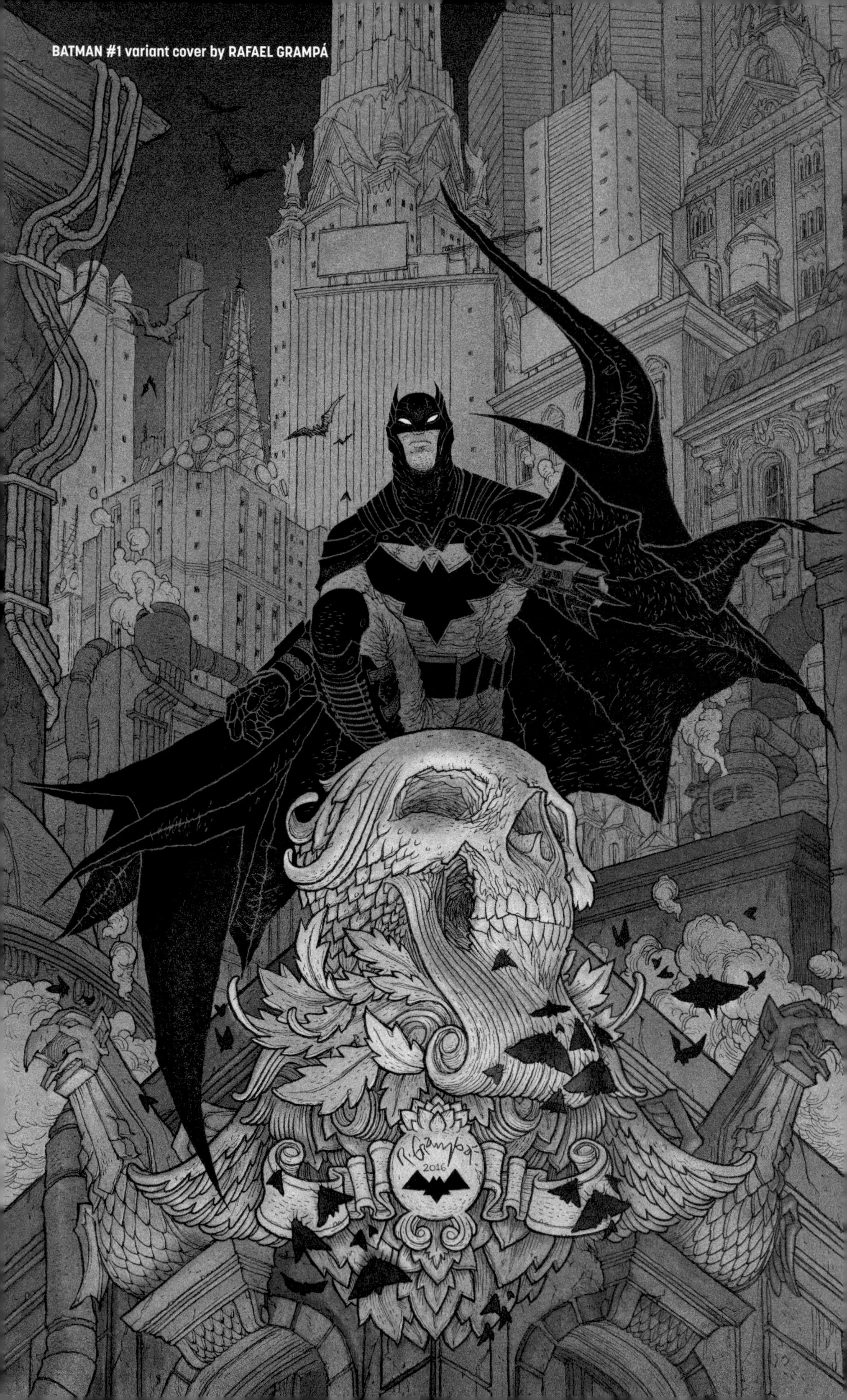
2016

BATMAN #1 variant cover by RAFAEL GRAMPÁ

BATMAN #1 variant cover by TONY HARRIS

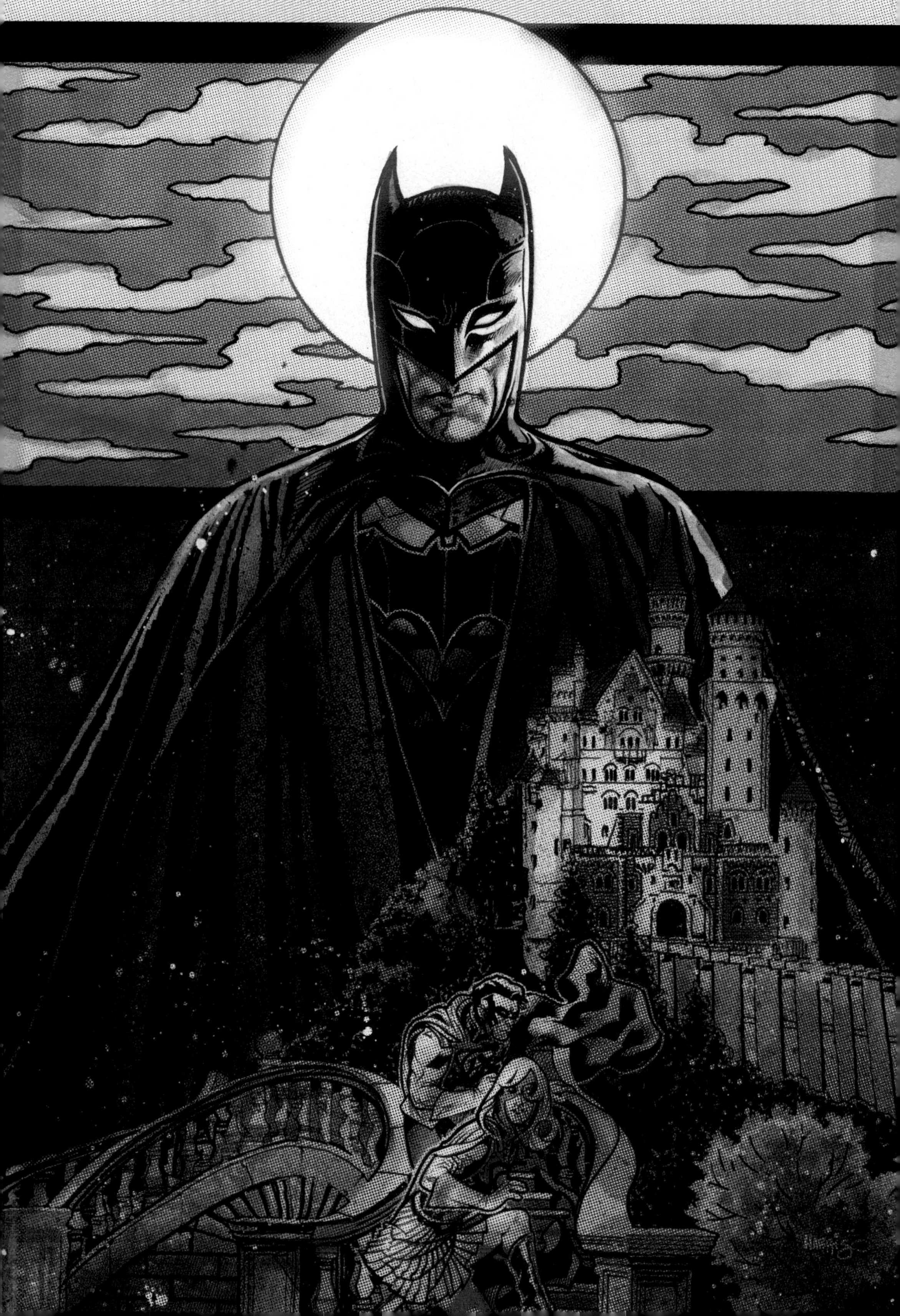

BATMAN #1 variant cover by TYLER KIRKHAM and TOMEU MOREY

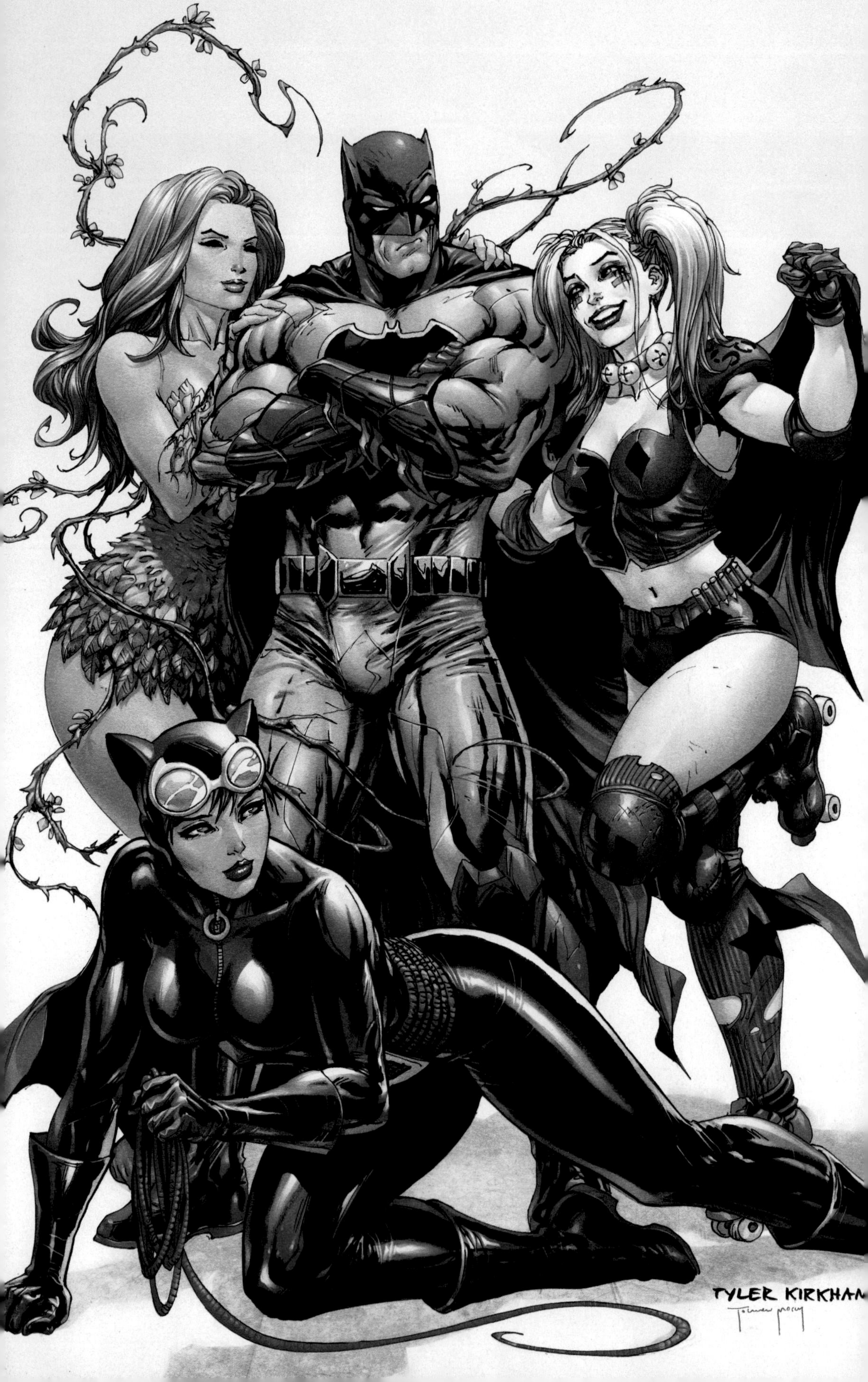
TYLER KIRKHAM

BATMAN #1 variant cover by BARRY KITSON and MORENO DINISIO

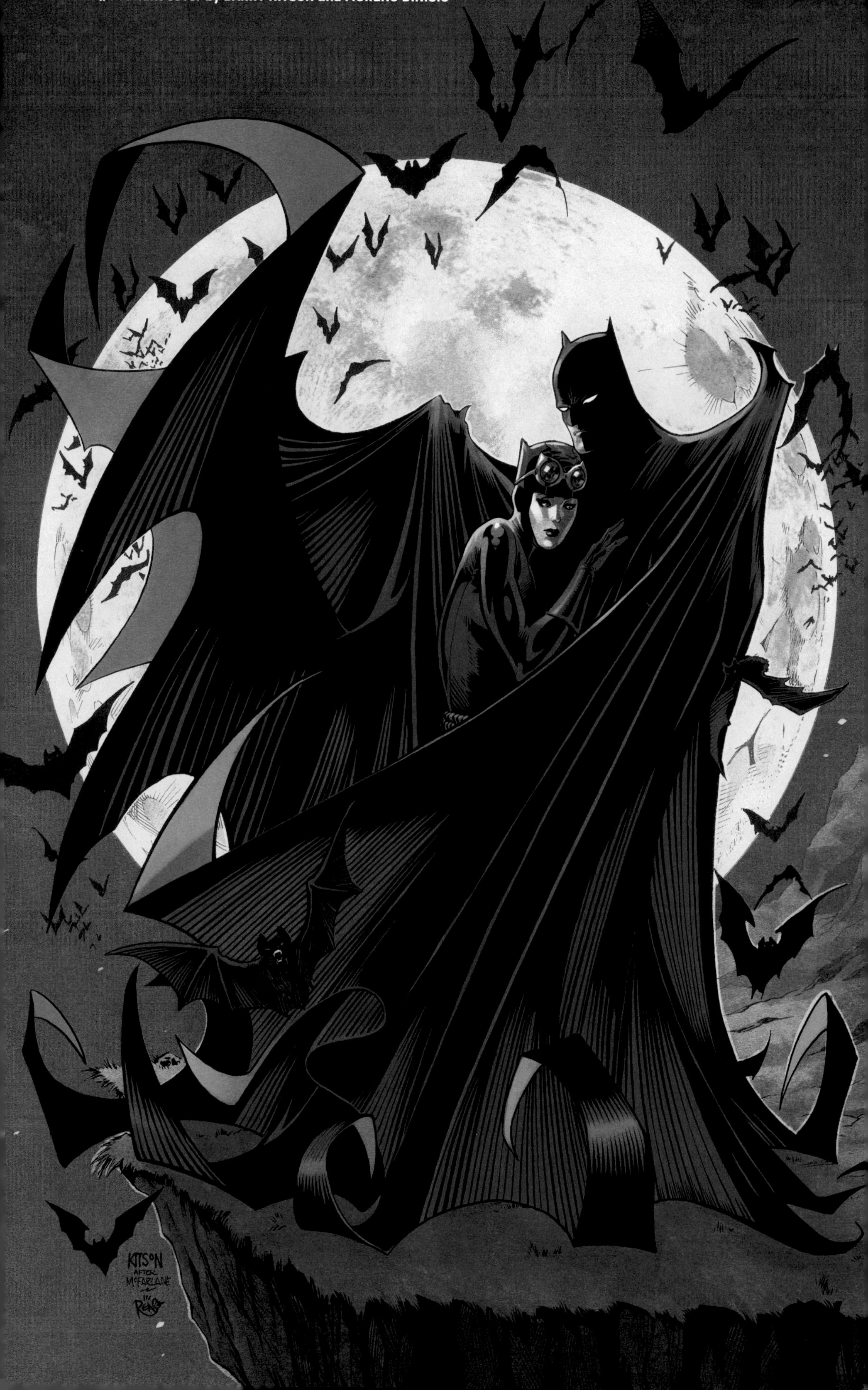
KITSON
AFTER
McFARLANE

BATMAN #1 variant cover by STANLEY "ARTGERM" LAU

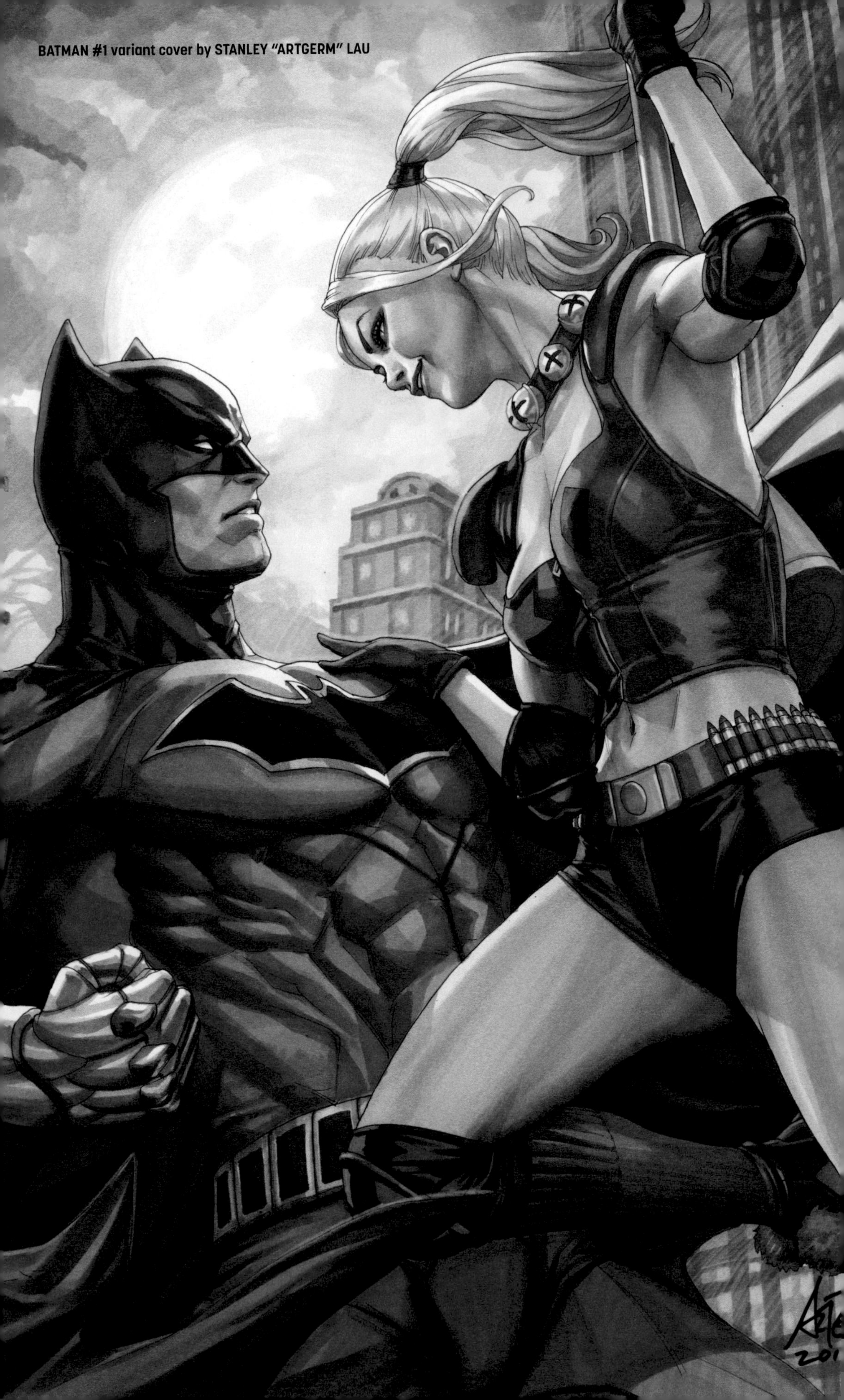

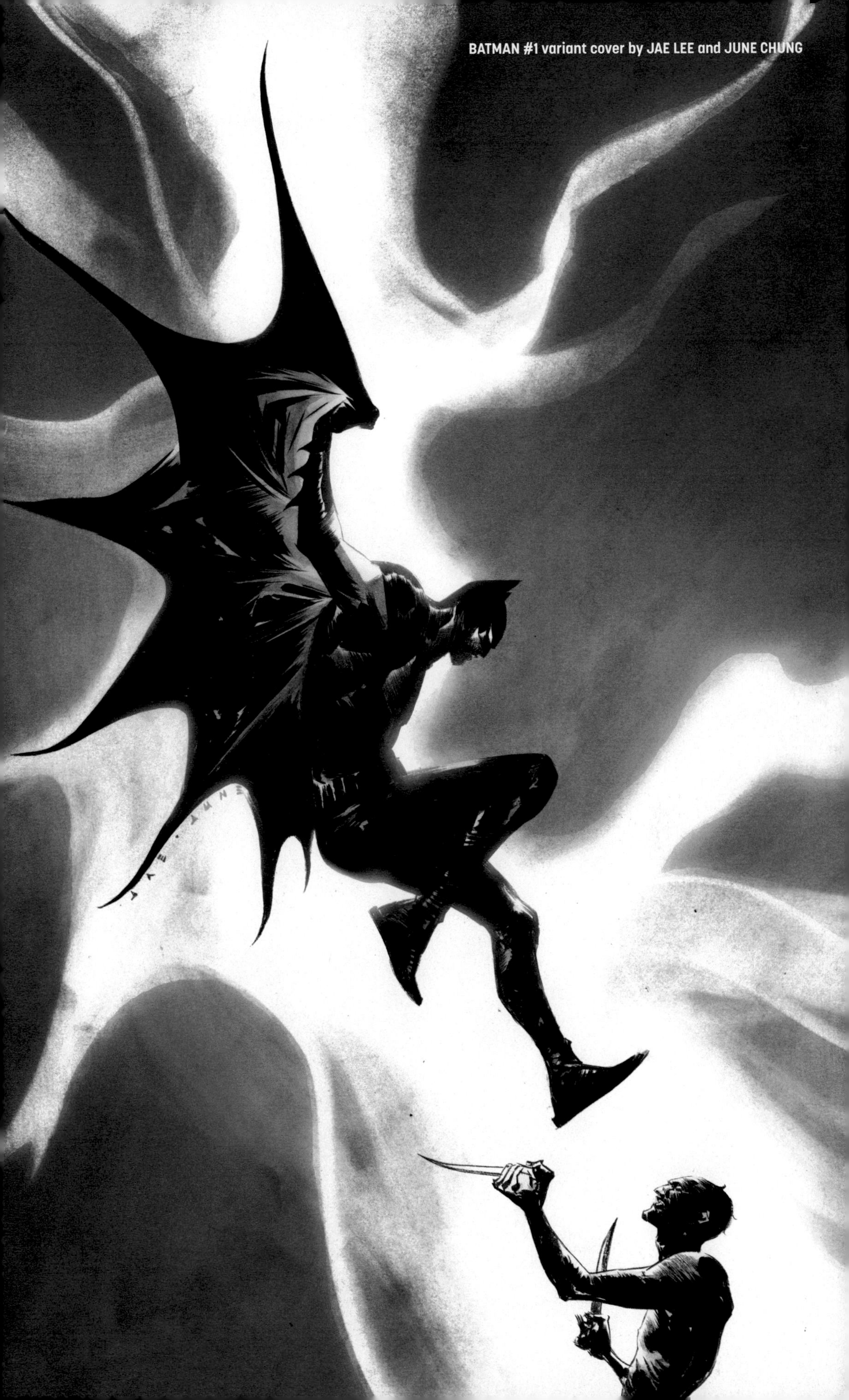

BATMAN #1 variant cover by JAE LEE and JUNE CHUNG

BATMAN #1 variant cover by ANT LUCIA

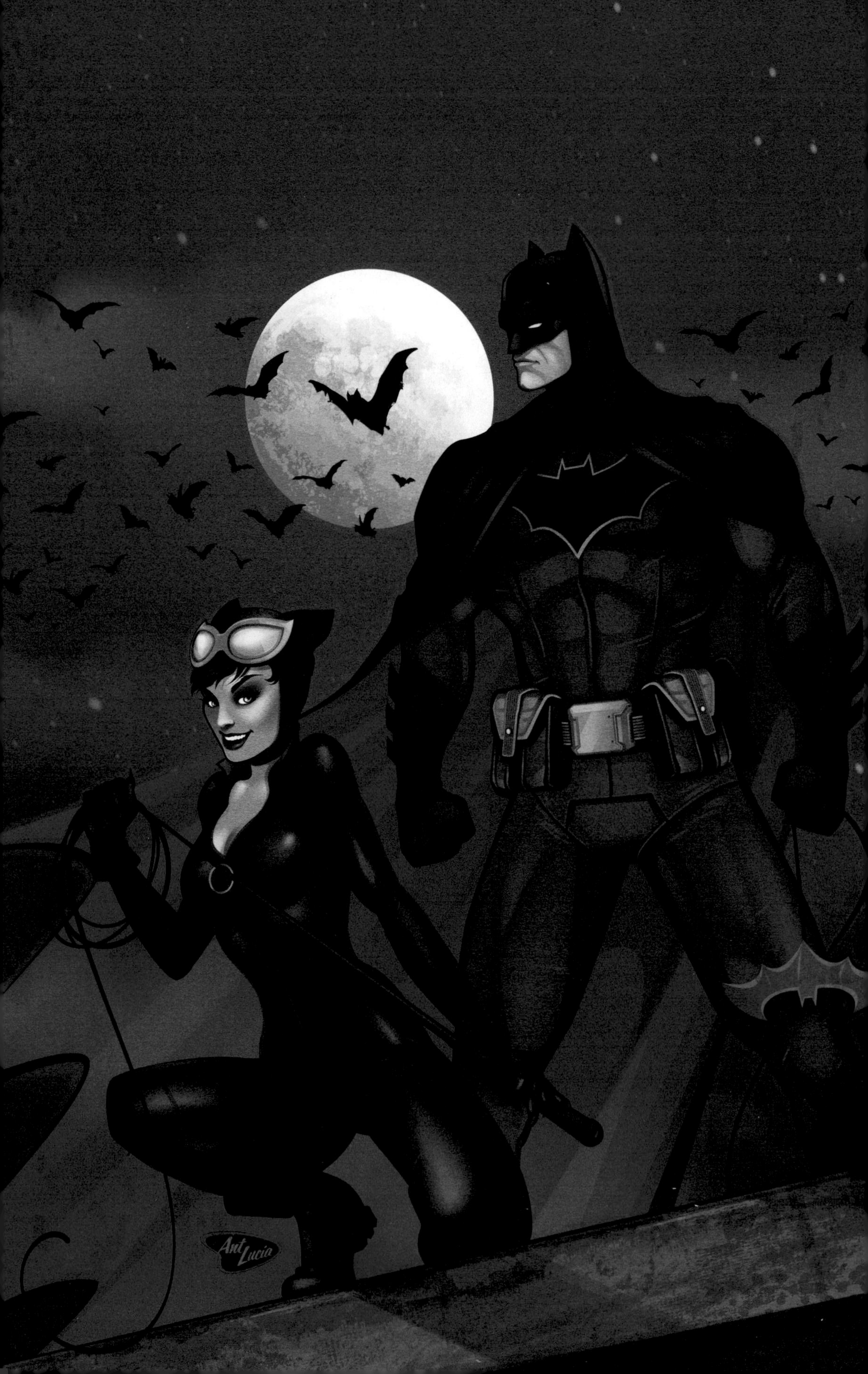
Ant Lucia

BATMAN #1 variant cover by GUILLEM MARCH

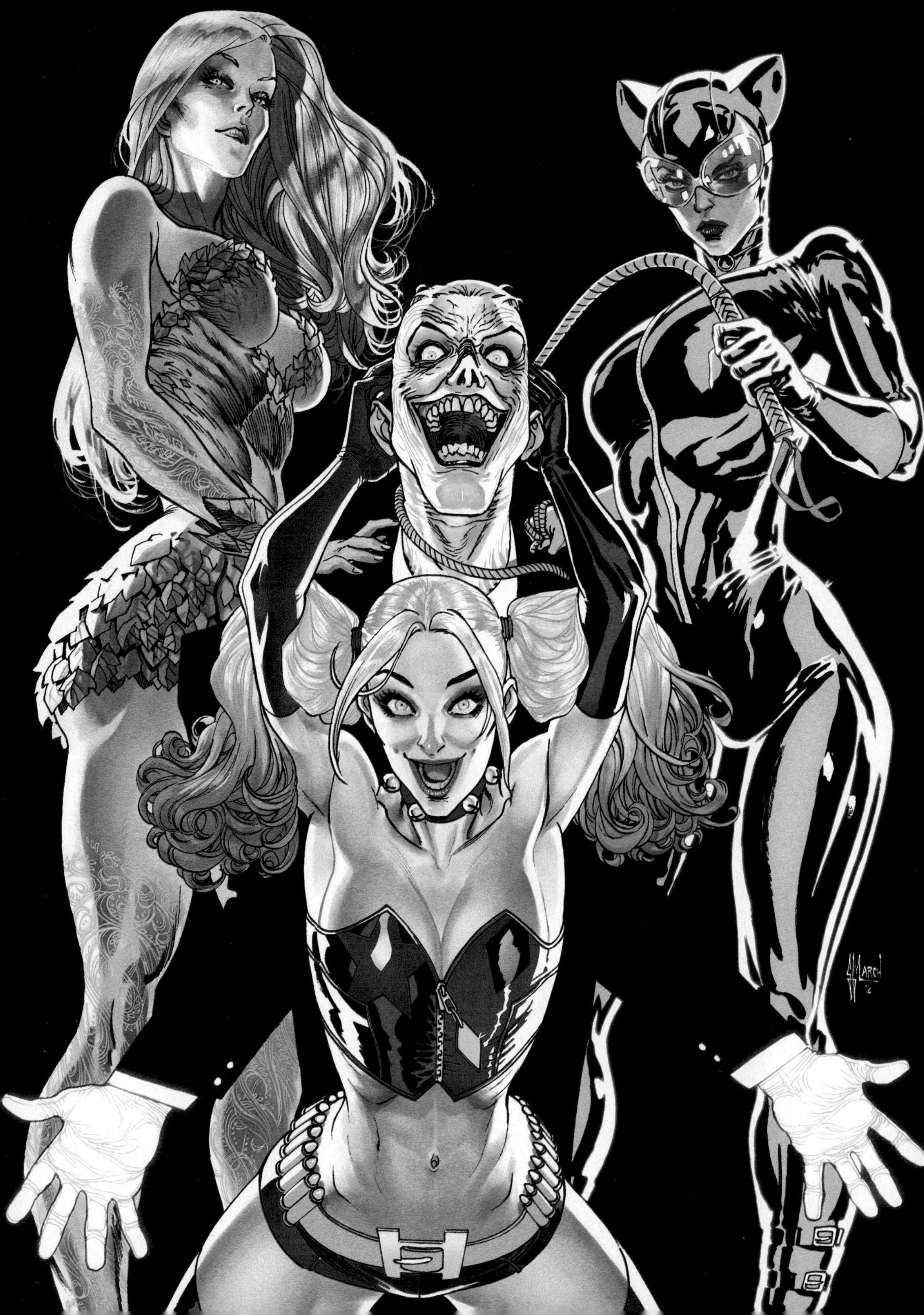

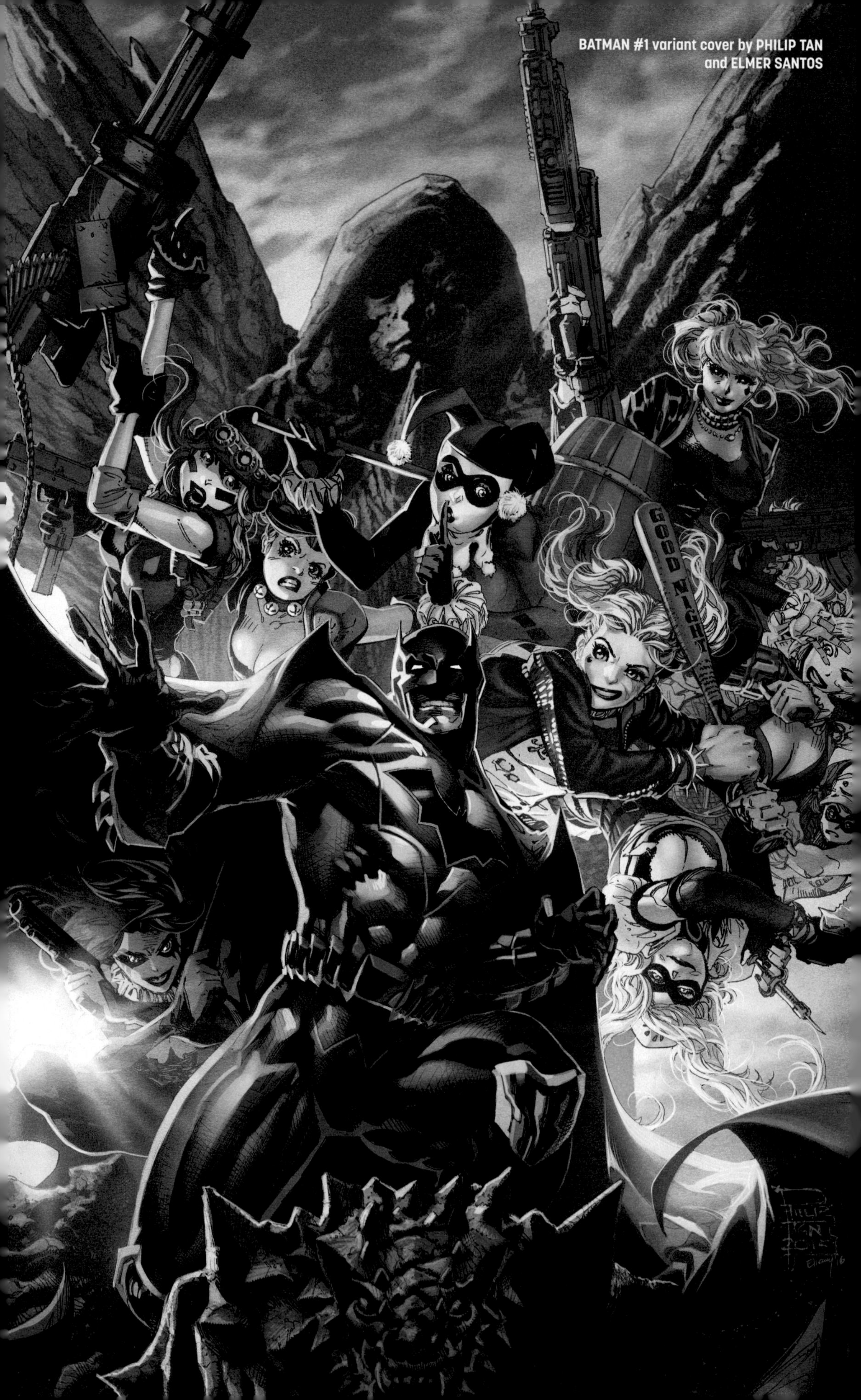
GOOD NIGHT

BATMAN #1 variant cover by PHILIP TAN
and ELMER SANTOS

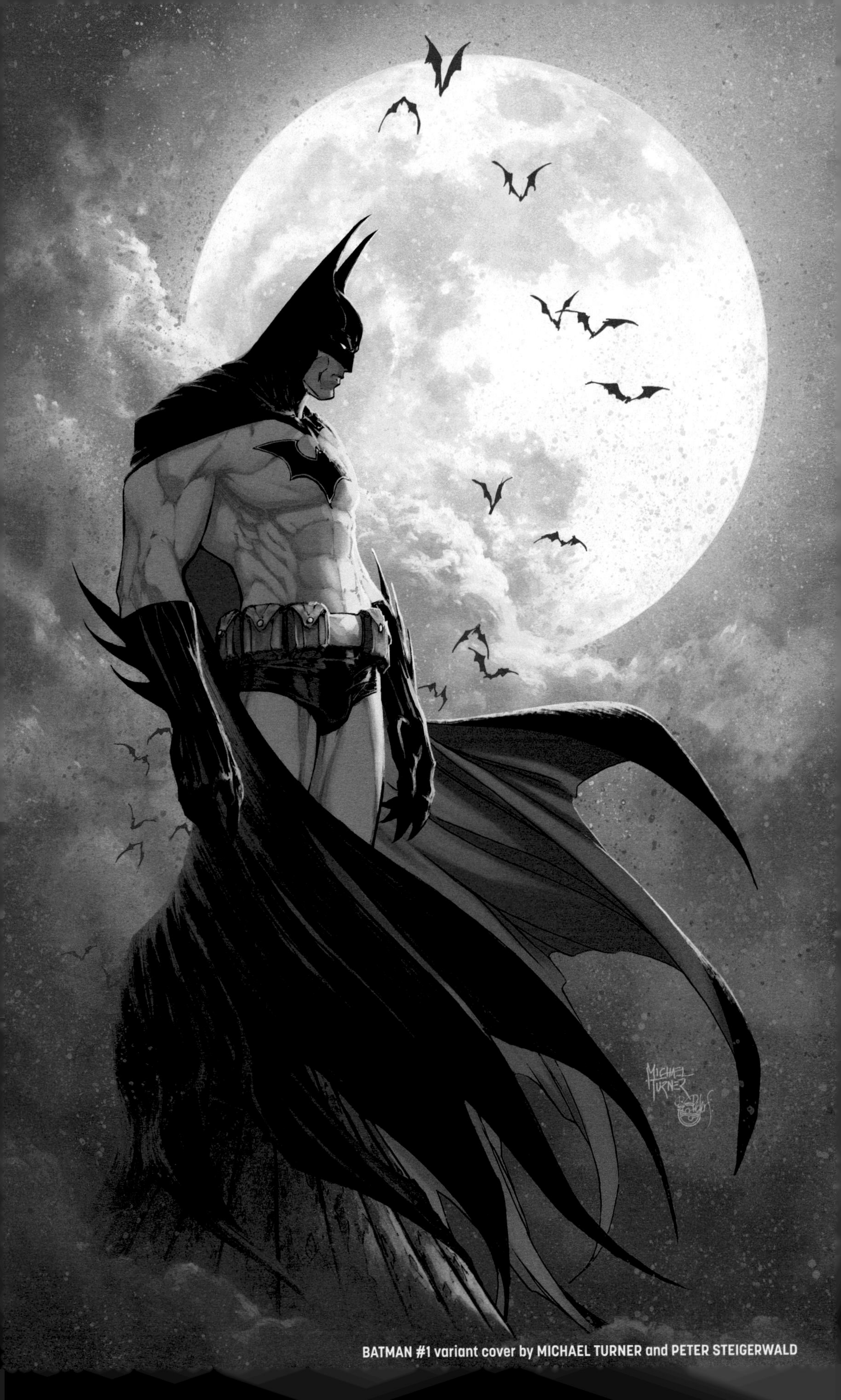
MICHAEL TURNER

BATMAN #1 variant cover by MICHAEL TURNER and PETER STEIGERWALD

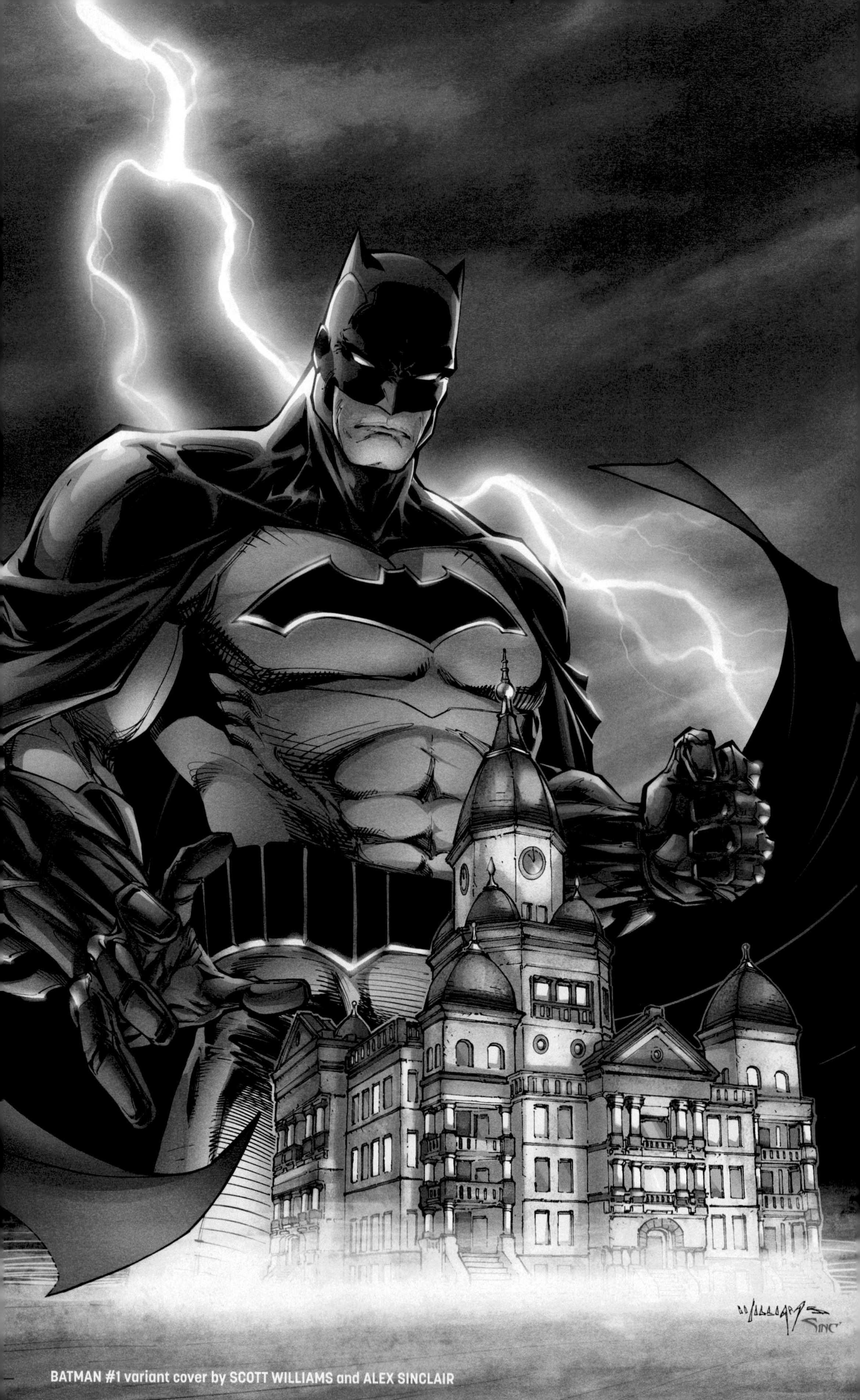

BATMAN #1 variant cover by SCOTT WILLIAMS and ALEX SINCLAIR

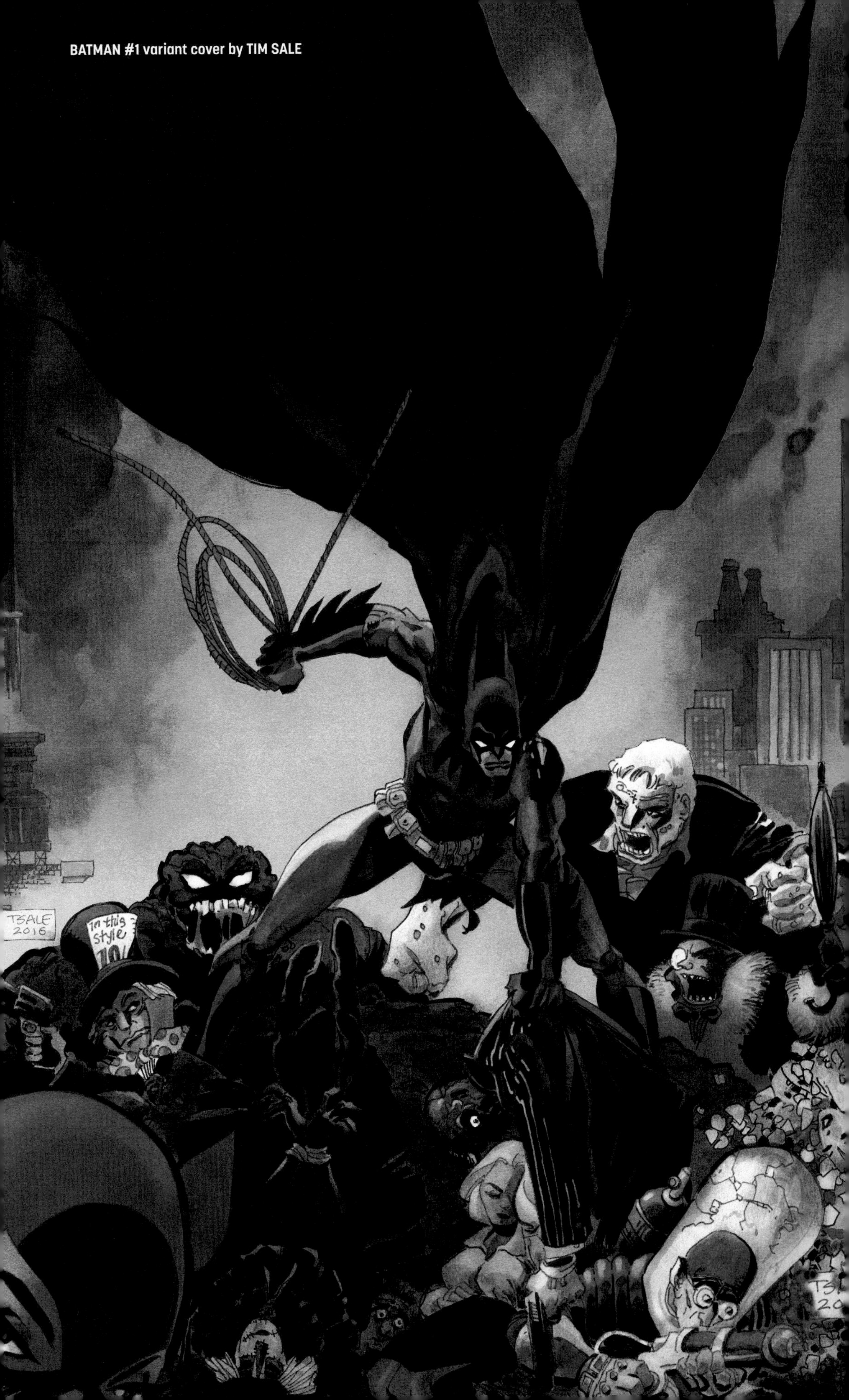
TSALE
2016
In this style

BATMAN #1 variant cover by TIM SALE

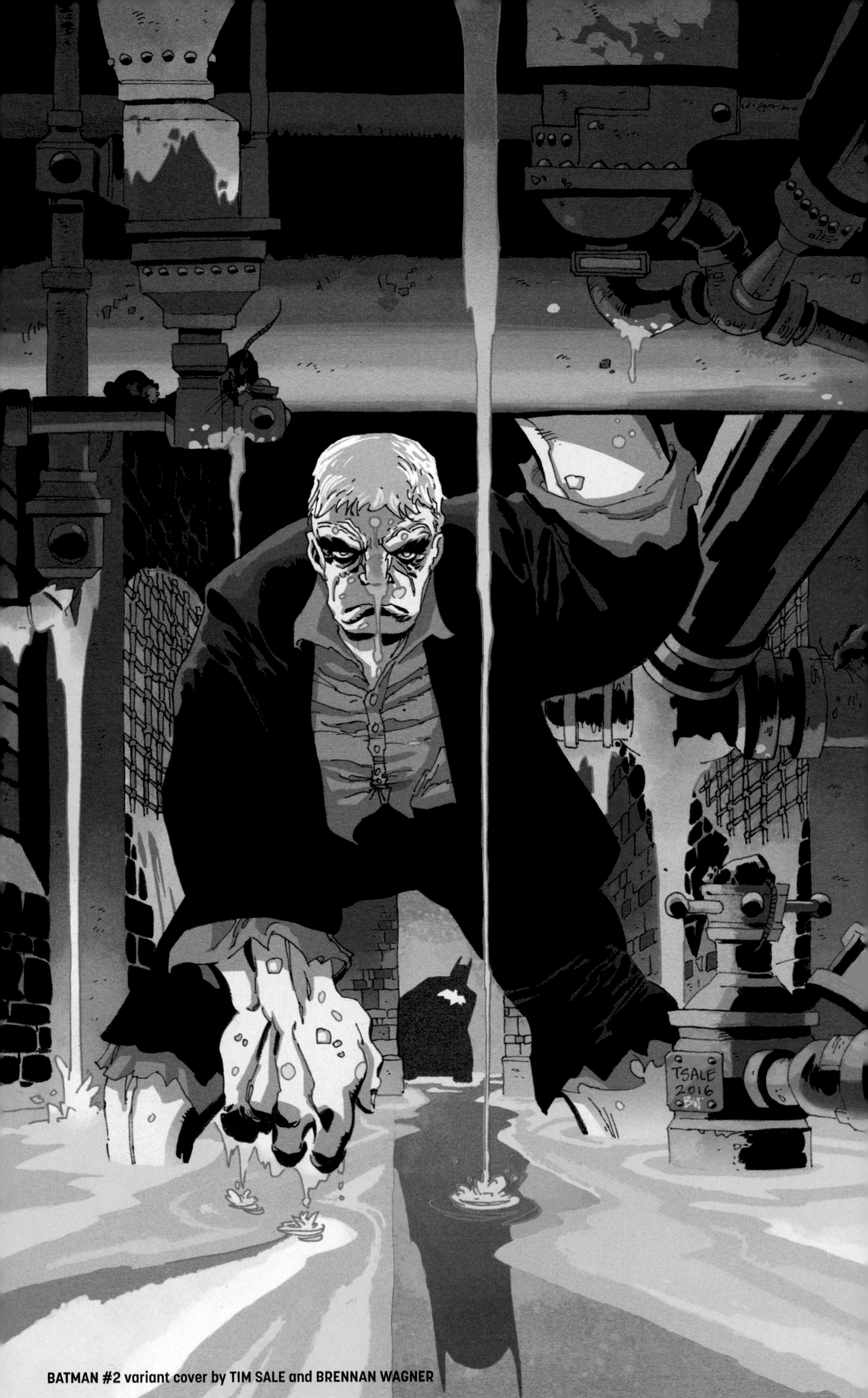
TSALE
2016
BW

BATMAN #2 variant cover by TIM SALE and BRENNAN WAGNER

BATMAN #3 variant cover by TIM SALE

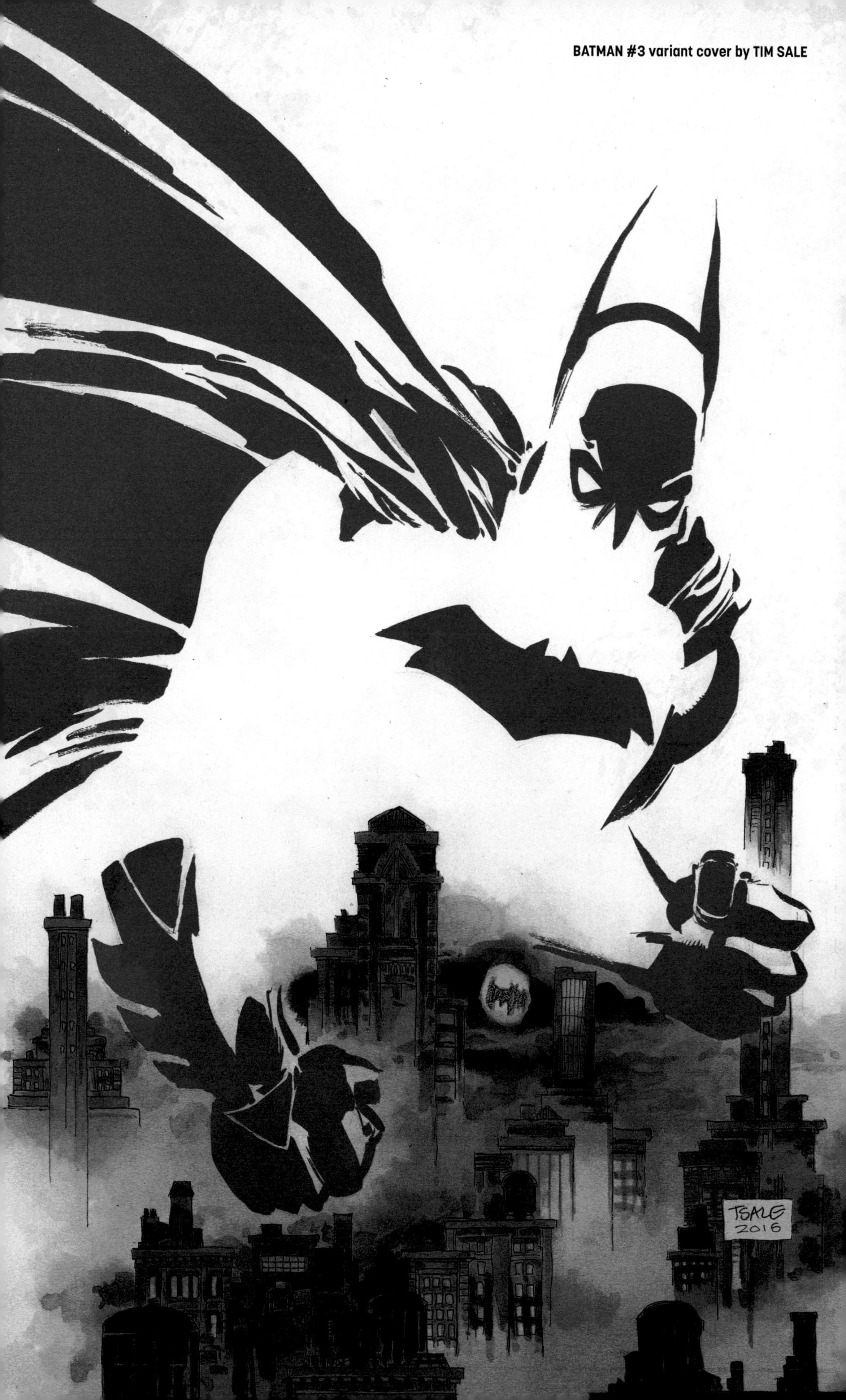
TSALE
2016

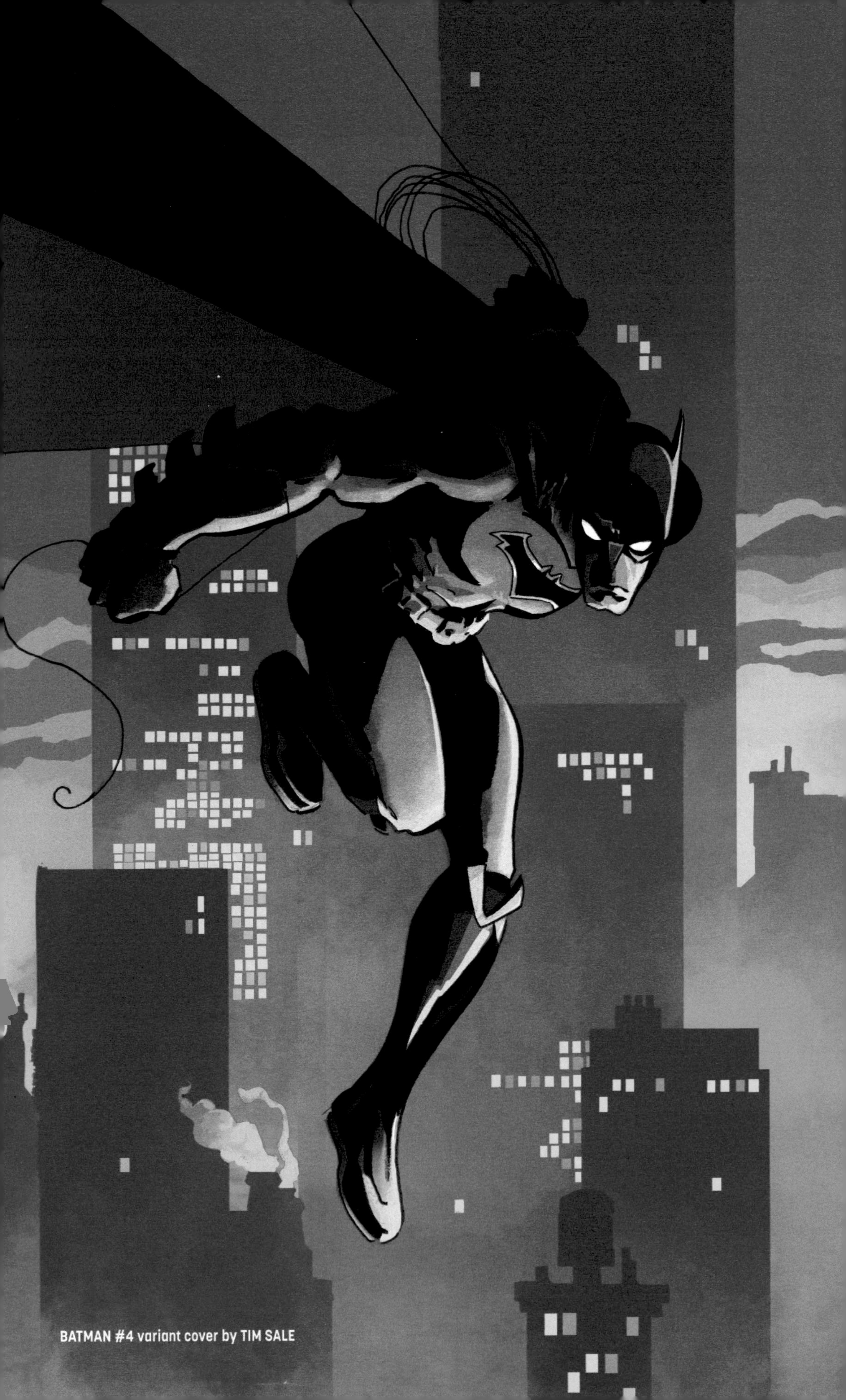

BATMAN #4 variant cover by TIM SALE

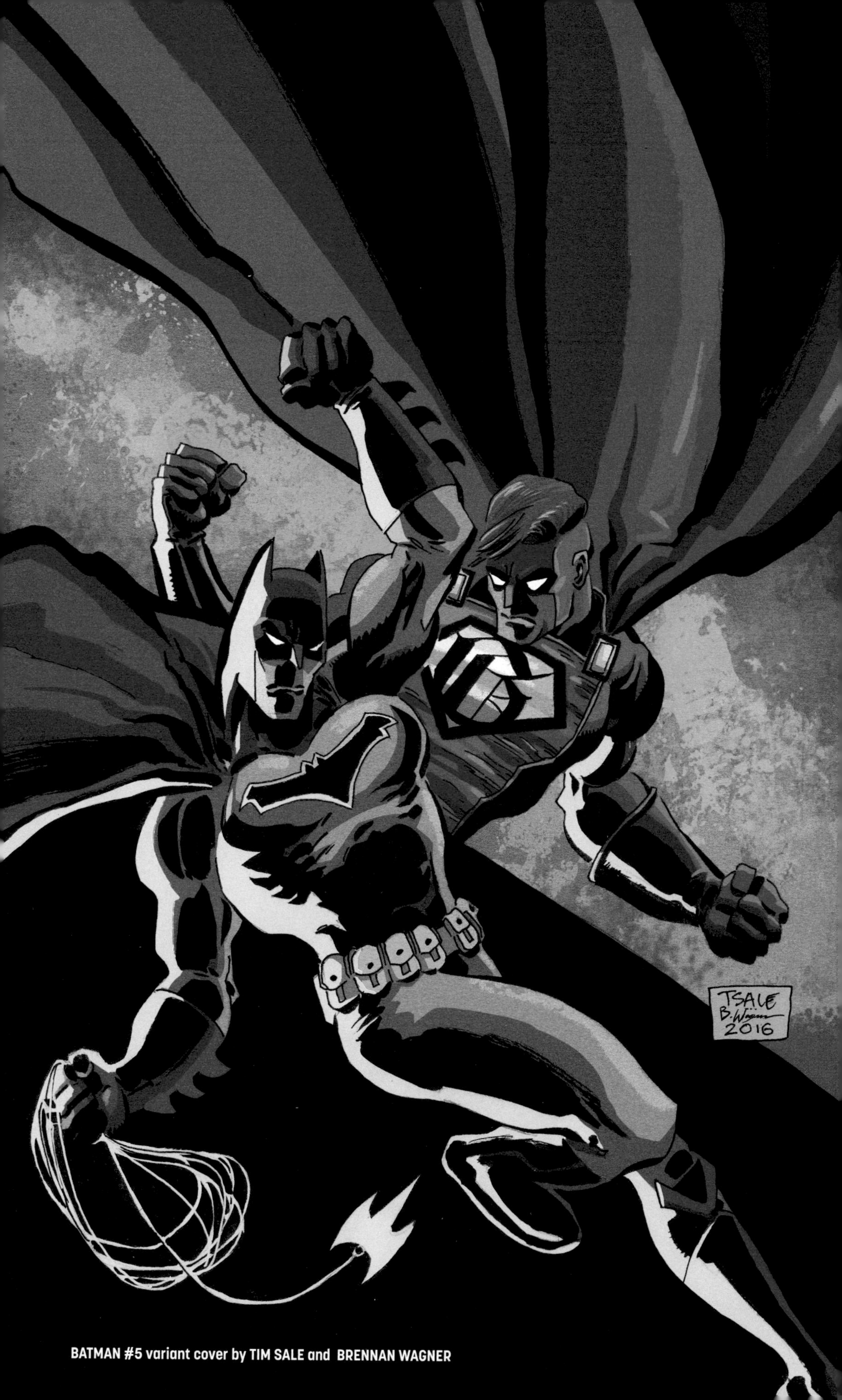
TSALE
B. Wagner
2016

BATMAN #5 variant cover by TIM SALE and BRENNAN WAGNER

BATMAN #6 variant cover by TIM SALE and BRENNAN WAGNER

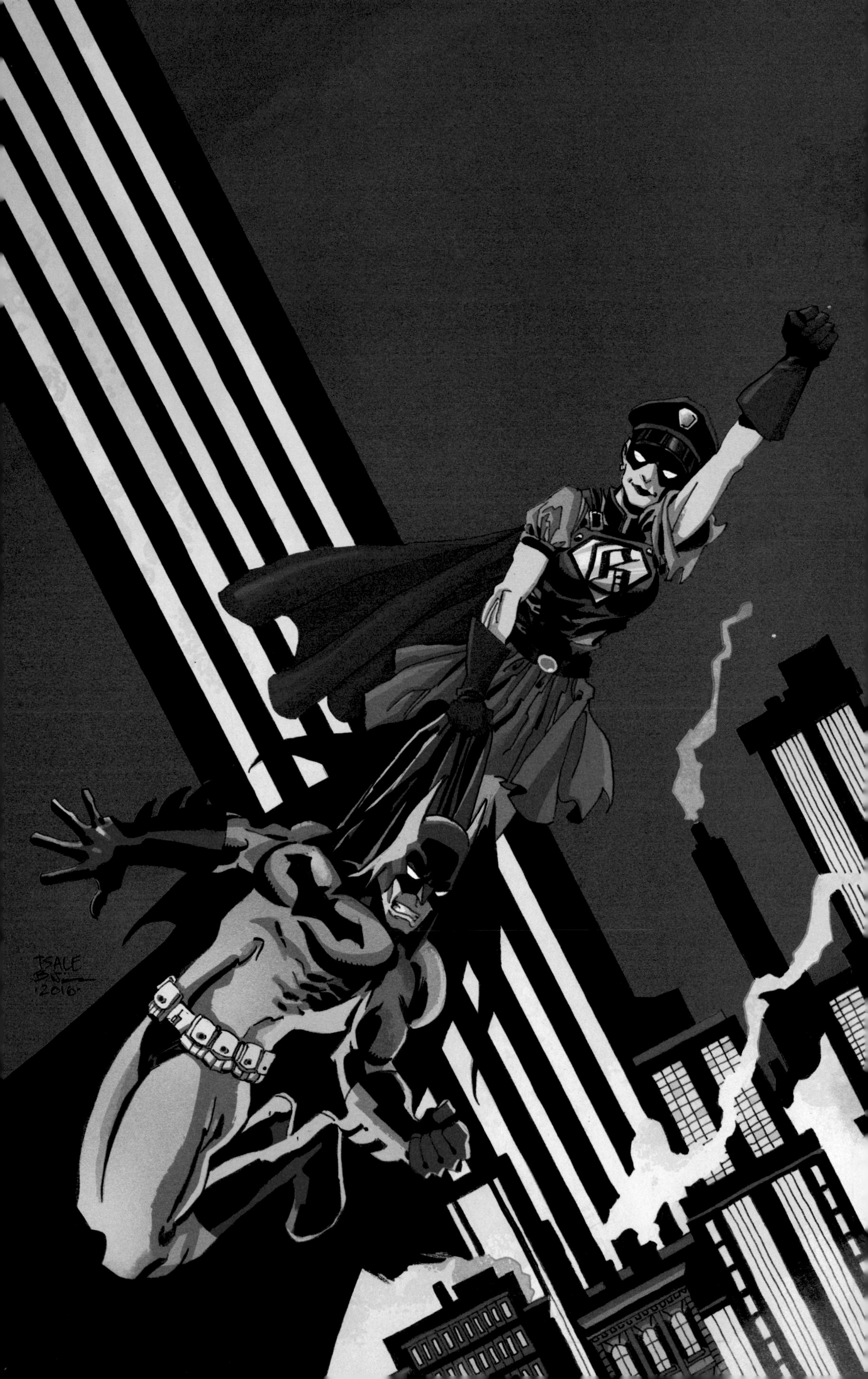

BATMAN COSTUME REDESIGN
by Greg Capullo

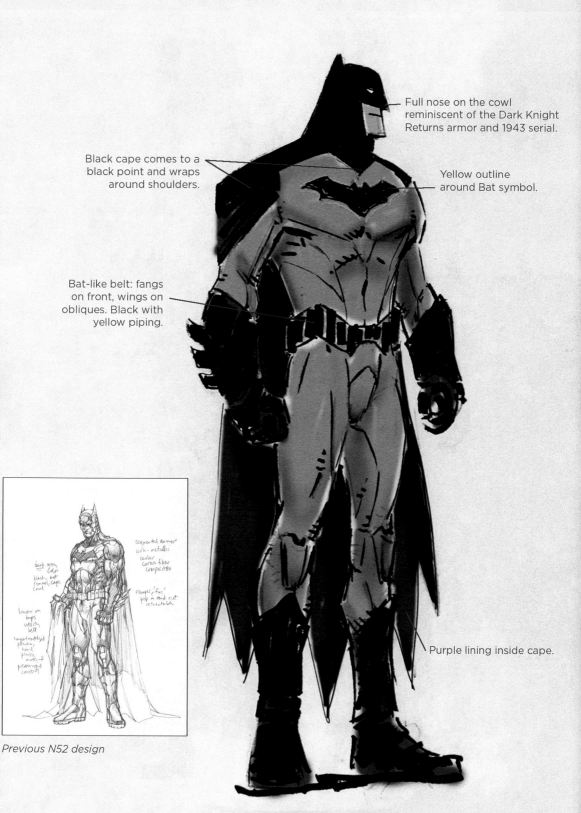

Full nose on the cowl reminiscent of the Dark Knight Returns armor and 1943 serial.
Black cape comes to a black point and wraps around shoulders.
Yellow outline around Bat symbol.
Bat-like belt: fangs on front, wings on obliques. Black with yellow piping.
Purple lining inside cape.

segmented armor
non-metallic
kevlar
carbon fiber
composites
dark grey color
black bat symbol, cape
cowl
Flanges, 'fins'
pop in and out
retractable
lower on hips
utility belt
compartmentalized pouches,
hard plastic material
pressurized contents

Previous N52 design

Illustration by Greg Capullo

DESIGNS FOR GOTHAM AND GOTHAM GIRL
by David Finch

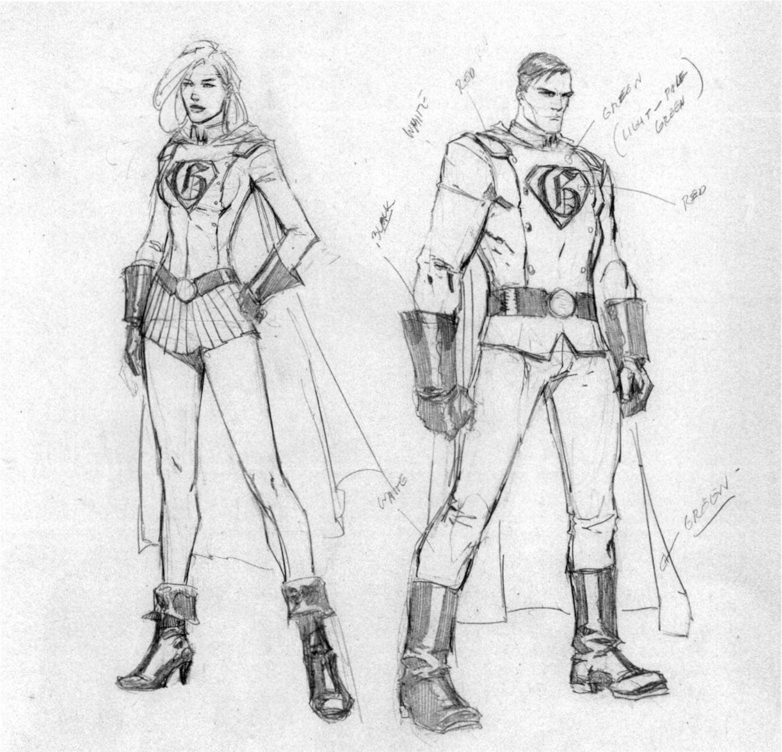
WHITE
RED
GREEN
(LIGHT-PALE GREEN)
RED
BLACK
WHITE
GREEN-

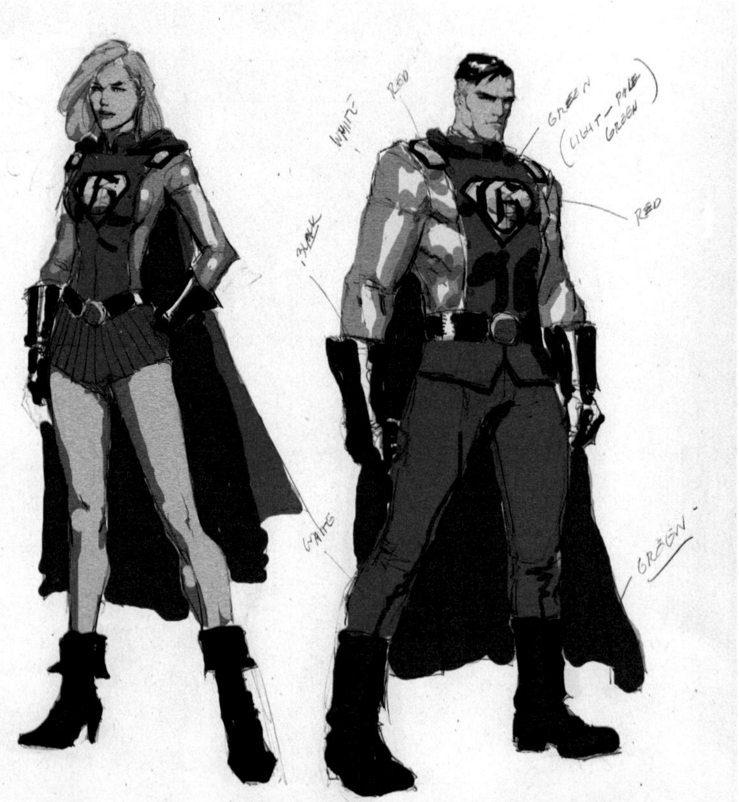
WHITE
RED
GREEN
(LIGHT-PALE GREEN)
RED
BLACK
WHITE
GREEN-

BATMAN #1 COVER
pencils by David Finch

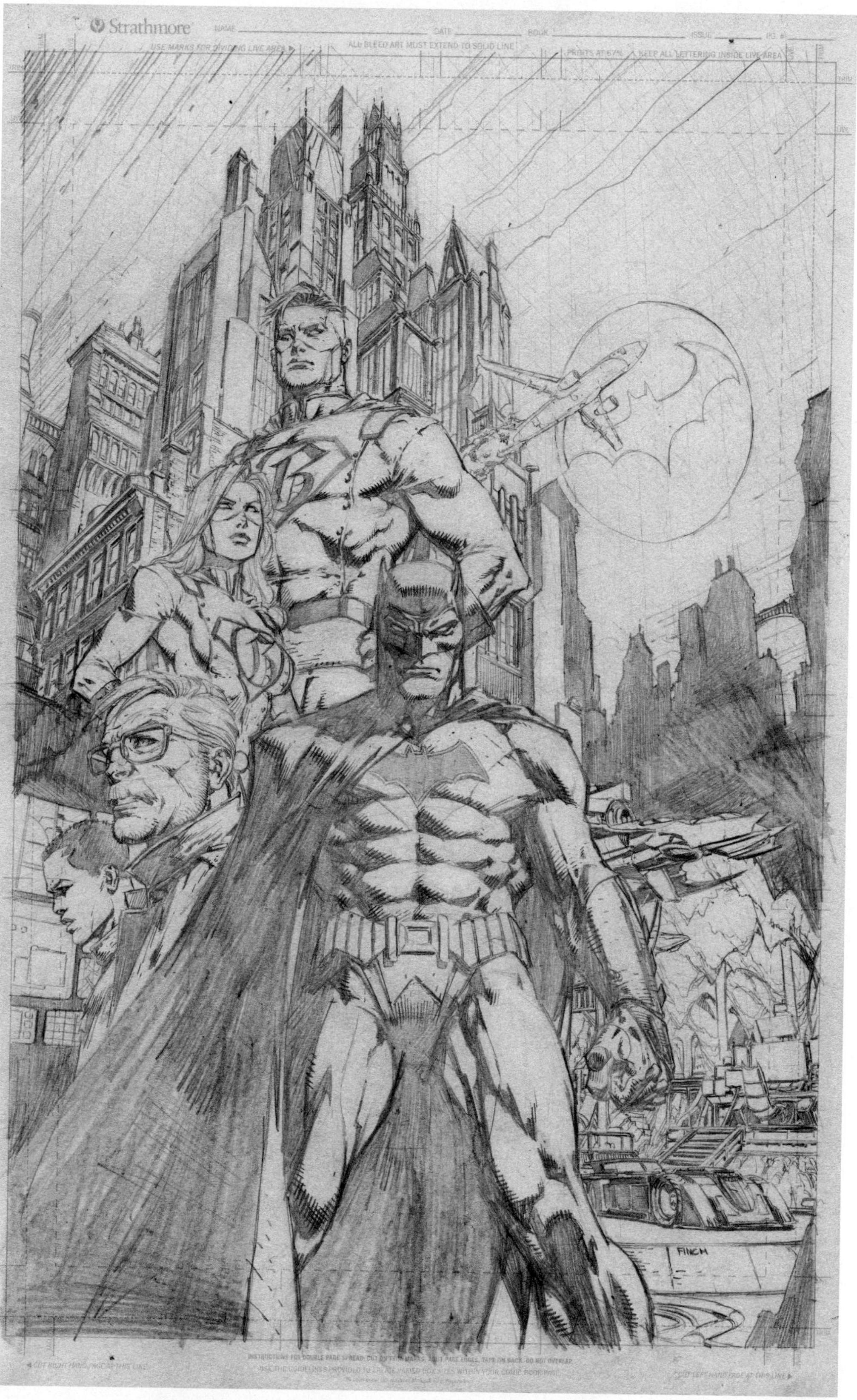
Strathmore
ALL BLEED ART MUST EXTEND TO SOLID LINE
FINCH

BATMAN #1 PAGES 1-4
pencils by David Finch

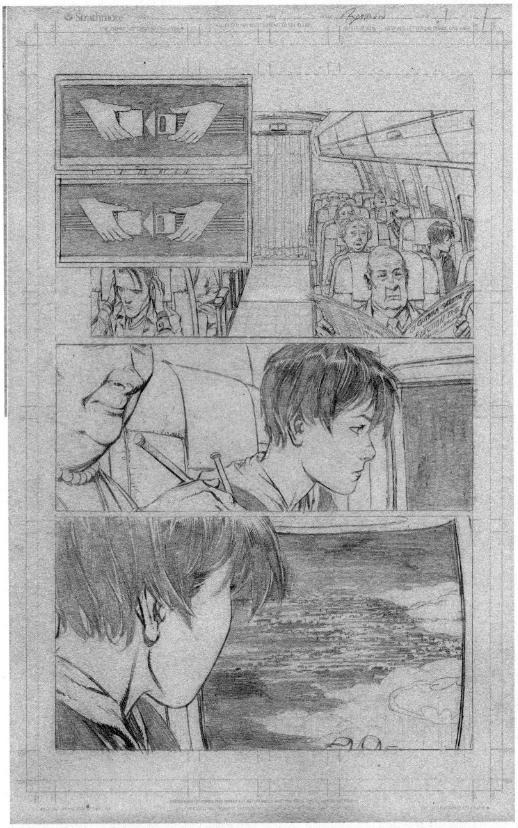

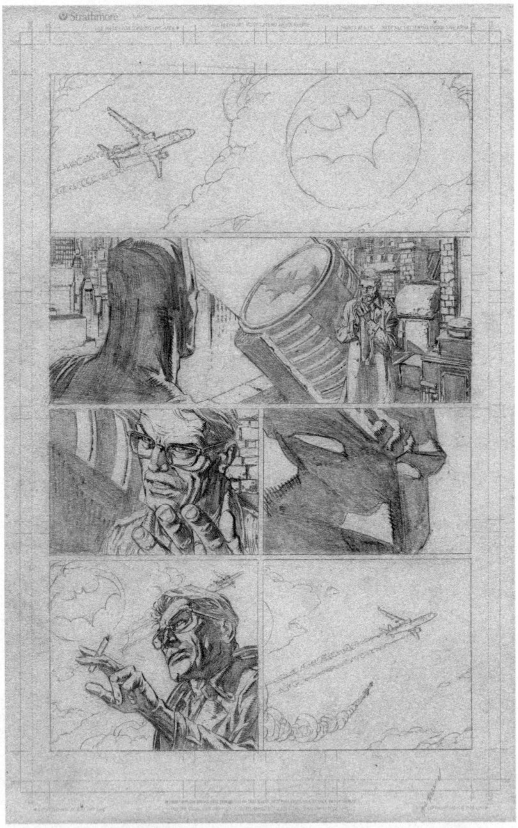

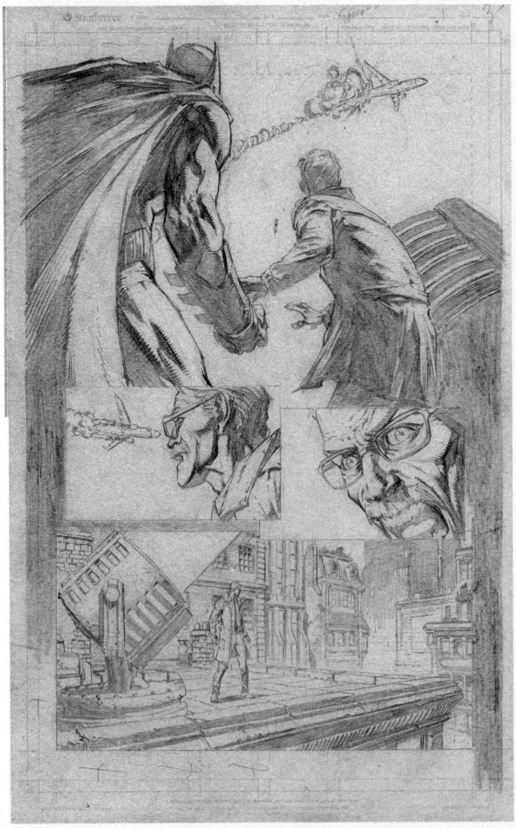

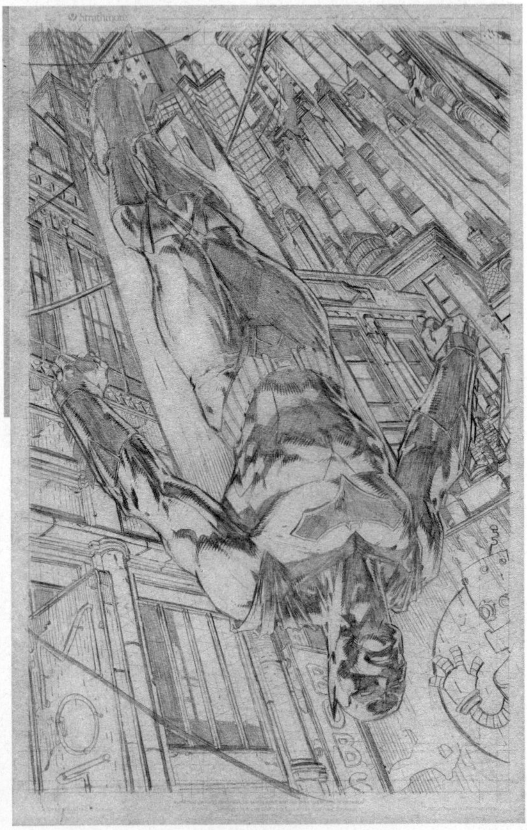

BATMAN #1 PAGE 15

pencils by David Finch

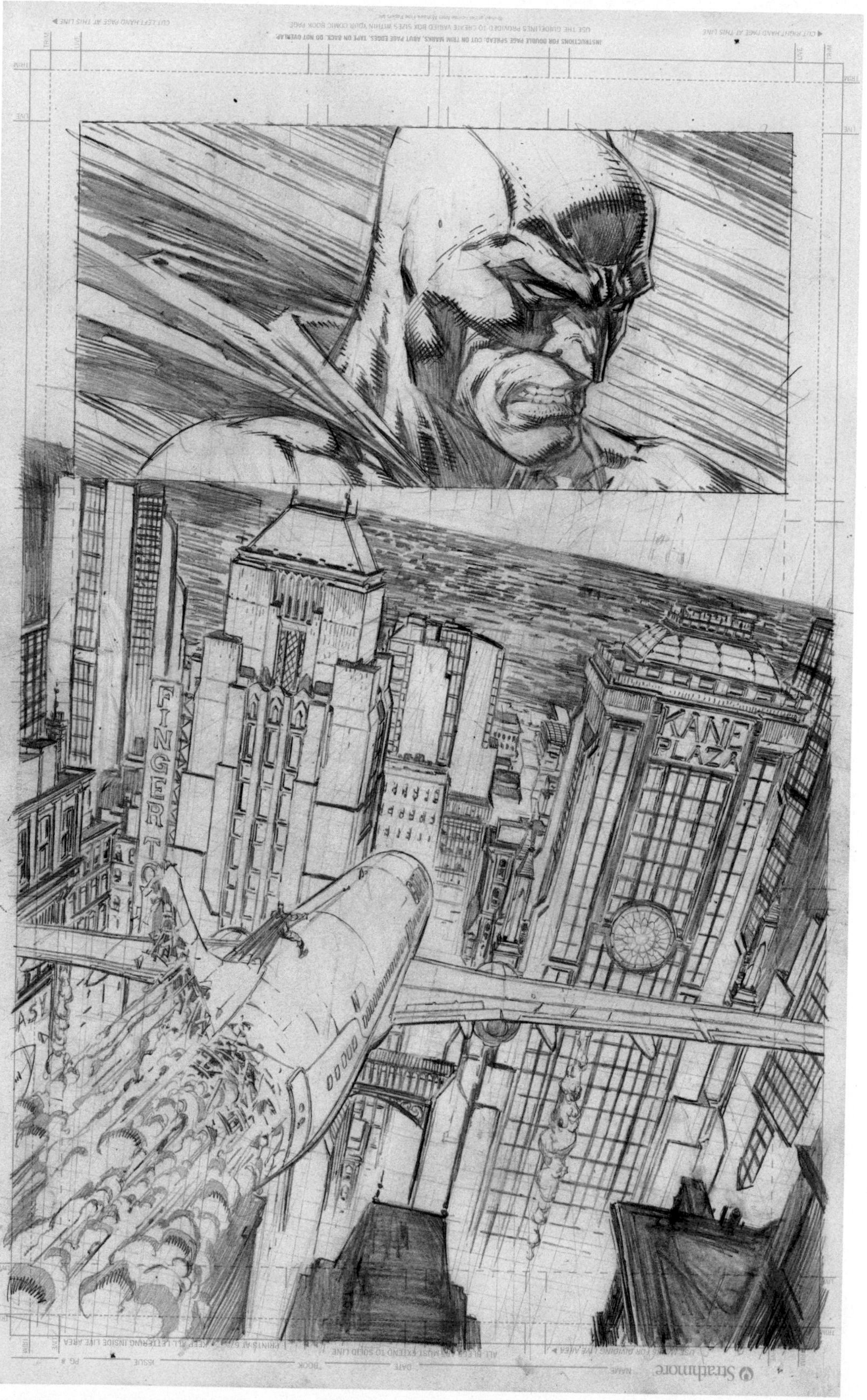
FINGER
KANE PLAZA

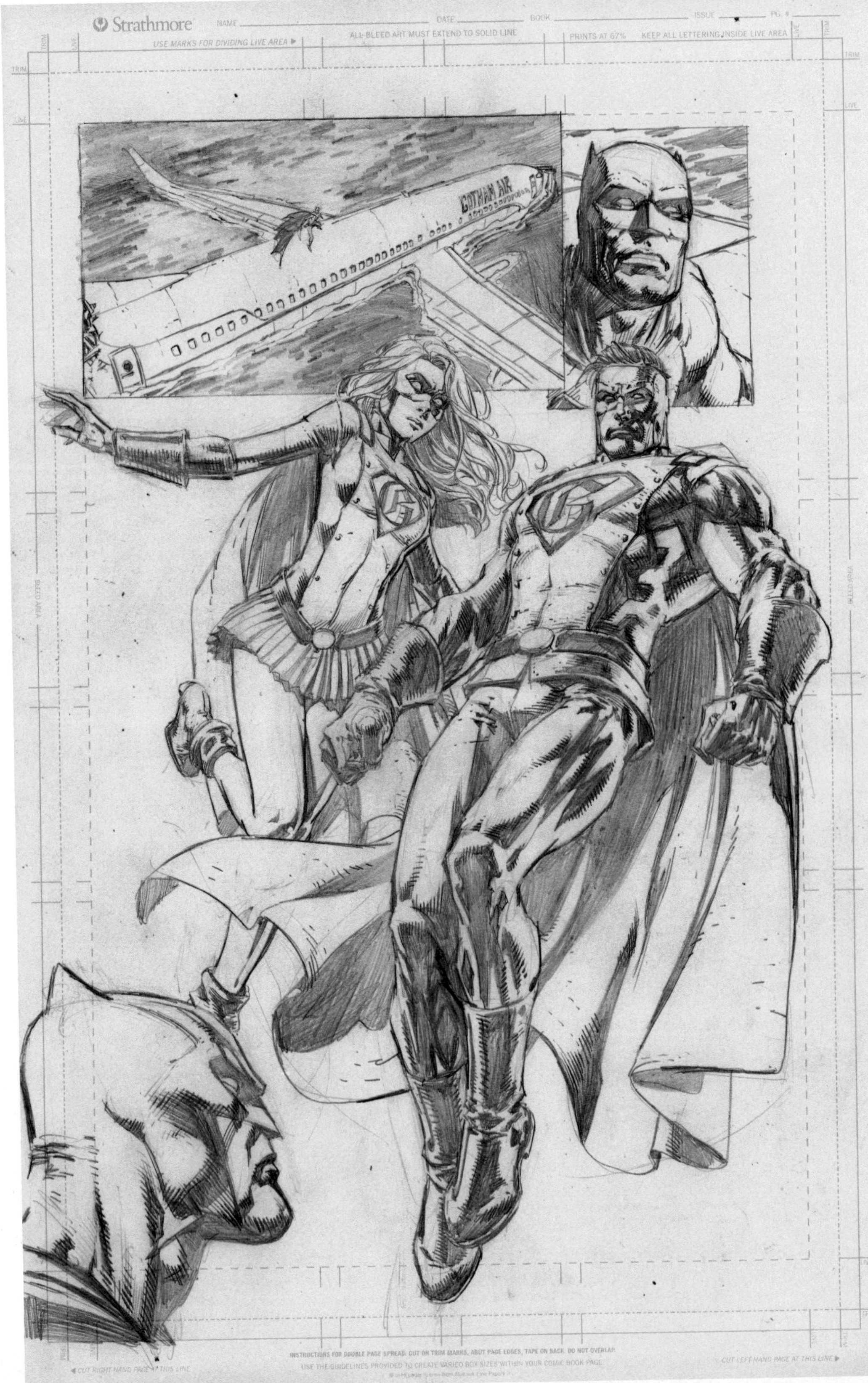

Strathmore
NAME
DATE
BOOK
ISSUE
PG #
USE MARKS FOR DIVIDING LIVE AREA ▶
ALL BLEED ART MUST EXTEND TO SOLID LINE
PRINTS AT 67%
KEEP ALL LETTERING INSIDE LIVE AREA
GOTHAM AIR
INSTRUCTIONS FOR DOUBLE PAGE SPREAD: CUT ON TRIM MARKS, ABUT PAGE EDGES, TAPE ON BACK. DO NOT OVERLAP
USE THE GUIDELINES PROVIDED TO CREATE VARIED BOX SIZES WITHIN YOUR COMIC BOOK PAGE
◀ CUT RIGHT HAND PAGE AT THIS LINE
CUT LEFT HAND PAGE AT THIS LINE ▶